Registered Childminding
-The Secrets of Success

SECOND EDITION

Written by
Tunja & Tamsin Stone

Published by T-Squared

ISBN 978-0-9543500-1-7

British Library Cataloguing in Publication Data
A catalogue record for this book is available in the British Library

Published by T- Squared,
451 Bideford Green, Linslade, Bedfordshire, LU7 2TZ

The authors would like to thank:

Karen Cox
Tracy Rose
and the members of UKChildminders

for their help, encouragement and support.

Contents

1. Childminding: An Overview

Registered Childminders are professional day carers working in their own homes to provide care and education for other people's children. They offer a flexibility of service that is difficult to find in other settings. Childminding is a proper job and is run as a business. A childminder's role involves more than just caring for children, regular accounting financial and medical records and paper work are essential and training must be regularly updated. Childminding is hard work but at the same time often very rewarding. In practice a childminder will care for children from birth until somewhere around fourteen years of age, when parents feel children can look after themselves after school.

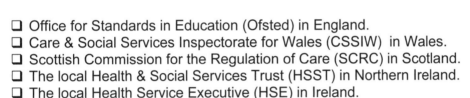

All childminders in the United Kingdom are required by law to register with their countries regulatory body. These are:

- ❑ Office for Standards in Education (Ofsted) in England.
- ❑ Care & Social Services Inspectorate for Wales (CSSIW) in Wales.
- ❑ Scottish Commission for the Regulation of Care (SCRC) in Scotland.
- ❑ The local Health & Social Services Trust (HSST) in Northern Ireland.
- ❑ The local Health Service Executive (HSE) in Ireland.

Note: In Ireland if registration is not required in your area, voluntary notification is recommended to obtain the benefits associated with registration.

Childminders are usually required to attend training courses before registration. Police and Social Service record checks are carried out on the childminder and all persons over 16 (10 in Northern Ireland) living in their home. The childminder's house is also checked for hygiene and safety. Registration is renewed annually. An inspection of the childminder's home by the regulatory body is conducted at specified intervals to check that standards are maintained. Registered childminders must also hold Public Liability Insurance.

Childminders are self employed. They are not employed by the parents they work with. They provide a childcare service which is available to parents and, as such, are legally responsible for keeping accurate business records and paying their own tax and National Insurance contributions. Childminders decide their own working conditions and calculate the fees they will charge for providing their childminding service.

History of Childminding

The forerunner of childminding was a 'day nursing' system formed as result of the industrial revolution of the 1830's. At this time there were no official regulations or checks. This system of care, called 'baby farming' since Victorian times, was open to abuse. Infants were often drugged on laudanum and neglect and starvation were frequent occurrences. By the 1870's public opinion wanted these 'minders' regulated and the ensuing Infant Life Protection Bill of 1872 contained a clause requiring registration and supervision of baby farms and those caring for children on a daily basis within manufacturing areas. This was the beginning of regulation. The act, amended in 1897, defined improper care of infants and empowered local authorities to locate baby farms and remove abused children.

Childcare demands during the First World War, to release women for work in munitions factories, encouraged childminders to fill the gap in childcare. They continued filling the gap from this time forwards. During the Second Word War an emergency scheme operated to recruit and subsidise childminders to free mothers for the war effort. By the late 1940's childminders became an important resource meeting working mothers need for extended hours of care.

The introduction of the 1948 Nurseries and Childminders Act brought private daycare under local authority control. Their duties in respect of childminders were minimal, only involving registration of premises and persons looking after three or more children unrelated to the childminder. There were no perceived training needs.

Throughout the 1960's childminder numbers rose to meet demand and provide wrap around care for the part time nursery provision. In 1969 legislation was tightened and included a new definition of childminding still in use today. Local authority powers were extended to cover the quality of care provided, although requirements still differed between regions.

In 1974 responsibilities for registering childminders changed from Local Health Authorities and Health Visitors to the new Social Services departments. In the mid 1970's childminders and local authority workers from around the country began meeting for the first time and exchanging information. By 1977 childminders were uniting to raise their profile, improve the standards of care offered and obtain better support services and a National Childminding Association (NCMA) was formed.

In 2001, Ofsted became the childcare regulator in England for children aged under eight, standardising the quality of care across England and raising parental expectations and all childminders became required to take a childminding training course.

In 2002 'Birth to Three Matters', a framework to support children, was launched. Childminders were among the first to receive the framework, although they were the last type of childcare provision to receive training due to a lack of accompanying funding. Childminders became seen as the new professionals as people gradually became aware of the increased training many childminders undertook and in 2004 accredited network childminders became eligible to offer Foundation Stage Education.

From 2008 all childcare providers in England will be required to deliver the Early Years Foundation Stage.

Considerations Before Registration

There are many points you must consider before applying to become a registered childminder. Childminding will have an impact on yourself, your partner and any other children in your home. You need to consider the change in routine, extra noise and how any children of your own may react to having to share their home, toys and you.

Would you enjoy being with young children during much of the week, do you have experience in caring for young children? Extra children can mean additional wear and tear on furniture and toys, childminders cannot worry unduly about untidiness.

Childminding does not just involve caring for children, you also need to understand you are running your own small business and will need to keep accounts and other records. You will not have the benefits of scale or business advantages found in group settings. You will however be able to offer the flexible home based care many parents want and are prepared to pay for, and run your business to suit your own family commitments.

Childminders Need to be Able to...

When deciding if you want to become a childminder you should consider whether you will be able to do all the things necessary to do the job in a way that is satisfying to yourself and provides parents and their children with quality childcare. You will need to be able to:

- ❑ Be welcoming to parents, treating them as individuals without being judgmental.
- ❑ Communicate effectively with all parents and with other agencies if required.
- ❑ Avoid gender stereotyping and promote equal opportunities.
- ❑ Prevent racism and promote cultural awareness.
- ❑ Provide a safe and secure environment.
- ❑ Learn about a child through observation and discussion with the parents.
- ❑ Provide care and attention for children's physical, social and emotional needs.
- ❑ Extend play and learning by adding resources and changing boundaries.
- ❑ Encourage intellectual development.
- ❑ Encourage a sense of responsibility.
- ❑ Foster self esteem and encourage independence.
- ❑ Provide motivation.
- ❑ Observe children's learning, including spontaneous play, and plan subsequent play and learning activities.
- ❑ Keep detailed records of individual children's development and progress.
- ❑ Share information on children's progress with parents, listening to and acting on contributions.
- ❑ Celebrate a child's achievements with the child and the parents.
- ❑ Provide a healthy and nutritious diet.

Registration - Overview

All people looking after unrelated children under eight years of age in England and Wales, under 16 years in Scotland, under 12 years in Northern Ireland or under six years of age in Southern Ireland where four or more unrelated children are present, for a reward of any kind (payment or gifts) must register with their regulatory body. The penalties for childminding without registration are a substantial fine, imprisonment or both.

When you apply for registration a Childcare Inspector, Officer or Social Worker, depending on your location, will discuss with you how you intend to provide a childcare service, the suitability of people who will be caring for the children will be checked, as will the premises where the children are to be cared for. You will have to complete a medical record form, to provide details to ensure that you are physically and mentally fit to be registered as a childminder. All members of the household over the age of 16 (over 10 Northern Ireland) must have a police check, and convictions and their relevance will be considered. The names and addresses of two referees will be required. Referees cannot be family members or parents proposing to place children in your care. If you do not own your own home, you may need to get permission from the owner of the property, e.g. your landlord or Local Authority Housing Department.

In England and Wales you can be registered for up to six children under eight, though not more than three of these should be under five. In Scotland registration is for six children under sixteen with no more than three not yet attending primary school. In Ireland registration is for six children under six, regulations apply when there are four or more unrelated children (these numbers are currently under revision). In Northern Ireland registration is for six children under twelve, of these only three can be under five. Any children of your own will count towards your total.The number of children you are registered for will be written on your registration certificate. Having more children in your care than you are registered for could result in the cancellation of your registration.

Offering a Professional Service

Childminders should offer a professional service to parents, and parents have the right to expect that your service is going to be of a good quality. Offering a reliable service will be very important to parents; they need to know that you will be available as stated in your contract. They must be able to meet their work commitments without having to worry about taking days off. You can help reassure parents by arranging for another childminder to take your minded children if you should need days off, for example, due to illness. (This will only be possible as long as the other childminder does not exceed his/her registration for numbers or children).

You must be committed to the well-being and safety of the children in your care. Parents are trusting you with their children and expect that you will care for them. It is important to keep parents informed about your routines, activities and how their child is doing. It is also just as important to listen to parents and respect their wishes for their child's care.

Keeping up to date with relevant knowledge and childcare practices and taking the opportunity to develop your knowledge through training courses, reading relevant materials or communication with other professionals will also help you deliver a quality childminding service.

You need to maintain your business and child records in a professional manner in order to comply with legislation regarding tax and businesses, to meet registration rules, and to ensure the well being of children.

Insurance

A variety of insurance policies including Public Liability will be required to ensure peace of mind and protect your pocket. (For more details see Section 6. Money Matters)

Retirement

Some childminders choose childminding as it allows them to stay at home with their children and they may move on to another job once their children have grown up, for others it becomes a career. It is always a good idea to seek independent advice on your pension options which ever choice you have made.

There is no set age for retirement, however, childminding is a physical job and you will need to be fit enough to lift children, push a pushchair or navigate a toy covered floor. You will also need to stay up to date with current legislation and regulations, training and safety requirements.

Registering bodies usually require a health declaration and whilst you are still able to meet their requirements and your National Standards there is no reason for you to retire from childminding until you want to!

Sources of Additional Information

You may find you need additional information on setting up and running your business. Further information can be obtained from: Inland Revenue, Children's Information Service, regulatory bodies Ofsted, CSSIW, SCRC, HSE, HSST, local childminding support groups, childminding associations NCMA, SCMA, NCMAI, NICMA, your local library, Citizens Advice centres and government web sites. (See also Section 19. Useful Organisations)

Grants for Childminders

In some areas Start-up grants are offered to encourage an increase in the number of registered childminders. They are funded by Central Government usually through the local Early Years and Childcare Partnerships (EYCP). The grant is mainly to promote childminding in areas where there is difficulty attracting childminders, so new minders in areas where there is no demand for new childminders are less likely to get a grant. Existing childminders who wish to provide an additional service, for example, caring for children with disabilities are also eligible for a grant. The Government also provides additional sustainability funding for new childminders living in 'disadvantaged' wards.

Grants will usually be paid to childminders when the Children Act Registration process is complete and on production of receipts. It is advisable to retain duplicate copies of your receipts, particularly for items of equipment under guarantee for your own records.

The grant could cover:

- ❑ Toys and equipment.
- ❑ Minor premises adaptation for health and safety reasons (guards, fences, safety glass, etc.).
- ❑ Membership of a Childminding Association/support Group.
- ❑ Insurance.
- ❑ Registration and inspection fees.

Currently the average grant funding is £300 per childminder. Although this can vary considerably from area to area. You should contact your local EYCP to find out what is available in your area. If you receive a grant and stop childminding within 12 months the money must be returned.

Applications are usually considered by Childcare Sub Groups on behalf of the Early Years Development and Childcare Partnerships. Availability of the grants has become subject to the Local Authority budget planning and may therefore not be available in all areas. The criteria for a successful bid include:

- ❑ Childminders that are becoming part of Family Link Schemes or who are extending their services in some way.
- ❑ Childminders from areas identified through the Children's Information Service as needing additional childminder support. Usually areas of deprivation decided by the local authority using a government provided index.
- ❑ Childminders from ethnic minorities and areas of high social deprivation.

Grants for Childminders in Wales
In addition to the start up grants existing Childminders in Wales can apply for a small equipment grant of £500.

Grants for Childminders in Northern Ireland
Start up grants of £400 are available from the 'Start a Business Programme'

Grants for Childminders in Southern Ireland
Under the Equal Opportunities Childcare Program, Department of Justice Equality and Law Reform childminders are eligible to apply for capital grants to build (Start Up Grant), renovate or upgrade their childminding service (Improving Services Grant). There is also a quality assurance grant available. You will need to demonstrate what you will be using the funding for. For example, how the funding will upgrade your premises and how many childcare places will become available. You will also need to show how you evaluated your needs and how the children will benefit.

Childminding Services

Within childminding there is the flexibility to offer different types of service. Some childminders prefer to cater only for school age children, others to provide care overnight or work together to provide holiday activities. You will need to decide what service(s) you want to offer.

Choosing What Age Children to Care For

When you are registered you will be given information on what age and how many children you can care for. This may be influenced by your own children, your experience and the space available. Within these constraints there is still some flexibility for you to decide the age children you want to care for. You may choose to focus on one particular age group or take children that are a range of different ages.

Some childminders may choose to take school age children, providing a service where they take the children to school in the morning and collect them in the evening. As these children are older less extra equipment is needed. If you are only caring for children before and after school you will need to consider what your policy will be on school holidays, for example, will you extend your hours or not work during the holidays?

Childminders are usually more limited on numbers when it comes to younger children. When caring for babies and toddlers extra equipment such as a pushchair, cot, extra car seats and stair gate will be needed, these are extra expenses you will need to consider. Space available in your house may also be an issue for storage of the extra equipment.

If you are caring for children of varying ages you need to ensure the care of an older or younger child does not adversely affect the care of another. Children will need to learn to interact with different age children. This may provide a home setting similar to that of families with siblings. Children from a one child family may need help adjusting to a setting with children of different ages.

Types of Service Provided

Childminding is a flexible role and some childminders also provide where demand is sufficient:

After School Clubs

For working parents the hours between the end of school and the end of work can be the most difficult to arrange care for. An after school service usually involves collecting the child, providing an evening meal and help with home work.

Holiday Clubs

Many parents struggle obtaining holiday care. Children often appreciate a structure to the day as this is what they are used to at school. A range of special activities, freely chosen activities, outings and ground rules the children help to produce create a smooth running service.

Overnight or Weekend Cover

Weekend and overnight care attracts higher fees although it also has more impact on your own family. Parents in professions such as nursing may require this service. Few childminders offer this service so it could be a niche market. You should check whether there are additional regulations you need to comply with.

Shopping Cover

Offering occasional use services for example, while parents are shopping or having their hair done is a service only available from childminders or crèche and can be a useful way to attract more permanent customers as satisfied customers spread the word.

Childcare and Education

Currently in England this is the provision of the Foundation Stage Education for which the childminder can receive funding when part of a network and is combined with more usual childminding care. From 2008 this will be the Early Years Foundation Stage (EYFS) a combination of Birth to Three, the Foundation Stage and the National Standards for Day Care and Childminding. It will be compulsory for all childminders, but only those associated with networks and Children's Centres will be able to claim the Nursery Education Grant for individual children and be able to offer free sessions to parents.

Childminding Standards and Other Legislation

Legislation affecting childminders registration and the standards they need to work to varies according to the country you are working in. The following outlines some of the legislation and how it is relevant to your practice.

The Children Act 1989 (applies to England, Scotland and Wales)

The Children Act 1989 brought together private and public law relating to children. It replaced what was complex and fragmented legislation with a single statute. A guide to the act was produced in 1997 to provide a clear statement of the requirements placed on local authorities. It discussed the implications for policies, procedures and practice. The following parts are of most relevance to childminders:

Chapter 6 Section D - Childminding: This covers childminding and the implications for both Social Services and the childminder. It is a very useful section, helping childminders to know their expectations and rights. This can also have advantages when disputes have arisen. It gives details on ratios, records, working with parents, suitable premises, equipment and toys.

Chapter 7 - Registration of Daycare Services: This gives details on the registration of day care and childminding. It defines a fit person, suitable premises, registration requirements, refusal of registration and maintenance of a register of day care service providers. It also covers applications for registration, cancellation of registration and emergency cancellation, certificates of registration and the appeals procedure, offences and re-registration.

Chapter 8 - Inspections: This covers the purpose and process involved in inspections.

Annex C: This defines the types of childcare available to parents.

Annex D: This includes fire safety requirements and fire safety guidance for childminders and food hygiene implications.

Childcare Act 1991 (applies to Southern Ireland)

These regulations contain the laws governing childminding in Ireland. They cover ratios and notification procedures to the HSE, together with the fact that notification is only required where four preschool children from different families are cared for. It also states the notification fee is waived for childminders.

Childcare (Pre-school Services) Regulations 1996 & Amendments 1997 & 2006 (applies to Southern Ireland)

These regulations explain the requirements and procedures for notification and inspection, together with the standards required.

The Children (Northern Ireland) Order 1995 (applies to Northern Ireland)

Volume X1 of this order is the most relevant for childminders. Ratios are defined, safety issues and relationships with parents covered and the need for observations and maintenance of records.

The Childminding & Daycare (Applications for Registration) Regulations (Northern Ireland) 1996 (applies to Northern Ireland)

These define the information required when applying for registration. This includes information on qualifications and experience and of people living at the premises who will come into contact with minded children.

The Care Standards Act 2000 (applies to England and Wales)

The Care Standards Act passed the responsibility for the regulation of childminding from Local Authorities to Ofsted and CSSIW, in order to standardise care.

The Act amended the Children Act 1989, adding part XA Childminding and Daycare for Children in England and Wales. This act defines what a childminder is, the requirement to register, and the cancellation of registration and inspections. Provision was also made for the creation of regulations governing childminders, which led to the English National Childminding Standards and the Welsh National Minimum Standards.

Regulation of Care (Scotland) Act 2001 (applies to Scotland)

This regulation passed the responsibility for the regulation of childminding from Local Authorities to the Care Commission and led to the Scottish National Standards.

Children Act 2004 (applies to England)

This act provided the legal underpinning for *Every Child Matters: Change for Children* a program aimed at transforming children's services. In this act children's well being was used to define the five Every Child Matters outcomes.

❑ Be healthy.
❑ Stay safe.
❑ Enjoy and achieve.
❑ Make a positive contribution.
❑ Achieve economic well being.

This act also established Local Safeguarding Children Boards to replace the Area Child Protection Committees.

Daycare & Childminding Regulations 2005 (applies to England)

This sets a schedule for inspections at three year intervals; requires childminders to inform parents of impending inspections; and details the requirements for providing parents with copies of the inspection report.

Childcare Act 2006 (applies to mainly to England and partially to Wales)

The act places a duty on the Local Authority to improve the five Every Child Matters outcomes for all preschool children, to secure sufficient childcare for working parents and provide better parental information services. For England only the act simplifies early years regulation and inspection arrangements providing for a new integrated education and care framework for preschool children and the new Ofsted Childcare Register.

Food Hygiene Regulations 2006 (applies to UK & Southern Ireland)

A European (EU) Food Hygiene legislation that has been universally applied. This means childminders will be required to register with the relevant authority, usually the local Environmental Health Department for a light touch approval as childminders are considered as low risk premises.

The Motor Vehicles (Wearing of Seat Belts/Amendment) Regulations 2006 (applies in the UK with EU regulations applying in Ireland)

This details the use of appropriate child seats and child restraints for all children less than 135 centimetres in height who are also under twelve years of age. In Ireland the height required is 150 centimetres or less than thirty-six kilos. (see Section 8. Out and About with Children).

National Childminding Standards

There are National Standards covering most areas of the UK and Southern Ireland. In Ireland the implementation of National Standards was postponed indefinitely, so the principles of Daycare have been included instead. Although there are variations they all cover the same basic principles. They set out the standards of care which a childminder must provide for parents and children. Note: The English standards are due to be amalgamated into the Early Years Foundation Stage (EYFS) during 2008 and an overview of the EYFS has been provided.

Standards are important as they set targets for childminders to meet and ensure that parents know that every Registered Childminder meets the same standards and their child will be in a safe environment.

The following are summaries of the standards for England, Wales, Scotland and Ireland. Standards are always going through an evaluation process and may be reviewed. If you are considering childminding you should obtain a current copy of the relevant standards and their guidance notes which will have much more detail for each standard. Throughout this book you will find information on meeting the standards.

English National Standards / EYFS Overview

Learning and Development Requirements: Children must be provided with experiences and support to help them develop a positive sense of themselves and others; respect for others, social skills and a positive disposition to learn. Childminders must ensure support for children's emotional well-being to help them know themselves and what they can do.

By the end of the EYFS children should achieve the Early Learning Goals (ELG's) (See Section 12, Foundation Stage/Phase and EYFS) for the six areas of learning and development.

Childminders must ensure they are observing children and responding appropriately to help them make progress from birth towards the ELG's and report progress and achievements to parents. Throughout the EYFS childminders should observe and assess children's achievements, interests and learning styles, using this to identify learning priorities and plan individually for each child matching expectations to the ELG's.

Assessment at the end of the EYFS is to be completed by the provider where the child spends the majority of time between 8am and 6pm in the final term of the year in which a child turns five.

The provider (usually a school) must ensure children are assessed against the thirteen scales in the EYFS profile throughout the year. Information must be shared with the Local Authority (LEA). Providers must permit the LEA access to observe implementation of the arrangement for completion of this assessment and take part in moderation activities specified by the LEA.

Parents must be provided with a summary of the child's progress against the ELG's and the assessment scales. A copy of the EYFS profile if requested and opportunity to discuss it and the results.

Where a child changes main provider in the year they turn five the provider should send the new provider on request within fifteen days any recorded EYFS profile data and an assessment in respect of the child. If there is no profile recorded the reason why it has not been carried out.

Safeguarding and Promoting Children's Welfare: Childminders must take necessary steps to safeguard and promote the welfare of children.

❑ **Information and complaints:**This standard encompasses legal requirements regarding the provision of information for parents including activities, routines, ratios, food and drink provided, policies and procedures including complaints and how to contact or complain to Ofsted, failure to collect a child and a missing child. The information required from parents, written permission to seek emergency treatment and access for them to their child's developmental records. It also stipulates the complaint record should be kept for at least three years.

❑ **Premises and security:** Premises, indoors and outdoors, must be safe and secure. Childminders must notify Ofsted of any changes in facilities that may affect space or level of care. Childminders must only release children into the care of individuals named by the parent. They must ensure children do not leave the premises unsupervised and take steps to prevent intruders entering the premises.

❑ **Outings:** Children must be kept safe whilst on outings. For each specific outing childminders must carry out a full risk assessment taking into account the nature of the outing.

❑ **Equality of opportunities:** All childminders must have and implement an effective policy ensuring equality of opportunities and for supporting children with learning difficulties and disabilities. All childminders in receipt of Government funding must have regard to the SEN code of practice.

Childminders must promote the good health of children, take necessary steps to prevent the spread of infection and take appropriate action when they are ill.

❑ **Medicines:** Childminders must implement an effective policy on administering medicines to include effective management systems to support individual children with medical needs. Childminders must keep written records of all prescribed medicines administered to children and inform parents. Childminders must obtain written permission for each and every medicine from parents before any medication is given (note: medicine must be prescribed by doctor, dentist, nurse or pharmacist).

❑ **Illnesses and injury:** Childminders must notify Ofsted and the Local Child Protection agencies of any serious accident, injuries, serious illness, death of any child in their care and to act on advice given. At least one person with current paediatric first aid certificate must be on the premises when children are present and at least one on outings. Childminders must have a first aid box with appropriate contents to meet the needs of children. Childminders must keep a record of accidents and first aid treatment. Childminders must inform parents of accidents and injuries whilst in their care and of any first aid treatment given. Childminders should discuss with parents procedures for children who are ill or infectious to include possibility of exclusion and protocol for contact if a child becomes ill or receives minor injuries.

❑ **Food and drink:** Where children are provided with meals, snacks and drinks, these must be healthy, balanced and nutritious. Those responsible for the preparation and handling of food must be competent to do so. Fresh drinking water must be available at all times. Childminders must notify Ofsted of any food poisoning affecting two or more children looked after on the premises.

❑ **Smoking:** Childminders must ensure that children are in a smoke-free environment.

Children's behaviour must be managed effectively and in a manner appropriate for their stage of development and particular individual needs.

❑ **Behaviour management:** Childminders must not give corporal punishment to a child for whom they provide early years provision and so far as is reasonably practical, shall ensure that it is not given by any other person who cares for, or who is in regular contact with children or by any other person living or working on the premises. A person shall not be considered to have given corporal punishment if the action was to avert immediate danger of personal injury to, or danger of death to any person including the child. Childminders must not threaten corporal punishment, nor use or threaten any form of punishment which could have an adverse impact on the child's well-being. Childminders must have an effective behaviour management policy.

Suitable People: Childminders must ensure that adults looking after children or having unsupervised access to them are suitable to do so.

❑ **Safe recruitment:** This covers employing others and ensuring they have CRB checks before they start work and checking them against the list 99. Records must be kept of such checks. Childminders must have effective systems in place to ensure that those likely to have unsupervised access to the children (including those living or working on the premises) are suitable to do so.

Childminders must inform Ofsted of:
- Any proposal to employ an assistant.
- Any change of persons 16 years or over.
- Any proposal to add overnight care.
- Changes to the premises which affect space or quality of childcare.
- Changes in name or address.
- Any criminal offence committed after registration

❑ **Alcohol / Other substances:** Childminders must not be under the influence of alcohol or any other substance which may affect their ability to care for children.

Adults looking after children must have appropriate qualifications, training, skills and knowledge.

❑ **Training:** Childminders must have attended a training course within six months or registration and must hold a current paediatric first aid certificate at the point of registration.

Staffing arrangements must be organised to ensure safety and to meet the needs of the children.

❑ **Ratios:** Childminders must meet the requirements for adult:child ratios. These remain unchanged. For childminders providing overnight care, required ratios continue to apply. Children must be close by and within easy hearing distance (this may be via a monitor).

Suitable Premises, Environment and Equipment: Out door and indoor spaces, furniture, equipment and toys must be safe and suitable for their purpose.

❑ **Risk assessment:** Childminders must conduct a risk assessment and review it regularly at least once a year. Risk assessment must identify aspects of the environment that need to be checked on a regular basis: childminders must maintain records of these aspects and when they are checked. Regularity to be determined according to the risk. Childminders must take all reasonable steps to ensure that hazards to children indoors and outdoors are kept to a minimum.

❑ **Premises:** Childminders must inform Ofsted of any significant changes or events relating to the premises. These include structural alterations or extensions. Something adversely affecting smooth running of the provision over a sustained period of time and changes to the outside of the premises such as adding a pond or taking down fencing. Childminders must take reasonable steps to ensure safety in the case of fire, and must have a clearly defined procedure for the emergency evacuation of the house. Childminders must have appropriate fire detection and control equipment (for example, fire alarms, smoke detectors, fire extinguishers and fire blankets) which are in working order. The premises and equipment must be organised to meet the needs of children and as far as is reasonable be suitable children with disabilities. Childminders must display public liability insurance.

Organisation: Childminders must plan and organise systems to ensure that every child receives an enjoyable and challenging learning and development experience that is tailored to meet their individual needs.

Childminders must promote equality of opportunity and ant-discriminatory practice and must ensure that children are not disadvantaged because of ethnicity, culture or religion, home language, family background, learning difficulties or disabilities, gender or ability.

Childminders must ensure there is a balance of adult led and freely chosen or child initiated activities, delivered through indoor and outdoor play. Childminders must undertake sensitive observational assessments in order to plan to meet children's individual needs. Childminders must plan and provide experiences which are appropriate to each child's stage of development as they progress towards the early learning goals.

Documentation: Childminders must maintain records, policies and procedures required for the safe and efficient management of the setting and to meet the needs of children.

❑ **Data:** Childminders must record for each child: their full name, date of birth, name and address of every parent and carer who is known to the childminder, which of these parents or carers the child normally lives with and emergency contact details. For those childminders in receipt of funding for the free EYFS entitlement they must also record and submit to their LEA for the census a child's full name, date of birth, address, gender, SEN status, the number of funded hours in the census week and the total number of hours (funded and unfunded) taken up at the setting during the census week.

❑ **Providers' records:** Childminders must keep the following information and documentation:
  • Name, home address and telephone number of anyone else who will regularly be in unsupervised contact with the children.
  • Daily record of names of children and hours of attendance.
  • A record of the risk assessment to include the date carried out, date of review and any action taken following a review or incident.

Where Ofsted notifies in advance an inspection parents must be informed. Parents must be provided with copies of the inspection report.

Note :These are the general legal requirements and childminders should also have regard to the statutory guidance.

Welsh National Minimum Standards
❑ **STANDARD 1: Information Outcome:** Parents have the information they need to make an informed choice about the childminding service they require.
❑ **STANDARD 2: Contract Outcome:** Parents have a written contract they have agreed with the childminder.
❑ **STANDARD 3: Assessment Outcome:** All children placed with a childminder have their needs and preferences identified and their parents know how these needs will be met.
❑ **STANDARD 4: Meeting Individual Needs Outcome:** Parents know that the childminder plans for and meets their child's individual needs and preferences.
❑ **STANDARD 5: Working in Partnership with Parents Outcome:** Parents are kept fully involved as partners in, and informed about, their child's activities and development.
❑ **STANDARD 6: Individual Records Outcome:** Parents and the CSIW have access as appropriate to a full range of records maintained by the registered person for the smooth running of the setting.
❑ **STANDARD 7: Opportunities for Play and Learning Outcome:** Children experience a range of activities which assist with their emotional, physical, social, intellectual language and creative development.

❑ **STANDARD 8: Behaviour Outcome:** Parents know that their child's behaviour is managed in ways they have agreed, and in such a way as to promote their child's welfare and development.

❑ **STANDARD 9: Health Care Outcome:** Children's health care needs are identified and addressed as appropriate by the childminder.

❑ **STANDARD 10: Medication Outcome:** Children receive the prescribed medication they require from the childminder.

❑ **STANDARD 11: Meals Outcome:** Children receive food that is wholesome, and eat in surroundings that promote their dignity and social learning skills.

❑ **STANDARD 12: The Childminder as Suitable Person Outcome:** Parents and children can be sure that the childminder and any assistant are suitable.

❑ **STANDARD 13: Adult: Child Ratios Outcome:** Children's needs are met through a ratio of adults to children which conforms with the required adult: child ratios.

❑ **STANDARD 14: Equal Opportunities Outcome:** All children receiving a service from a childminder are treated with equal concern and respect.

❑ **STANDARD 15: Financial Procedures Outcome:** Children and their parents are safeguarded by the childminder operating sound financial procedures.

❑ **STANDARD 16: Quality Assurance Outcome:** The children and their parents receive a childminding service that is effectively monitored.

❑ **STANDARD 17: Complaints Outcome:** Children and their parents are confident that their complaints will be listened to, taken seriously and acted on.

❑ **STANDARD 18: Child Protection Outcome:** Parents have the confidence that the childminder takes all reasonable steps to protect children from harm.

❑ **STANDARD 19: The Premises Outcome:** The children receive a service in premises that are safe, secure and suitable for their purpose.

❑ **STANDARD 20: Equipment Outcome:** Children benefit from access to furniture, equipment and toys that are appropriate and suitable for their needs.

❑ **STANDARD 21: Safety Outcome:** Children have their needs met in settings that are safe.

Scottish National Care Standards

❑ **STANDARD 1:** Each child or young person will be welcomed, and will be valued as an individual.

❑ **STANDARD 2:** The needs of each child or young person are met by the service in a safe environment, in line with all relevant legislation.

❑ **STANDARD 3:** Each child or young person will be nurtured by staff who will promote his or her general well being, health, nutrition and safety.

❑ **STANDARD 4:** Each child or young person will be supported by staff who interact effectively and enthusiastically with him or her.

❑ **STANDARD 5:** Each child or young person can experience and choose from a balanced range of activities.

❑ **STANDARD 6:** Each child or young person receives support from staff who respond to his or her individual needs.

❑ **STANDARD 7:** In using the service, children, young people, parents and carers experience an environment of mutual respect, trust and open communication.

❑ **STANDARD 8:** You will be treated equally and fairly.

❑ **STANDARD 9:** You can be confident that the service contributes to the community and looks for opportunities to be involved in the community.

❑ **STANDARD 10:** You can be confident that the service keeps up links and works effectively with partner organisations.

❑ **STANDARD 11:** Each child or young person has access to a sufficient and suitable range of resources.

❑ **STANDARD 12:** Each child or young person receives support and care from staff who are competent and confident and who have gone through a careful selection procedure.

❑ **STANDARD 13:** You can be confident that the service will evaluate what it does and make improvements.

❑ **STANDARD 14:** You can be confident that you are using a service that is well managed.

Irish (Southern) National Quality Framework Standards

- ❑ **STANDARD 1: The Rights of the Child:** Ensuring children's rights are met and they are enabled to choose and use initiative as an active partner in their own development and learning.
- ❑ **STANDARD 2: Environments:** Enriching of environments indoor and outdoor. Materials and equipment to be well maintained, safe, available, accessible, adaptable, developmentally appropriate, challenging, stimulating.
- ❑ **STANDARD 3: Parents and families:** Proactive partnership approach, valuing and involving parents and families, demonstrated by clearly stated, accessible policies and procedures.
- ❑ **STANDARD 4: Consultation:** Ensuring inclusive decision-making promotes participation, seeking out and acting on views and opinions of children, parents and staff (childminder) as appropriate.
- ❑ **STANDARD 5: Interactions:** Policies, procedures and practice based on mutual respect, equal partnership and sensitivity.
- ❑ **STANDARD 6: Play:** Allowing time for free play with well-resourced, developmentally appropriate, accessible opportunities for exploration, creativity and meaning making for themselves, other children, or with supportive adults.
- ❑ **STANDARD 7: Curriculum:** Use of a verifiable, broad-based, documented and flexible curriculum or programme to encourage holistic development and learning.
- ❑ **STANDARD 8: Planning and Evaluation:** Use of cycles of observation, planning, action and evaluation undertaken on a regular basis to enrich and inform aspects of practice.
- ❑ **STANDARD 9: Health and Welfare:** Provision of nutritious food, opportunities for rest, secure relationships characterised by trust and respect and protection from harm.
- ❑ **STANDARD 10: Organisation:** Use of written philosophy and clearly communicated policies and procedures to guide and determine practice.
- ❑ **STANDARD 11: Professional Practice:** Maintaining skills, knowledge, values and attitudes with regular reflection upon practice and undertaking further supported training.
- ❑ **STANDARD 12: Communication:** Having policies and procedures and actions that promote proactive sharing of knowledge and information with respect and confidentiality.
- ❑ **STANDARD 13: Transitions:** Close involvement of parents and, where appropriate, relevant professionals. Policies, procedures and practice promoting sensitive management of transitions including liaison and transfer of relevant information (with parental consent).
- ❑ **STANDARD 14: Identity and Belonging:** Defined policies and procedures to promote positive identities and strong sense of belonging , confidence and a group identity and develop a positive understanding and regard to the identity and rights of others.
- ❑ **STANDARD 15: Legislation & Regulation:** Meeting or exceeding relevant regulations and legislative requirements.
- ❑ **STANDARD 16: Community Involvement:** Procedures and actions which extend and support all adults and children's engagement with the wider community.

Irish (Northern) Principles of Daycare

- ❑ **STANDARD 1:** A child's welfare and development are paramount.
- ❑ **STANDARD 2:** A child should be treated and respected as an individual whose needs, including special educational needs, are catered for.
- ❑ **STANDARD 3:** The values deriving from different backgrounds - religious, racial, cultural and linguistic, should be recognised and respected.
- ❑ **STANDARD 4:** A child has the right to safe and secure surroundings in which to grow and develop independence and social skills.
- ❑ **STANDARD 5:** A child has the right to learn and when young this is done through a wide variety of play.
- ❑ **STANDARD 6:** A child has the right to companionship of other children, individually and in groups.
- ❑ **STANDARD 7:** A child has the right to the company, protection and stimulation of adults in a manner which promotes development and independence.

❑ **STANDARD 8:** A child has the right to question and to be given answers at a level they can understand.

Quality Assurance

Quality Assurance schemes help childminders improve quality and increase marketability. They support childminders through mentoring, offering advice and help in thinking about how you work and how you can improve. They help you evaluate yourself, a helpful attribute for completing regulatory bodies self evaluation forms.

If you are a network childminder you will already be partaking in a quality assurance scheme. In some areas there may be a quality assurance scheme or Kite Mark which is provided for or suitable for childminders run or funded through the Local Authority.

The NCMA also has a quality assurance scheme, specifically for childminders, based on the NCMA Quality First Standards with three levels of attainment. During the assurance process a childminder has to complete reflective materials and build a portfolio with the support of an NCMA mentor through phone and email, and receives a home visit from an assessor to observe their interaction with the children they care for. The completed portfolio is sent to another NCMA assessor for assessment against specific criteria. Certificates awarded are valid for three years. This scheme is available for childminders in England, Wales and Northern Ireland.

Childcare Induction Standards (CIS - CS) (will apply to England)

These are a set of common induction standards to be used across the different areas of the English childcare work force. The standards will support the principles of Every Child Matters. These Standards were piloted in the Autumn of 2006, and two childminders were included within this. However considerable work will be needed before being launched to make them compatible with all childcare settings. These standards will link with other childminder specific standards to ensure they acknowledge that childminders work from home. Links will also be made to related qualifications. A work book for new childminders will be available to enable childminders to plan and record their induction and is likely to cover the following seven areas:

❑ Understand principles and values essential for working with children
❑ Understand role as worker (employed or self employed)
❑ Understand health and safety requirements
❑ Know how to communicate effectively
❑ Understand child development
❑ Safeguard children
❑ Develop yourself

2. Registration & Inspections Uncovered

All childminders must register with the appropriate regulatory body with the exception of Southern Ireland where for most childminders registration is still currently voluntary. In England the regulator is Ofsted; in Scotland it is The Care Commission; in Wales, the Care Standards Inspectorate; in Northern Ireland,The Health and Social Services Trust; in Southern Ireland, it is the Health Service Executive for both registration and voluntary registrations.

Ofsted (England)

The Office for Standards in Education (Ofsted), officially the Office of Her Majesty's Chief Inspector of Schools in England, is responsible for inspecting all early years child care and education, including childminders, in England. Their role is to enable the protection of children, to ensure the National Standards are met, to ensure that children are well cared for and can take part in activities that contribute to their development and learning and to provide parents with reassurance.

Ofsted's regulation of childminders covers registration, inspection, investigation and enforcement. Ofsted works actively with registered childminders to advise them what is expected of them. Childminders in turn are encouraged to seek advice from Ofsted about the compliance with requirements.

Ofsted has three regional centres as follows: Southern counties, Bristol; northern counties, Manchester and for the midlands, Nottingham. Each regional centre has a regional manager and three teams with different roles. The teams comprise of:

❑ Inspection support (called AIS teams).
❑ Complaints investigations and enforcement (called CIE teams).
❑ General administration, including applications and processing (called Business teams).

The regional centres support the work of the home based Childcare Inspectors and the Senior Childcare Inspectors (CCIs and SCCIs). Each SCCI will lead a team of six to ten inspectors in a small geographical area. At Ofsted's headquarters in London they have a secretariat and provide a national overview on policy and quality. This policy division is responsible for developing and maintaining Ofsted's national protocols.

CSSIW (Wales)

The Care and Social Services Inspectorate for Wales (CSSIW) is an operationally independent part of the National Assembly for Wales. It is responsible for registration, inspections, complaints and enforcement in Wales. They also organise the pre-registration information meetings for prospective childminders. Their National Headquarters, based at Parc Nantgarw, has a coordinating role and is home to the Chief Executive.

The CSSIW have eight regional and three local offices. Each region has a regional director to coordinate and support the local team. Each regional office covers an area base on those of the Local Authority/Local Health Boards. Regional offices are located as follows: Northwest region, Caernarfon; Northeast region, Mold; Southeast region, Pontypool; Southwest region, Swansea; Mid Wales region, Llandrindod Wells; West Wales region, Camarthan; Cardiff area, Tremorfa; Vale & Valleys region, Parc Nantgarw.

Care Commission (Scotland)

The Scottish Commission for the Regulation of Care (SCRC) or Care Commission was established in 2002 as an independent regulator. Part of its role is to regulate childminders through registration, inspection, investigation of complaints and by taking enforcement action. The national headquarters of the care commission is based at Dundee.

The SCRC has five regional offices and a number of local resource centres. Regional offices are located as follows: South West region, Hamilton; South East region, Musselburgh; Central West region, Paisley; Central East region, Dundee; North region, Aberdeen.

HSST (Northern Ireland)
The Health & Social Services Trust (HSST) in Northern Ireland are responsible for registrations, inspection, monitoring and support of childminders. Trusts central offices are located in these four areas:Northern area, Ballymena; Southern area, Armagh; Eastern area, Belfast; Western area, Londonderry.

HSE (Southern Ireland)
The Health Service Executive (HSE) in Ireland have the responsibility for ensuring the health, safety and welfare of preschool children (children under six, not attending school) through their preschool services inspectorate. All areas of children's services, including early childhood education and care, come under the auspices of the Minister for Children.

There are currently ten HSE areas and these are divided into four administrative areas, South, West, Dublin mid Leinster and Dublin North East. Regional offices are located as follows. Within the South area: Southern region, Cork; South Eastern region, Kilkenny; Within the West area: Mid Western region, Limerick; Western region, Galway; North Western region, Manor Hamilton; within the Dublin mid Leinster area: Midland region, Tullamore; South Western region, Naas; East Coast region, Bray; within the Dublin North East area: North Eastern region, Kells; Northern region, Swords.

Registration

Registration of childminders is the process of checking that prospective childminders are suitable to care for children and that the premises they want to be registered at are safe and suitable.

Ofsted expect it to take approximately three months, from the date they receive your application, for them to accept or reject you for registration. Both the SCRC and the CSSIW expect the process to take six months. It may take longer if you have areas that need addressing before you can be registered.

To start the registration procedure or for more information on registration you need to contact the Children's Information Service (CIS) in England, or for Scotland, Wales and Ireland contact the registering authority.

The CIS may send you Ofsted's book about childminding, 'Is Childminding For You?', and an information sheet on the CIS and the services they offer. Other authorities will supply information leaflets and booklets. You will also get a letter from the National Childminding Association (NCMA), a training body or from your registering body informing you about pre-registration information sessions and the dates they are held, together with a reply slip. The pre-registration meetings are held at varying locations across the UK and Ireland so there should be one near you. You need to return your reply slip to book your place on a pre-registration meeting.

At pre registration sessions application forms and the registration process are usually explained and any questions you have will be answered. Prospective childminders can receive their application packs at the meeting if they decide to proceed. You may be given information about your regulatory body and, the requirements you must comply with as a childminder, and possibly a start-up grant application form which may help you with purchasing necessary equipment. You may also receive an invitation to an pre-registration course such as the Introducing Childcare Practice (ICP) course. Ofsted for example, recommend that suitable training is preferably taken during registration but it must be completed within six months of being registered. Your application is formally made when the regulatory body has received the forms completed to their satisfaction. Regulatory bodies require information on both the applicant and members of their family to check their suitability for caring or being in contact with children.

Application packs usually contain an information leaflet, an application form, references request, other person's notification, health declaration and criminal record check (disclosure). If you need extra copies you can photocopy the blank forms.

Information Leaflets

Leaflets contain details of where information and support can be obtained and details of helpful documents to read before making an application. They also contain a checklist of forms you will need to submit.

Application Forms

These forms ask for details including previous experience and qualifications (verification such as certificates may be required), previous employment history and usually request two references. The form may ask for details of the premises where you plan to childmind and information about any other people who live or work on those premises.

You must also fill in sections relating to previous criminal convictions. You are normally required to sign a form consenting to a variety of checks for example, with the police, your doctor, social services and, to references being followed up.

References for Application

These are character references, similar to those you may require when applying for a job. Regulatory bodies are looking to see if you have qualities suitable for someone who will be caring for small children, e.g. caring or sociable, or qualities that would be less desirable, such as a short temper.

They will be using these references to help them form an opinion as to whether you can be classed as a 'fit person' to be caring for children.

References should be from someone who knows you well, and has known you for some years but is not a family member. Your bank manager, for example, is not suitable unless they are also a family friend, but someone you regularly babysit for would be ideal.

Other Persons Notification

This form asks for brief details which will enable a regulatory body to carry out any necessary checks on a persons suitability to look after, or to be in contact with children.

You need to submit the details of every person aged sixteen or over (ten or over in Northern Ireland) who lives or works on the premises where you intend to childmind, including anyone who will look after children with you.

Health Declaration

A health declaration will include questions about your health and ask for permission to contact your doctor or other medical practitioner. This is to help a regulatory body check you are mentally and physically suitable to care for children. Prospective childminders and anyone else who will look after the children, e.g. assistant childminders, will need to complete and sign this declaration.

When your form is received a request for a medical report may be sent to your doctor. Some doctors will charge for providing this service. You are entitled, should you wish, to see the medical report before it is supplied to a regulatory body, and to ask the doctor to amend anything which you consider to be inaccurate or misleading. If the doctor declines to amend any information, you are entitled to attach a written statement of your views of the reports contents or withhold your consent to the report being supplied to the regulatory authority. If you withhold consent, they may not be able to satisfy themselves as to your suitability.

Whether or not you decide to see the report before it is supplied to the regulator the doctor is obliged to keep a copy of the report, for a period of at least six months after it was supplied, and you are entitled to have access to that report if you would like to view it at a later date.

Criminal Record Check (Disclosure)

You and everyone aged sixteen years and over (ten in NI), that lives or works on the premises you intend to childmind at, including anyone who will look after children, will need to obtain a criminal record check. In Southern Ireland, although not yet compulsory, a Garda clearance would be good practice.

Prospective childminders in England, Wales and Scotland will be checked under the Enhanced Disclosure police check. In Ireland this would be undertaken by the Garda.

Ofsted has registered as an 'umbrella body' of the Criminal Records Bureau (CRB) and will carry out criminal record checks on your behalf. You will need to complete the relevant forms before your registration visit. CSSIW deal with the Criminal Records Bureau forms in Wales and the SCRC in Scotland.

Regulatory bodies with the exception of HSE in Ireland will send you a letter containing guidance on how to apply for your check. Ofsted will also send the unique number for Ofsted as a registered 'umbrella body'.

When you receive your disclosure form you should check the details that have already been entered and add any additional information that is requested. Return or retain the form as requested. The inspector or yourself will dispatch the completed form to the CRB and both yourself and the regulatory body will receive a copy of the disclosure from the CRB.

For other members living or working on the premises the process is the same, you may contact the CRB on their behalf if you have their relevant details to hand or alternatively they can contact the CRB personally.

Prospective childminders and individuals subject to the criminal records check, disclosure or Garda clearance will be asked to provide original documents (not photocopies) to verify identity, date of birth and any name changes. These could include a passport or birth certificate to confirm identity and marriage certificates or deed poll papers where appropriate to confirm any changes of name.

An Enhanced CRB Report, as required by childminders, will include details of all convictions recorded including 'spent' convictions, cautions, reprimands and warnings. It will include any information from the DfES and Department of Health lists of persons deemed unsuitable for work with children and will include checks made with your local police (Garda) force.

The results of police checks and other information supplied will be taken into account by a regulatory body in assessing the suitability of a person for contact with children.

Registration Inspections

During the registration inspection the inspector will be gathering information to check that you, as a prospective childminder, are suitable and ready to be registered and that your premises are also safe and suitable for children.

Preparation for a Visit

In preparation you should read your National Standards and any guidance for them. This will help you prepare and give you information on what the inspector is looking for.

Heath and Safety: You should conduct your own health and safety inspection of your home. It may help to consider this from a child's perspective. Try sitting on the floor to check from a child's point of view and remember not all children are 'little angels'. It is helpful to consider one room at a time and cover all areas children will have access to. Whilst checking your premises consider the following, and read Section 7. Health Hygiene and Safety for further details.

This is not an exhaustive list and you may notice factors that have been omitted that are relevant to your particular premises and working practices.

Lounges, Dining Areas, Sitting Rooms, Play Rooms

- ✓ Heating Appliances - These need to be protected with fire guards or similar, including radiators unless they run at safe temperatures.
- ✓ Glass - Safety or laminated glass is required for floor height windows or safety film used. Safety glass or safety film is also necessary for accessible glass doored cabinets, tables etc.
- ✓ Cupboard/Drawer Contents - Check these are suitable for small children or secured with safety catches to prevent children's access. Unsuitable contents might include alcohol, drinking glasses or plastic bags.
- ✓ Electric Sockets - If these are not in use they should be protected with socket covers.
- ✓ Tablecloths - Ensure these are not dangling where small children can pull them off together with the table contents.
- ✓ Curtains/Blinds - Check for dangling cords, children have been known to strangle themselves accidentally in these.
- ✓ Floor Covering - These should be kept clean and be well fitted. This is to ensure hygiene and prevent tripping.
- ✓ House Plants - Make sure any poisonous varieties, eg Dieffenbachia (dumb cane), are 'up higher' out of reach of children.
- ✓ Playthings, toys and learning materials - These should be clean and unbroken, pens and crayons should be non toxic and with safety caps and all should be suitable for the age and stage of development of the children you intend to care for.
- ✓ Equipment - This needs to be clean, safe and in good condition, e.g. highchairs should have a safety harness to prevent children falling out.
- ✓ Electrical Appliances - Make sure these are safe from prying fingers, e.g. that a child can't post their toast in the video slot.
- ✓ Pets - These should be under control at all times and good natured and remember to a crawling child, cat biscuits look really tasty!
- ✓ Trailing Flexes - Make sure these are not a hazard, or that children can't pull a lamp down.

Kitchen

- ✓ Glass - As for living areas.
- ✓ Cupboards / Drawers - As for living area, but also be aware of dangerous items including knives, skewers, string, cling film, freezer bags, washing powder and cleaning products.

✓ Fire Blanket - These need to be sited appropriately to be useful, e.g. not over the cooker or other potential sources of fire, as if a fire occurs in these areas access to the fire blanket will not be possible. A large sized fire blanket can help smother flames if a child clothes are burning.

✓ Electrical Socket - As for Living areas.

✓ Electrical Equipment - This type of equipment should be kept out of reach and electrical leads should be short enough that children cannot pull appliances off work surfaces.

✓ Fridge/Freezer - Make sure these run at manufacturers recommended temperatures, usually 4 -5°c for fridge and -18°c for freezer, to ensure food remains fresh.

✓ Waste Bins - These should be maintained in a clean, hygienic way and should be kept closed.

✓ Animal Litter trays - These are not suitable to have in areas to which a child might have access.

✓ Kitchen in general should be clean and hygienic, fridge contents should be regularly cycled, with all food covered and raw meat stored below cooked meat to avoid contamination. There should be room for storing minded children's food from home where appropriate. A gate or barrier to the kitchen may be appropriate in some circumstances to prevent children from accessing dangerous areas, e.g. a hot cooker.

Halls, Stair Wells and Landings

✓ Stairgates - These should be correctly fitted in accordance with manufacturers instructions and appropriate for age of children you intend to care for.

✓ Smoke detector - These must be fitted on every floor of the house and be tested weekly, batteries should be replaced annually, (write the date on the battery and in your books to help you remember and choose a memorable date).

✓ Glass - As for living areas, glass panelled doors at the bottom of stairs may be hazardous.

✓ Floor Coverings - These should be clean and securely fitted.

✓ Banisters - Check that children cannot climb up or through handrails.

✓ Doors - Closed where appropriate.

Bathrooms, Cloakrooms, Toilets

✓ Cupboards - If contents are not suitable for small children they should be secured with safety catches. Unsuitable items include cleaning products, medication, razor blades, toiletries and cosmetics.

✓ Equipment - Should be maintained in a clean and hygienic fashion. Useful items to have include, toilet seat, potty, step stool and changing mat.

✓ These areas in general should be maintained in a hygienic condition and good hygienic nappy changing and disposal routines should be followed.

Bedrooms

✓ Heating Appliances - As living area.

✓ Glass - As living area.

✓ Cupboards / Drawers - As living area, unsuitable items could include medications, toiletries and cosmetics.

✓ Power Points - Socket covers fitted.

✓ Equipment - Cots should be clean and in good condition and each child should have separate linen and bedding.

Gardens and Outside Areas

✓ Washing Lines - Hanging lines and uncovered rotary dryers are a hazard.

✓ Hazardous Plants - These might include poisonous plants, those with sharp edges as with some grasses or thorns. They should be away from areas where children play or have access to.

✓ Play Equipment - This should be kept clean and in good repair, and regularly tested for faults. Large equipment must be secured according to manufacturers instructions, for example, swing frames should be concreted into the ground. Play equipment should be suitable for the age range of children you intend to care for. Sandpits and water must be covered to ensure hygiene and safety.

✓ Security - Fences and gates must be secure, there should be no access for the children to tool sheds or garages. Greenhouses, steps, ponds and water hazards may need barriers to prevent children accessing them.

✓ Pets and Wild animals - The garden or outside area should be free from animal waste and pets cages/runs should be secure.

✓ Equipment - Pushchair/buggies should be clean and in good repair, they should have full five point harnesses, to prevent children wriggling out. Car seats and restraints should meet current British or European standards.

The Visit

Before your visit an Inspector will contact you to confirm the date and to make sure you will have all necessary documents to hand. These must be originals and may include passport, birth certificate, marriage certificate, driving licence, CRB form and child protection procedures. You will receive a list of documents that they require in advance.

During the visit the inspector will be checking that your premises are suitable, safe and ready for children to begin attending and that you meet all your National Standards. They will do this by checking all rooms and any outdoor spaces are safe and hygienic, that equipment is safe and appropriate for the age and developmental needs of the children, and through discussion with you.

Inspectors will check food preparation areas for safety and hygiene requirements, including those required by environmental health departments, for example fridge temperatures.

They will check animals on the premises will be housed appropriately and controlled while the children are present.

Where a vehicle is to be used for transporting children you will need to show the inspector that it is roadworthy (MOT), taxed and insured (including insurance to cover business use), and that appropriate child seats and safety restraints are used.

Inspectors are also required to confirm a prospective childminder is qualified and prepared to begin caring for children on the premises. In order to do this inspectors will discuss aspects of your proposed childminding practice, including how you will cover the following points:

❑ Promotion of equality of opportunity and anti-discriminatory practice
❑ Managing children's behaviour
❑ Establishing good relationships will parents
❑ Child Protection Issues

Suitable Person Interview

The inspector will conduct what is referred to as a suitable person interview. During this the inspector discusses all aspects of the National Standards with you and the kind of activities you intend to offer the children. The inspector is checking you will offer a wide variety of experiences to the children which will help them develop physically, socially, emotionally and intellectually.

The inspector will also be checking that you are aware of the necessity for your premises and practices to meet hygienic requirements to ensure children's good health. They will check that there are arrangements for administering and recording of first aid and medicines, and the procedures you will follow should a child become ill. The inspector will also check on your understanding of child protection issues.

During the registration visit the inspector will be assessing your all round suitability and will use this together with the space available on the premises to assess the number of children you can be registered to care for.

Throughout the inspection the onus is on you to show how you intend to meet the standards and you will need to demonstrate that you have identified possible risks to health and safety and what you have done to minimise these risks.

This is a good time to fill in your start-up grant application, your inspector may offer suggestions for required equipment you could purchase.

You will be required to attend a Childminder Induction Course. An example would be the Introduction to Childcare Practice (ICP), this is the first step to the nationally recognised qualification, Diploma in Home-based Childcare (DHC). Most Early Years teams expect training to be completed before registration but this varies from area to area.

Feed Back

Before an inspector leaves your premises they will provide you with verbal feedback, so you will know if they will recommend your registration.

If further action is required before a recommendation for registering can be made an Agenda for Action, with appropriate time scales, will be discussed and mutually agreed between your self and the inspector, together with any conditions which will be imposed on the registration.

An example of action required might be:' Ensure children do not have access to sharp knives': You as the applicant will decide how to achieve this as the inspections are outcome based. Most actions required will have several options you can use to comply. For example, in this case, you could fit cupboard catches to drawers containing knives in the kitchen, move the knives out of reach, or fit a gate across the door to the kitchen.

An example of a condition might be, 'children are to be accompanied while playing in the garden'. Conditions are always phrased as statements and in the present tense.

Inspectors must ensure that any action they require is proportionate to the risk involved in the safety and welfare of the children and that compliance with the action does not result in major costs.

After the visit an inspector has to produce a summary of recommendations which will be reviewed by a senior staff member. If there are actions to be made, as discussed at your registration visit, you will receive a letter detailing the work needing to be done to meet the National Standards and the time period which you have to complete the actions.

When the required actions have been undertaken you should notify your regulatory bodie's regional centre in writing, within the stipulated time frame. An additional registration visit may be made to check the actions carried out are satisfactory.

Registration Approval

When your application is approved a letter will be sent to you, stating the decision to register (notice of intention) and any conditions that will apply. You do have the right to object to any conditions imposed.

Registration Refused

If your registration is refused, a letter will be sent to you stating the intent to refuse your registration and giving the reasons for the decision. You have the right to object. If no objection is received within the stipulated period the notice of refusal will be issued. You still retain the right of appeal.

There are several reasons why a regulatory body may refuse to register a prospective childminder. These include not being qualified for registration or the prescribed fee for registration has not been paid.

Objections

If you wish to object to a condition being imposed, or to the refusal of a registration you must inform your regional centre, in writing, within the prescribed period. If a prospective childminder has raised any issues regarding the decision to register, they will be discussed by the applications team and the issue of the certificate may be delayed.

Registration Certificate

If registration is approved a certificate is normally issued fourteen days after receipt of your written acceptance of any conditions imposed.

Inspections for Existing Childminders

Inspections provide a regular check to ensure registered childminders are continuing to meet the National Standards. Inspectors will report on the standard of care provided and check that the childminder is still qualified to provide daycare, enabling regulatory bodies to reassure parents that their children are cared for in a safe environment. A copy of the report will be provided to the registered childminder and the process will be repeated approximately every three years in England and annually in both Scotland and Wales. These reports will identify strengths and weaknesses of the childminding provision so that quality can be maintained and improved upon.

During the inspection the inspector will be checking that the premises and equipment are suitable. They will check that the children are safe and well cared for and being provided with activities which will promote their development and learning, also that parents are kept well informed and discuss their children's needs.

Inspectors will be rigorous but with the minimum of bureaucracy and disruption (i.e. the children in your care will come first). You should keep in mind that Standards are written as outcomes and therefore the onus is on the childminder to demonstrate how they meet the standards.

Before an Inspection

The inspection support team from your local regulatory regional office will notify you by phone or letter when your inspection is due. In exceptional circumstances some inspections might take place without notice. Childminders are likely to be asked about changes to household members, building alterations not previously notified and any changes in the number and age of the children cared for.

You will be notified of a time period of when the inspection will take place. Childminders may be asked about holidays, day trips and outings if known within the inspection time frame so inspectors can call at a time when the childminder is likely to be in and childminding. Childminders will receive very little or no notice of the exact date/time of inspection. Prior to the inspection the inspector will check previous reports, conditions imposed at registration and complaints received to see if any action is required.

If you receive prior notification you should inform the parents of the children you care for, you are being inspected. It can be helpful if they would like to write something for you, which you can share with the inspector, on how they and their children view the service you provide and the quality of your childcare provision.

Preparing for the Inspection

The guidance to your National Standards will help you prepare for an inspection visit. You should make sure all documents are available for the inspector to view during the visit, a list will be provided for you by the regulatory bodies regional support team when a visit is due.

You might find a portfolio of your policies and practices will be helpful (see Section 17. Maintaining a Portfolio and Policies).Your certificates for training attended could also be stored here and may help an inspector form a positive view of your practices.

Self Evaluation or Self Assessment

Self evaluation gives you the opportunity to explain how you feel you are meeting outcomes and standards set out in law during your every day childminding practice. It helps you become a reflective practitioner and, to think about what you are doing and why you do it and wether you could improve your practices. If you consider each standard or expected outcome in turn it can be helpful to write down a sentence on how you achieve them and where possible illustrate with a photograph (NB: good practice dictates permission for photos of children is obtained). You may like to include thank you letters; references from parents and pictures or comments from the children to share with the inspector. These can be grouped together for ease or in England into the Every Child Matters headings (see Section 14. Observation, Assessment and Evaluation for more information). Self evaluation should be a continuous process and can demonstrate good practice which may not be obvious in an inspection which is only a 'snap shot' of your practice.

Grading (England & Scotland)

In England Ofsted grades childminders practice using the terms: Inadequate, Satisfactory, Good and Outstanding. Satisfactory is for childminders whose practice is effective with scope for improvement. Good is for those whose practice is worth reinforcing and developing. Outstanding is reserved for childminders whose practice is considered exceptional.

In Scotland the Care Commission grades specific areas giving each a mark on a scale of 1-6 with six being excellent. This comes with an explanatory and detailed report on how and why the grade was agreed. To achieve top marks childminders will need to show how parents are included.

As a registered childminder the normal standards of your care and safety should meet all the requirements that an inspector will look for, so there should not be much preparation that you need to do. It may help to read through 'Preparing for a Registration Visit' to reassure yourself you haven't missed anything.

Integrated Inspections

These occur where both care and education are being provided and the education side is inspected at the same time. Inspectors look for evidence of observation led planning and recording of progression. In England this is towards the 'Foundation Stage, stepping stones'.

During the Inspection

All regulators undertake an inspection although criteria may vary. Before you admit an inspector to your home remember to check their credentials, they should be carrying ID proving they are an inspector. If you are in any doubt leave them on the door step while you check with your regulatory body.

A typical inspection should take approximately two to three hours, an integrated care and education inspection will take longer. The inspector will be gathering evidence and information as in the registration visit. This evidence and information will be provided by the childminder through discussions and their provision of relevant documents. Information is also gathered by the inspector by observation of what the children are doing, the way the childminder is relating to them, the quality of care and the resources provided for their learning. The intention throughout the inspection is to check you are meeting your National Standards and to consider what it is like to be a child at your childminding setting. In England Ofsted will be using the 'Every Child Matters' outcomes (see the Children Act 2004 in Section 1). In practice this will mean the inspector will be looking at how the experiences and activities you provide enable the children to meet these.

You may find that taking your inspector on a tour of your premises and pointing out how you have made each area safe, hygienic and suitable for children will help you to cover the points needed. Include what stimulating activities take place in each area incorporating equipment and play provisions. Remember to include outside areas.

Cloakrooms and bathrooms are good areas to discuss your hygiene practices, health, prevention of infection and also remember to talk about exclusion of sick children and first aid.

Kitchens are good places to discuss hygiene, healthy diets, religious and cultural preferences and regular meals, drinks and snacks.

In play areas discuss what toys and activities are available, how the area is made safe and how you make sure toys are suitable for the age ranges you care for. You can also discuss your equal opportunities provision.

You will need to explain to your inspector how you would deal with challenging behaviour and how you reward good behaviour. The inspector will also need to know how you promote equal opportunities for all children, including those with special needs.

Inspectors also need to ensure that you work with parents to meet their children's needs, e.g. information is gathered and used regarding a child's routine, preferred diet, religious preferences, and that time is provided for parents to discuss a child's day.

In the UK the inspector will also look at how you implement the 'Birth to Three' practices if you have children under three and the 'Foundation Stage' if it is a combined inspection. From 2008 Birth to Three, the Foundation Stage and the National Standards will be combined to form the Early Years Foundation Stage (EYFS) and then all childminders in England will be inspected against the EYFS.

The inspector will also inspect your prepared documents, your portfolio and policies (if you have them), your accident/incident book, records of medicine administration, records of evacuation/fire practice records, complaints procedure and complaints, your records of children's attendance, proof of contracts and child records.

Feed Back

At the end of an inspection you will receive oral feedback from the inspector as to whether or not the registration will continue and in England what grading you will receive.

If the standards have not been met an action plan will be mutually agreed with time scales for completion and you will receive a letter detailing what is required. Failing to meet the standards may also result in new conditions being put on the registration.

When you have taken any necessary actions you should inform you regulatory body in writing. An additional visit may occur to check the actions.

Inspection Report

After the inspection you will receive a written report and you should check that it is factually correct. After any changes have been made the final report will be sent to you. You are expected to make copies available for parents to read. In England childminders are now required to provide a copy of the report to parents within five days of receiving the report. The cost of reproducing a report can be charged at cost to the receiving parents.

The report will summarise the inspector's findings and clearly state your registration status. Where applicable it will include anything that must be done, and by what date, to meet the National Standards. It will also include any recommendations to enable you to improve your practice.

Notice of Intent

A notice of intent sets out the conditions of registration that will apply. It will detail conditions imposed, varied or removed and you have a right to object to these.

Variations and Conditions

The registration certificate may impose conditions or a variation of terms. A registered childminder must comply with these conditions in order to remain qualified for registration. They will include standard ones, such as supplying a regulatory body with information, and may include conditions imposed at registration, such as actions required to ensure National Standards are fully met.

Regulators can decide after an inspection, during an investigative visit, follow up or monitoring visit that a registered childminder's registration can only continue if new conditions are made or existing conditions altered.

Where circumstances change, registered childminders can apply to have conditions varied or removed. Examples would be where a condition has been met within the required timescale or an extension provides more room for children to play.

Requests to vary or remove conditions must be sent in writing to your regional regulatory office, who will then make a decision to agree or refuse such an application. If they do not find in your favour you have a right to object.

Where a new condition has been imposed or existing conditions have been varied you may receive a visit from an inspector to check you are complying with the conditions.

Receiving a Compliance Notice

If you are found to be in breach of regulations relating to the National Standards or the keeping of records you will be given the opportunity to comply, i.e. they will request you meet the standards and keep appropriate records. If you do not comply, the regulatory body will impose or vary your conditions of registration. Failure to observe these conditions will result in the issuing of a compliance notice instructing you to do so. You will be given a date by which to comply. You have no statutory right of appeal. If you fail to comply with the notice by the date due, you will be committing an offence, and may be prosecuted or have your registration cancelled.

Intent to Cancel Registration

When a decision has been made to cancel your registration following an inspection, you will receive a letter stating the intention to cancel and giving the reasons. You have the right to object to a cancellation.

Cancellation of Registration

Regulatory bodies can cancel a registered childminder's registration for the following reasons:

❑ If they consider you have ceased or will cease to be qualified for registration.
❑ If the annual registration and inspection fee has not been paid when invoiced.

When a regulator imposes a condition on a registered childminder to make changes to their services, equipment or premises, they can only cancel that registration on the grounds of defects in the service, equipment or premises for the following reasons:

❑ Time set for actions has expired or lapsed.
❑ It can be shown the defects are due to the changes or additions having been made.

Objection

If you want to object to a condition imposed, varied or removed, or to a cancellation of your current registration, inform the regulatory bodies regional centre in writing. This has to be written within 14 days of receiving the notice of intention. The conditions will not take effect until after the period of appeal has lapsed or is heard, the conditions will apply if you do not object. Decisions made by regulators will be provided in writing.

Registration Certificate

If you already have a registration certificate a new one will usually only be issued where conditions have been imposed, varied or removed. If this is the case then a new certificate will be received approximately 14 days after they receive your written acceptance of any changes.

Between Inspections

Between inspections you should be maintaining your records including an attendance register, accident and incident logs, medicines administered, fire practice and evacuation records, complaints records, risk assessments, diaries (providing a detailed record of happenings and visitors etc.), details of courses attended, information sheets on children's individual needs, parental contact details, children's doctors, tax records and any policy statements you produce.

Duties to Regulators

You are required to notify regulatory bodies if there are any significant relevant changes between inspections to your premises, family circumstances or significant injuries, harm or communicable diseases. Where it is not possible to notify a regulatory body in advance, they must be notified as soon as possible and no later than fourteen days after the event occurs.

Notifiable events might include change of address, conversion or extension to your home and changes of the hours you provide childminding for e.g. changing from part time to full time.

You are required to notify a regulator if you change your name, e.g. get married or the people living or working in your home change, e.g. you take in a lodger, or when a person living in the home reaches the age of sixteen. You will need to supply full details so a check can be made. You must also notify a regulator of any matter which may affect a person's suitability to be in regular contact with children.

Regulatory bodies require notification of infectious disease considered serious by the doctor, serious injuries, illnesses or death of children and persons living or working on the childminding premises. Regulators should also be notified where there have been allegations of serious harm or abuse by persons looking after children, living or working on the premises. In general they should be notified of any serious matter or event which may affect the welfare of children on the premises.

In line with the Children Act and to comply with regulatory bodies the records you should be keeping are as follows:

❑ Name, home address and date of birth of each child
❑ Name, home address and telephone number of a parent for each child
❑ Parent or guardians place of employment and contact telephone number
❑ Name, address and telephone number of child's GP
❑ Records of medicine administered to children, including date, circumstances, who administered, parents consent (this record needs to be kept for two years)
❑ A record of accidents occurring on the premises
❑ An attendance register noting if an assistant and not the childminder is caring for the children
❑ Name, home address of the registered childminder and any other person regularly in unsupervised contact with the children, and of any other person living or working on the premises
❑ Complaints records including details of complaint, standards referred to and outcomes
❑ Records of evacuation and fire practices

Resignation

If you decide to stop childminding you should resign your registration. The registration certificate should be returned to your regulatory bodies regional centre together with a covering letter.

Registered childminders cannot resign their registration where regulators have issued a notice of intention to cancel the registration.

Regulators and Childminder's Assistants

Registered childminders are required to notify regulatory bodies of any staff they propose to employ. Once a prospective assistant has been found and before they begin working you will need to obtain and submit the relevant paper work to your regulatory body.

A form of notification of involvement with a registered childminder will be required, full details can be found under Registration Section 2. An application for an enhanced criminal records disclosure will be required and the registered childminder will be responsible for verifying the identity details of the prospective assistant and will have to produce a signed declaration to that effect.

A health declaration form will also be required by the regulator who will seek information from the prospective assistants doctor if they have any concerns arising from the supplied information.

The registered childminder will be required to show that their assistant will be suitable and able to comply with National Standards. In addition regulators will check that the proposed assistant does not appear in the list of people banned from working with children under the Protection of Children Act 1999.

The decision of whether an assistant is suitable to employ is the registered childminders, who should take into account any concerns about the suitability of the prospective assistant reported to them by the regulatory team. You should be aware that regulators will take into account your assistant when they consider your qualification and fit person status as a registered childminder.

Don't Panic, Inspectors are Human!

Inspectors should conduct your inspection according to set requirements and guidance produced by their regulatory team, and they will have a complaints procedure should it be required.

Inspectors should treat childminders with courtesy and sensitivity while minimising stress and bureaucracy. They will be acting with the best interests of the children and adults, so if you need to feed or change a child, that should come first. Inspectors will be evaluating your provision objectively against the standards, they have to report honestly and fairly, anything recorded must accurately reflect your achievements and actions.

Your inspector is human; talk to them and ask questions if you do not understand something. Ask them to explain and give examples or instances to help you follow their reasoning. Discussions will help you develop a professional relationship with your Inspector, which is a positive step for future meetings.

Complaints

As a registered childminder you must provide parents with a means of addressing complaints about the service or care you provide. Discussions with the parent are usually sufficient to resolve any complaints or problems. You should also have a policy for recording all written complaints from parents and record all outcomes. These complaint records need to be retained for ten years. Occasionally this is not enough and a parent may complain to a regulator (it is also not unknown for parents to make false accusations in order to avoid payment).

Regulatory bodies investigate complaints they receive of non-compliance with the standards, regulations or the conditions of registration. Complaints are usually viewed as an opportunity for a provider to improve the quality of their service, a complaint may highlight an area where an improvement can be made.

Complaints are usually dealt with a minimum of delay whilst respecting confidentiality. Whilst some complainants may wish to remain anonymous, regulators will suggest that should the complaint proceed their identity may be disclosed. Names are preferred to prevent malicious complaints.

If a complaint has been made against you the details will be restricted on a need to know basis. Regulators will consider all complaints as allegations until they are proved. They will gather evidence to enable them to produce an informed conclusion.

Unless a complaint involves or might involve child protection issues, when it will be dealt with by the Local Safeguarding Children Board (England), Child Protection Committee (Wales & Scotland) or the Health Board (Ireland), regulators will investigate. Where child protection issues are involved you may be asked to stop childminding while the investigation is in progress.

Most non serious complaints will be referred back to the registered childminder for them to look into and regulators will expect written details of the outcome, for example actions taken to resolve the problem, and may check this and your complaints procedure at their next visit.

Investigations

An investigation may be made when a complaint has been received, an allegation made or a breach of requirements has been submitted or reported. For example, if you have been reported as having more children in your care than your registration allows. However the majority of complaints will be referred to yourself for investigation.

Information gathered or received on registered childminders forms part of the evaluation as to the continued suitability for registration.

It is quite common for a visit or phone call to be made in order to check the facts of the complaint. The regulatory bodies inspectors have a statutory right of entry to your premises at any reasonable time of day if they believe a child is being looked after in contravention of requirements (including the premises of unregistered child carers) but they must produce authorising documents. Obstructing the registered inspector is an offence.

Should you be unfortunate enough to have such an investigation you should be aware that these officials have certain rights to gather evidence.

❑ They can inspect your premises.
❑ They can inspect records and relevant documentation, they can take copies of these but not the originals. Note: you should obtain a receipt for any items removed from the premises.
❑ They can remove documents or materials when they have reasonable grounds to think they contain evidence of failure to comply with any condition or requirement. Note: obtain receipts for any such items.
❑ They will expect you to cooperate.
❑ They can take measurements and photographs.
❑ They are able to inspect children being looked after and check on their welfare. Important note: ensure they are genuine officials first.
❑ They can interview you and can interview in private any other person looking after children living on the premises who consents to an interview. Note: children should be accompanied by an appropriate adult and adults may request an independent witness.

When gathering evidence regulators must make clear and accurate records. Detailed notes and records of phone calls made to you are usually kept by the regulator and checked to ensure there is a mutual understanding of what was said or has taken place. You might like to make records to keep for your own use.

Where regulatory bodies believe the result of the investigation will lead to enforcement action then they need to ensure that the evidence they have will stand up in court or at a tribunal. For a tribunal their evidence must prove that in all likelihood the offence probably happened, should the case be a criminal one then the evidence they collect has to prove 'beyond any reasonable doubt' that the offence occurred.

If you are to be interviewed you can request the presence of a friend, supportive person or legal representative. You do not have to be interviewed alone.

When the results of any investigation requires action to be taken then a regulator may take enforcement action.

Enforcement

Regulators have powers of enforcement which they use when registered childminders fail to meet or are in breach of standards, regulations or conditions of registration, or when an unregistered person has been childminding. Regulators use a range of enforcement practices and will use what they consider to be the most appropriate to match the situation. Sanctions vary from non-statutory measures, civil sanctions and imposition of conditions, through to cancelling a childminders registration. As a last resort a regulator may begin criminal proceedings resulting in prosecution for the offence.

Non-Statutory Enforcement

Non-statutory methods are typically employed where a registered childminder is not fully complying in a minor way with their National Standards or conditions of registration. Examples of methods employed include use of formal explanations as part of feedback after an inspection where the childminder is deemed receptive and regulators believe it will be sufficient to rectify the problem. Regulators could also require an action to be taken within a set time scale which will be notified by letter. Once the actions are complete and the registered childminder has informed their regulatory body an additional visit may occur.

If a registered childminder fails to respond favourably to these non-statutory methods regulators may resort to statutory means of enforcement.

Statutory Enforcement

Regulators have a range of statutory powers of enforcement or civil sanctions. They can:

❑ refuse to register an applicant.
❑ cancel a registered persons registration.
❑ impose new conditions of registration, vary or remove existing ones from registered childminders.
❑ serve a compliance notice.
❑ suspend a registered childminders registration.
❑ apply to a Justice of the Peace, Justice of the District Court or, Sheriff to obtain an emergency order to cancel a registration, impose or vary existing conditions where it could be construed that a child is suffering, or would be likely to suffer serious harm.
❑ serve an enforcement notice on an unregistered person acting as a childminder.

Justice of the Peace, District Court and Sheriff

A Justice of the Peace (JP) is a civil officer, a lay magistrate who has been appointed to hear minor cases and grant licences (England & Wales). A Justice of the District Court (JDC) is a judge who can issue court orders under the Childcare Act 1991 (Ireland). A Sheriff is a judge with ministerial powers and can serve judicial writs (Scotland).

Regulators can make an application to the JP, JDC or Sheriff without giving notice to the childminder. They will support this application with a written statement as to why they feel it is necessary. The JP, JDC or Sheriff will need to be satisfied there is a risk of significant harm to children in the registered childminders care before the application is approved.

If having satisfied themself, the JP, JDC or Sheriff will make an emergency order. They must serve it on the registered childminder with minimal delay. The order should be accompanied with copies of any statement by the childminding regulatory body as to why they made the application together with information explaining the registered childminders rights for appeal against the use of these emergency powers.

Regulators will also alert the Child Protection teams where they have concerns regarding child protection.

A regulator may also decide to begin ordinary cancellation of a registration at the same time as using its emergency cancellation powers.

Suspension of Registration

Ofsted, CSSIW and the Care Commission have the power to suspend a childminder's registration during an investigation if they have reasonable concern there could be danger to children for safety or welfare reasons and where emergency action is not appropriate.

You have a right to appeal against suspension and if allegations prove to be unfounded you may be able to claim compensation for loss of earnings.

Where Ofsted (England) serves an enforcement notice on an unregistered person acting as a childminder the notice lasts for a year from the issued date, this notice still applies even if the unregistered person moves house. If this notice is ignored, and the person continues childminding without becoming registered, Ofsted will have grounds to prosecute them.

Criminal Prosecutions

If a regulatory body decides to take criminal proceedings against you it is strongly suggested that you seek professional legal advice. If you have legal insurance you should contact your provider immediately. Advice can also be found by using the NCMA legal advice line (England & Wales), the Citizens Advice Bureau or similar agencies. You may find there is an childcare development officer or similar within your local area who can offer support.

Regulators should only undertake prosecution where evidence gathered is 'beyond reasonable doubt' and therefore criminal sanctions are only applicable in limited circumstances.

If an Ofsted inspector suspects that an offence has been committed the registered childminder must be cautioned according to Police and Criminal Evidence Act requirements. Where an offence has been committed the childminder should always be cautioned. You are entitled to have legal representation present at any such interview.

What Constitutes an Offence

❑ Contravening or failing to comply with imposed conditions without reasonable excuse.
❑ Failure to comply with or contravention of National Standards and regulations without reasonable excuse.
❑ Continuing to childmind unregistered after an enforcement notice.
❑ Continuing to childmind when disqualified.
❑ Making misleading or false statements knowingly in applications.
❑ Being a registered childminder who employs a disqualified person.
❑ Wilfully obstructing regulatory bodies registered inspectors during their right of entry.

A person that commits any of these offences is liable for prosecution. Regulatory bodies have a responsibility to investigate these offences with a view to criminal proceedings. In each scenario convictions may result in a fine.

Ofsted will bring proceedings for offences within six months of the date they have collected sufficient evidence to satisfy the prosecutor.

Care Standards Tribunal (England & Wales)

If you have written to Ofsted or the CSSIW to object to something and are not happy with the outcome you have a statutory right of appeal to the Care Standards Tribunal in the following circumstances:

❑ Ofsted/CSSIW refused your application for registration.
❑ Ofsted/CSSIW cancelled your registration.
❑ Ofsted/CSSIW removed, varied or imposed conditions.
❑ Ofsted/CSSIW refuses to grant you an application to remove or vary conditions.
❑ Ofsted/CSSIW has suspended your registration.
❑ Ofsted/CSSIW has applied to a Justice of the Peace for the issue of an emergency order.

The tribunal should be composed of persons who are aware of childminding and childcare issues and decisions taken by the tribunal have immediate effect. A tribunal has the power to confirm Ofsted's/CSSIW's taking of steps or orders. It also has the power to direct that steps or orders shall not have effect, or should cease to have effect on the registered childminder. They also have the power to impose, vary or cancel conditions.

Applications to the tribunal will have to be in writing and within 28 days of the Ofsted/CSSIW decision you are objecting to (this only applies to childminders in England and Wales). Ofsted/CSSIW should provide you with the necessary application forms for your appeal.

Threatening to Report You

When a parent threatens to report you it is usually because they are unhappy about something they believe you have said or done, or something they have misunderstood. In the first instance, most regulators will expect you and the parent to discuss the problem and where possible to come to an amicable arrangement. Unless the parent believes you have done something which affects the well being of the children in your care, in which case a regulatory officer will contact both yourself and the parent to discuss what happened.

If you are operating within the law you should have nothing to worry about. Document all grievances parents have and any solutions. A complaints procedure document is particularly helpful in these circumstances. If you have evidence contradicting the grievance remember to store it safely in case the parent decides to proceed with an official complaint.

A common reason, unfortunately, seems to be that the parent does not want to pay the bill. Even if they previously thought the childminder was wonderful, when they get the bill, they argue that the childminder was horrible. By threatening to report the childminder they hope that they will waive the charges in order to avoid the parents speaking to their regulatory body. If you believe this is the reason the parent is threatening to complain, do not back down. Regulators are there to support childminders as well as parents. Regulatory officials are aware of the ruse and will investigate any complaint with an open mind. Keeping full records of any conversations, bills presented, etc. can be valuable in such cases. You may find "Thank you letters" or conversations with other parents in which they praised your care to be useful evidence for their feelings prior to their non payment (also see Section on Investigations).

Been Reported ?

If you have done something wrong and been reported to the regulatory body you may find it helpful to contact the NCMA advice line for example, or obtain other legal advice. Ofsted's role, and that of other regulators, will be investigation to ascertain the correct details of allegations reported and the reasons behind them. They may visit you to do this or talk on the phone.

You will need to ensure you can provide them with the facts relevant to the issue or allegation, and be as helpful as possible. Regulatory bodies, including Ofsted's role is not to close down childminders for minor misdemeanours but to ensure your service is brought up to standard.

3. The Art of Getting Customers

The amount of energy you need to put into advertising will be dependant on the competition in your area. If there is a shortage of childcare places then a hand written note in a shop window may supply all the customers you need. If there is competition from other childminders, nurseries and after school clubs you will need to put more effort into both advertising and persuading the people that respond to your adverts you are the person they should choose to care for their children.

It may take sometime to find customers, so it is important to plan ahead. If you know a contract is ending or a child is starting full time school from a certain date, advertise in advance so you are not left with a gap with no customers. The notice period in your contract is important because it sets how long you have to find a new customer if one leaves. Make it clear when you are discussing your services with new customers what date they can start from.

If you are a new childminder, it is a good idea to start planning your advertising during the registration process so you can start your search for customers quickly. When you first become registered it may seem to take weeks or even months to find the right customer. It is important not to give up, try a different method of advertising or a different place.

Before designing and putting up your adverts, it will help to spend some time on planning your advertising campaign.

Who are your Potential Customers?

Thinking about who will use your childminding services will help you target your advertising at the right people. Once you know who your potential customers are, you can design your advertising to attract them. If you're planning your advertising to attract parents looking for full time care for infants your adverts may be very different to ones attracting parents looking for after school care. If you have a vacancy for a baby then targeting your advertising at new parents through baby clinics may be more effective than an advertising campaign targeting schools.

Consider the type of vacancy you have to fill; is it full-time, part-time, over-five, or to fit around existing school pick ups? What type of customer would fill it? Potential customers for a full time vacancy would probably have children under four and may include new or expectant mums or parents just going back to work. Potential customers to fill a before and after school vacancy are likely to live within a close radius of the school, may be returning to work, just moved into the area or already have older children at the same school.

If you do not have very specific requirements for filling your vacancy it will still help to think generally about the type of customers that will be looking for your service in your area. Ask yourself questions like: What's your catchment area and who lives there? What are their main places of employment? What schools are in the area?

What do your Potential Customers Want?

You know your potential customers want childcare, but what exactly are they looking for that will make them choose one service over another? You need to know what your potential customers need, want, like, dislike, expect and can afford. As you have worked out above, there are different types of customers and they will want different things. A new parent may consider the most important thing your experience with babies, where as distance from school might be important to the parent of a school age child. If you know what your potential customers want you can make sure that when you advertise or talk to them you promote those aspects of your service.

Ask yourself why a potential customer should choose you instead of another childminder or childcare provider. What do you offer they cannot get elsewhere? These unique selling points are different for each childminder, for example home cooked meals, a large garden, proximity to a local park or school, play equipment, overnight care, your experience or qualifications. Childminders in general also have some unique selling points over other forms of childcare including being home based, having high child to adult ratios and being able to pick up/drop off children from school or nursery. You need to know what makes you a good choice so you can tell potential customers about these points. Your selling points may change depending on the type of customer your are targeting.

Things that might influence parents choice of childcare providers include the following:

Distance
Parents often choose settings that are local or easy to get to on their way journey to work. This means something as simple as advertising locally, and making in clear on your advertising that you are local, may help you find customers. Highlighting transport links for working parents may also encourage customers.

Reputation
Many parents choose settings by the reputation or on recommendation. It can be difficult to build a reputation when you are not a large setting but you can use testimonials from existing/past customers as recommendations and to show what they thought of your service. It's important you are always professional and friendly as this reflects on your reputation. For example, if people see you in the playground with happy children and being friendly this will help you form a good reputation and may help you get recommendations.

Qualifications
You can also highlight any courses you have attended, your first aid training and qualifications such as the DHC or an NVQ3. You could also note any courses you are working towards.

Safety
Parents want to know their children will be safe with you so make them aware you are registered and inspected by the relevant regulator such as Ofsted and show any relevant safety certificates and insurance.

Where to Advertise for Customers
Now you have a better idea of who your customers are going to be and what they want you need to find out where those people 'hang out', where do they stand waiting, where do they pick up leaflets, who do they go to for advice, what places do they visit? Putting your adverts in the right place is just as important as what information you put on them. You need to target

Ask Yourself...	Possible Answers
Where do they visit?	School, Playgroup, After School Clubs, Activity Centres, Leisure/Community Centres, Shops.
Where do they go for advice?	Job Centres, Children's Information Service, Library, Citizens Advice Bureau, Nurse, Doctor, Midwife, Health Clinic.
Where do they wait?	Doctors/Dentists, School Playground, Shopping, Picking Children up from Clubs, Banks, Post Office , Fish & Chip Shop Queue.
Where do they pick up leaflets?	School, Library, Information Desks, Hospital.

locations where your potential customers will see the adverts. Once you've made a list of your target customers consider where you can find each of these groups of potential customers. Don't just rely on where you think people will go ask others, particularly the people you are targeting. Friends, family, staff and existing customers may all have helpful ideas you hadn't thought of. You can refine your advertising locations by looking at the response you get from each area.

Other locations:

Children's Information Service
This service is a national body that holds details for all types of childcare. It is often a first contact for parents looking for child care. Registering your details is free. When filling in your form include the areas that you are close to as searches are done by computer. Most also offer the opportunity to add an overview of your services; always fill this in. Think about how you word it, as this can make your entry stand out to potential customers. You need to update your details regularly as your vacancies change.

Local Childminding Association
Your local childminding association may help parents looking for vacancies, if they have a vacancy list ask for your details to be included. Experienced childminders may be able to pass on tips for finding customers and the best places to look.

Word of Mouth
A lot of customers come through word of mouth so make sure your friends and family know you have vacancies. Let other childminders in the area know you have vacancies so they can pass your details on to parents that contact them if they have filled their vacancy, or the parent's requirements do not match their vacancies. A badge or logo on your clothing or car that identifies you as a childminder can be a good form of advertising. Always have business cards with your contact details ready. Attending local childminder drop in centres may help to get you known to other childminders in the area.

Your Competitors

Your competitors are people that offer the same service as you, other childminders, and also those who your potential customers may perceive as offering the same services as you e.g. nurseries and after school schemes. The aim isn't to copy your competitors, instead by looking at your competitors you can find ways to be unique from them, in both the appearance of your advertising and your selling points.

❑ What advertising materials do they produce? What colours, sizes, shapes, styles do they employ and what don't they use that you could?
❑ Where do they distribute their advertising materials?
❑ What are their selling points? What do they list as the benefits of their services? Is there something they don't have that you do?
❑ Is there a part of the market that your competitors don't cover? A niche market that you could target?
❑ How do their prices compare to yours?
❑ What are their strengths and weaknesses from a customers point of view?
❑ Are they they full up to capacity on childcare places or short on numbers?

Designing an Advert

The first thing your advert must do is catch the eye of the reader. You can write a brilliant advert but if no one ever notices it then it won't do you any good. Try glancing at an advertising board in a shop or adverts in your local paper and see which adverts catch your eye. These are likely to be ones that are different to the other adverts for example they have a bold colour that makes them stand out or an attention grabbing phrase. You can use colour, size, shape or pictures to make your advert stand out. Remember people may be standing several feet away so your poster should be clear from a distance.

Heading

Make sure readers can instantly tell what you are advertising by using a phrase like "Registered Childminder", "Childcare Vacancies" or "After School Childcare". This should be the most eye catching part of the advert, so use a big font or colour to make it stand out.

Images

If you add pictures make sure they don't detract too much from your text. The pictures should support your posters message so pictures of happy children work well. If you are including photographs get written permission from the parents of the children in them.

Contact Information

Another important part of your advert is instructing people what to do if they are interested in your services, for example "Call Now on 00000 000000". Make sure your contact details are clear and easy to read. You can also include your general location (not your address), nearby schools if you are advertising before/after school vacancies and transport links.

Facilities

When writing about your facilities you could include your selling points such as a garden, playroom, separate sleeping room, hot food, play equipment, computer or going on outings. You need to sell yourself, for example, if you have a garden, say if it is large or what sort of toys you have outside and that it is child friendly. Tailor your adverts to where you are putting them. If you have a particular vacancy to fill you may also want to look specifically at that vacancy not just your services in general. For example if you are putting an advert up on a school notice board phrases like "Before & After School Care" or "School Pickups" would be appropriate. In a mother and baby class "Highly Qualified & Experienced Homebased Childcarer." might be what new parents are looking for. Mentioning qualifications you have or are working towards can help portray a professional image.

Registered Childminder

Inspected By Ofsted

Before/After School Childcare

(Based Near Woodbridge Lower School)

- Breakfast & Dinner Provided
- Help with Homework & Reading
- Large Garden & Playroom
- Carer Qualified to Level 3

**Contact Jenny on 0000 000 000
to arrange a visit**

Under 3's Childcare Place

(Based in Town, Near Junction x of M)

- Healthy Home Made Meals
- Safe Environment
- Experienced & Qualified Carer
- References Available

**Contact Jenny on 0000 000 000
to arrange a visit**

Little Tot's Holiday Care

(Based in Area Name)

- Home Cooked Meals
- Arts & Craft Activities
- Large Garden & Playroom
- Visits to Local Attractions

**Contact Jenny on 0000 000 000
to arrange a visit**

Be Honest!

Be honest and specific on your advert. If you only have a part-time vacancy then state that on your advert. Generating lots of calls doesn't help if the customers are unsuitable. It just wastes your time and theirs.

Fees

The cost of your services often depends on the number of hours etc. so it is often easier to discuss this in person or on the phone rather than on an advert. If you do put a cost remember to say it is only approximate.

Appearance

Your advert should be eye catching, friendly and professional. Using a computer is a good idea otherwise make sure the writing is neat and easy to read. People will only read a few lines so keep the text short and use colour and font size to emphasis the most important parts so they will be read first. Other ways to make your adverts look professional include: do not use all capital letters, leave gaps around text and images, check your spelling and only use one or two different fonts - do not go crazy. Do not make it look like a rainbow; it makes it hard to read. Some coloured fonts are particularly hard to read such as yellow or lime green. Red is useful for emphasis in moderation.

Business Cards

Business cards can be left at places where parents go such as health visitors clinics, doctors surgeries or mother and toddler groups. Parents who may not have the time to search for a pen to copy a number down if their child is demanding attention, will find it easier to just pick up a card. It is possible to buy business cards on a sheet that will go through most home computers so producing cards need not be expensive, try your local computer shop. Alternatively you could try slips of paper or postcards with your details on.

Newspaper Advert

A small ad could be placed in the classified section. This is not usually too expensive. 'Registered Childminder has vacancies' and a telephone number is the basic information needed. You could add keywords like experienced, Ofsted registered, or qualified depending on your particular situation.

Internet

Many childminders now have their own web site. There are also many sites that hold directories of childminders you can enter your details into. The CIS also offers the option for you to put your details online. When putting up your advert think about what words parents will use to search for childcare in your area and use these in your advert/website for example 'childcare in Nottingham', 'childminding in Nottingham' or 'after school care near Woodbridge lower school'.

Other Ideas

There are lots of other ways you can advertise, here are just a few:

- ❑ Put up a poster on the window of your car.
- ❑ Ask local businesses about putting an advert on the employee notice board.
- ❑ Attend meetings with parents such as mother and toddler groups and local school meetings.
- ❑ Put a notice in places where people have to wait such as dentists, doctors, bus shelters, and places where people have to queue.
- ❑ Advertise in other groups newsletters, such as schools and support groups.
- ❑ Put business cards next to baby changing facilities in shops/community centres.
- ❑ Offer to run the toy stall at a local fate in exchange for having your posters up on it.
- ❑ Handout business cards along with treats at Halloween.

Don't forget advertising costs are tax deductible!

Advertising Feedback

During your childminding career it is likely you'll have to advertise more than once. To help future advertising campaigns, find out what locations produced the most enquiries. Advertising in the newspaper maybe worthwhile if it generates lots of enquiries but if you do not get any you know not to spend money on it in future. To help you learn what works and what does not make sure you ask anyone enquiring where they got your details from.

Your existing customers, both children and parents, are a valuable source of information and ideas. Why did they choose you? What do they like/dislike about your services? How did they find you? What points about your service/childcare do they find most important? Use the feedback you receive to alter your adverts to be more effective next time you advertise.

First Contact

Having run a successful advertising campaign your telephone is, hopefully, ringing off the hook with potential customers. Don't relax yet though, you still have to convert these potential customers into paying ones.

Your first contact with a prospective customer is often by telephone. Make sure you, and any other family members, always answer the phone politely, as you never know when it may be a potential customer calling. Have a clear and friendly answer phone message for missed calls and a pad by the phone for messages.

When a parent calls the first thing to establish is whether they are a suitable customer to fill your vacancy. Check whether you can fit in the hours required, school/playgroup pick ups and child's age. If the parent hasn't used a childminder before it may be helpful to give a summary of how you work. Explain what a childminder is and how they differ from a nursery or other types of care. Parents will often want to know about your fees, it maybe helpful for you to have these written down ready to make it easier for you to explain. Once you have answered their questions, if they are still interested in your services, arrange for a meeting date, don't forget to tell them how to get to you. Ask for their telephone number in case you need to contact them. For example you may have to reschedule the meeting if you have sick children or a family emergency. If they mention the children's names write them down, greeting the children by name at the door gives a good first impression. Also make a note of anything a parent asks about such as outside facilities so you can discuss these points when you meet them. You might find it helpful to have a list of questions to ask or topics to cover next to the phone so you can easily remember all the points you need to make.

Meeting Prospective Customers

When meeting a prospective customer you need to demonstrate that your childminding service is the best available and, if they are undecided which type of childcare they are looking for, that childminding is best. Parents looking for a childminder may not have experience of selecting childcare and may need guiding through the various forms of care available and the benefits of each.

Encourage parents to bring their child with them to meet you. Some parents may prefer this to be on a second visit after they have met you separately. Allow prospective customers plenty of time for their visits, don't rush them. Meetings when minded children are present have both advantages and disadvantages. It can give a good indication of how you interact with them and hopefully how contented they are. However, the danger is that the demands of giving attention to existing children may act as a distraction. Deciding on a time will depend on the needs of the children present, you may like to have an 'out of hours' meeting first and suggest they may also like to visit during the day at a later date.

Parents will be looking for a variety of points and first impressions are very important, after all they are proposing to leave their most treasured possession with what to all intents and purposes is almost a complete stranger. Expect them to inspect those areas where their child might eat, sleep and play both indoors and outdoors to ensure that they are clean and safe. This does not mean they are nosey, they are just being good parents. They should be checking that there are plenty of toys appropriate to the children present and sufficient equipment if their child was to come to you. Some parents will feel nervous about looking around your home so take them on a tour and show them all your facilities, point out areas and explain how you use them. For example, in the kitchen you may point out that the children enjoy helping you make cakes or you may point out that you have a potty in the bathroom cupboard for younger children.

You need to discuss any special arrangements that might be needed. If the child needs picking up from playgroup, for example, you need to make sure you can fit this into your routine. You also need to know about any special dietary requirements, facilities or care the child will need.

Some parents may have difficulties asking questions. They may feel they are imposing on you or intruding on your privacy. Help them overcome this by having a chat over coffee, and tell them what you have to offer. They may find it helpful to know how long you have been childminding and what experience and qualifications you have. Describe the activities you can provide and, if you take the children out during the day, the type of places you visit. Providing information on the other children that their child will play and socialise with can be very important (remember not to breach confidentiality). The prospective customer will need to know who is to provide meals and snacks and if you are providing these then give details, home made cooking can be a deciding factor. Show them your portfolio and explain your behaviour management policy to them, they will often be looking for someone with similar house rules, you may need to be flexible. The information you have provided will help them form a picture of you and the service you offer. It is up to you how you paint this picture but it will influence their choice of childcare.

The first visit is also for you to decide whether the prospective customer is right for you, not just for them to judge whether you are suitable. This is an opportunity to size up both the child and parents as well. Will the child's behaviour fit in with your existing children, do the parents appear reliable, will they turn up on time, will they pay on time?

Parents often find references from parents whose children you have cared for previously helpful. If you can offer references this may also sway a parent in your favour, to know someone else is happy with you and your services can be very reassuring. An existing customer may provide references for you. If your existing customers are too busy to write references, then ask if they mind if prospective customers phone them for a chat about your childcare services. If you are a new childminder then consider references from when you were a baby sitter or looked after a friends child. Parents also like to see what you have to say about your services, a statement about the care you will give and your standards may prove helpful.

Providing parents with written information gives you the opportunity to state clearly your policies and back up the information you have given them verbally. It will also help them remember you when they are choosing their childminder. Do not forget when your prospective customer leaves to thank them for coming and give them your phone number in case they think of anything else they would like to know (or have lost it as happens sometimes). This gives the parent an image of professional childminding at its best, helping persuade the parent to choose you. You may find it helpful to request parents contact you with a decision within a mutually agreed time frame.

What are Visiting Parents Looking for?

Parents will be looking for a childminder that has good personal qualities as well as professionalism, they will want to leave their child with someone they 'feel' they can trust. They will also be looking at the environment their child will be staying in. The ages of the other children present at the time their child may attend may also be important to them. They may want their child to have the chance to interact with similar age children, or they may want to consider the impact caring for other children will have on the attention you give theirs. Parents may also want to consider what experience you have with caring for needs similar to their child, this may be particularly important if their child has any special needs. Many parents will also be looking to see if your care is flexible enough to fit around the hours they work, this will be particularly important to shift or part time workers.

After the Visit

Parents usually visit several childminders before making up their minds. If they do not choose you it does not mean they thought you were a terrible childminder, it is just they found a childminder more suitable to their situation. When they contact you to let you know their decision you may like to ask them why they choose/did not choose you, it can help you in your future meetings.

Sometimes after a visit a parent may not contact you to let you know whether or not they want to use your services. Try not to take this too personally, parents may have forgotten or just not bother to let you know, possibly because they feel uncomfortable with telling you they have gone elsewhere. Occasionally they may contact you months later for a place because their work situation has changed or their childcare arrangements were not satisfactory.

4. Working in Partnership

Partnership

As a childminder you will work in partnership with parents and in some cases other professionals such as speech therapists, physiotherapists, Social Services and teachers. A partnership is a living, changing relationship, within which issues change. The secret to making a partnership work is for trust and honesty between partners and for all parties to meet commitments and to communicate. Changing circumstances and issues that arise should be quickly addressed. Monitoring and evaluation through contract reviews and frequent discussions make partnerships work.

When working in partnership with parents remember they are the most knowledgeable authority on their own children and should be able to participate in all aspects of their child's education and care. Make sure you use a preferred method of address from the first contact e.g. Some parents prefer to be addressed as "Mrs Smith" rather than by their first name. Parents can provide a role model and a view point and should be seen as the first and continuing carers and educators of their children. A parent is almost always the person who is responsible for their child and they have certain parental rights and responsibilities.

Parental Responsibility

Having parental responsibility means having a duty to care for and protect a child as a parent would and to make decisions regarding their future. For example, they can consent to medical treatment or choose a form of childcare.

Where a child's biological parents are married both parents hold equal responsibilities. Should the parents become divorced then both parents continue to have parental responsibility even when the child lives with one parent exclusively. If parents remarry, the step parent will not have parental responsibility unless it is conferred through a Section 8 Residence order under the Children Act 1989 or they have adopted the child.

Where parents are not married then only the mother has parental responsibility. The father will have no parental responsibility unless he has applied for a court order or made a formal agreement with the mother on a special form registered with the Principal Registry in London. This means the father may not sign for medical treatment for their child or demand access to a child in the event the relationship breaks down.

Adoptive parents and legal guardians have parental responsibility. Where a child is fostered the foster carer may share responsibility with the biological parents and / or Social Services. Parents only lose their rights of parental responsibility on the death of the child, if they have given the child up for adoption or a court has revoked their responsibility.

It is important for childminders to be aware of who holds parental responsibility when they obtain signatures for permission forms and when ascertaining who can collect a child.

Balancing Professional and Personal Relationship

In creating a professional relationship with parents it is important to be aware of the boundaries that the relationship sets. Boundaries govern what is acceptable and unacceptable behaviour within your relationship. Boundaries can be both physical and emotional. The type of work a childminder does means they often become an extension of the family and working in their own home means that boundaries can be harder to define than in more formal settings.

Whilst many childminders and parents become good friends it is also important to maintain a good business relationship. Maintaining contracts, prompt payment and records are an essential part of a good business relationship.

You must be careful to maintain boundaries so that neither party takes advantage of the friendship, such as extending working hours just because the parent is a friend when you would rather not. Likewise the childminder must not take advantage of a friendship such as asking the friend to take time off work.

Information Needed or Desired by Parents

In a childminding setting effective exchange of information between parent and childminder is the key to working in partnership. Mutual exchanging of information should occur at your preliminary meetings prior to a child starting and will continue throughout their contracted period. Information can be verbal, in which case you should allow time for parents to write down information, or you may have written information to give them. A mix of these is often the best solution. You should also encourage them to ask questions. Some information parents require will be detailed in their contracts.

Information likely to be required by parents includes:

❑ Details about your setting/childminding premises and it's layout.
❑ The child/adult ratio.
❑ What the fees are.
❑ What happens about fees if they go on holiday.
❑ What happens when a child leaves the setting/childminders.
❑ Opening times and what happens if they are late arriving, or collecting children.
❑ Settling in arrangements.
❑ Arrangements for handing over, or collection of children.
❑ What happens if their child is ill, or taken ill.
❑ Other emergency procedures.
❑ Details on rules and boundaries.
❑ Policies and procedures.
❑ What items a child needs to bring, e.g. nappies and school uniform.
❑ Information about meals.
❑ Details of routines and activities available.
❑ Whether their child will have access to outdoor activities.
❑ Whether the children are taken on outings.

Information provided must be accurate, to prevent undermining of the parents confidence in you, and easy to understand. Written information should be simply written, avoiding abbreviations and technical terms. Written information provided should not be too lengthy or it may not be read thoroughly.

Other topics of information parents need or desire once a child has joined the setting will include information on: their child's health and welfare; their daily routine and activities; negative events (tantrums, biting etc.); their child's progress and achievements and how they are interacting.

There are many organisations that you can refer parents to for further advice e.g. health visitors, family doctors and the Citizens Advice Bureau.

Supporting Parents

Childminders can be a great source of support to parents, who may seek advice on childcare or behaviour problems, or use them as someone to discuss their child's progress or other worries they have. When giving advice ensure it is accurate; give parents details of further contacts rather than passing on second hand information. When giving advice you should consider that parents may have different ideas of how they would like things done. Your suggestions, though valid, might not be something they would consider. Parents know their child best and giving instructions rather than offering advice can undermine parent's confidence. Giving information that allows parents to come to their own decision helps them bring up their children using their own methods rather than yours.

You should bear in mind when offering advice if it is wrong and the child comes to harm you may be liable and the parents could sue.

Where you have problems with parents considering their circumstances will enable a more sympathetic approach, with solutions produced by mutual agreement. Where parents become upset it is almost always because they are under emotional stress of some kind. What may seem trivial to the childminder may be the last straw for a parent after a stressful day. In this instance the parent should be encouraged to move to a quiet place to talk, or a meeting or phone call arranged after hours.

Poverty, stresses and pressures of living conditions, lack of experience in parenting and lack of self confidence, or experiences of discrimination such as racism, sexism and class discrimination will influence how parents behave towards their children and you. These factors will also affect their ability to communicate and form relationships with their children and other adults.

Parental Feelings of Guilt

Some parents cannot wait to drop off their children and have a break, other parents would prefer to stay at home with their children. Parents may be forced to work for economic reasons and staying at home with their children is not always possible, parents may suffer terrible feelings of guilt for 'abandoning' their child. You should reassure them that this is a normal feeling.

Parents feelings of guilt usually lessen with time when they realise that their child is happy and well cared for. Some parents feel the need to compensate for their guilt by bringing presents for their child either to have while they are at work or for when they collect the child. Unfortunately some children do play on this and use it as a lever to get their own way.

There are some children who recognise the mother's feelings of guilt at leaving them and they will deliberately turn on the tears as the mother is leaving. This can have the effect of upsetting the parent, even to the extent of making them cry. You should reassure the parent that the child will be fine shortly, probably as soon as she is out of sight, and that you will phone her to let her know how the child is later. Encourage them to look through the window before ringing the door bell, on collection, so they can see how their child is normally.

Working with New Mums and Dads

Often childminders may care for a baby from a relatively young age when a parent returns to work after maternity leave. Leaving their child in the care of someone else for what may be the first time can be a difficult time for mums and dads. You can help to make this time easier and support parents in a range of ways.

Encourage a gradual settling in period. It may take several weeks for a parent to become comfortable enough to leave their child in your care. Encourage the parent to make visits where they stay with their child so they can get to know you. Explain that you don't mind if they phone you to see if how their child is doing or that they can pop in occasionally. Keep a diary to be passed between you and the parents for them to detail the child's daily routine, for example, sleeping and eating pattens.

Parents may like to visit during their lunch break to reassure themselves that you are caring well for their child. Try to understand the parents' point of view and don't see it as them trying to undermine the way in which you care for their child, or that they don't think you are doing your job in the right way.

Communication is important; Encourage parents to discuss with you how they feel the child is settling in and whether the arrangements are working for them as well.

Working with Young Mums and Dads

In some areas special schemes are being set up where a childminder provides childcare and support for young parents. In this role a childminder plays the part of not only a carer for the child but also a support role to the parent. Childminders work equips them with the knowledge of how to care for children, something which can seem very daunting to a new parent particularly if they are only a teenager themselves.

The childminder will be able to offer advice and provide a friend to the new parent. Young parents may find asking for advice from a childminder easier than someone from a Local Authority, especially once a good relationship has developed between the parent and childminder. Parents may fear that the child will be taken away or they will be judged if they need to ask advice from a more official source.

It is important that you are not judgmental of the young parent and that you are not condescending when offering advice. Sharing the problems you may have encountered and how you dealt with them can be a good way to communicate without the parent feeling you are giving them instructions rather than advice.

They may need reassurance that they are doing things in the right way and it is important to focus on the things they are doing well in addition to anything that you feel needs to be done differently. When offering advice also give the reasons behind the advice not just instructions. For example, if commenting on the importance of keeping equipment clean explain why this is necessary.

It can be helpful to keep a detailed diary of the routine you and the parent follow regarding feeding, sleeping etc., this may help the parent with maintaining the routine. Writing down things like the length of time a child slept gives the parent a reference point if they are worried about sleeping when at home.

Parents may also find it helpful to spend some time with you whilst you are childminding so they can see how you do things and work with the children. Be sure to point out that everyone does things differently, and even if they don't do things exactly like you it doesn't mean they are wrong.

When Children Leave

Childminders and the children they care for do form bonds and inevitably when a child who has become part of the childminding group leaves there will be some sadness. This can be felt most keenly by children within the group who are from a one child family, they will have formed attachments and for some they will feel the loss almost as a bereavement of a sibling.

Children can be helped by preparing them where possible for the departure. They may enjoy making a scrapbook for the child who is leaving to include pictures and photos they produce for them. This can also be beneficial for the child leaving, who may also be feeling sad, and for yourself. It can be both helpful and educational to remain in touch. Children can write to each other and send pictures, they may even be able to email or visit each other.

Communication

Effectively communicating with parents is an essential part of a child's care and education. Where a parent is unable to stop to talk regularly, making opportunities to talk to them will be necessary. A family's social, environmental and cultural background will need to be taken into account when developing relationships with members of the family, remembering that family values and practices do vary between different groups in society and also within them. Where a child and their parents have a distinct culture or language, this must be respected. Only with some insight into a parent's background will good communication be possible, the words and actions they may use may only be fully understood within the context of their beliefs and circumstances.

When communicating with parents they should be treated as individuals; they should be listened to and their views valued and respected. The way you communicate with parents can then be adapted according to their interest, knowledge and confidence. If a communication problem proves hard to resolve, you may need to seek outside help or guidance, that could include other family members, social workers, interpreters and audiologists.

There are many barriers to effective communication, some parents will offer information and ask questions without prompting, others may feel it is not up to them to provide input. Parents with negative childhood experiences of care/education settings may not want, or expect, to share information. Difficulties in communication occur for many reasons including, differing backgrounds both socially and/or culturally, English not being the first language, impaired hearing, parents feeling intimidated by the professional jargon or parents having unrealistic or negative expectations. Some parents find it hard to express themselves without anger. You should not argue or become defensive. Listening to what the parent says is important, critical or aggressive language should be responded to in a neutral way. A parent may only require further reassurance or there may be another problem. Improving communication will help, a parent should be assured that every effort is being made to understand and rectify the problem.

Some difficulties in communication are easy to identify and remedy. For example - if a parent is suffering a hearing impairment it may make it difficult to hear sometimes, a quiet area to talk, talking slowly and clearly and using visual aids can help. Having no shared language - here photographs visual aids and an interpreter will solve the problem. Other difficulties in communicating are not so obvious, for example, the language may be the same but culture differences can lead to misunderstandings. Where there is a difficulty in communication, recognition of the failure to communicate is essential and steps must be taken to rectify the situation. Other factors to be considered are: ensuring you are not always too busy to talk; not being judgmental about people who do things differently and taking into account gender differences. Men and women communicate very differently. Including the number of words they use to communicate information. Try not to become over anxious where there is difficulty understanding a parent as this will make matters worse.

Listening to Parents

Communicating with parents involves not only the ability to get your point across, but also listening to parent's points of view.

It is important when listening not to have a predetermined idea that what they say isn't going to be important, will be repeating something previously heard, or that you already know their view. In other words it is important to really listen, not 'switch off'.

When listening it is important to:

❑ not interrupt. It is hard to make a valid point or remember what you are saying if someone constantly interrupts you.
❑ show interest in the person speaking, not something other than the speaker or be gazing around the room instead of looking at them. If children are being distracting arrange a time to talk when they are not present.
❑ allow the speaker to finish their own sentences. Finishing them is rude and disconcerting. Allow them time to speak and don't rush them.

Parents and Discussions

The information that parents offer helps you to build up an accurate understanding of an individual child, their family and their individual needs. Time should be given during preliminary meetings for discussion and a 'swapping' of information. During these meetings a mutual agreement can be reached on your policies, taking account of parental preferences and adjusting where possible to take account of areas where family values differ from yours. Policies to be considered could include routines, boundary setting, emergencies, collection of the child, meal arrangements and use of preferred names. The use of these policies should be explained to parents, in that they are there to help ensure the safety, welfare and happiness of their child while maintaining a smooth running efficient service.

Ideas and expectations of what good childcare should be like varies widely and may be dependent on family values. It helps to have an appreciation of what a parents expectations are. Parents should be provided with clear, accurate information about what is done in your setting and why. Where parents have expected formal 'teaching' activities, explain that children can learn through play. It can be helpful to point out some of the differing things that activities 'teach'. Where parents have the opportunities to talk about activities to participate or repeat them at home they find it easier to understand that mathematical concepts for example, can be learnt through a variety of games and 'fun activities' and that even playing with water and sand are learning experiences.

Parents should be encouraged to ask for information and explanations about what their children do in your childminding setting and to discuss any concerns. Parents may like to share information about routines, activities and incidents. They may like to know what their child is doing when they are not there to see. This will help them to understand what a child tells them and gives them a greater insight and confidence in your childminding abilities.

Information on rules, procedures and your philosophy can be explained to parents through conversation so that they relate them to their child, or provided in the form of a brochure. This is intended to help their understanding of what behaviour is acceptable, how unacceptable behaviour is dealt with, how stimulating a child's day was, where the child spent her day (inside/outside), what they have done during the day (meals/sleeps/stories/outings/play activities etc.) how and why their routines are organised, what equipment and toys are available, what play activities they enjoy and what they are learning from them.

Parents will build up an understanding of how your setting is organised, its aims and what can be offered by visits to discuss expectations, and standing invitations to come and spend time with you to see what their child is doing. Regular discussions with every parent, displays of work, the provision of photographs for parents of their child at various activities and outings can be used to foster this understanding.

Ways of managing a child's behaviour should be discussed with parents so that a shared approach is developed. The handing over periods at arrival and going home are grey areas. While the child is still within the setting, the carer has responsibility, but where a parent is taking charge and putting on coats and shoes they assume responsibility (unless the child runs off). Then a cue could be given to help the parent regain control e.g. Mummy will not be pleased if you do that. Can you help her find your things to pack and show her how helpful you are?

Confidentiality

Confidentiality means not sharing privileged information, concerning children and their families, which parents divulge to you either through the records they contribute to, or during casual conversations. An example of a casual conversation could be information revealed on their partner's employment status. Both verbal and written information provided by parents is given in trust.

When parents sign or look at records, care should be taken to ensure only their child's records are on view, those of other children should be covered or folded behind to ensure you are maintaining their confidential nature. Care should also be taken when sharing information to parents by email. An email to all parents includes their email address which may, unless you have taken precautions, be visible to others. All records should be stored safely so that access is restricted to those with a 'need to know'. Where there are assistants it may be helpful to share or exchange this information, for example, diets, allergies, religious rituals, or if the child is to be collected by someone else.

Occasionally there may be circumstances where the responsibilities to the child's welfare will outweigh the responsibility to the parent and information may need to be shared with other relevant authorities. A child who is in need of protection will have needs which override the parents right to confidentiality.

Information given by parents should not be used for gossiping with colleagues and other parents as this amounts to a breach of trust. If you have a non child protection issue you need to discuss or need guidance on, for example at the childminder drop in, then talk about it in general terms and without names. E.g. "What would you do if you had a toddler who bites?" Not "James bit Susan on the arm yesterday and there were teeth marks and her mummy, the school teacher Pat, was very cross and his mum said "well boys will be boys".

Confidentiality or the lack of it can seriously impact on parents and their children. If they feel you have betrayed their trust in talking about privileged information you will have damaged your working relationship. They may feel they cannot trust your judgement on other issues.

Parents may not want issues from their private life shared with others. This is how rumours and misinformation can be spread. Misinformation can lead to parents and children being discriminated against. Confidentiality should always be respected unless there are child protection issues and then only information relevant to an investigation should be shared with relevant professionals.

Complying with Data Protection Legislation

The Data Protection Act 1998 governs the use of personal information. As childminders personal information is required to run the business and so the Act must be complied with. Information about living identifiable individuals such as; names, addresses and medical history fall within the remit of the legislation.

The act contains eight principles of good information handling. Those most relevant to childminding practice are keeping accurate information, up to date relevant information, information for childminding purposes only, information while the child is in your care, information for the regulatory inspection bodies recommended time frame only. The information must be stored in such a way as to protect it from unauthorised individuals. Examples of this include using a locked filing cupboard or where on a computer having the information password protected.

If your records are solely paper based then there is no requirement to notify the Information Commissioner's Office. However if you have records on the computer and add to these or produce bills for parents on the computer then you are considered to be processing the records electronically and there may be a requirement to notify and an annual fee may be applicable. You may have to ensure all computer records are password protected.

Understanding Parent's Feelings

Parents leaving children in your care may experience a range of different feelings. It will help your relationship if you consider these feelings and the effects they may have on the way a parent communicates and works with you.

Placing a child into a childminding setting may be a stressful event for parents. They may be experiencing feelings of guilt. They will be concerned that the setting is suitable for their child. They may be having misgivings about leaving or entrusting their child to someone else. There may be fears that carers will 'replace them' in a child's affections. They may feel undermined. These manifestations of parental anxiety require reassurance; parents need to feel confidence in you and your setting. New parents may find it helpful to talk to parents of other children in your care. This may naturally occur as parents and children discuss the day's events each evening.

Parents may feel guilty, frustrated, angry or upset. They may have preferred to stay at home with their child but be forced to work through financial pressure. They may also feel jealous of the time that you get to spend with their child, that you get to see their child develop, the way their children interact with you or that you are able to stay at home with your own children.

Some parents are much more concerned about leaving their children than others. This anxiety may show itself in unexpected ways such as rudeness, excessive criticism (of the child or setting), abruptness, anger (at the child or childminder), excessive questioning about the child's welfare, an appearance of 'not caring' or brushing off the child's demands. These feelings should be responded to calmly and in a non judgmental fashion. Discovering the reasons behind the behaviour by talking may be helpful.

Parents may express their feelings in ways that are not always obvious and you will need to recognise these feelings and support parents in dealing with them. Parents may also worry that you consider them bad parents, that the child will love you more or that the child will consider them bad parents. Parents may drop their children late or collect them late, they may avoid discussing their child's day with you, or be uncomfortable with their child expressing excitement over activities they have done. They may also want to discuss everything about their child's day in detail or provide overly strict instructions about how you should care for their child. You can help parents deal with these feelings by providing support and communicating with them to help them sort out these feelings.

Parents may feel that they are the only parents to feel like this. They may even feel guilty for feeling angry or frustrated. Encourage them to talk to other parents in a similar situation. You could do this by arranging a social event for the parents of the children you care for. This could be meeting with the parents and children for a barbeque, or going for a meal in a restaurant. If you have used childcare for your children, it may help to explain the feelings you had.

Encourage parents to tell you how they deal with situations at home, so they do not feel that you are undermining their authority or that you consider them bad parents. Ask them how they deal with the child's different behaviours and what activities their child enjoys. Reassure them that you know that they know their child best. Parents may need to feel that you approve of them, and are not judging them as parents.

Remember to thank parents when they pay on time, change arrangements to accommodate an activity or outing, or remember to bring the equipment you asked for. Let them know that you appreciate them.

Try to take into account the stress that parents may be under, particularly single parents. Their work load and the lack of time they have for leisure activities can cause stress and this may affect the way they deal with you. They may not have as much patience and the little things that would not normally upset them may get blown out of proportion.

If the child has talked about an activity they enjoyed with their parents, tell the parents about what the child said. This helps them realise that the child loves being with them too.

If a child reaches one of the important 'mile stones' in their development, such as talking or walking for the first time, you may prefer not to tell the parent and allow them to see it for themselves. Share in the parents excitement when they arrive the next day and tell you.

Assertiveness

What is Assertiveness?

Assertiveness means:
- ❑ Expressing your opinions, beliefs and points of view in a direct and honest way.
- ❑ Listening and negotiating to come to an agreement in which the needs of both parties are met.
- ❑ Not allowing others to violate your rights or 'get away with' something or to make you feel like your opinions, values or emotions are less important than theirs.
- ❑ Saying no if a parent makes unreasonable requests of you, asking for help when you need it, admitting when you are wrong and trying to come to agreements that encompass the interests of all parties involved.
- ❑ Not forcing your opinions on others or bullying them into agreement.

Assertiveness will help you deal with and prevent conflicts between you and parents, assisting you in finding a solution that is agreeable to both parties.

Being Assertive

Some people are more assertive than others and becoming assertive will not happen overnight. It will take time and practice. You will become more used to explaining yourself clearly and your responses will come more naturally. If you do not manage to get your point across do not worry, you can always try again. Think back over why it did not work and how you could explain yourself differently.

'I' Messages

'I' messages contain three points: the behaviour in question, its' effect on you and the way it makes you feel. A statement consisting of these parts will help you to put across your point, and an explanation of why you feel like that.

E.g. Jack's mother is usually late bringing him, this means the children are late for school.

You could: Ignore the situation, perhaps trying to get the children to walk faster so they make it to school on time. By doing this, however, you have avoided the situation and let your, and the other children's, feelings and rights become less important than Jack's mother.

Or say: "You keep being late, you should come on time." This is an accusation, and is likely to make Jack's mum angry and has not explained why this behaviour is unacceptable to you.

Or say: "When you bring Jack late, it makes all the children late for school and I feel frustrated." Here you have explained what effect her being late has on the other children and why you have a problem with the behaviour. You could then go on to discuss ways to solve the problem, perhaps by her dropping Jack earlier, or meeting you at the school.

Think Before you Speak

Remember the old adage 'Think before you speak'. It is very useful to keep in mind. If you know you need to discuss something with a parent when they come later, consider what points you need to get across and how you are going to say them.

If you are angry or upset then allow yourself time to calm down. Likewise if the person you are talking with is angry or emotional suggest you talk later when you have both had a chance to calm down.

Be Clear

When talking with someone use facts rather than your judgements. 'I don't think children should have lots of sweets,' is your opinion whereas 'lots of sweets will rot children's teeth,' is a fact.

Do not exaggerate. If you exaggerate then your view and opinions will not hold so much credence. If a parent has paid late the last two weeks do not say 'You always pay late.' instead say 'I noticed you have paid late the last two weeks, would it help if we discussed other payment options.'

Be specific. If you need a parent to pay the next day then say so. "I need your fees tomorrow, so I can go into town and pay the bills," lets the parent know you need the money the next day, whereas "Are you going to pay tomorrow?" leaves the choice of payment in the parents hands.

It can also help to explain what you do not mean. Ask whether they understood what you asked or your point. "Do you understand what I mean?" or "Is their anything I did not cover?" gives other people the chance to clarify anything they did not understand or go back over points they missed.

Attitude

Making your point clearly, through words, will not help if you do it whilst standing over a parent, waving your arms at them, not looking them in the face or acting aggressively. Make sure you are both on the same level. Standing over someone sitting down, or making them stand on the doorstep, is threatening and will not encourage the person to listen to you. You must also convey your assertiveness through appropriate gestures.

Maintain eye contact, so they know you are listening to them and so they know you are confident in what you are saying.

Talk calmly but firmly, raising your voice or talking with obvious angry tones will not help a reasoned conversation to take place.

Responding to Requests

If parents make requests outside the normal contract, such as asking you to take a child on a different day to usual or collecting a child from a club, you do not have to automatically accommodate them. You should consider your own needs and the needs of other children first. Do you have time? Will it make extra work for you? Do you want to? Use assertive language such as "Collecting Millie from hockey will make dinner late for the other children, I don't feel that it would be fair on them."

If you find yourself regretting things you agree to on the spur of the moment in future offer to call back later, when you have checked your calendar or diary, with the answer.

Dealing with Criticisms

People may criticise because they have had a bad day, are having trouble dealing with feelings such as guilt or jealously or because they genuinely believe you are doing something wrong.

When responding to criticism it is helpful to acknowledge the person's view and then respond with your opinion. Acknowledging their view lets them know that you have listened to what they said.

Example: "You shouldn't give them burgers. Junk food isn't good for children."

Response: "Yes, I agree good nutrition is important for children. I try to provide a balanced diet. We don't have burgers very often and they always have salad with them."

Another method of dealing with criticism is asking the person what they would do in that situation. You may find they have they have a good solution and it is OK to admit you are wrong.

Criticism: "You shouldn't give them sweets for a snack, it's bad for their teeth."

Response: "I have trouble thinking up snacks. What sort of things do you provide at home?"

Affirmation

Affirmation means recognising and accepting your own worth and the worth of others, and that your feelings and views have value.

Such as saying or thinking "No matter what anyone says, I know that the job I do is worthwhile."

Aggressive People

Some people have a more naturally aggressive demeanour. They may not realise the way they stand or speak seems aggressive to you, particularly if it is the way their parents behaved.

When dealing with aggressive people try not to raise your voice as this may be viewed as a sign of aggression. Remember to smile and not duplicate any aggressive body language they display.

If you feel intimidated and you feel you can discuss this with them do so. Remember you are offering a service they want.

Should parents become aggressive over a contract dispute, suggest they discuss it over coffee. If they decline to discuss it in a calm manner then ask them to put their complaints in writing to you. Do not be provoked into an argument or a slanging match. Remember the children are listening. Tell the parents this is not in the best interests of the child.

Resolving Common Conflicts

Issues and conflicts arise in every relationship or partnership. If partners find themselves confused by something unforeseen or in conflict then time is of the essence to prevent a break down in the partnership. Prompt diagnosis of the problem followed by rectifying action will be required.

Causes of Conflicts and Grievances

There are many causes for conflicts and stress between parents and childminders, examples may be due to, or might include, the following factors:

❑ **Low morale:** This may occur particularly where childminders feel unsupported and undervalued.
❑ **Confusion:** For example over individual roles where assistants are employed and/or parents wishes keep changing.
❑ **Responsibility:** For example inappropriate responsibility given to an inexperienced assistant, or possibly responsibility for ill or disadvantaged children, with insufficient help and guidance.
❑ **Communication:** Poor communication skills or lack of adequate communication between childminders and/or parents.
❑ Ambiguity: Misleading instructions received, or possibly a difficulty with prioritising of tasks.
❑ **Work load:** Excessive work, too much else to do, or too many children accepted into the setting.
❑ **Feelings:** Of personal insecurity, inadequacy or personal problems.
❑ **Criticism:** Destructive in nature, of work, setting, personality and/or culture.
❑ **Feedback:** Not positive and lacking in praise.
❑ **Discrimination:** Usually occurs where someone is different, i.e. they do not conform to someone else's idea of 'norm' and so they discriminate against them. Often due to racial origin, cultural differences, disability and gender.

Where personal problems are affecting your performance and relationship with others, you may need the opportunity to talk, possibly on a one to one basis, and share your difficulties and concerns. Where possible seek help. Do not keep your problem to yourself. Local childminding support groups can be a good place to start.

Conflicts between childminders and parents need resolving quickly so they do not affect the child. This sort of conflict is often caused through a lack of communication and not having made allowances for parental circumstances.

Where criticism is given to assistants, or parents are being told of behavioural problems etc. it must be constructive and identify their good practices or points. This will help reinforce parents and assistants self confidence preventing feelings of resentment or inadequacy.

Conflicts must be resolved as rapidly as possible without disrupting the childminding service. Children are very sensitive and notice conflicts. Unresolved problems can be detrimental to their welfare. Grievances and complaints should be settled, preferably at an early stage through discussion. People need to be consulted about their feelings, or they may brood on the problem. Conflicts cannot be resolved where they are managed by aggression or ignored, it only causes complications. Where solutions have been proposed for a reduction of the conflict childminders and parents should attempt to compromise with a flexible, positive attitude to enable the childminding service to continue operating in an effective manner.

Assistants and parents have a right to seek redress for grievances and must have been told how to proceed during discussions. In this situation written complaints policies are particularly helpful.

Inappropriate Behaviour from Parents

Inappropriate behaviour from parents is not always intentional, cultural differences and their own upbringing may influence their behaviour. Some people are naturally more 'touchy, feely' than others, if you find this uncomfortable then talk to the parents and explain that you do not like it. If you are uncomfortable discussing it then write them a letter instead.

Inappropriate behaviour from parents toward their children should be recorded in your incident book or diary. You should also be aware if there are any child protection issues when you are recording details.

If parents are smoking, swearing or using 'bad language' it should be noted that this may be acceptable in their household and a polite request to refrain while on your premises and an explanation that it is in the best interests of the child is usually successful. This can be followed up in writing.

Where parents arrive inebriated to collect a child it may be appropriate to call the emergency contact. Explain this is in the child's best interests, particularly where motor vehicles are involved. If this is a regular occurrence then this may be a child protection issue.

Different Standards than Parents

Standards are the level of quality or principles of behaviour we expect a child to conform to. When we set 'house rules' or 'ground rules' we are setting standards which we require children to follow. Each parent or childminder will have a different set of standards that they apply to the children they care for. One person may find watching television an acceptable activity another may not. One person may forbid wearing shoes in the house where as another finds this perfectly acceptable. Children are expected to comply with the standards set down by their carer.

There are no set ways to bring up a child; family, culture and religion may all play a role in the standards of behaviour expected of the child. What standards are set and how they are applied will vary from parent to parent, childminder to childminder, and childminder to parent.

Children are usually very adaptable and can easily work within two different standards, they can understand which behaviour is acceptable or required in their own home and which behaviour is required at their childminder's. For example, they may know they are allowed to eat dinner in their room at home but at the childminders, must sit at the dining table.

It may take children a while to settle in and learn the new standards expected of them. Parents often choose childminders with similar standards to themselves as they feel it helps the child having a consistency between home and the childminder. Problems can occur when parents are picking up or dropping off children, as children may be unsure of whose standards apply, as both the childminder and the parent are present. Making it clear that your standards still apply until they have left the premises will help.

Inappropriate Clothing

Childminders and children take part in a range of activities. This might vary from going to the playground, taking children to school, painting or playing with toys. For some of these activities some clothing is more appropriate than others. For example, sandals are not very good for walking to school if it is winter and raining.

If a child repeatedly comes with inappropriate clothing this can make extra work for you and prove awkward for the child. You should first consider whether there are social circumstances affecting the parent's ability to provide suitable clothing. If they are on a low income you may have to make allowances for the fact they may not be able to afford new or extra clothing. In this situation it may be helpful for you to keep a small collection of spare clothing which can be borrowed. This is also helpful for the occasions when any parent forgets appropriate clothing. Nearly new sales and charity shops are a good source of inexpensive backup clothing.

Two other common causes for inappropriate clothing are a lack of awareness from the parents and pressure from the child.

It can be helpful to have a clause in your contract detailing required items. This could include outdoor coats, hats, gloves, outdoor shoes or boots and a change of clothes. It may even be helpful to have a separate handout for parents suggesting items.

If you are planning particular activities or outings then parents should be reminded in advance, either verbally or with a written list. This will give them time to think about and pack the night before if necessary, preventing a last minute panic in the morning. Reminding children what they need to bring can also help as they may remind parents or collect their own necessary clothing.

If parents have acceded to children's whim or given the child free range over their choice of clothing the child may have decided on inappropriate items, such as turning up in a party dress or high heels on the day you plan to go to the adventure playground. If the parents have not prevented the child from doing so, there are several things you can do that might help:

❑ Send the parents back home to collect the recommended 'gear'.
❑ Lend the child something suitable.
❑ Take the child but do not allow them to participate in activities that may be dangerous or cause damage due to inappropriate clothing or footwear.

The last option should only be used if the child is old enough to understand when you explain why they cannot participate. You should also explain to the parents in advance that the child will not be able to fully participate for health and safety reasons. You should also be aware that some cultures will have clothing 'rules' and you will need to take these into account when planning activities. In these circumstances it would be inappropriate to remove such items of clothing from a child. (Some examples can be found under Section 10. Equal Opportunities, Religion and Culture). Parents will be the most knowledgeable on their child's dress code.

Necessary Items not Provided (e.g. nappies, clothes)

Items that parents are required to bring for their children should be detailed in the contracts, if they are not then you should discuss adding them with the parents when you review your contract.

Even if they are detailed parents may forget, and you may have to remind them. A slip of paper with the items required as an aid to their memory may help. If the children are old enough then they may be able to help their parent by reminding them.

If the parents persistently forget important items then try sending them home for the required items or ask for payment for the purchase of required items. Asking for the cost of items can be particularly useful with items that get used up quickly such as nappies or baby milk, you could suggest a regular fee in exchange for providing these items.

Having a few spare sun hats, woollen hats and gloves can be useful as they can be purchased inexpensively (are tax deductible) and are some of the most frequently forgotten items.

Person Collecting Children

Each child you care for should have a contract, this should state who will collect the child. Children's records should also detail any relevant circumstances such as custody battles and exclusion orders affecting who may collect the child.

If someone is to collect the child who was not present at the signing of the contract you should make arrangements to meet them in advance. Photographs of grandparents or other people who may occasionally collect children could be added to a child's file.

If the person who normally collects the child will not be available, prior notice should be given, unless it is an emergency. If it is not someone known to you, you should be given a name and if possible a photograph. Parents may also like to give you a password that people unknown to you will use so that you will know they have parental approval. Note, once used a password should be changed.

If someone unexpected or unfamiliar comes to collect a child, you should not let them onto the premises, first phone for confirmation from the parents. If no one comes to collect a child, you should continue with activities and meals as required and offer the child reassurance. If attempts to contact the parents or other emergency contacts are unsuccessful, after a reasonable length of time, Social Services should be notified.

Collecting Children Late

Unfortunately some parents are not as prompt at collecting their children as childminders would like. Some parents may regularly collect their children ten minutes late, some even later. Your first step should be talking to the parents, find out if there is a reason for them being late. Make sure they realise that this behaviour is not acceptable. If you have not said anything they might not realise that their being late is causing you a problem. You can help prevent this by clearly stating in your policies that children should be collected on time, and you should be notified by phone if they are unavoidably delayed.

Being late is not always deliberate. Parents may have misjudged the time in which it takes them to get to your home after work or their work patterns may have changed since they signed the contract. In this case it would be a good idea to review the contract allowing for a later pick up time.

Charging an overtime fee may help dissuade parents from being late or taking advantage of your services. This rate is often higher than usual hourly rates and can be divided to be charged for every fifteen or twenty minutes they are late. If you are intending to charge an overtime rate you should clearly state this in the contract and any policies you have.

It will help to read our section on assertiveness, when talking to parents use 'I' messages to explain the behaviour you have a problem with and the effect it has on you. For example, "When you are late, I get frustrated as I can't get on with the jobs I need to do and cooking a meal for my family." You can follow this with suggesting a solution or arranging a convenient time to discuss the problem further. For example, "Would it help if we discussed changing the contract so you collect the children later?" It can also help to explain the effect their behaviour has on the child, that they worry when the parent is late, or are tired and would like to go home.

Bringing Children Late

Depending on circumstances it may not be a problem if a parent brings a child late, they may have arranged to pay from a certain time so they can bring their child earlier some days than others, this may happen particularly if a parent has a flexible work pattern. This should have been discussed when the contracts are signed.

If a parent brings a child late and it is a problem, for example, you need to leave the house at a certain time for a school run, or to catch the bus for shopping, your first step should be to talk to the parent. They may not realise that you find it a problem, after all they may think they are paying you for that time, why should it bother you what time they actually come? Explain to them why you need them to arrive on time, and the effect it has when they are late.

If they continue to bring the child late and you need to be at school or playgroup at a certain time, suggest they meet you there to drop the child, that way you will not be late with other children's commitments. You could also point out that you have to leave at a certain time and if they are not there they will have to wait until you return. This may encourage them to make an extra effort.

Allowing Children to Bring Inappropriate Items

There are some items you may have requested children do not bring to your home. This may be because you do not believe them to be suitable for all the children present or you feel they may lead to undesirable behaviour, such as arguments.

There are several options open to you which may vary according to the item in question and will also depend on your relationship with parents.

Sweets and 'treats' - Parents may not be aware of your views on sweets. This will vary between childminders; some have no strong views, some prefer no sweets, some only allow them to be eaten after a meal and others only allow sweets if the parents provide sufficient for all the children present. You should discuss your views with parents.

Where sweets are brought as treats, if you do not approve you could return them to the parent or child to 'eat later', or suggest they bring an alternative healthy snack such as fruit.

Some parents use sweets as compensation for leaving a child, you should be aware of parents feelings, (see Section on Parents Feelings). If you do not approve of sweets or feel an alternative would be better for the child, then offering suggestions of what 'Mrs Bloggs round the corner' found very successful, e.g. cuddles and quality story time may be the answer.

Some parents may be using sweets as a hasty breakfast, you may like to offer breakfast at an additional charge or suggest cereal bars or toast can be eaten on route and may be a healthier option.

Toys or equipment - If you have strong views on toys brought from home, toys that are not shared, cause arguments, or are not suitable for other children present you should discuss this with parents.

Transitional items - You should be aware that some 'cuddly toys' are used by children as 'familiars' or 'comforters' and they may not justifiably wish to share these.

If unsuitable toys continue to arrive after discussion with the parents then consider the parents may be allowing the child to bring them to avoid arguments and confrontations. Sometimes it can be very hard to say no to a difficult child, especially if you are in a hurry to get to work on time.

Help the child to understand ground rules on toys. Discuss with the child (if they are old enough to understand) that toys need to be shared and why some toys might not be suitable.

If these ground rules are not complied with make sure the child understands that their toy will be returned to the parent for safe keeping, placed in a box by the door or out of sight in a cupboard to keep them safe ready for when they go home.

Taking Advantage of You

You may occasionally have the feeling that you are being taken advantage of, some times this may just be due to a misunderstanding. It is always easier to avoid the opportunity of someone taking advantage of you or misunderstanding you than it is to solve the problem.

When dealing with parents you should always be business like, professional and discuss your way of working with parents and share your policies. This will help parents understand your working practices. Ensuring the contract is understood and that incidentals are itemised in the information you provide parents minimises the risks of misunderstandings.

There should be some leeway for 'give and take' in all relationships, where it becomes 'all take' then you are being taken advantage of. Remembering that it is a business arrangement and that they are your clients for whom you provide a service may help you to be firm when you have reminded them of the contractual agreement and they continue to bend the rules.

Suggesting they may like to review the contract and negotiate to cover the changes they are trying to make can help, e.g. if they are always ten minutes late, suggest extending the contract ten minutes, possibly at an enhanced rate. Parents may agree and you have successfully solved the issue, or it may encourage them to arrive on time, or in some case they start arriving five minutes early!

If you are being taken advantage of, do not let it continue. It is harder to counteract the longer you allow it to happen, with some parents the the more leeway you give them the more they will take advantage of you (you may find the Section on Assertiveness helpful).

Working with Other Professionals

Childminders may work with a wide range of other professionals, including those from education, health and Social Services departments. As with working with parents, good communication will be essential in forming a successful relationship. Information needs to be exchanged regularly and regular assessments of how the relationship is working will also be helpful. Within the relationship all parties should have a clear understanding of their roles, this prevents misunderstanding about who does what. Listening and respecting each others views creates an environment which allows the free exchange of information.

Backup Childminders

It is very useful to have at least one backup childminder who, if their numbers permit, can take the children you care for to cover you in an 'emergency' or when you are unable to have the children. Situations may include, you or your child being ill, a doctors appointment where it is inappropriate to have a child present, the dentist, or a childcare course.

Backup childminders should be known to both the minded children and their parents. Should you be ill the parents can then contact the backup childminder to see if they can accommodate their child or whether alternative arrangements are needed. In order for the backup childminder to be covered for the children, they might like to have an 'open' contract with the parents.

Payment options can include the parent paying the backup childminder (rather than you) when you are unavailable or paying you as usual and then you paying the backup childminder. If you pay the backup childminder remember to get a receipt as this is a tax deductible expense. A childminder you use as backup must be registered, insured and keep within their numbers unless it is a genuine emergency, such as you being rushed into hospital.

Employing Childminding Assistants

Some childminders choose to work with assistants. Having an assistant will enable you to discuss problems, share the work load and can remove the isolation sometimes felt by childminders who work alone. However you will also have to consider whether you can afford to pay an assistant, as by law they must be paid at least the minimum wage, and will be entitled to annual leave. You will have to share your home and discuss daily plans. An assistants salary and circumstances will affect whether you need to register with the Inland

Revenue as an employer and deduct tax and National Insurance. Contact the Inland Revenue for more details.

You should check with the relevant childminding standards and regulator, such as Ofsted, whether your assistant can be left in sole charge of the children. There may be conditions such as a time limit or written permission from parents if this is allowed. Assistants must be police checked.

Family members may be registered as assistants, husband and wife teams or parent and son/daughter teams are not uncommon. The Children's Information Service may be able to help you find a suitable assistant if you decide to find an assistant by advertising the job

Interviewing Assistants

When interviewing someone for the role of childminding assistant, you will find yourself looking for many of the qualities a parent will look for in a childminder. You should choose someone with similar policies on behaviour and childcare to your own, someone you feel will be reliable and that you can build a good working relationship with, they must interact well with children and have good communication skills for dealing with parents and other adults.

You should discuss with them their previous experience, the age of children they have cared for and in what settings. You may like to ask them about qualifications they have and whether they are willing to take part in training courses in the future. To find out whether your working practices are similar you may like to ask them how they would deal with a particular situation, for example, two children arguing or an angry parent.

When you have found someone you think will fit the requirements you have for an assistant you may find it helpful to have a trial period, for a few days, to check you work well together.

5. Keeping Effective Records

Childminding involves paper work as well as caring for children. Although this can seem quite daunting at first as you become more practised it will become easier. You will need to keep a range of records, from daily attendance to contracts and letters.

Records are an essential asset. As a childminder you can use your records to make important decisions, generate revenue, for marketing, operational guidance enabling your business to function day to day and for reporting to regulators and parents. Childminding records give accountability, providing verifiable evidence and they can ensure compliance with regulation, legal and financial requirements. Compliance with relevant data protection requirements and confidentiality will underpin effective record management.

Attendance

Planning Numbers

It can be handy to make a chart of which children you have when, especially if you are looking for customers. When someone phones, you can see at a glance whether they would fit in around your current children. It can also be helpful if you have lots of children coming for short periods.

The example chart shows clearly when the childminder has spaces, and which children she has when. By making a chart with the correct number of columns per day for the number of spaces available the childminder can also ensure she doesn't exceed her numbers.

	Monday			Tuesday			Wednesday			Thursday			Friday		
7-8															
8-9															
9-10															
10-11															
11-12															
12-1															
1-2															
2-3															
3-4															
4-5															
5-6															
6-7															

	Anna (age 7)		Billy (age 8 months)		Sarah (age 4)

The chart could be developed to allow only the correct ratios according to age, this could be done, for example, by allowing three columns for under fives and three for over fives a day. Where children attend school part time the time absent for school could be hatched or a list/chart made of collection times.The chart does not replace an attendance register, it is an aid for you when you are advertising for customers or organising your day.

Attendance Register

An attendance register is a requirement of most regulatory bodies, including Ofsted, and needs to record the actual times a child is present, not the times they are booked in for. This is important so that if you have to check back in your records for what time a child was picked up, you have the actual time not the one they were booked for. Remember a parent still pays for the hours they have booked (contracted hours) even if they pick their child up half an hour early. Keeping accurate records also show when a child was in your care. This is important, for example, if it is claimed a child was injured during hours you were contracted to care for them. If you can show they were not in your care you cannot be held responsible. The register can also highlight where an additional payment for overtime or late collection is due when you produce your bills and to demonstrate you are operating within your registration numbers and ratios. There are many ways in which you can set out your attendance register, below is just one example. Generally you will need one page for each child but if two siblings attend at the same time you may share a page between them, you will need to note however if one child is not attending or attends at a different time to the other.

Month : January 2007 Child's Name: *Jacob Smith*					
Date	Arrival	Departure	Arrival	Departure	Hours
Monday 6th	*8.05am*	*8.45am*	*3.30pm*	*5.55pm*	*3hrs 5mins*
Tuesday 7th	*8.00am*	*8.45am*	*3.30pm*	*5.40pm*	*2hrs 55mins*
Wednesday 8th	-	-	*3.30pm*	*6.05pm*	*2hrs 35mins*
Thursday 9th					

The above example is for a child cared for before and after school, if you are caring for a child without a break then you will only need one arrival and one departure column.

Remember: unless you care for a child at the weekends you will only need to include weekdays on your chart. You may be able to purchase a preprinted attendance register from a childminding association or childminding insurance provider if you do not want to design your own.

Contracts

A contract is an agreement that defines the terms of care and payment between a childminder and the parents/carer. If necessary, a contract may be used as evidence in court seeking recompense for non-payment if it is breached (broken). Once the contract is signed it becomes a legally binding document, it is designed to protect both parties. A written agreement or contract setting out the terms and conditions you have agreed to work with a family is an essential childminding record.

You may find it helpful to get the parents to fill in the details on your copy and you on their copy. This way if they dispute the contract they cannot argue that they did not know what they signed. All contracts should include the following:

❑ Name, address, phone number of child and parents or guardian.
❑ Payment rates, fees, deposits.
❑ Time of care - days, dates and times.
❑ Termination procedures, length of notice needed.
❑ Signatures of parents/guardians.
❑ Signature of childminder and the date.

Contract/Agreement Between
Parents and Registered Childminder

Two copies of this form should be completed, one copy to be kept by the parent(s) the other by the childminder. Each parent should receive a copy of the Childminding Policies, these are an integral part of the contract. Your signature on this document signifies that you have received and read the Childminding Policies.

Child's Name:
Address:

Telephone:
Date Childminding Agreement is to Start:
Hours:From am/pm   To am/pm
Days:
Meals to be provided:

Fees:	Contracted Hours	Weekly	£	per week
		Hourly	£	per hour
	Additional Hours (8am to 6pm)		£	per hour
	Additional Hours (before 8am or after 6pm)		£	per hour
	Weekends or statutory Public Holidays		£	per hour

Charges for Absence:

	Due to child's or parent's sickness	as hourly/daily rate
	Due to childminder's sickness	no charge
	Parent(s)' occasional days off	as hourly/daily rate
	Parent(s)' annual holidays (wks/yr)	as hourly/daily rate
	Childminder's annual holiday (_____wks/yr)	no charge
	On statutory Public Holidays	as hourly/daily rate

Name of Parent Responsible for Payment:
Pay day: in advance.
Notice required of holidays (on both sides) :
Parents to provide:
Childminder can take child on outings:
Any special arrangements:
This agreement is subject to review every   months. Date of next review:

Notice of termination   weeks or full fee in lieu of notice (this applies to both childminder and parent).

Signed   Parent 1   Date:
Signed   Parent 2   Date:
Signed   (T V Stone)   Date:

Please note that I cannot normally undertake the care of sick children

Contracts should also set out which hours/days/months you will provide care, who will be responsible for collection and payment, if there is a fee for late pickups, whether you charge for days when children are ill or on holiday, whether you charge for days when you are ill or on holiday, what notice is required for holidays, whether there be an extra charge for meals or nappies, or other supplies and what items parents need to supply. Who will pay for toddler group, nursery, playgroup, outings and entrance fees can also be included. To prevent misunderstandings all parties involved in picking up and dropping off should read and sign the contract. If you make additions or alterations to a contract then these must be signed and dated by all parties to show agreement.

You may supply some of this information as a separate document that also needs to be signed by the parents.

Note: The above is an example contract. Contracts may contain a variety of different points to suit your particular business practices.

Commercially available contracts can be purchased. Public liability insurance companies such as that for the NCMA may have contract conditions if you want to take advantage of their legal team in a contract dispute.

Start Date

Your contract needs to include the date that the care will commence.

Contracted Hours

These are the usual core working hours agreed between parent and childminder. Subject to any external influences, these are the hours that a childminder guarantees to look after the child. Parents should generally expect to pay for these hours, irrespective of whether or not the child is present.

Outside Contracted Hours

If you are able to provide additional care outside of the contacted hours you may decide to charge a premium rate; this should be specified in the contract. However, you must comply with the statutory limits on the number of children in your care.

Generally, parents shouldn't expect unused contracted hours to be offset against overtime hours, unless this has been specified in the contract.

Statutory Holidays (Bank Holidays)

Where a statutory holiday falls on a contracted day, often the normal fee will be charged however childminders will not normally be available for work on these days. If you do work on these days you may wish to negotiate an enhanced rate which should be detailed on the contract.

Contract Review

This gives parents and childminders the opportunity to update the contract on issues that may arise as the child develops, and to check the agreement is working well for everyone.

The date for the review of the contract is not the date on which the contract ends. The contract remains in force until a new contract is agreed and signed or until notice of termination is satisfactorily completed.

Retainer Fee

This is a fee used to reserve an existing place for future use by a child. The retainer fee is a proportion of the normal fee (often 50%) and is to be paid on the same basis (e.g. monthly/weekly) as the service to be provided. The purpose of the retainer is to recompense the childminder for potential loss of earnings during the retained period and to reserve a place and reassure a parent that you will not take on another child. It is not a credit against future fees. Whilst you are being paid a retainer, you may not fill the slot the child would usually fill. You may, if parents have a need, provide childcare during the retained period, the full childminding fee would be payable for any such period. If you take on a short term contract for another child during a retained period you should not continue to charge a retainer fee as the place would not be available.

A contract will be needed to cover any retained period. Without a retainer fee you do not have to guarantee a place for a child at any time in the future. If a retained place is not taken up by the parent, the retainer fees are not refundable. Retainer fees should not be taken for babies until after they are born. Your policies on retainer fees should be made clear on the contract.

Deposit

This is usually a one off fee paid to show parents intend to take up a place. The deposit is used to secure a place that is to become available. For example, if you have a child leaving next month, you could ask for a deposit (just like booking a hall for a party) from a prospective customer to reserve the vacated place for their child. It is usually then deducted from the first week/months fees or returned at the end of a contract. If parents change their mind about taking up a place the deposit is not normally returned. However, if you are unable to take the child the deposit must be returned.

Annual Holidays

If you take an annual holiday or take a certain number of days off a year, this should be specified in your contract. If the holiday is not between set dates you will also need to specify the notice period.

School Holiday Retainers

If you are caring for a child that only attends during the school term, you may wish to charge a retaining fee during the holidays. You can only charge a retainer fee if you are available to care for that child. If you do take the child during the holidays, the normal fee is payable (not the retainer!). If you are on holiday or you take on a child that fills the place a retainer fee is not applicable.

Payment

Fees for the contracted hours are normally payable in advance on the due date, this prevents trouble with parents not paying. Overtime payments are normally paid in arrears, with the advance payment for the next period, or on collection of the child. Parents may ask for a receipt (see Section 6. Money Matters).

Termination of Contract

Notice of termination of the contract by either party must be given in writing and should not include a holiday period. If it is necessary to end the agreement straight away then payment in lieu of notice must be made. In ordinary circumstances both the childminder and parent should serve the appropriate notice. The length of notice should be specified in the contract.

In some cases there may be reason for immediate termination of the contract. In the childminder's case, if the child's behaviour is or becomes such that the safety and well-being of other children in their care are threatened. In the parents case, if they feel you are failing to provide reasonable and safe care for their child. In this situation you should suggest the parents state their reasons in writing as soon as possible and also advise your regulatory body of their action and reasons. Parents may sometimes use false accusations to avoid paying termination fees.

Second Child Discounts

Some childminders offer a reduced fee for the second, or additional children in the family. When deciding whether this is something you want to do you must consider whether you can afford to charge less for a child that will take the same amount of care as a child paying full fee. However the parent may not be able to afford to have several children minded at full fee. If you do decide to charge a discounted rate make it clear that if the first child leaves, for example to go to school, the full fee is then applicable to the second child, or discount the older child. Remember, if you do not want to offer discounts you don't have to. As a self employed person you decide what fees and discounts you apply.

Playgroups/Nursery

If a child attends playgroup or nursery and you are still responsible for them, for example, if they become ill and you will have to collect them, then your fees should still be paid whilst the child attends. A contract can also detail who will be responsible for paying the fees for playgroup or nursery sessions.

Extras

Most parents provide items like nappies. If the parents wish you to provide these, you may wish to charge an extra fee. You will also have to decide whether your fees include meals, car journeys (for picking up from school) etc. What your fees include/exclude should be set out clearly in the contract.

Doctors, Clinics, Dentists

When you are negotiating your contract you may like to consider whether you are prepared to take a child to the hairdressers, doctors, health clinic or dentists. These events will all require prior parental permission. Note: If you have not included this into your contract you will require a letter from the parent giving you permission to take the child.

You cannot give permission yourself for any treatment or practice considered invasive even if you have permission to take the child. The health or other practitioner will require separate permission from the parent. Examples of such treatment include: inoculations, lancing wounds, painting teeth with fluoride, fillings for teeth and cutting of hair.

Policies & Procedures

If you have policy documents that give further information on your care provision you may want to acknowledge these in your contract.

Disputing Contracts

Contract disputes frequently arise from misunderstandings. Taking time to discuss contracts and having contract information notes covering as many points possible which parents can refer to helps eliminate this problem.

When a dispute arises with a parent discuss the problem in a calm manner, do not shout or raise your voice, while discussing the problem. Remember people who are losing an argument generally resort to shouting to try and get their point across. Always refer them back to the contract and point out the relevant details. If they or yourself are not complying with the contract then there will be a breach of contract and the contract could be deemed terminated. E.g. If they fail to pay you they are in breach of contract and could be liable for all outstanding fees plus fees for notice of termination.

Remember to keep all copies of letters relating to contract disputes as these can be used as evidence in court if the need arises. (See also sections on contract, correspondence, Section 6. Money Matters, where parents don't pay and Section 4. Working in Partnership, assertiveness.)

Record of Information

As a requisite of the Children Act, and similar regulations, records must be kept for the children in your care. These should include: the child's name, date of birth, address and home telephone number; the name of the parent or guardian and their place of employment and telephone numbers; other responsible persons details where appropriate; and the child's doctors name, address and phone number.

Record of Information for a Minded Child

Child's Name   Date of Birth
Home Address
                                            Tel No.

Mother's Name
Mother's Place of Work
                                            Tel No.

Father's Name
Father's Place of Work
                                            Tel No.

Emergency Contacts
Name of Person(s) who will Collect Child
Child's Doctor
Doctor's Address
                                            Tel No.

Immunisations:
☐ Diphtheria   ☐ Tetanus   ☐ Whooping Cough   ☐ Meningitis
☐ Hib   ☐ Polio   ☐ MMR   ☐ BCG
Infectious Illnesses
Health Clinic
                        Tel No.

Health Visitor
Am I to take Child to Clinic? Yes/No
Playgroup/School address   Tel No.

I give permission for my childminder to seek any necessary emergency medical advice or treatment required in the future. Parents Signature_____. (If you do not wish to give permission because of religious or cultural reasons, please provide written instructions about your wishes overleaf.)

I would like the following specific non - prescription medications to be administered to my child when required due to health reasons. Parents Signature _____
☐ Calpol Paediatric   ☐ Calpol six plus
☐ Teething gel   ☐ Sudocrem
☐ Cough syrup   ☐ Other please specify _____

Please specify overleaf any special needs of your child (Cultural, Religious, Dietary, Allergies, Health Problems etc) and anything else I need to know about your child (e.g. Fears, Likes, Dislikes, Routines)

Other helpful details might include information on health, medications and immunisations. The child's Health Visitor, playgroup/school attended with appropriate contact phone numbers. Details of any special needs including cultural, religious or health needs. Space for other details is also helpful, such as likes, dislikes, fears, routines.

Failing to Provide you with Necessary Information

Most of the necessary information you require is statutory and you will need to make parents aware that you are required by law to have the information. Some parents can feel intimidated by form filling and may like help to fill in your child record forms, they may like you to fill them in as they answer your questions. It also helps to explain why you need each piece of information.

Lack of provision of information can often stem from forgetfulness and parents need reminding that the information is required and that the children cannot be cared for without the statutory information.

Information on children's needs and dietary information should also be discussed. If the parent does not want to write the information you should explain that the information is necessary to help you provide the very best care for their child. This information can also be written by the childminder from information shared by the parent where the parent finds this easier or more acceptable.

Permission Forms

Permission forms are a means of ensuring your practice is approved of by parents, protecting yourself should there be an accident, and to comply with legislation and regulations. When producing permission forms common sense should be applied. Parents will not wish to sign vast numbers of forms and only those most relevant or required by your regulator are required.

Forms can be written in several ways. They can be added to the bottom of a contract or child record form and the text included 'In signing this contract you give permission for...' They can also be written as a separate form, either as optional statements 'I do/do not give permission for...' or as on the contract, that in signing the form parents give permission. They can be combined in a document with boxes to tick or initial to indicate a parent is in agreement and a signature and date for the document as a whole. Some permissions can be amalgamated in policy documents which parents sign to signify approval. For example, outings to the park will include the use of the swings and slide. Some example permission forms are included in the following text.

Outings & Transport Permission Form

This is to give you permission to take children on outings, using a car, train, bus etc. It could have room for parents to write the types of transport they give you permission for. It needs to be signed by the parents/carer.

Obtaining permission to take a child on public transport, even when not normally used, means you are covered if your car breaks down, or you have to use a taxi or a bus in an emergency.

I give permission for my childminder to take my child(ren) on outings, during day to day routine and local excursions, using public transport, car, or on foot (e.g. school/nursery runs, feeding the ducks, park visits, shopping trips etc.) If outings outside the normal area are planned separate permission will be sought.

Parents Signature_____

Administration of Non Prescription Medicines Permission

This is to give you permission to give a child medicine such as Calpol if necessary. It should have room for parents to write what medicines, lotions and creams, including sun cream, they give you permission to administer.

I would like the following specific non - prescription medications to be administered to my child when required for health reasons.
Parents Signature _____

☐ Calpol Paediatric   ☐ Calpol six plus
☐ Teething gel   ☐ Sudocrem
☐ Cough syrup   ☐ Other please specify _____

Permission for Emergency Treatment

Permission to give first aid in an emergency, to take a child to hospital or call an ambulance. This is required by some regulators. In practice in an emergency, if parents are unavailable a doctor will assume responsibility. Having discussed this with parents will however alert you to their wishes. For example, a preferred hospital.

I give permission for my childminder to seek any necessary emergency medical advice or treatment required in the future.
Parents Signature_____.
(If you do not wish to give permission because of religious or cultural reasons, please provide written instructions about your wishes.)

Permission Form for use of Photographs

This might be just for taking photos for your personal use, e.g. a photo album of the children you care for or to display on the wall, for your course work, children's or your own portfolio. You may also like to consider whether you will need or be using DVD or video materials. If you plan to use photographs for advertising by yourself, on a website or for local publications you need to state this, so parents have the option of saying no. Some training providers also require a copy of this permission if you are submitting photos as part of an assignment or project.

Parents may not want you to take pictures of their children or may limit the ways in which they permit you to use them. You should respect their wishes. However, this is unlikely to affect whether or not you feel you can care for their child.

Other

Other permission forms you may wish to consider may include:
☐ Outdoor play equipment - trampoline/climbing frame/large play equipment in the garden or park
☐ Internet/computer use
☐ Walking unescorted to and from childminder's house and school
☐ Persons authorised to collect children
☐ Consent for observations
☐ Washable nappies
☐ Contact with family pets
☐ Leaving minded children with registered assistants
☐ Face painting

Parent Refusing to give Permission

If a parent refuses to sign a permission form you will have to consider whether you can work without doing the things they refuse to give permission for.

If they refuse to give permission for outings how will this affect you? It may depend on the length of time the child is with you and the other children in your care.

If they refuse to give permission for non prescription medicines you may be able to discuss other options, for example that they give permission if approval is sought by telephone first, any conditions should be added to the form in writing, signed and dated, not just made verbally.

Keeping a Diary

It can be helpful to keep a diary of any unusual occurrences, for example, you could note when you had to pick up a child from school or that a parent was late collecting. It is also a sensible precaution to keep a log of all your visitors. This additional information you collect will help to cover yourself in the event of queries or allegations which may occur. You might keep a separate book for this or note it in the margin of your attendance register.

Accident and Incident Records

These records are used to record any accident or incident, from a cut or bruise to a fall or major incident. You should fill in an entry every time an incident happens or a child comes to you injured. It should also be used to describe any long term treatment a child may need/take and medicine that is administered. Records should also record incidents, such as if a child has had to be restrained by you or if they have injured another child in your care (e.g. biting).

These records are very important and it is vital you keep them up to date. There are many times when the information may become particularly important. If a child protection issue is raised you will have a record of all injuries that happened to the child in your care and also injuries they arrived with. If a parent makes an allegation against you then having records can help clarify the situation. If an incident occurs that needs reporting to a regulatory body such as Ofsted or child protection you will have the details ready, and if you are asked several weeks or months after the event you will still have a clear account of the incident.

You can purchase Accident/Incident and Medication Record Books, that you may find helpful for keeping records or you can make your own forms and store them in a folder. However you record accidents you must ensure that a parent viewing their child's notes cannot read other entries, as this would be a breach of confidentiality.

Accident/Incident Records

Your records should include the full name of the child/children involved, the date, time and place of the accident or incident, as well as a description of the circumstances and injury caused and any first aid that you administered or action that you took, such as calling a doctor or taking the child to hospital should also be recorded. There should be space for both your signature and that of the parent or guardian. You may also note any witnesses to an accident or injury.

Child's Name : *Ann Smith*	
Date and Time of Accident/Incident: *2.30pm 23rd September 2007*	
Place of Accident/Incident Occurred: *The garden, at childminder's.*	
Description of Circumstances: *David and Ann were playing in the sandpit, David threw sand over Ann and some got in her eye.*	
Description of Injury: *Sand in left eye.*	
Action Taken: *Ann was comforted and her eye washed out with luke warm water. This cleared the sand.*	
Signature of Childminder:	Date:
Signature of Parent:	Date:
Witness: *n/a*	

Existing Injuries Records

These are used to record any injuries a child has sustained when not in your care, for example whilst at school or playgroup or they arrived with in the morning from home.

You should record the full name of the child, the date, the cause of the injury and a description of the injury. There should be space for both your signature and that of the parent or guardian.

Child's Name: *Shan Jones*	
Date: *1st December 2007*	
Cause of Injury: *Accident in playground at school*	
Description of Injury: *Small graze to right knee and left palm of hand.*	
Signature of Childminder:	Date:
Signature of Parent:	Date:

Administration of Medicines/Treatment

Whether medicines are given as a one off event or part of a course of treatment, each dose needs to be recorded. Similarly with treatment, such as massage, it should be recorded each time it is given.

The record should include the full name of the child, the full name of the medicine, the dosage, the time it is to be given and duration the treatment should continue for. In the case of a treatment not including medicine a description of the treatment should be given and the time and duration.

Child's Name: *Joseph Coll*				
Date: *21st October 2007*				
Reason for Treatment: *Ear infection (non - contagious)*				
Name of Medicine / Description of Treatment: *Amoxycillin, 5ml once a day*				
Duration of Treatment: *1 week from 21st October 2007*				
Signature of Parent:			Date:	
Record of Each Dose:				
Date	Time	Dosage	Parent Signature	Childminder Signature
21st October	*12pm*	*5ml*		
22nd October	*12pm*	*5ml*		
23rd October				

Correspondence

Childminders may need to write a range of letters. The following are some of the basics.

Put your address on the top of your letter on the right hand side, the address of the person to whom you are writing should be set below this and on the left hand side of the page. Include your phone number, fax number and email address if you have them so you can be contacted easily if your letter needs a response. You should also include the date, the month is usually written as words, e.g. '27th October 2009'.

23 Lane Road,
Trumpington,
Kent,
MH67 56Y
Tel:1234-567891

45 Garden Road,
Trumpington,
Kent,
MH67 45R

4th April 2007

Dear Ms Smith

May I draw your attention to my invoice, dated 31st January, in respect of care I provided to Adam Smith for the week beginning 26th January.

Please note the sum of £123.50 is still outstanding despite a telephone reminder.

I would be grateful if you could now arrange prompt payment. If there are any queries regarding this invoice which are delaying payment, then I would ask that you contact me at the telephone number above.

Yours sincerely,

Set your letter out clearly in paragraphs. Try not to make your sentences too long, average about 15-20 words, although you can use occasional shorter or longer sentences. Try to keep your letter clear and to the point, use language that will be easily understood.

If you are on first name terms with the person you are writing to, the letter can be addressed 'Dear Annie' and finish with 'Yours sincerely'. Otherwise use Dear 'Mr Bridge' or 'Dear Mrs Bridge'. If you are unsure whether a women's title is 'Miss' or 'Mrs' use 'Ms'. If you do not know the name of the person you are writing to use 'Dear Sir', 'Dear Madam' or 'Dear Sir or Madam'. These should all be finished with 'Yours faithfully'. You can also finish letters with 'Regards'.

If you are writing a reply to a letter you have received then start your reply with an acknowledgement of the letter, such as 'Thank you for your letter of 27th October.'
When your letter is finished read through it and consider whether you have made all the points that you needed to and whether they will be clear to the person reading the letter. Check that you have answered any questions. Check that your letter has been polite, impolite letters are likely to be ignored or only partially read. If you are angry or emotional put the letter away overnight and re-read it the next day or ask someone to check it for you.

Organising your Office

Childminders all have paper work to do. You may have a room in your house that you use as an 'office' or you may just use the dining room table. Wherever you work, it can help to have some organisation. You will need somewhere to store paper work. Equipment such as pens, paper and calculators should be to hand so you don't have to get up and look for them.

Being organised will save you time, you won't need to go looking for the information or equipment you need. It can also help motivate you, paperwork can seem daunting or boring and having an organised office will encourage you to work on it.

If you are just starting childminding and you haven't done much paperwork before you might need some new equipment or supplies. This could include hole punch, stapler, ring binder or cardboard folders, pads of paper, notelets, envelopes, sticky labels, a filing cabinet or box, calculator, waste paper bin. If you are setting up an office in a separate space or room you may also need a desk and chair.

If you already have a 'office' area, have a sort out. Remove anything you do not need, and organise it in a way that allows you to find everything easily.

How you organise your paper work is up to you. You may find it helpful to have a folder for each child or family containing contracts, record forms etc. or you may prefer to keep all your contracts in one place and just separate out the one relevant to the family for discussions to ensure confidentiality. However you organise your paperwork and records, data protection issues and confidentiality should be taken into consideration.

6. Money Matters

All registered childminders are required to keep records of the money they earn like any other business. You will need to keep accounts recording the money parents pay you (income), the money you spend to help you look after the children e.g. buying food and toys (your expenditure). You will use these totals to work out your profit (income less expenditure). You may need to pay tax on the profit you make.

Setting Fees

As a self employed childminder you are free to decide your own fees. You need to ensure you will be left with a reasonable amount of money after you have deducted your expenses. Like any business you will run up costs, the fees you charge should reflect this. This can be a difficult decision. Your fees can depend on a range of different things. Generally childminders charge a higher rate for part time (before and after school) than for full day care. Parents receiving Childcare Tax credit can claim up to 80% of their childcare costs back, up to a maximum amount depending on the number of children they have. This is based on a 40 hour week by working out the hourly rate this may give you a general idea for fees. Some childminders may charge more than this and some less. The fees can also depend on the area you live in. Your local childminding association may be able to give you an idea of the range of fees in your area, or your local Children's Information Service may be able to help.

If may also help you to find out what the local nurseries in your area are charging. This may vary slightly between nurseries but will give you an idea of what parents expect to pay in your local area.

You do not have to charge different families in your care the same fee, if you are expected to collect and take a child to school, you may want to charge more than if the child is dropped and collected from your house, this reflects the increased expenses you will have. Another example would be if you are supplying baby's essentials, such as nappies and milk meaning you will have more expenses than if the parents supply these.

Minimum Wage

As a self employed person you are not entitled to receive the minimum wage and it is not intended as a guide fee per hour. If you employ an assistant however, they should be paid the minimum wage or above.

Retainer Fees

Retainer fees reserve a place for future use by a child (For further information see Contracts in Section 5. Keeping Effective Records).

Annual Increase

During the year running expenses may rise. It is helpful to have written in your contract a date when the contract can be reviewed and fees examined. This will prevent you running at a loss or with slim profit margins. Many expenses rise annually, e.g. water rates, rent, gas, electricity, insurance and publications. Others can increase more subtly, e.g. food and petrol. Monitoring these can help you calculate increases required.

It can also be helpful to monitor the cost of living indexes both the underlying and headline rates and the average wage rises as these may influence your decision on fees and help you predict rises in costs for the following year. Cost of Living Indices are published in the financial papers and will be quoted on the television during news and magazine programs. It is often discussed at budget time or when the Bank of England discuss bank rates.

In setting your fee increase and profit margin remember to consider market forces. Market forces are factors which will influence how much you can charge for your services without deterring customers. Examples would include level of unemployment, local economy, average wages in your area and competition.

Payment

Methods of Payment

You need to discuss with parents a payment method and schedule that suits both of you. If they are paid monthly, it may be easiest for them to pay you monthly, or if they are paid weekly, to pay weekly. If they are forgetful and the fees are the same each month it may help for them to set up direct debit payment from their bank account into yours for the set amount, then any extra fees can be paid by cash or cheque at the end of the month. You could also take full payment by cheque or cash.

Non Monetary Rewards

If you exchange childminding services for a non monetary reward, such as in exchange for some work done to your house, this must also be declared in your accounts. You need to work out the value of the service and record it as income.

Providing Receipts

When a parent has paid they may ask to be provided with a receipt. You can buy receipt books at most stationers or make your own.

Little Tots Childminding	*Receipt No: 0012 Date: 03/01/08*
32 Little Lane, *Broomhill*	*Parents/Carers Name:* *Joyce Brown*
Payment for the period: *01/01/08 - 14/01/08*	*Amount:* *Forty Four Pounds & 50p*

Receipts should include the date, the amount received, your name and the person you received the money from and what it was in payment for. You might also include a reference number if you are handing out lots of receipts.

Payment Record

You need to keep a record of when a parent pays and how much. It needs to be filled in each time a parent pays, whether weekly or monthly. It should include the date of payment, the amount and the signature of the parent and yourself. You don't need to divide up the payment for each child within a family. You will need an individual record for each family to prevent other parents from viewing the records.

You will use these figures to work out the income for your monthly or weekly accounts. In the example the 'Jones Family' pays weekly so you will need to add together the weeks totals to get a monthly total.

Payment Record For Jones Family			
Date	Amount	Parent Signature	Childminders Signature
25/02/08	£50.50		
4/03/08	£57.50		
11/03/08	£56.00		
18/03/08	£59.00		

Late Payment

As a childminder you are offering a professional service and as such you should be able to expect parents to pay fees on time. Unfortunately some parents do not pay on time, they may be forgetful or they might be taking advantage of your good will.

To encourage parents to pay on time and prevent a problem occurring make your payment policies clear from the start. The way in which fees are paid and who is responsible for payment, and whether an additional fee for late payment applies can all be written into the contract or given as a policy sheet.

It is important to discuss late payments with parents, there may be a problem that you can resolve together, such as a different payment date that corresponds better with the date they are paid. (See the Section 4. Working in Partnership, Assertiveness for discussions with parents.)

If a parent is forgetful there are several things you can do to help: provide a written bill each month/week detailing the amount due and the date it is due on. Or, help them set up a direct debit as detailed in methods of payment, that way they don't need to remember and can just pay for any extra hours by cash or cheque.

To encourage prompt payments, particularly for regular late payers, you may also like to charge a late payment fee. This is a fixed amount for each day the payment is overdue. You should also set a period of time after which you will not accept the children into your care until the fees are paid. Any late payment fees and policies should be outlined in your contract.

Accounts

Retaining Accounts

You need to keep your accounts for at least six years before disposing of them (accounts for the current tax year and the five preceding years). This is a legal requirement by the Inland Revenue and the Irish Revenue for income tax purposes.

Calculators

You will find a calculator useful for doing your accounts. It is possible to work without one but they will speed up the process. A basic calculator will work fine, is very cheap, and tax deductable.

Computers

Some childminders use computer programs to do their accounts. If you have some computer knowledge this may be an option for you, or you may find your local college offers computer courses. If you do use a computer make sure you keep back up files and print copies. Under the Data Protection Act you can keep accounts and records on computers but these must not include personal data, such as addresses and names, as this may contravene the Data Protection Act.

When Accounts Start

Accounts can be done on a monthly or weekly basis. If the end of a week finishes in the start of the next month, finish that week in the previous month's accounts.

Where to Keep Accounts

You can keep your accounts on lose sheets of paper in a file, or in an account book available from most stationers, some childminding associations also offer childminding account books. However you choose to keep accounts they should be organised so it is easy to find the right pages, so you do not lose bits, and legible so you can read what they say.

Keep your accounts where you can find them easily but not where things can be spilled on them or children can 'decorate' them. Any accounts containing personal data should be kept secure. Receipts can be hole punched and put in date order in a file or each months receipts could be stored in a separate labelled envelope, the idea is that you can easily find a particular receipt if you need it.

Free Milk

Childminders can claim for the cost of ⅓ of a pint of milk per day for children under five in their care. Applications are processed by the Welfare Food Reimbursement Unit (WFRU), the Children's Information Service (CIS) will be able to provide you with contact details.

National Insurance

All childminders need to inform the Inland Revenue Office or Irish Revenue that they are self-employed. Depending on your yearly income you may be able to apply for a small earnings exemption certificate, which means you will not have to pay class 2 National Insurance (NI) or in Ireland Pay Related Social Insurance (PRSI) contributions.

The Inland Revenue or Irish Revenue can provide you with information so you can make a choice, as you may opt to pay contributions to ensure your eligibility for certain benefits and pension. It is also possible to pay voluntary, class 2 or S, contributions even if you have an exemption certificate. Additional benefits include incapacity benefit, retirement pension, widows pension and maternity benefits.

Class 2 NI: These are paid monthly by direct debit or can be billed quarterly to be paid by cheque or direct debit. You can get a refund on your contributions if you subsequently do not earn enough and could have applied for an exemption certificate. To reclaim contributions you will need to provide proof of earnings in the form of receipts and expenditure, or your profit and loss accounts.

Class 4 NI: These fees are paid on the profit, above a given level, on your self employed income. Fees are calculated on any profits above the current rate of personal allowances and will be collected at the same time as you pay income tax.

S Contributions: The self employed are exempt from Health Contributions where the income is below the Irish Revenue thresholds, self employed PRSI contributions have a minimum payable fee.

Tax

Childminders have to pay tax if they earn over a certain amount, after expenses are deducted, the same as any other self employed person. However not all childminders earn enough to become liable for tax. It is important to keep accurate accounts of the money you are earning and your expenses (the money you have to spend to run your business), so you do not have to pay more tax than you are due.

In Southern Ireland there is a special tax relief for childminders who care for no more than three children. Relief applies while their gross annual income, their turnover, stays below a given threshold meaning they will have no tax liability.

Allowable Expenses

Allowable expenses are those expenses used legitimately to run your business. Household expense such as water, gas and electricity are based on the hours you work, this is the number of hours you work each week not the total for each individual children's care. For example, using the grid for attendance shown in Section 5. Keeping Effective Records the childminder works for ten hours on Monday, Wednesday and Thursday, seven hours Tuesday, six hours Friday giving a total of forty three hours per week. Full time is anything over 40 hours per week. If you are working full time you can deduct the following from your earnings before calculating profit or tax due:

Allowable Expense	Fraction	%
Heating and Lighting	1/3	33
Water Rates	1/10	10
Wear and Tear	1/10	10
Council Tax	1/10	10
Rent	1/10	10

If you are working part time (under 40 hours per week) then you can claim a proportion of what you would claim if you were working full time.

Working out fractions, percentages and proportions is not as confusing or difficult as it first seems.

Calculating Fractions and Percentages (%)

Percentages are parts of a whole, like dividing a cake into pieces. A whole cake is 100%, if dividing a cake into two equal parts (two halves) each would be 50%, because 100 divided by 2 is 50.

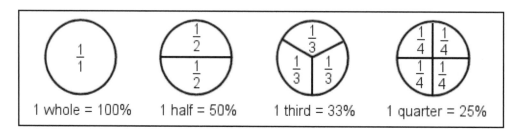

1 whole = 100%   1 half = 50%   1 third = 33%   1 quarter = 25%

Percentages can also be written as fractions. Fractions are one number written above another number with a line between: ½ is a fraction, in this example it is said 'half', one is the top number and two the bottom number. The bottom number is the number of pieces the cake was divided into (in this case two) and the top number is the number of pieces we are referring to. For example if I ate ½ a cake I would mean I ate one of the two pieces the cake was divided into. ½ is the same as 50%.

Working Out Percentages (%)

To work out a percentage of a figure you first need to work out what 1% would be by dividing the whole number by 100 (because there is 100% in a whole). Next you multiply by the percent you need. Example: What is 20% of £200?

[figure] ÷ 100 x [percentage] = Answer
£200 ÷ 100 x 20 = £40

Working Out Fractions

To work out a faction of a figure you need to divide the figure by the number of pieces it was divided into (the bottom number) then times it by the number of pieces you want (the top number). Example: What is ¾ of £200?

[figure] ÷ [bottom number] x [top number] = Answer
£200 ÷ 4 x 3 = £150

Turning Fractions into Percentage

If you find it easier to work with percentages than fractions you can convert fractions into percent. To do this 100 by the bottom number of the fraction and then multiply that by the top number. Example: Turn ¾ into a percentage.

100 ÷ [bottom number] x [top number] = Answer
100 ÷ 4 x 3 = 75%

Once you have turned your fraction into a percentage you can then use it to work out your sum.

Proportions

If you work less than full time (under 40 hours per week) you will claim a proportion of the allowable expenses a full time childminder would.

If, for example, you are working 20 hours per week, you would claim half as much rent allowance as if you were working full time. A full time child minder can claim 1/10 or 10%, so you would claim 1/20 or 5%.

Working out fractions of a fraction, or percentages of percentages can be confusing. It is easiest to work out what a full time childminder would get and then work out your proportion.

Example: Your rent is £340, a full time childminder can claim 1/10 of their rent as an expense.

So, first work out 1/10 of £340

340 ÷ 10 x 1 = £34   So a full time childminder can claim £34.

You only work 15 hours a week though. So you can claim less.

To work out how much you can claim, divide how much money a full time childminder can claim by the number of hours they work (40), this gives you the money per hour. Next you can times it by the number of hours you work. In this case a full time childminder (working 40 hours) can claim £34, and you work 15 hours.

£34 ÷ 40 = 0.85p per hour
0.85 x 15 = £12.75   So a childminder working 15 hours can claim £12.75

Rounding Numbers

Sometimes when you are working out fractions or percentages the numbers do not come to whole pence. You might get an answer like five pounds and three and a half pence, which would look like £5.035 on a calculator. As we don't have half pence or any amount below 1 pence you need to round the number up or down to the nearest whole penny.

To decide whether to round a number up or down you need to look at the first extra number after the whole penny. If we needed to round £5.035 we need to look at the 5 as this is the number after the whole numbers, £5.03 wouldn't need rounding.

If the first extra number is between 0-4 then you round down, this just means you remove the extra numbers from the end. If the extra number is between 5-9 then you round up, this means removing the extra numbers and adding one to the last whole number.

In the case of £5.035 the extra number is a five so we round up. To do this we remove the extra numbers, which gives us £5.03 and then add one to the last whole number, which gives us a final answer of £5.04.

Tax Deductibles

In addition to set allowable expenses you can also claim other expenses (tax deductables). Other expenses should be itemised, and receipts retained for items over £10. This could include things like toys, food, equipment, books, childcare courses, art and craft materials and insurance. You can claim things that are for use by the children, for running the business or furthering your training relevant to your childminding.

The following are examples and not an exhaustive list.

Disposables - Toilet rolls, tissues, baby wipes, kitchen roll, rubber or latex gloves, changing mats, nappies, nappy sacks, air freshener, soap, washing up liquid, hand cream, disinfectant sprays and wipes, cleaning products (window cleaning products, toilet cleaner, carpet cleaning fluid,) window cleaners, carpet cleaner hire, flannels, towels, bibs, floor cloths, mops.

Equipment - Cots, cot bedding, prams, pushchairs and bedding, sleeping mats, high chairs, safety straps, walking reins, wrist reins, spare children's clothes and wellies, cups, plates and bowls, step stools, potties, toilet seats, car seats.

Safety equipment such as cupboard catches, drawer catches, stair gate, fireguard, anti slam devices, closed circuit television, smoke detectors and carbon monoxide detectors.

First Aid Equipment such as supplies and box, first aid training, book and a thermometer.

Toys, Games and Activities - Books, tapes and videos for the children. Toys, puzzles, games, outdoor play equipment and batteries.

Art and Craft materials such as paper, paint, chalk, printing accessories, pencils, crayons, felt pens, glue and sticky tape. Extras for children's activities such as ingredients for cooking, plants/seeds and plant pots for growing things.

Business Equipment - Text books on childcare, play activities, curriculum planning or similar. Subscriptions to childcare magazines. Stationery such as envelopes, paper, folders, pens, pencils, paperclips, staples, stapler, hole punch and calculator.

Training expenses not paid for by other sources, e.g. Child Protection, Early Learning Goals, Equal Opportunities, Child Development, First Aid, NVQ and safety.

Public Liability Insurance, Group Membership, Membership of a Childminding professional body.

Outings - Travel such as a car as capital allowance, running costs or mileage allowance, bus fares, train fares, taxi fares, car parking fees, road or bridge tolls.

Outings such as meals out, entrance fees (only for you and minded children, not your own children).

Meals - Meals (it may help to calculate this for a month and work out a weekly percentage/fraction). Drinks, snacks, ice-cream and squash. Some people include the cost of meals in their hourly rate, others charge a set fee per meal. It is up to you how you decide to cover your costs.

Advertising - This could include advertisements in shop windows, newspapers, web sites or similar and your phone calls to organise them.

Working Out Profit

Profit is the money you have left after you take away the amount you had to spend (expenditure) from the money you made (income).

So if you were selling cakes the profit would be the price you sold them for (income) less the cost of the ingredients (expenditure).

income - expenditure = net profit
net profit - tax allowance = taxable profit

Weekly Accounts

Doing accounts weekly, particularly for expenses, is much easier than having to work out all your figures at the end of the month/year. At the end of each week you should work out how much expenditure you have had, you can keep a note throughout the week, or work it all out at the end. This is where you should itemise your allowances.

First work out the figures for allowable expenses: Heating and Lighting, Water Rates, Wear and Tear, Council Tax and Rent (if you pay it). Then list extras underneath, these might be things that occur every week such as food and drinks or one off items such as a new pushchair.

Expenditure for Week Beginning 4th March 2008	
Heating and Lighting	£ 8.20
Water Rates	£ 0.93
Wear and Tear	£ 17.92
Council Tax	£ 2.50
Rent	£ 24.00
Food and Drink	£ 23.56
Travel Costs	£ 12.30
Art and Craft Materials	£ 10.78
Pushchair	£ 78.89
Toiletries	£ 5.00
Miscellaneous	£ 12.34

Total	£196.42

When writing down lists of numbers to add up it helps if you keep the decimal points (dot that is between the pounds and the pence) in line. It helps to make it clearer whether numbers are hundreds or just a few pounds, or pence. Don't forget to double check your totals. If you are paid weekly you can also make a list of your weekly income.

Monthly Accounts

These should contain a summary of the total weeks expenditure and income. You need to list the weekly totals from your weekly expenditure sheets and your income. The totals from each month will be used to make the yearly accounts so check your work each month.

Accounts for March 2008	
Income	
Hobson Family	£450.00
Smith Family	£ 36.78
Jones Family	£230.00

Total	£716.78
Expenditure	
Wk Beginning 4/3/08	£196.42
Wk Beginning 11/3/08	£120.34
Wk Beginning 18/3/08	£114.00
Wk Beginning 25/3/08	£ 99.50

Total	£530.26
Income - Expenditure = £716.78 - £530.26	**Profit £ 186.52**

Yearly Accounts

Yearly accounts summarise the monthly income and expenditure. If you have done your monthly accounts this should just involve copying the totals across and adding them together.

Accounts For Year 2006 - 2007			
Month	**Income**	**Expenditure**	**Profit**
April	456.00	287.00	169.00
May	245.78	145.00	100.78
June	345.67	206.56	139.11
July	345.67	197.32	148.35
August	467.00	289.98	177.02
September	367.89	167.00	200.89
October	509.00	309.00	200.00
November	145.89	157.00	-11.11
December	324.00	208.67	115.33
January	335.12	207.00	128.12
February	387.69	200.00	187.69
March	267.89	178.00	89.89
Total	**£4197.60**	**£2552.53**	**£1645.07**

Using a table like this will help you double check your sums. In the columns labelled income and expenditure fill in those totals from your monthly accounts. In the right column box work out the profit (income - expenditure) the answer should match the profit you worked out for each month.

On the bottom row is the total income, expenditure and profit for all the months. The total profit should equal the same whether you add up the profit column or you take the total expenditure from the total income. If they aren't the same re-check your sums.

If you have more expenditure than income your profit will come to a minus (-) number, when adding up the column just take that number away instead of adding it.

You will be able to use your figures for your income and expenditure to fill in your self assessment tax return. If you are earning less than fifteen thousand pounds these will be the only figures required for the business. You will need to keep all your records and calculations as the tax office can ask to look at them up to six years after you have submitted your tax return. The tax year runs from 6th April in one year to the 5th April the following year.

Self Assessment Tax Returns

The Inland Revenue (IR) will automatically send you a tax return once you have registered as self employed. Having to fill in a tax return sounds very difficult but try not to put it off. The Inland Revenue will help you with any problems you have and it comes with a question by question guide to help you through it. If you keep records of your income and expenditures, which you should be doing as a childminder, then filling in the form should be easy. You will need to fill in your yearly totals and work out how much profit you have made. They also ask about any other income you have had, such as casual work, or work you have done whilst being employed by someone else. The tax year runs from 6th April one year to 5th April the following year, you may have to add up your monthly totals for this period if your yearly totals don't cover the same dates.

Self Assessment Tax Returns received in April should be completed no later than the following 31st January to avoid penalties imposed by the IR. If you return your forms by 30th September the IR will calculate your tax and class 4 NI if applicable and they will then notify you of any tax or NI due by the 31st December giving you thirty days before the payment is due at the end of January.

The first eight pages of your Tax Return form requires information on your personal savings and income from pensions. and allows you to claim any allowances and relief you may be entitled to. You will also need to complete the Self Employed supplementary page for your childminding business. Note: all the money earned from your childminding business is referred to as your turnover.

When Parents Don't Pay

Sometime during their childminding career many childminders will experience parents that do not pay the fees that are due.

The following section will guide you through a fictitious case in which Annie Jones neglected to pay a week's fees for the care of her son, Sam Jones, then gave notice that she would no longer require her childminder's services. The contract they had signed agreed a four week notice period.

Letter to State Outstanding Fees

If a parent ignores verbal requests for money due, the first step is to send a letter detailing what they owe. This allows you to set out what is owed and when it needs to be paid. As with all your correspondence this letter should be polite and include your contact details and the date. Send the letter recorded delivery as this can then be tracked and you will know if parents have signed for it.

Dear Annie,

With reference to your telephone call to me today, I was disappointed to learn from you that my childcare service for Sam is no longer required. I hope your future arrangements will prove as successful as I feel Sam's time with me has been.

Your verbal notice of termination is effective from today (15th September 2007) as is your instruction that my care is to cease immediately. I would however draw your attention to the outstanding monies, detailed below, owed to me, both for the childcare already provided and as payment in lieu of notice (as provided for by the contract we agreed). Should you wish I can continue to provide you with childcare, as per the contract, during the notice period. I would also point out that the payment terms agreed in the contract are weekly in advance, your payments are therefore already overdue.

Invoice

Care Provided
To supply care for Sam Jones
8th to 12th September (8am to 5pm basic weekly rate) £123.75
Meals: Five meals @ £1.00 each   £5.00

Total for care provided   £128.75

Payment in lieu of notice (Four weeks)
Payment in lieu of notice for 4 weeks @ £123.75/week   £495.00

Total due in lieu of notice   £495.00

Invoice Total   £623.75

Should you wish to dispute these charges please contact me on the telephone number above, otherwise prompt payment, no later than 26th September, would be appreciated. As indicated above, payments are already overdue.

Regards
Mary

The Parent's Response

Hopefully after receiving your polite letter the parents will promptly pay the amount due. For the sake of the example we will assume the parent responded as follows:

The parent sent a letter and a cheque for £128.75. The letter stipulated that acceptance of the cheque would be on the condition that it was full and final payment.

The parent might also have responded by refusing to pay any fees or not responded at all. If the parent does not respond resend the letter by recorded delivery.

At this point the childminder has two options: she could accept the cheque as the final payment and write off the fees that were incurred in the notice period, or she could decline the cheque and try to obtain the full amount. It is advisable to obtain legal advice at this point, the Citizens Advice Bureau and various other organisations including your public liability insurance company may provide free legal advice or you may prefer to consult a solicitor.

In this case the childminder decided she would not accept the cheque and wanted the full amount due. She responded by returning the cheque with the following letter. Note address and date were included.

Dear Annie,

I have received your letter dated 17th September 2007 and the enclosed cheque for £128.75.

As you are aware, under the terms of the contract we agreed and signed, the sum you owe to me is £623.75. Your token payment, made on condition that I accept it as full and final settlement of my claim, is woefully short of that sum and is not acceptable as full and final settlement. I therefore return your cheque uncashed.

Your attention is drawn to my invoice dated 15th September 2007 and I would remind you that payment is overdue. I look forward to receiving full settlement on or before the 26th September 2007.

Settling this matter amicably would be preferable, but I am prepared to initiate proceedings through the County Court if necessary.

Regards
Mary

In the letter the childminder set out the reasons why she would not accept the cheque and also notified the parents she was willing to take the case further if necessary. Informing the parents that you are willing to take the matter further will often encourage them to pay, especially if they realise that they are in breach of the agreed contract terms and conditions. The childminder still kept the letter polite and the parents still have time to settle the amount.

If the parents still refuse to pay the amount due, you have two options: writing off the money or, pursuing a claim through the county court.

Deciding Whether to Pursue a Claim

When deciding whether to take a parent to court you should consider whether the possible expenses and risks involved outweigh the possible benefits. There may be stress involved in preparing for a court case, paper work involved in filling out the claim forms and preparing documents. If you lose you will also have to pay court fees and expenses incurred. If the amount due is small, less than £100 it may not be worth pursuing the fees further. If you win, however, the parents will be ordered to pay the fees, expenses and court costs. You will also have to consider whether if you win the case the parents will be able to afford to pay.

In this case the childminder decided that the possible benefits outweighed the risks, and that the evidence she had supported her claim. After not receiving payment following her second letter she responded to the parents with the following letter.

Dear Annie,

Final Demand

I would remind you that the amount of my Invoice, dated 15 September 2007, is still outstanding.

In view of your refusal to offer full payment, I have prepared a County Court Summons, for the sum of £671.98 (the amount you owe plus interest at 8% as allowed by the Court) plus £40 court fees. I have enclosed photocopies of the court papers for your reference. This summons will be submitted to the local County Court unless I receive full payment of my invoice, £628.75, before midnight on Wednesday 8th October. I regret that at this stage I cannot accept payment by cheque.

Regards
Mary

Small Claims Court

You can issue a claim in any county court or the district court in Southern Ireland, you will need to fill in a form, this comes with guidance on how to complete it.

There is a fee, this is dependant on the amount you are claiming for, however if you win, the defendant (person you are claiming against) will be ordered to pay this. In addition to the money owed you can also claim interest. The form will include details on how to work this out.

Once you have filled in the form and returned it, the court will send a copy to the defendant along with a response pack, with details for them on how they can respond. They have the choice between not responding at all, admitting that whole or part of your claim is owed or disputing the whole or part of your claim.

If the defendant disputes your claim they must return a form within 14 days. If that happens the court will send you a copy of the defendant's completed form.

Preparing Claim Details

When going to court you need to collect evidence to support your claim. In a small claims court the Judges or Registrar's decision is largely based on the written submissions. This means you should take the time to present your evidence in a clear and logical manner with an index. Depending on the claim you might include the following:

❑ Contracts signed by you and the parents
❑ Attendance record for the child
❑ Correspondence between you and the parents
❑ Testimonials from relevant witnesses
❑ Other records with information from parents
❑ References such as quality assurance reports demonstrating the quality of your care.

You can also prepare a statement to read detailing your claim, the reasons behind it and what the evidence shows.

Getting the Defendant to Pay

Even if the court finds in your favour and orders the defendant to pay there is still no guarantee that you will receive the money owed. If parents still refuse to pay there are several options. You may have to pay extra to use these methods and there is still no guarantee of payment, however if you do receive payment any extra costs you incur will be added on to the amount the defendant owes.

In Southern Ireland you can send the court order (Decree) to the Sheriff for execution. There is a fee for the service, refundable if the Sheriff succeeds in obtaining the money owed.

Warrant of Execution - This gives court bailiff's the authority to collect goods to the value of your claim to be sold at auction.

Attachment of Earnings Order - If the person you are seeking money from is employed this asks the employers to retain an amount from their earning each pay day to be sent on to you through a collection office.

Garnishee Order - This freezes the defendants bank account and if the funds are available pays you from the account.

Charging Order / Judgement Mortgage Affidavit - This prevents the defendant from selling their assets such as their house or investments without paying you the money owed.

Benefits

Child Tax Credit UK

Child Tax Credit is administered by the Inland Revenue who will be able to provide details of their latest version of this tax benefit. It is for families with at least one child, with an additional element for each child in the family. Parents will receive a higher amount if there is a child under one. There is also an enhanced rate for disabled children.

Working Families Tax Credit

This is a tax credit for people in paid work including those working as a self employed person. Eligibility, and the amount received, if eligible, is dependant on the amount of time worked each week, earnings, the number of children and childcare costs.

This tax credit is made up of a series of elements:
❑ Basic adult if you meet criteria
❑ Extra element for single parents and couples
❑ Extra element for working 30 hours or more per week
❑ Extra element if you are working and have a disability
❑ A childcare element

Childcare Tax Credit payments are based on parents' annual childcare costs divided by the number of weeks in the year. This means holiday periods, (when childminders may be looking after their children for more or less time than usual) will be taken into account in the calculations, but the amount a parent receives will not vary between term time and holiday time. Parents can receive up to 80% of their childcare costs.

The childcare element is paid to parents in money or offset against tax depending upon the tax status of the family. It can be paid to eligible families through the wage packet by employers as part of the Working Families Tax Credit or directly to those who are self employed.

Childminders may be contacted by the Inland Revenue to ensure a parent is using them for childcare before paying or continuing to pay this benefit.

Jobseeker's Allowance / Benefit

You can only claim this if you are working under 16 hours a week and are looking for a full time job. It is not available for becoming self employed so having vacancies does not entitle you to this benefit.

Income Support / Supplement

You may be able to claim this if you are on a low income and earning below a certain amount. Your savings and the number of hours you are working per week also impact on whether you can receive this benefit and the amount you can receive. Childminders who are single parents may also be eligible.

Housing and Council Tax Benefits

If you are on a low income your Housing or Council Tax Benefits may be paid on your behalf by the local council. Your Local Authority will be able to tell you whether you are eligible and if so how much for. In Southern Ireland a rent supplement may be available from your Local Health Office.

Back to Work Bonus / Enterprise Allowance

You may be eligible for this if you have been claiming benefits which stop when you start childminding. This is a one off lump sum that you may be able to claim if you were previously claiming Income Support but this stopped because you started full time work. In Southern Ireland this is paid on a weekly basis.

Incapacity / Illness Benefit (if you become Unable to Work)

If you become unable to work for health reasons you maybe able to claim Incapacity Benefit, to claim this you will need to have paid the right level of National / Social Insurance Contributions. You may be able to claim even if you are only unable to work for a short period, as well as longer periods.

Sources of Benefit Information
❑ Benefits Agency Office
❑ New Deal Advisor or your Job Centre
❑ Tax Enquiry Centre
❑ Inland Revenue
❑ Citizens Advice Bureau / Citizens Information Board

Insurance

As a childminder you may need public liability, car and house insurance. When purchasing insurance it is good practice to 'shop around' for the best deal. Points you may want to consider when choosing a policy include: ease of making a claim; flexibility; what is protected (covered); the excess (what you pay out towards the cost of money claimed); whether payments can be made in installments; reputation of the insurer and the total cost of the policy. The limit of indemnity they quote is the amount of money up to which an insurance company will pay when a claim is made.

Insurance policies can be purchased direct (you contact them), through a broker, who will compare prices and policies for you but will charge a fee for this service, or through a membership organisation e.g. a childminding association where the Public Liability Insurance may be linked to the membership fee.

Public Liability Insurance

You should obtain Public Liability Insurance cover. This covers childminders in situations where they may be liable for any loss or damage caused to a third party, or the property of a third party during the course of their childminding activities. Depending on the insurance, accidental injury to a child or assistant, damage or loss of customers property and loss or damage to toys on loan may be covered. Litigation claims are becoming far more common and compensation claims can run into millions of pounds for an injured child so it is essential to check you are adequately covered.

Car Insurance

A minimum of third party insurance is required by law. This will however only insure you against loss and injury to others, i.e. if you cause an accident the insurer will only pay your liability to other people involved in the accident and not your car repairs. Comprehensive cover will provide cover as in third party policies but will cover you for damage repairs to your car and replacement value if your car is stolen. If you use your car to transport your minded children you will need to ensure your policy includes business use. Ofsted for example, will check for this on your insurance certificate.

House Insurance

This is often broken down into contents and buildings although some companies offer combined policies. Buildings insurance covers the structure of the house and provides for site clearance and rebuilding costs. Some policies will cover alternative accommodation for yourself and pets. Contents insurance covers personal possessions. If you choose a 'new for old policy' deductions for wear and tear are not made and if something is not repairable it can be replaced with a new one. It is a good idea to choose a policy that includes accidental damage, then if a child puts toast in the video recorder slot or spills glue on the carpet you will be covered for cost of repair, professional cleaning or replacement. You will need to inform the insurers you are childminding as this may affect your policy. Some companies will charge a different rate for childminders, some may refuse accidental damage cover and some will provide cover providing you do not exceed a specific number of minded children.

Personal Accident

This provides insurance protection from financial hardships if you injure yourself and are unable to work, for example, if you break your leg.

Pensions

You will need to ensure you have considered your pension. Home Responsibilities Protection (HRP) can help protect your state pension, reducing the number of years you need to contribute. HRP cannot reduce this to less than twenty years. For every full year you receive Child Benefit for a child under sixteen, twelve in Southern Ireland, you will automatically receive HRP. For more details see your Family Allowance book. In the UK opting to pay class two National Insurance provides contributions towards your state pension at a minimal cost, check with the Inland Revenue for more details.

You may like to consider a private pension plan to top up your state pension. There are many such schemes on the market including the stakeholder pensions. Relevant information on these should be obtained from an independent advisor before making your final choice.

7. Health, Hygiene and Safety

Considering aspects of children's and your own health, safety and hygiene, both in and around your setting, is good practice. It will help you to provide a professional service and meet any imposed standards and legal obligations.

Health

Medicines

All medicines should be stored in their original packaging, clearly labelled and out of reach of children. Medicines can pose a serious risk to children if they are taken by accident. If a child does accidentally ingest medicine, medical help should be sought immediately.

Childminders need to have written permission from parents before they administer any medicines. Parents may have signed a permission form in advance indicating which non prescription preparations they will allow you to give their child if the need arises such as teething gel or medication to reduce temperature. As a matter of courtesy it is still a good idea to call a parent before administering any medication (except where this has been agreed for prescribed medicines). If the parents have not signed a permission form you are not permitted to give the child medicine.

You need to make it clear to parents that you should be informed of any medicine prescribed by the child's doctor and be given written permission to administer the medicine if required. Prescription medicines should have the child's name on the bottle. Do not administer medicine with another persons name on. Remember to check when the child received the last dose and when the next dose is due to prevent accidental overdoses.

Childminders need to keep accurate written records including the times and dates of any medicines administered, which should be signed by the parents even if the medicine is one which the parents have already signed a consent form for. Note: under the EYFS only medicines prescribed by doctor, dentist, pharmacist or nurse can be administered. However, there is no mention of preventative preparations within the guidelines.

Sick Children

Childminders do not normally care for children that are ill, and this should be made clear to parents in advance. Parents should be asked to inform you if their child has been ill within the last twenty-four hours before attending so you can decide whether they pose an infection risk. Parents are not always aware of the reasons for you not accepting a child that has been ill. They may greet you with phrases like 'He was throwing up last night, but he's fine this morning.' If a child has been ill in the last 24 hours, 48 in the case of sickness and diarrhoea, you should not accept them into your care. You risk the illness spreading to other children or yourself which may mean you are unable to accept any children and must take days off. If a parent becomes difficult about a child, give them a copy of the communicable disease exclusion periods (example within this section)and show them your National Standards. It is helpful if you have clearly stated your policy on sick children when they signed their contract. The decision whether or not to accept a sick child for care is up to you. For example, if there is no risk of infection (e.g. an ear infection) you may take the child for that day. You might also take a child with chickenpox if you have no other children that day and are not pregnant.

When caring for a child with a long term illness you should make sure you have a thorough understanding of the condition and any treatment you need to give. If the treatment for a long or short term illness requires specialist or technical knowledge you should be instructed by a qualified health professional in the required procedures.

Under no circumstance should you accept a child with a notifiable infectious disease, because of the risk of infecting other children or yourself.

What to do if a parent tries to deliver a sick child

You should have a policy in place for how you will deal with sick children and parents should have a copy for reference. The policy should contain details of any exclusion policies you enforce.

There is a great temptation for parents to take advantage and deliver a sick child due to the pressures of work. They may feel you will not notice when the child is delivered and will be reluctant to call them back from work. You should be consistent in your approach. Infectious children pose a risk to both other children and you and your family's health, point out to parents that if you become ill you will be unable to care for their children.

Firmly refuse admittance in accordance with your policy. Explain that a sick child is better off at home, where they will not have to travel and can rest and recuperate. If a child is delivered and subsequently found to be unwell, you may decide that it is in the best interest of the child and others present for the child to be collected and taken home. In this situation you should contact the parents and request the parent collects or arranges for the collection of the child as soon as possible. You should have an 'emergency' contact agreed who can pick up a child if you cannot contact the parents, e.g. grandma or aunt. (See Section 4. Working in Partnership, Assertiveness).

Accident / Injury Records

Childminders are required to keep accident/injury records. These should contain a description of the injury and be countersigned by both parent and childminder. An entry should be completed when a child arrives with an injury or is injured whilst in the childminders care. These records are a statutory requirement and are there to protect the children from any danger of abuse. They are open to inspection by your local Social Services Department and childminding regulatory bodies.

Accidents and Emergencies

Parents should be informed of any accidents or injuries to their child, where these are minor e.g. scrapes or bruises they can be informed when they collect the child. These should be detailed in the accident record book for the parents to sign. If a child needs to attend a doctor the parents should be contacted to arrange whether you or the parents are to take them, or you are to meet them there with the child. Parents should be offered reassurance, particularly while phoning, to prevent panicked reactions and be given the information they will need to make a decision about treatment. Remember you cannot agree to any treatment a child may need; in an emergency a doctor will take that responsibility.

In the event of a serious accident your regulatory body, such as Ofsted, and your Public Liability insurer should also be informed. Note: in England you must also notify the local Child Protection Team.

It is a good idea to have a back-up minder, a registered childminder you know (and preferably the children know) that you can leave children with in an emergency.

Reassuring Children in an Emergency

Comfort, reassurance and possibly distraction should be given to the injured child and other children present, some of whom may panic during an emergency, or at the sight of blood. The safety of all the children should always be kept in mind. 'Helping' can be useful to distract children to prevent panic, e.g. collecting a favourite toy for the injured child, explaining what you are doing and why may also be calming and reassuring.

Children will follow your example, so try to keep your voice and expression calm and reassuring. Smile and give clear instructions, speak loud enough to be heard especially if your instructions are important to the safety of the children.

First Aid Kit

All childminders must have a first aid kit. First Aid kits and boxes should always be kept in the same place and should be easily accessible to adults but not children. An additional first aid box may be kept in the car for outings.

The contents should be replaced when used and any out of date items replaced routinely. Remember the contents of the first aid box and the box itself are tax deductible. Do make sure you know how to use the contents of your kit. There are no set contents but here are a few suggestions, all of which should be available from your local chemist.

- Crepe bandage
- Large open weave bandage
- Small open weave bandage
- Eye pad with bandage
- Scissors
- Sterile gauze swabs
- Small sterile pads with bandage
- Triangular bandage
- Hypoallergenic tape
- Sterile non-adhesive pads, perforated film absorbent dressings (x2)
- Finger bandage and applicator
- Disposable gloves (latex)
- Safety pins (optional)
- Disposable laerdal face shield (for resuscitation if trained)

There are also some optional extras that you might find useful:

- Ear thermometer, electronic thermometer, or 'hold to head' Strip thermometer
- First Aid book or similar instructions
- Special cuddly toy
- Stickers for 'brave' children
- Disinfectant spray (for cleaning up, not for use on children)
- Disinfectant wipes (for cleaning up, not for use on children)
- Body fluid disposal kit inc : disposable gloves, apron and waste bags, absorbent crystals, plastic scraper, paper towels

Note: Childminders in Wales are required to have the contents of a 1-20 persons employee kit which dictates contents including how many bandages and safety pins are required.

Disposable gloves should be used when dealing with blood, vomit and other bodily fluids for preventing the spread of infectious diseases, including HIV and Hepatitis. Appropriate anti-bacterial cleaning fluids should be used to sterilise areas where blood and other bodily fluids have been spilt.

Recognising Illness

It is important you can quickly recognise signs a child is ill so appropriate action can be taken. Signs and symptoms of illness can include physical symptoms and changes in behaviour, or a combination of the two. Recognising a child is ill can explain their change in behaviour and the severity will determine the course of action required.

Physical signs of illness can include one or more of the following: high temperature, flushed and hot, sweating, shivering, increased pulse or respiration rate, swollen glands, sunken eyes or dark shadows beneath the eyes, aversion to light (photophobia), pale skin colouration (may appear greyish in black or Asian children), rash, blood in the urine, vomiting and/or diarrhoea, pain or runny nose.

Rashes occur for a wide variety of reasons including the following: heat rash, allergies, viral infections, insect bites, nettle rash, 'slapped cheek' virus and chicken pox. Blood in the urine can also occur for a variety of reasons including kidney or urine infections and thread worms.

Changes in behaviour may include one or more of the following: loss of appetite, fretful and irritable, crying, high pitched whine or cry, unusually quiet, listless, withdrawn, refusing to play, more clingy than usual, needing more sleep than usual, rocking, unnaturally aggressive and complaining of pain or of being ill.

The importance or significance of symptoms will vary according to the age and stage of development of the child, as will their criticality. For example, at ten months a child with fingers in their mouth and crying may mean they are teething, however, if the child was seven years old it might mean they have a tooth ache, a mouth ulcer or have bitten their tongue. High temperatures for children under the age of four can lead to a child developing Febrile Convulsions, older children will usually withstand high temperatures without this added complication.

In addition to your own general knowledge help can be gained for identification and responses to symptoms from reference books, illustrated texts, health visitors, doctors, practice nurses, parents and other similar sources.

Dealing with High Temperatures

Children frequently develop high temperatures due to viral infections, but occasionally they can be a sign of a more serious illness.

In order to make a child with a high temperature more comfortable while you wait for a parent you could do the following:

❑ remove excess clothing
❑ sponge face with tepid water or offer a cool flannel
❑ give plenty to drink
❑ request permission from parent to use paediatric paracetamol or administer if permission previously obtained (and record time and dose for parents to countersign when they arrive).
❑ If the temperature is still not reduced after an hour bathe in tepid water and leave to air dry, or place close to a cool fan if one is available.

If tepid bath or fan, and medication do not reduce the temperature and it is running at or above 40^0c immediate medical advice should be sought.

Exclusion Periods For Communicable Diseases

Communicable diseases are infections or illnesses caused by microbiological agents comprising of bacteria, viruses, fungi, parasites or prions which can be passed from person to person, both directly or indirectly.

Some communicable diseases must be notified, in accordance with the Public Health Act of 1984, to the Consultant at the Communicable Disease Control Unit (CCDC). Each local Health Authority will have a consultant in communicable disease to whom you can talk concerns over with and to whom information should be supplied where a child's doctor has not already done so.

Examples of notifiable diseases are as follows: Anthrax, Cholera, Diphtheria, E. Coli, Food Poisoning, Hepatitis, Leprosy, Malaria, Measles, Meningitis, Mumps, Plague, Poliomyelitis, Rabies, Rubella (German Measles), Salmonella, Scarlet Fever, Shigella (Bacterial Dysentery),Tetanus, Tuberculosis, Typhoid/Paratyphoid Fever, Whooping Cough and Yellow Fever. Which diseases are considered notifiable can vary slightly according to region. For example, in Scotland and Northern Ireland Chicken Pox and Rabies are also notifiable.

The following are exclusion periods for communicable diseases.

Infection	Exclusion	Notes
Athlete's Foot	None	Treatment recommended.
Chickenpox	5 days from onset of rash	It's not necessary to wait until spots have healed or crusted.
Cold Sores (Herpes simplex virus)	None	Many healthy children and adults excrete this virus at some time without having a 'sore.'
Conjunctivitis	Until treated	If an outbreak occurs, consult Consultant in Communicable Disease Control (CCDC).
Diarrhoea and Vomiting	Until diarrhoea and vomiting has settled (no symptoms for 48 hrs)	Often there will be no specific diagnosis or treatment.
E coli and Haemolytic Uraemic Syndrome	Dependant on type of of E. coli	SEEK CCDC's ADVICE
Fifth Disease	See Slapped Cheek Disease	
Flu (Influenza)	None	Flu is most infectious just before and at the onset of symptoms.
German Measles (rubella)	5 days from onset of rash	Most infectious before diagnosis, and most children should be immune due to immunisation so that exclusion after the rash appears will prevent very few cases.
Giardiasis	Until diarrhoea has settled (no symptoms for 48 hrs)	There is a specific antibiotic treatment. No swimming for five days.
Glandular Fever (Infectious Mononucleosis)	None	
Hand, Foot and Mouth Disease	None	Usually a mild disease not justifying time off school.
Head Lice (nits)	None	Treatment is recommended only in cases where live lice have definitely been seen.
Hepatitis A	There is no justification for exclusion of well, older children with good hygiene who will have been much more infectious prior to the diagnosis. Exclusion is justified for 5 days from onset of jaundice or stools going pale for under 5's or where hygiene is doubtful.	
Hepatitis B or C	Although more infectious than HIV, Hepatitis B and C have only rarely spread within a school setting. Universal precautions will minimise any possible danger of spread of both Hepatitis B and C.	
Herpes simplex virus	See Cold sores	
HIV/AIDS	HIV is not infectious through casual contact. There have been no recorded cases of spread within a school or nursery.	
Impetigo	Until lesions crusted/healed	If lesions can reliably be kept covered, exclusion may be shortened.
Infectious Mononucleosis	See Glandular Fever	
Influenza	See Flu	
Measles	5 days from onset of rash	Measles had become rare in the UK, but with some parents choosing not to vaccinate it may become more common.

Infection	Exclusion	Notes
Molluscum contagiosum	None	A mild condition.
Meningococcal Meningitis/Septicaemia	Until recovered	There is no reason to exclude siblings and other close contacts. The CCDC will give advice on any action needed.
Non-Meningococcal Meningitis (viral)	Until recovered	Once the child is well, infection risk is minimal.
Mumps	5 days from onset of swollen glands	Most infectious before the diagnosis is made, and most children should be immune due to immunisation.
Nits	See Head Lice	
Parvovirus	See Slapped Cheek Disease	
Pertussis	See Whooping Cough	
Ringworm (Tinea)	Until treatment commenced	Proper treatment by the GP is important. Scalp ringworm needs treatment with an antifungal by mouth. This infection is caused by a skin fungus and not a worm.
Roseola	None	A mild illness, usually caught from well persons.
Rubella	See German measles	
Scabies	Until treated	Outbreaks have occasionally occurred in schools and nurseries. Child can return as soon as properly treated, including all the persons in their household.
Scarlet Fever	5 days from commencing antibiotics	Treatment recommended for the affected child.
Slapped Cheek Disease (Fifth Disease /Parvovirus)	None	Exclusion is ineffective as nearly all transmission takes place before the child becomes unwell.
Salmonella	Until diarrhoea and vomiting has settled (no symptoms for 48 hrs)	If the child is under five years or has difficulty in personal hygiene, seek advice from the Consultant in Communicable Disease Control.
Shigella (bacillary dysentery)	Until diarrhoea has settled (no symptoms for 48 hrs)	If the child is under five years or has difficulty in personal hygiene, seek advice from the Consultant in Communicable Disease Control.
Tinea	See Ringworm	
Tuberculosis (TB)	CCDC will advise on action	Generally requires quite prolonged, close contact for spread. Not usually spread from children.
Threadworm	None	Treatment is recommended for the child and family.
Tonsillitis	None	There are many causes, but most cases are due to viruses and do not need antibiotics. For one cause, Streptococcal infection, antibiotic treatment is recommended.

Infection	Exclusion	Notes
Warts & Verrucae	None	Affected children may go swimming but verrucae should be covered.
Whooping Cough (Pertussis)	5 days from commencing antibiotics or 21 days from onset of illness if no antibiotic treatment	Treatment (usually with erythromycin) is recommended though non-infectious coughing may still continue for many weeks.

In some cases different action may be needed if there are vulnerable children in your care or you, your assistant or spouse are pregnant.

Vulnerable Children

Some children have medical conditions that make them especially vulnerable to infections that would rarely be serious in other children. For example, children being treated for leukaemia or other cancers, children with AIDS or HIV, children on high doses of steroids (not including inhalers) and children with conditions which reduce immunity. You should have been made aware of any of these conditions by the parents. You will need to discuss with them what will happen in situations where a child would not normally be excluded but their inclusion may affect the child. Parents will also need to be informed promptly if you think their child has been exposed to any infectious diseases. Chickenpox, Shingles and Measles in particular may pose a problem to vulnerable children.

Pregnancy

Some infections, including Chickenpox, German Measles (Rubella), Measles and Slapped Cheek, pose a danger to an unborn baby if exposed during pregnancy.

Chickenpox: If a pregnant woman, who has not previously had Chickenpox, is exposed early in pregnancy (before 20 weeks) or in late pregnancy (the last 3 weeks) she should contact her GP and/or midwife.

German Measles (Rubella): Many people are immunised against Rubella, a test is possible to ascertain immune status.

Measles: Exposure during pregnancy can result in premature birth and occasionally loss of the baby.

Slapped Cheek Disease (Fifth Disease, Parvovirus): This can occasionally affect an unborn child if a woman is exposed in early pregnancy (before 20 weeks).

A pregnant woman exposed to any of these diseases should contact her doctor/midwife for advice. If you or any parents that may visit are pregnant you should take precautions to ensure you or parents do not come in contact with these infections.

Meningitis

There are several types of meningitis, it can be caused by a bacterium or a virus. It causes swelling in the membranes that surround the brain and spinal cord. Bacterial meningitis can be very serious, if treated promptly most people make a full recovery, however in some cases it can be fatal or lead to a permanent handicap.

Children may have been 'off colour' for a few days, but it can develop very rapidly. The symptoms include headache, vomiting, fever, stiff joints, a dislike of bright lights and a rash of reddish purple spots or bruises **Note:** these 'spots' do not disappear if a glass is pressed against them. The rash can be harder to detect on dark skin, spots are more easily seen on paler areas such as palms, soles of feet, stomach and the roof of the mouth.

Babies and small toddlers may also have the following symptoms: Pale or blue tinged blotchy skin, refusal to eat/feed, irritability with refusal to be held, stiff body and jerking movements, floppy or unable to stand, high pitched moaning cry.

Meningitis symptoms can appear in any order and not everyone will get all of the symptoms. If you suspect meningitis seek urgent medical assistance.

Head Lice

Head lice are insects that live on the scalp and in the hair. They cannot jump or fly and are spread by close contact and can be detected by using a fine tooth comb on very wet hair. If no lice can be found after combing shampooed hair from the roots then there is no need for treatment even if other children in your care have lice present. Lice can be treated by 'wet combing', washing the hair then using conditioner and combing through from the roots to remove lice. This should be repeated for two weeks every 2-4 days, or by using lotions recommended by a pharmacist.

Dehydration

Symptoms of mild dehydration include thirst, dry lips and mouth, tiredness, irritability and headache. To alleviate increase fluid intake.

Moderate dehydration has all the above symptoms and the skin will not bounce back quickly when pressed. The eyes may become sunken (in babies so will the soft spot on the head, fontanel). Urine production will be limited and dark yellow. There may be cramps, stiff and or painful joints, severe irritability, tiredness and severe headache. Medical advice should be sought in these circumstances.

Severe dehydration has all the above symptoms plus blue lips, blotchy skin, confusion, lethargy, cold hands and feet, rapid breathing, dizziness, fainting, high fever, inability to pass urine or cry and disinterest in drinking water. Emergence medical treatment is required in these circumstances.

Thread Worm

Thread worm is a common condition, children are particular susceptible due to their poor hygiene practices. To prevent the spread, hands should be washed with soapy water and each person should have a separate towel/flannel. Kitchen roll on a dispenser can save on the washing. Children should be discouraged from putting their hands in their mouth. The toilet area, including seat, handle and door handle should be disinfected regularly and rooms should be dusted and vacuumed regularly. Your doctor or a pharmacist will be able to advise you on treatment which should be taken by the whole family, on the same day, to prevent re-infection.

Teeth

Milk teeth cannot be replanted if they are knocked out, however adult teeth can and should be placed into a glass of milk if available or placed inside the cheek to be replanted by a dentist.

Tooth decay is where the tooth enamel has become damaged causing cavities to form. The risk of tooth decay is increased by a high sugar intake. If the teeth are not brushed plaque forms on them. When sugary drinks or foods are eaten the plaque turns the sugar acidic, increasing the risk of damage to the tooth enamel.

Dentists suggest regular brushing should take place before breakfast and last thing at night before bedtime. This should mean that the majority of children's teeth will be brushed by the child's parent or carer at home.

If children are cared for overnight or the parent has insufficient time in the mornings, they may request that you clean their child's teeth for them. It such cases they should provide the child with their own toothbrush. Each child should have their own toothbrush and these should not be stored touching, to prevent cross infection.

The teeth should be cleaned using a pea sized quantity of children's fluoride toothpaste (this is important as young children may not be able to spit the paste out and could ingest too much fluoride). Brush the teeth in a circular motion at an angle of 45° to clean all the surfaces. Children should be encouraged to spit out spare toothpaste and water. Avoid rinsing to leave a film of fluoride on the teeth to protect them from acid attacks. Children with sufficient coordination should be encourage to have a turn at brushing their teeth. This will help them learn the correct way to look after their teeth.

Drinking sweet drinks and sucking sweets all day should be discouraged to help protect the teeth. It can be helpful to restrict sweets and sweet foods to mealtimes and choose healthy snacks and non acidic drinks (milk, water) for between meals. Where children are old enough to understand, then the reasoning behind the restrictions or choice can be explained so children learn about healthy eating habits.

Smoking

There is over whelming scientific evidence to indicate smoking is harmful to children's health. A report by the Royal College of Physicians,'Passive Smoking' (2005), estimates that 50 children under the age of five are admitted to hospital every day in the UK with illnesses resulting from passive smoking; including: bronchitis, pneumonia, coughing and wheezing, phlegm, asthma attacks, middle ear and meningoccocal infections. They also state it causes cot death, stunted growth and reduced lung function.

If you do smoke, then you can minimise the risks to minded children in the following ways:

❑ Try to only smoke outside. If you must smoke inside, limit smoking to a room where you can open windows to allow adequate ventilation.
❑ Never smoke in children's sleeping areas or rooms where children spend a large proportion of time.
❑ Never smoke in the car with the windows closed.

You should not smoke in the presence of childminded children and you cannot leave them unattended while you smoke.

In England, as set out in the new Welfare Requirements of the EYFS, childminders are required to ensure that children are in a smoke free environment and this would include both the house, outside play areas and your vehicles. Only in exceptional circumstances can children use areas where smoking has occurred and then there must be adequate ventilation to clear the atmosphere.

In other areas you can smoke, after hours when children are not present, in rooms that revert to domestic use when you close, but not in rooms solely used for childminding such as a purpose built play room.

If you do smoke then you should have a written policy to give to parents that states when and where you smoke and what precautions you take to ensure it does not have a detrimental effect on the children present. It may also be helpful to include in your policy whether parents are allowed to smoke in your house, it is strongly suggested that this is not allowed and you have a smoke free policy. If a parent smokes in your house against your wishes politely ask them to put their cigarette out or go outside. Remember a non smoker can detect the smell of cigarette smoke on adults, children, clothing, hair and furnishings days after the event.

Your Health

Isolation and Depression

Childminding is often described as an occupation where childminders work in isolation. You are not really alone. In 2006 there were 71,500 childminders working in England. (Ofsted), 6,051 in Scotland (Care Commission), 3,627 in Northern Ireland (HSS trust) and 2,384 in Wales (CSSIW). There are also 500 who have chosen to notify the authorities in Ireland that they are working.

A childminding development officer or the CIS can put you in touch with other childminders in your area. There are often small groups of local childminders which you can join. These self help groups tend to meet frequently and can offer coffee and someone to talk to. They may also arrange outings and events. Many childminders like to meet up to talk about anything from childminding to where they went on holiday. If you cannot find a group local to yourself then the NCMA, for example, can provide information on starting one. You only need to find 3 or 4 other childminders. In many areas there are also county or unitary groups of childminders who meet up for a variety of events.

Having someone else to talk to about problems with your work or life eases the burden and helps prevent depression and loneliness setting in, 'a problem shared is a problem halved', or even eradicated. Never bottle up your problems, share them, someone somewhere will have been there before and be able to offer advice and support.

There are many other groups that childminders are welcome to take the children or join in with. These include Mums and Toddlers groups, tumble tots, story time, 'drop ins', Meet a Mum and the National Childbirth Trust. These groups allow both childminder and children to socialise.

Stress

Childminding is a stressful job. Feeling stressed does not mean you are weak or that you are inadequate for not coping. Almost all childminders will feel stressed at some point throughout their career. Signs of stress include mood swings, tiredness, trouble concentrating, changes in eating and sleeping patterns, feeling run down and low self esteem. Everyone will show different signs when they are stressed and will find different ways that help them deal with it.

There are many ways to help prevent and reduce stress. Make sure you take care of yourself, get adequate sleep, take time to relax and eat a healthy diet. You may have to turn down parents that want late hours so you have time to do necessary jobs and get to bed on time. Take time out to relax, spend time doing non work related things, reading a book, going for a walk, clothes shopping, whatever you find relaxing. Eat a balanced diet, don't rely on 'junk' food just because its quicker. Take some exercise, this doesn't have to be going to the gym, walking or swimming are also good for you.

If you are feeling stressed then there are lots of things you can do to help.

❑ Plan a messy activity with the children, such as painting and join in creating your own picture too.
❑ Treat yourself to a massage or facial.
❑ Think about what you have accomplished rather then the problems that are causing your stress.
❑ Talk about how you feel with another childminder, or a friend.
❑ Spend some time doing something special with your child(ren).
❑ Listen to relaxing music and put your feet up for a while.
❑ Slow down, consciously stop yourself from rushing.
❑ Have a relaxing bath.
❑ Find something amusing to read or watch.

You should also consider why you are feeling stressed and try to take positive action towards dealing with the problem. This book provides helpful suggestions on dealing with many of the common problems that a childminder may face. If you need more help talk to your regional regulator, childminding professional body or your childminding development worker.

Contact your local college they may have stress management courses that will provide information on managing stress.

If you feel you cannot deal with your stress, consider talking to your doctor about it. They may be able to refer you to a counsellor who will help you work through your problems.

Unsupportive Family Members

Before you start childminding you should discuss with other members of the household or family the impact childminding may have on them. If your partner had no objections at this point but has become unsupportive you should discuss the reasons for this.

Partners may appear unsupportive because they have had a busy day, are tired, or because they do not appreciate what childminding involves. They may assume that because you were 'at home' you spent the day 'drinking coffee and playing with the children'. If they do not appreciate what childminding involves discuss what you do with the children, how much paper work you do or let them borrow this book! It may also help if your partner spends a day at home to see what work you do.

If your partner is at home while you work they may also feel jealous of the attention the children receive or that you spend time after hours doing paper work. Try to involve them in activities, such as asking them to read a story or lead the tidying up while you make a cup of tea or snack. Make sure you allow time to talk about each other's day at work.

Self-Esteem

Having self-esteem is about valuing yourself, your work and your opinions and recognising your achievements.

When you have had a problem with a parent or are experiencing difficulties with your studies or something is just 'not going right' for you, you may feel low in self-esteem. You may have feelings like, 'I'm not a good childminder'; 'I never get anything right'; 'Everyone else seems to do better than me'. Almost everyone feels like this sometimes.

You can help yourself deal with these feelings by thinking in a different way. Instead of focusing on what you have not achieved, consider what you have succeeded with. Acknowledge your strengths, you might find writing a list will help 'lift your spirits' these could be things like being a good listener, being good with animals/children, taking good photographs, helping people with a problem or making really yummy cakes. Be patient with yourself; you don't have to achieve things at the same time as others, recognise things that are an achievement for you without comparing them to whether they are an achievement for someone else. Think of the things you achieve each day, getting dinner for three children, doing the washing up or getting the children off to school are all achievements. Reward yourself when you do achieve something, this could be an extra five minutes to put your feet up, ordering a takeaway so you don't have to cook or going on holiday! Be assertive do not let people belittle your opinions or beliefs.

You may find it helpful to have a few inspirational quotes or things that make you feel positive such as thank you letters from happy customers or photographs from a fun day out to look at.

Nutrition and Diet

Children often continue the eating habits they develop while they are young throughout their lives. This makes it very important to talk about food and help children develop healthy eating patterns whilst they are learning. Children need to learn which foods are healthy options and why.

Providing a well-balanced diet, encompassing any religious, cultural or medical requirements, is an important part of ensuring healthy development in children. A balanced diet must include vitamins, minerals, protein, fat, carbohydrates, fibre and water.

Vitamins

There are a range of vitamins necessary for the healthy functioning of our bodies.

Name	Used For	Found in
Vitamin A (Retinol)	Helping your eyes adjust to changes in the light and keeping your eyes, and skin moist. (Yes, carrots can help you see in the dark!)	Egg yolk, cheese, liver, carrots, and spinach.
Vitamin B	Production of blood cells, healthy muscles and nervous system.	Liver, fish, green vegetables & eggs.
Vitamin C (Ascorbic Acid)	Helping the body to repair damage and strengthen the immune system. Its also helps the body absorb iron.	Fruit and fruit juice, especially orange, and green vegetables.
Vitamin D	Absorbing calcium which is important for healthy teeth and bones.	Fish, cod-liver oil, egg yolk & some cereals.
Vitamin E	Helping to keep the circulatory system healthy and aids in wound healing.	Vegetable oil, cereals, peanut butter & whole grain products.
Vitamin K	Blood clotting; it stops bleeding when you get a cut. Its also plays a role in bone growth, and kidney function.	Dark, leafy green vegetables, liver & cheese.

Minerals

The main minerals required are listed in the following table. Other trace minerals needed include zinc, sulphur, magnesium, phosphorous and potassium.

Name	Used For	Found In
Calcium	Keeping your bones and teeth healthy, and your heart and nerves functioning properly.	Cheese, eggs, milk, yogurt & green leafy vegetables.
Fluoride	Decreases incidences of dental caries in children.	Water.
Iodine	Lack of Iodine can cause brain damage and mental impairment	Water, sea food & salt.
Iron	Iron prevents anaemia and keeps your red blood cells healthy	Red meat, green vegetables, pulses (beans, lentils, chick peas), egg, liver and dried fruit (apricots, sultanas, raisins).
Sodium Chloride	Regulation of fluid balance.	Table salt, bread, meat & fish.

Protein

Protein is used by the body for growth and repair. Protein foods contain a range of amino acids. Meat products contain all the amino acids needed. Individual vegetables only contain some of them, a vegetarian diet must contain a wide range of vegetables to ensure all amino acids are available.

Sources of protein include: meat, fish, chicken, dairy products, nuts, pulses, soya and tofu.

Carbohydrates

Carbohydrates are used for energy. There are two types: starches and sugars. Starches produce energy more slowly than sugars which provide a quick source of energy.

Sources of starch include: cereals, potatoes, pasta, beans and lentils.
Sources of sugar include: sugar, fruit, vegetables, honey and milk.

Fat

Fats also provide energy for the body. They come in two types, saturated and unsaturated. Too much saturated fat should be avoided along with trans fats (unsaturated fats created during processed food production).

Sources of saturated fat include: butter, cheese, milk and meat.
Sources of unsaturated fat include: fish oil, olive oil and sunflower oil.

Fibre

Fibre is found in plants; it provides the body with roughage. It does not have a nutritional value but is used to keep the digestive tract working healthily. Sources include wholemeal bread, brown rice, pears and bran. Too much fibre can reduce the amount of minerals children can absorb such as calcium and iron.

Water

Water is necessary to maintain healthy levels of fluid in the body to prevent dehydration. Children aged 1- 3 years need approximately 1.3 litres (5.5 cups) and children aged 4 - 8 years need approximately 1.7 litres (7.5 cups) daily. Children may also drink up to 50% more liquid when it is flavoured.

Providing Children with a Balanced Diet

Children are growing, so they need large amounts of protein to build new cells. They also need carbohydrates to provide them with the energy they need for their daily activities. Vitamins and minerals are also important in keeping their bodies healthy.

A suggested daily intake would comprise of:
❑ two portions of meat or proteins
❑ two portions of protein from dairy products
❑ four portions of cereal foods
❑ five portions of fruit and vegetables
❑ six cups of fluid

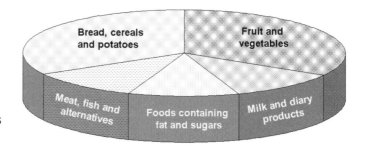

Sugar and Children's Teeth

Children like the taste of sweet sugary foods, however they often have very little nutritional value and can cause tooth decay. Sugar does not need be banned completely; occasional sweets and sugar as part of puddings are acceptable. Children under one should not be given things sweetened with honey as their gastrointestinal tracts are not sufficiently developed to cope with the C. Botulinum spores it may contain.

Nuts

Children under five should not be given nuts as they may cause choking. Pureed nuts as part of cooking ingredients or spreads are fine, provided you have checked an allergy is not present. However it is recommended that children under the age of two are not given peanuts in any form.

Milk

Children younger then five should not be given skimmed milk and children under two should not be given semi-skimmed milk. This is because it lacks the fat soluble vitamins A and D.

Salt

Salt should be kept to a minimum in young children's diets as their kidneys cannot cope with the amount adult kidneys can. Avoid salty snacks such as crisps and processed meals which have a high salt content. When cooking do not add salt to children's meals.

Special Dietary Requirements

When taking on a new child you should check whether they have any special dietary requirements. These could be for religious, cultural or medical reasons. You should respect the parent's or child's requests and provide food meeting their requirements, you will have to discuss with the parents how best to do this. It may involve them supplying some of the food or ingredients.

More details of cultural dietary requirements can be found in Section 10. Equal Opportunities.

Vegetarian

Vegetarians may not eat any meat, poultry, game, fish, shellfish, or the by-products such as animal fats. They may do this for a range of reasons, cultural, religious or through an awareness of animal rights.

It is not an uncommon misconception that by cutting meat out of a child's diet they are missing important nutrients. Well balanced vegetarian diets actually provide all that a child needs to grow healthily. A vegetarian diet is appropriate for infants and children and provides all the nutrients required for normal growth and development. Vegetarian children are similar in height and weight to non-vegetarian children and are less likely to be obese or overweight. (Report Vegetarian Vitality Written by Andy Bond Published January 1995 by The Vegetarian Society)

Young children need a lot of energy to grow and support their active lives, this means they need a high calorie diet. Vegetable oil can be added to cooking, nuts and seeds e.g. peanut butter (see information on nuts and children's ages), cheese, yogurt and avocado are all high energy foods. Bread, rice, pasta and potatoes are also good sources of energy.

Our section on a balanced diet contains sources of all the nutrient needs for children and adults, all of which can be found in foods without meat. Not all foods are obvious in their use of animal products, gelatine is a good example of this, it is made from animal products but often found in sweets or jelly.

If you are caring for a child on a vegetarian diet after seeking advice from the parents you may also like to look for books in the library covering food alternatives and recipes.

Vegan

A vegan is a vegetarian who in addition does not eat any products that come from animals, e.g. dairy products or eggs. Most vegans also do not eat honey.

It is possible to provide a balanced diet containing all required nutrients within these guidelines. There are some nutrients, e.g. calcium and vitamin D, that would normally be obtained from dairy or meat products and you will need to make sure these are supplied. Dairy products can often be replaced with soya alternatives (where recommended by the child's health visitor or GP), many of these products are fortified with essential vitamins.

If you are caring for a child on a vegan diet after seeking advice from the parents you may also like to look for books in the library covering food alternatives and recipes.

Food Allergies

You should ask parents to inform you of any allergies a child has when they first come into your care. Allergic reactions can be very serious, even life threatening, so it is important to ensure that a child with an allergy does not have the wrong food.

Some allergies are more easily catered for than others. Foods such as wheat appear in many different foods whereas shrimps appear in few. Parents may be able to provide you with special foods for their child, cookbooks and contacts for more information.

It is important to also teach the child about which foods they can eat and which to avoid. You must be careful that children do not share food amongst themselves that could contain the allergen.

Hygiene

Hygiene is important to keep children and adults healthy. Good hygiene prevents the spread of germs that can cause illness.

Hand Washing

Washing hands is important as germs can easily spread to and from things we touch. You should wash your hands before you prepare food, before you eat or feed a child and before you care for an ill child or administer first aid. You should wash your hands after handling raw foods (and between handling other foods), going to the toilet, changing nappies, cleaning up bodily fluids, handling or cleaning animals, coughing or sneezing, and gardening.

When washing hands use hot water and soap, and make sure you wash thoroughly. The areas often missed are thumbs, finger tips, under nails, between fingers and backs of hands. Dry

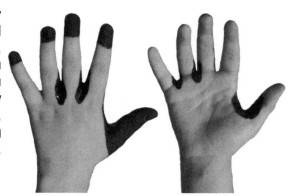

Most frequently missed areas marked black.

your hands after washing, as germs are more easily spread on damp hands. Use a clean dry towel or a disposable paper towel.

It is important that you explain to children why they need to wash their hands and remind them to do so. It may help to have a notice on the toilet door reminding them. To teach children about washing all parts of their hands try giving them a blob of water based paint and suggest they close their eyes and pretend to wash their hands. When they've done you can discuss which bits they have missed.

Germs can also be hard to explain to young children. Try using some playdough to explain, give all the children one colour and you have a different colour (the germs). Everyone moves around shaking hands and exchanging a piece of playdough, but when they shake hands with you and get a piece of playdough theirs will include a different colour which will it turn be passed on to the next person. By the end everyone will have a bit of the germs and the children can see how one person can spread germs to the others if they do not wash their hands.

Noses

Hands should be washed after wiping a child's nose to prevent cross infection. Disposable paper tissues are more hygienic than cotton hankies which need washing at 60-90°c to destroy germs.

Small paper tissues are most cost effective, they can be used once and disposed of. This prevents finding 'snotty' tissues lying around creating a health risk. Encourage the children to put them in the bin themselves.

Keeping the Kitchen Clean and Hygienic

It is important to keep the kitchen clean. You should have a thorough clean regularly during which you wash inside of cupboards, drawers etc. and also clean daily all surfaces and food preparation areas. It is important to clean as you work as well. Do not leave dirty implements in areas where you are preparing foods or on clean work surfaces as these can cross contaminate other foods. This is particularly important in the case of raw foods, such as uncooked meat or fish, which could contaminate ready to eat foods such as sandwiches.

When cleaning use the appropriate detergents, anti-bacterial solutions or disinfectants for the job. Use a different cloth for floors than for work surfaces and separate water. If you are not using disposable clothes soak them in bleach to clean and disinfect them.

It is important to keep the floors clean, especially with children who are still crawling, as they will be moving on their hands across the floor and often put fingers in their mouths.

Washing Up

When washing up use hot water and washing up liquid. Wash the cleanest things first and if the water becomes dirty change it. Rinse items afterwards in clean hot water.

Tea towels can be a source of contamination; use a clean towel each time you dry up and clean the cloth on a hot wash cycle. Do not use the same towel you dry your hands with to dry washing up. Leaving items to drip dry is a more hygienic alternative.

If you use a dishwasher use the recommended amount of salt and detergent and a hot wash cycle.

Rubbish Bins

Empty bins regularly; you may need to increase frequency in summer. Use a bin with a lid and liners. Be careful not to spill contents when emptying. Clean the top and inside of the bin regularly with disinfectant or bleach solution.

It is not uncommon for children to find swing bins interesting and want to play with the lid or to try posting toys in. This should be discouraged and any toys that end up in the bin should be thoroughly cleaned and disinfected.

Pest Control

Pests such as flies, ants and mice are most attracted to kitchens. Cover food to prevent flies and use an electronic fly killer or sticky fly paper to catch them. Do not use anti-insect sprays in the kitchen as it can contaminate food and preparation areas. If you have an infestation your local environmental health department will be able to offer advice and assistance. If food is contaminated by pests throw it away.

Storing Foods

Foods will need to be stored according to their type. The packaging should give guidance on where food needs to be stored, the temperature and how long it is possible to store it for. Do not store food in original containers (e.g. tins) once its been opened. Transfer food into covered containers or cover with silver foil or cling film. Do not reuse foil or cling film for different foods. Use non-PVC cling film, especially on foods with a high fat content. The PVC chemicals can leach into fatty foods.

Make sure you do not store raw foods such as meat or fish in a way that it can contaminate fruit, vegetables or ready to eat food. Meat should be covered and stored on the bottom shelf in a fridge so that it cannot drip on to foods below, it should not be stored touching ready to eat foods.

Fridge/Freezer

Use a thermometer to check regularly that both fridge and freezer are operating at the correct temperature. Fridges should be below 5°C and freezers below -18°C. Defrost your fridge/freezer regularly and carry out any maintenance according to the manufacturers instructions. Clean shelves, insides of doors, door handles and other surfaces regularly.

Use By/Best Before

The majority of foods carry either a 'use by' or 'best before' date. A 'use by' date is generally given to foods with a short life span and 'best before' to those that can be stored for longer. These are the dates that unopened food can be used until. Once opened the food should only be eaten within the time specified on the packaging (e.g. use within two days).You should check these dates before using food, however do not rely upon this as always being right, if a food smells, looks or tastes like it has gone off, or you are not sure, then throw it away. Use up older items first.

If the packaging is damaged or the safety seal broken then do not use it. Remember you may be able to return it for a refund.

Food Preparation

Good hygiene practices when preparing foods helps to prevent the spread of infections. You should always wash your hands before preparing food. There are also other precautions you should take:

❑ Use clean utensils and wash surfaces before starting to prepare food. When possible use utensils rather then hands for handling foods.
❑ Clean hands, surfaces and utensils thoroughly between working with raw and ready to eat foods.
❑ Do not use the same utensils for raw food once it has been cooked.
❑ Wash vegetables and fruit thoroughly whether it is to be eaten raw or cooked.
❑ Avoid preparing foods if you are ill.
❑ Re wash hands if you have to do something else in the middle of preparing foods, between working with raw and cooked food or handling eggs.
❑ Cover cuts or sores with waterproof plasters (blue if available).

Note: Blue plasters, although not required by law for childminders, are a sensible precaution and not a fashion statement. As food is rarely blue they are easy to spot if they fall off during cooking. These plasters are required, by law in the UK, for the catering industry.

Bottles

Hygiene is particularly important for bottle fed babies to prevent infections such as gastroenteritis. Hands should be washed before the preparation of feeds, this prevents the contamination of both teat and milk. Equipment used for bottle feeding will need to be sterilised; check with the parents on their preferred methods of sterilising. If you are sterilising, always follow the manufacturers guidelines. If you are using sterilising fluid check that equipment is fully submerged and no air bubbles are present as these trap germs leaving unsterilised areas. Parents may prefer to supply sterilised bottles for you.

Water for feeds should be boiled and then covered as it cools to prevent contamination. Cooling can be hastened by placing the container of boiled water into cold water. Normally each bottle should be freshly made for each feed. Storing made up formula may increase health risks as powdered milk is not sterile. Where prepared bottles, including breast milk, are provided by parents store them at the back of the fridge and not in the door to reduce the risk of bacterial growth.

Defrosting and Cooking

Always follow carefully the instructions on food packaging for defrosting or cooking. Ensure food is thoroughly defrosted before cooking and do not re-freeze once it has been defrosted. If you are reheating foods make sure they are hot right through and do not reheat them more than once.

Cook foods until they are hot right through to the centre. Check chicken and pork are not still 'pink' in the middle (and other meats if being served to young, sick or elderly) and that, if you stick a knife in, the juices run clear not red.

Nappies

You should wash your hands and nails before changing nappies to prevent cross infections. It is also recommended that you wear disposable gloves when dealing with nappies. These prevent cross infection and protect the wearer as well as children. These are inexpensive and available from most chemists.

Babies should be changed on a changing mat or plastic sheet to prevent urine or faeces contaminating surfaces. These should be disinfected between changing children to reduce the risk of cross infections.

Using baby wipes or similar will neutralise the ammonia in the urine and help prevent nappy rash. Parents may provide cream to apply in case of nappy rash. Where the nappy is soiled, solids should be removed from the skin using wipes or damp cotton wool. All soiled materials can be rolled into the disposable nappy and taped closed using the adhesive tabs. These should then be placed into a nappy sack along with the gloves. This should then be sealed and placed into the outside refuse bin to prevent smells and contamination.

Washable Nappies

Washable nappies require soaking in sterilising solutions, in accordance with manufacturing guidelines, in lidded buckets to prevent cross infections. Buckets must be inaccessible to children, as the solution used can be harmful. Nappies need washing at a minimum temperature of 60°C to destroy germs, washing at 90°C can help them stay whiter in appearance.

Using a nappy liner removes the need to scrape off faeces as this can be flushed away with the contents. Air drying nappies in sunlight also helps to destroy germs and keep the nappies soft and white. You may find there is a local nappy laundering service in your area which collects dirty nappies and delivers clean ones to your door.

Potties

Potties should be emptied and disinfected immediately after each use in order to remain hygienic.

Medical Waste

When dealing with spills of urine, faeces, vomit or blood you should keep in mind the risk of cross infections to yourself and others. Children should be kept away from the area while you clean up.

You need disposable gloves, kitchen roll or similar, plastic bag (not a carrier bag as these have holes in the bottom) for rubbish and disinfectant. You may also be able to purchase granules from you local chemist designed to soak up fluids which enable the mess to be easily scraped up. Once the area has been cleared it should be washed and disinfected, anything that has been contaminated should be sealed in a plastic bag and placed in the outside rubbish bin.

If you are dealing with a wound you should wear disposable gloves and any swabs used should be sealed and disposed of in an outside bin. Should you be required to administer drugs using a syringe, remember these cannot be disposed of in your bin. You will require a sharps tin for used needles, this must be kept out of reach of children and should be returned to parents or your local doctor's surgery for disposal

Fire Safety

Fire Exits and Evacuations

You should consider how you would evacuate the house in an emergency. You should plan in advance what you will use as exits. You need to consider how your escape routes may vary depending on the location of the fire. Exits should not be blocked by equipment such as buggies or bags and the keys should be within reach of the door or window. Should a fire occur you will need to be able to get outside quickly and safely from what may be a smoky environment making it hard to see.

You should practice the fire drill regularly so that all children know what to do. They should know where to go to be let out if they hear the fire alarm or you tell them there is a fire. Explain to them about needing to leave their toys and coats behind. Make sure children are aware of what the practice is for, explain that they are practising in case there is a fire. Use age appropriate language - don't frighten them! If children know what to do if a fire should occur they are less likely to panic and more likely to get out safely.

It is good practice to keep a log of practice evacuations. You can note the date, which exit you used and which children were present. You can use this to ensure practices are regular and all children, including babies, have taken part.

If a Fire Occurs

Close the door of the room that contains the fire, and close other doors behind you as you leave. If you have to open a closed door to escape test it with the back of your hand first, if it is warm the fire is behind the door so do not open it. Do not stop for valuables or children's possessions. Remain calm and follow your planned escape route. If possible use a phone to call the fire brigade or take a mobile phone with you, however, do not put yourself in danger to get to a phone. Once outside you can use a neighbour's phone or a call box.

If the fire prevents you from leaving the house, shut the doors between you and the fire. If the room is filled with smoke crawl along the floor as there will be less smoke lower down. Choose a room furthest from the fire with a window, and plug any gaps around the door with towels or material to stop the smoke. Reassure children and try to keep them calm. Open the window if you have access to one and attract the attention of others who can alert the fire brigade.

If you are in immediate danger from the fire, i.e. it is in the same room as you and you are in danger of being burned, and the room is not too far above the ground, drop cushions or bedding from the window and lower children by their hands as far down as possible before dropping them feet first. Lower yourself until you are hanging full length before dropping to the ground. Only do this if there is immediate danger as falling can cause injuries, especially to small children.

If you have to escape by breaking a window cover any jagged glass with towels, thick clothing or bedding. Do not go back into a burning building until the fire brigade has made it safe and given you permission to do so.

There are a variety of ways of reducing the risks of a fire occurring or reducing its effects:

Smoke Alarms

Smoke alarms detect smoke, providing early warning of fires. When they detect smoke they sound a loud warning noise, some may also have a flashing light. A smoke alarm should be fitted on every level of your home, including the loft. They should be tested regularly and the batteries should be replaced annually. They can be purchased from almost all DIY stores and are designed to be easy to fit. You need to choose an alarm that conforms to British Safety Standard BS5446 Part 1 and has a Kitemark, these will both be marked on the packaging.

If you care for children with impaired hearing you may need to consider an alarm that has flashing lights as they may not be alerted by an alarm sound. You will need to choose an alarm that conforms to BS5446-3.

CO Detector

CO stands for Carbon Monoxide, a lethal gas that can be produced from miss-functioning gas appliances. This gas has no discernable smell. A CO detector will sound an alarm if the gas becomes present in the room.

Gas/Other Fires

Children should not be left unsupervised in a room when these are in use to prevent accidents. They should be fitted with a suitable fire guard. Do not leave clothing or papers on the fire guard or near the fire. If you are going out turn off the fire or in the case of a real fire use a spark guard.

Chip Pans

Chip pans and deep fat fryers are a common cause of fire. To help prevent a fire, never fill them with more than a third full with oil/fat and never leave them unattended. If the oil starts to smoke do not put food in, turn off the heat, leaving the oil to cool.

If a fire should start, do not try to move the pan or throw water on it. Turn off the heat if you can reach the switch safely but do not lean over the pan to do this. Cover the pan with a damp cloth, towel or fire blanket and leave for at least 30 minutes to cool.

If you feel that you cannot put out the fire safely, leave the room closing the door behind you and call the Fire Brigade.

Matches / Lighters

If you have matches or lighters they should be stored out of reach of children. Beware of lighters left in coat pockets or bags. Note: only safety matches should be kept in the house.

Fire Blanket

Fire blankets can be used to put out fire on a child or their clothing. When wrapped around the child they smother the fire. The fire blanket should be large enough to wrap a child in and conform to BSEN1869.

Hazards

There are many potential hazards to children in any home. As a childminder you need to identify possible hazards and take steps to minimise risks.

❑ **Doors:** Outer doors should be escape proof to prevent children opening them unaccompanied. Any steps should be safe and well built. Inner doors can have 'anti-slam' devices to stop children catching fingers and children should be discouraged from playing with doors.

❑ **Windows:** Windows above ground floor level should designed to prevent children climbing out; this may involve locking handles (note: keys should be accessible in an emergency). Curtain/blind cords should be out of reach of children to prevent strangulation.

❑ **Cupboards/Drawers:** These should be fitted with door catches if they contain items dangerous to children.

❑ **Glass:** All furniture that contains glass, such as book cases, coffee tables and green houses should either be made from safety glass, covered with safety film or be out of reach of children.

❑ **Fires:** These should have safety guards, firmly attached to the wall, to prevent children from knocking them over during play or when pulling themselves up to stand. Guards should be large enough not to become too hot to touch when the fire is in use. They should not be used to dry washing on as children may knock this into the fire.

❑ **Heating:** Hot radiators or pipes should be inaccessible or guarded. Heaters should be guarded and in a safe place away from materials that might catch light.

❑ **Electrical Sockets:** These should be covered with plastic socket covers. You should also be aware of where your mains switch is in case there is an emergency.

❑ **Cleaning Fluids:** These should be stored in cupboards out of children's reach, with safety catches on doors where necessary.

❑ **Toilets:** If the door has a locking device, this should be designed so it is possible to get inside if a child has locked it.

❑ **Equipment:** All toys and equipment should be checked regularly for rough edges, cracks, loose screws or anything that could cause harm. Anything which is worn or damaged should be repaired or replaced as necessary.

❑ **Kitchen:** Appliances should have short flexes so children cannot pull them off a worktop. Knives and sharp tools should be stored out of reach of children, and kept towards the back of work surfaces when in use. There should be a fire blanket available. Any cooking should be supervised. The handles of pots and pans should be turned towards the side or back of cookers so they cannot be reached. Children should not be allowed to play in the kitchen area whilst you are cooking.

❑ **Plants:** Hazardous plants should be out of the reach of crawling babies and toddlers. Older children should be taught not to eat plants without prior permission.

Safety Equipment

Safety equipment, including stair gates and harnesses, should be appropriate to the developmental levels of the children you care for. You should adhere to the manufacturers recommendations and guidelines when using them, to prevent accidents occurring from the miss-fitting or miss-use for which you could be accused of negligence.

All safety equipment should comply with the appropriate British Standards. You should retain any instructions or guidelines for use and maintenance instructions for future reference.

Outdoor Play Areas

Children should be closely supervised at all times whilst in the garden. Outside play areas should be securely fenced to stop children leaving the premises. Before the children are allowed outside you should double check gates are closed and that any tools, such as rakes, secateurs, trowels or spades, are not left lying around. Any tools or other dangerous equipment should be stored safely away from children. Sheds or garages containing dangerous or unsuitable tools and materials should be kept locked.

Plants that have poisonous leaves or berries, spines, sharp edges or similar should not be within reach of children. Common poisonous plants include caladium, monkshood, ivy, poinsettia, rhododendron, larkspur, laburnum, bleeding heart, foxglove leaves, hydrangea, lily of the valley, yew berries, and many bulbs including daffodils, narcissus, hyacinths and snowdrop. Children should be taught about the dangers of eating berries or fungi which you have not specifically given them to eat.

Chemical fertilizers, slug pellets, weed killers, and insecticides should not be used where children play. Natural alternatives are safer for the environment and children. Your local library will have gardening books with appropriate information on alternatives.

If children are helping with the gardening, do not let them use tools that are too big for them. Most tools are available in a child sized version. It is also important to teach children how to use tools safely.

Water can be very hazardous; even a bucket of water can be dangerous to a child. Turn containers upside down so they do not fill with rainwater, cover larger areas of water securely in a way which will help to prevent harm if a child should fall on top of the cover or restrict access to areas where water may pose a hazard.

Play equipment should be checked regularly for damage. Climbing frames and similar equipment should have a soft surface underneath to help prevent injury in case of a fall. All equipment should meet current safety standards.

Safety in the Sun

It is important to protect children from sunburn and over exposure to the sun. In children under fifteen years these are the major risk factors attributing to skin cancer in later life. Children should wear factor 15 or higher, sun cream or lotion, which should be applied every few hours.

You can ask parents to provide this, but it is also handy to have a spare in case it is forgotten. Remember to check with parents first that their child is not allergic and ask for permission to apply your sun cream. Children over four should be encouraged to rub in their own suncream.

Children should also wear sun hats and if they are out for long periods or when playing in water such as in a paddling pool an old t-shirt will also help prevent sunburn. Explain to children the importance of not getting burnt and why you are making them use sun cream or wear a hat. You can also encourage them to spend time in the shade. If your garden has little natural shade you could erect a tent or make a 'hidey hole' which will provide a shady area. Remember to keep children out of the sun at the hottest part of the day i.e. between eleven and two.

Teaching Children to be Safe

When teaching children about safety they will be more likely to follow your advice if you explain why you are giving it and the consequences of not following it. Young children find it difficult to associate actions with consequences. For example, when explaining scissor safety, when telling a child not to run with scissors you should explain that if they do they could fall over and injure themselves or another child. Topics to cover might include water safety, playground safety, kitchen safety, stranger danger, fire safety, road safety and garden safety.

Every day activities and unplanned learning opportunities can be utilized to help children learn to keep themselves safe. For example, on seeing a fire engine you can discuss what firemen do and what should happen if the fire occurred in your house.

Risk Assessment

There are many areas in the home that contain potential risk of harm to the people in it. The aim of risk assessment is to consider the current steps in place to reduce these risks, and to address any areas which could be further improved. There are five steps, identifying possible dangers (the hazards), deciding who might be harmed and how, estimating the chance of an injury happening (the risk), deciding on any measures to prevent or reduce the risk and reviewing and updating regularly.

Do not over complicate your risk assessments, for many childminding scenario the risks are well known and the necessary control measures easy to apply. The table below demonstrates the thought process involved in assessing risks, writing out risk assessments for all hazards is not necessary, however it may help to keep a note of improvements that you are intending to make.

Hazard	Steps to Garden
Control Measures already in Place What safety measures are in place that have reduced the chance of somebody being harmed by the hazard?	Children always supervised, step edges marked in yellow.
Risk Factor What is the likelihood that something could happen? High (could occur quite easily) Medium (could occur sometimes) Low (unlikely, although possible)	Medium - Could occur if children are rushing or excited. Could become slippery if wet.
Further Control Measures What more can you reasonably do to reduce the likelihood of an accident happening.	Add a hand rail and tread to steps to reduce risk when wet.

When thinking about risk there are several important considerations you should keep in mind. Children's abilities can develop very rapidly; what might be safe one week could pose a threat the next, hence the need to review regularly. You should continually reassess potential hazards to ensure the risks are minimised as much as possible. You should always prepare for the unexpected. Children think and act differently to adults and may not behave in a predictable manner. Children cannot always understand the consequences of their actions. Things that an adult would know to avoid because of the possible risks may not be apparent to children.

Risk and Children's Development

The nature of learning requires 'risk' taking. Children would never learn to walk or socially interact without being allowed to take risks. Risk management is in part dependant on the age and development of the children you care for. Children under three do not understand the risks involved in some activities and it is hard to explain them in a way that they understand. Young children will also test to see what happens which may or may not be appropriate.

Once children are over three they are more likely to understand instructions such as 'don't touch the cooker because it's hot'. This does not mean you can relax your supervision; they will not always remember instructions and may still test to see if what you say is right.

❑ **Babies** - Before a child is able to crawl they will be able to wriggle, so keep them away from high surfaces they may fall from. Keep things away from surface edges to prevent a child pulling something onto them. Remove all mouth sized object and toys from reach. Once a child starts to crawl beware of them falling down steps. Make sure furniture and toys will not tip over if a child pulls themselves up to standing using them.

❑ **Toddlers** - Children will be able to open cupboards and containers. Cupboards containing hazards or unsuitable items should be fitted with door catches. Toddlers will also be able to work switches, make sure gas switches for example are inaccessible. Their coordination will still not be fully developed and as they learn to walk and climb the risk of accidents will increase.

❑ **Pre Schooler** - Once a child is three they generally stop putting things in their mouths so toys with small parts are safer. Stairs can pose a danger, children may be able to climb up them but getting down can still be a problem. Children should be closely supervised when using playground equipment to ensure they do not fall off or injure themselves. Older children may start using scissors, these should be designed for children so they are less likely to injure themselves.

❑ **Primary School** - Once a child is five they have a better understanding of what is safe but may not always remember when they are distracted or busy playing. Children may start riding bikes and going swimming (only two under eights swimming per childminder) but these activities should still be closely supervised. Children will also start to try to impress their friends which can lead to other risks.

❑ **By eight years old** - By eight a child will understand and remember safety rules but still needs reminding occasionally. They may be able to cross quiet roads on their own, but children under twelve cannot accurately judge the speed and distance of oncoming traffic.

❑ **By ten years old** - Children are more reality orientated. If they have been allowed to take 'risks' they will have a sense of which risks to avoid and which risks to take.

After an Accident

Where there has been an accident in your setting you are likely to feel guilty. This is a natural reaction and is quite common even when you were not to blame.

A common reaction is to consider the 'what if' or 'if only' followed by 'why' scenarios, these can be a helpful way to consider things that may need altering to prevent recurrences. You should not however allow these thoughts to become overbearing and affect your sleep or care.

You should use the accident as part of a learning curve, record it, evaluate how it could be avoided next time, look at risk assessment for future reoccurrences and take any necessary and suitable precautions required.

Considerations when Keeping a Pet

Before choosing a pet it is important to research its needs and ensure you can meet them. A new Animal Welfare Act was introduced in 2007 setting out a duty of care towards pets. This includes: providing a suitable place to live, with or without other animals (as appropriate) where the pet can exhibit normal behaviour patterns; to provide a suitable diet; and to protect them from pain, injury, suffering and disease (this includes seeking veterinary treatment if they are ill). The Royal Society for the Protection of Animals (RSPCA) can provide information leaflets to help you and the children learn about different pet's needs.

You need to ask yourself if you have the space a pet requires both for housing, storing equipment and keeping it separate from children if necessary. You also need the time to look after it, including exercise, cleaning out, trips to the vet or to buy supplies. Finally can you afford the cost of owning a pet? This includes housing, bedding, food and any vet bills that may arise.

It is also important to ensure that the type of pet you select is suitable for your home and the extra conditions imposed by childminding. You need to ensure that any animals you keep will not affect the health and safety of the children you care for. Animals and children should always be supervised when they are together. Both are unpredictable and could cause accidental injury to the other. Children under four have not yet developed control over emotions and aggressive impulses that could endanger themselves and pets. Some children have allergies to animals so you should inform prospective customers of any animals you have. Any allergies should be noted on the child's information record.

Feeding bowls should be kept out of reach of younger children who may try sampling the food. The floor should be washed after animals have been fed, especially if there are crawling babies present. Feed bowls, water bowls/bottles should be washed separately from other crockery and cooking utensils. Children should wash their hands after handling animals, and should be supervised to make sure it is done thoroughly. Litter trays and areas animals use for toileting should not be accessible to children. Animals can carry parasites that can be transmitted to children, so they must be vaccinated, wormed and treated for fleas regularly as appropriate.

It is not necessary to have 'a pet for the children'. There are many ways to introduce children to animals that do not involve owning one yourself. Activities can be based around wildlife such as bird watching or spotting animals on walks. There are also animal orientated places to visit, such as farms, animal sanctuaries, zoo's, pet shops, veterinary practices or pet shows, which can be used as educational experiences. A pet should only be obtained if it's going to be welcomed by all the family not purchased specifically to entertain the children you are caring for.

Pets

The following is a general overview of the considerations for the most common types of pet; it is not an exhaustive guide. Remember individual animals have individual temperaments, for example just because you have previously kept, or know someone with, a friendly hamster does not mean all hamsters are friendly.

❑ **Dogs** - Dogs may put off potential customers, particularly if they are large or boisterous. Dogs that appear on the dangerous animals register, for example Pitbull Terriers, may affect your registration. Even if your dog has a nice temperament it should never be left unsupervised with children. You will also have to consider how you will arrange walking the dog; can you safely supervise children while out and a dog? Is it possible to prevent access to any garden areas used as a toilet by the dog?

It is important that dogs are well trained and socialised with children. The Kennel Club 'Good Citizen Scheme' provides training courses on several levels that cover important points for dogs living as family pets and will help reassure potential customers.

❑ **Cats** - Cats may scratch children if provoked, but if the cat is used to children or spends most of its time outside they often co-habit well. If the cat has a litter tray this needs to be inaccessible to children. The garden will have to be checked and cleaned regularly if the cat uses it as a toilet.

❑ **Hamsters, Mice & Rats** - Hamsters sleep during the day and are active at night this means children rarely get to see them. Hamsters may bite if children put their fingers into the cage and others will bite whilst being handled. Hamsters and mice are small making it hard for younger children to handle them gently, but they can be interesting for children to watch. Despite their reputation as vermin, pet rats carry no more diseases than other animals. Rats are less likely to bite than hamsters. They are awake during the day and are easier to handle. They need larger cages than hamsters and being very intelligent need lots of stimulation and prefer to be kept in pairs or larger groups.

❑ **Rabbits** - Rabbits need large runs and hutches, and can be as expensive to keep as cats and dogs. They are active during the day. They may be hard for children to handle as they do not always like being carried, however once sat on a child's lap they may enjoy being groomed.

❑ **Guinea pigs** - Guinea pigs need a hutch and run. They thrive best when kept in pairs or larger groups. They are quite active and may nip if mishandled. Being smaller than rabbits they may be easier for children to pick up and hold. They enjoy sitting on a lap to be groomed and petted.

❑ **Fish** - Though children will not be able to handle a fish they often find them very interesting to watch. Watching fish can also be very relaxing for both childminder and children. Fish tanks are often made from glass, so you should ensure that tanks cannot be reached by children or are made from safety glass. Also beware of thrown toys that could break the glass leaving fish, glass and water all over the floor. It is a good idea to have fish tanks with a lid or covers to prevent toys and fingers from access to the water.

❑ **Reptiles** - Reptiles can carry salmonella so it should be ensured that children wash their hands thoroughly after handling them. There are a wide range of reptiles and some may be very unsuitable for children to handle.

❑ **Birds** - Allergy to feathers should be considered. Birds are usually kept in cages or aviaries and as such not handled by children but they can be interesting to watch.

If you are intending to get a pet, you may like to consider adopting an adult from a rescue centre rather than buying a baby. This way you will be given an idea of the temperament before you take it home.

8. Out and About with Children

Childminders take children on a wide range of different outings. It is equally important to prepare for mundane trips, such as a visit to a shopping centre, as it is for special outings, such as a zoo or learning centre. Preparing in advance allows you to consider and address any safety concerns and make sure outings are pleasant activities for all involved.

Outings should be suitable for the children in your care, in terms of safety and their development. Young children tire easily and may be overwhelmed or frightened by something an older child might find fun. Lengthy car journeys or large amounts of walking may not be suitable for young children, or some children with special needs. You also need to consider the increased levels of supervision that might be needed in a crowded or open environment. You may find it helpful to increase the number of adults by going with a friend, or another childminder. If parents are free they may also enjoy accompanying you on the trip. Many childminders become good friends with parents and meet socially as well.

It can be helpful to remember that the eyes and ears of the world will notice you when you are out. Make a note in your diary of any unusual events or those which could be misconstrued to protect yourself in the event of any complaints, including malicious ones, reported to regulators.

Permission

General permission for outings should be obtained when contracts are agreed. You should still inform parents of journeys that are further afield than normal in advance. This also helps parents provide any additional items needed for the trip such as suitable clothing, pocket money or travel sickness medicine. You may need to ask special permission for some activities such as swimming, theme park rides or films.

Items That May Be Required

These will depend on the developmental level of the children and may include safety equipment, provisions and outdoor clothing depending on the type and length of the outing.

Items that might be required include: spare clothes, sunhats, food and drink, tissues and wetwipes, children's medicines, snacks, nappies and changing equipment, a blanket to sit on, pushchair, contact numbers for parents, money including spare for emergencies, first aid kit, spouted cups, plastic bags for rubbish or wet clothes, sun cream or lotion, waterproof/wellies, car safety seats, camera, walking reins, potty and a mobile phone.

How Not to Lose Children

No one likes to contemplate the possibility of a child going missing from their care, but the best way to prevent this is to assess the risk so you can take precautions. It is important to consider 'losing' a child whilst out as a risk to be assessed and how to minimise the risk, not as something that could never happen to you.

There are many precautions you can take to help ensure that children remain safely in your care and do not wander off. Young children should wear reins or a wrist strap to ensure that they are kept close; it is much easier to let go of a hand than reins. The youngest children should hold your hand rather than the hands of other children. If you are travelling with other adults, parents or childminders discuss in advance who is responsible for which child, so no one mistakenly assumes that someone else is watching out for a particular child.

Before you go out take a minute to note what each child is wearing, if they do go missing you will need to be able to describe their clothing.

Older children may remember their home contact details and should practice these regularly, but they may not remember your contact information if they become lost. If you are going on a trip you may want to use a 'kiddie band', a brightly coloured wrist band which has your contact details on. These can be purchased or made from paper.

You can prepare children by giving instructions on what to do if they do get lost. Simple instructions can be taught even to young children: 'If you can't find me, stop and look around. If you still can't see me then go to the nearest shop and ask the person behind the till, they will help you find me'. You will need to explain the importance of finding someone that works in a shop, not just asking a stranger. Children can identify shop keepers or people working at an activity centre or similar by their uniforms or name tags. Make a game of spotting people who would be safe to ask for help so children can learn the difference.

If you do lose a child, it is important not to panic. First stop and look around and call their name. Check where you last saw the child and ask at the nearest shop or place where the child may have gone if lost. Check dangerous places first such as water and roads. Listen carefully for public announcements. If you are in a shopping centre or similar find the nearest information desk or member of the security staff, they will know if anyone has found a child and will send people to look for them. If you are out on the street or in an open place call the police using a mobile phone or from the nearest shop or call box.

Stranger Danger

When explaining to children about the dangers of strangers, one of the key concepts to get across is what a stranger is. They are not scary monsters that can be spotted from a mile away, they look just like ordinary people and can appear very friendly and nice. Children should understand that anyone they do not know is a stranger.

Strangers may use lures such as sweets, asking for directions or searching for a lost item, and children should be made aware of this. Kidscape produce activity leaflets you can use to encourage children to take the right action if they are approached by someone they do not know (for more information see Section 9. Child Protection/Safeguarding Children).

Car Outings

If you transport children in your car you need insurance to cover the use of your car as part of your business. The car should be well maintained and have an up to date MOT certificate.

When putting children into or taking them out of the car, you should do so on the kerb side of the road to keep them away from other cars. It is a good idea to unstrap children, and leave them sitting in their seats while you unstrap the others so that children are not left alone outside the car while you are concentrating on undoing the restraints of the others. Take the most mobile children out last so they do not come to harm while you are unloading the others.

Never leave the children alone in the car unsupervised, even for short periods. Turn off the engine while you unload/ reload the car. If you have equipment or shopping to load into the car, load the children first so you can ensure their safety. Never move the car whilst the children wait outside to make loading easier. Load them through an alternative door, secure them, then move the car to load.

Use child safety locks so that doors can only be opened from the outside, this prevents children opening doors whilst the car is moving.

Child Car Restraints/Seats

You should ensure that all children are strapped in securely with appropriate restraints for their size/weight. Child car seats should be checked regularly for wear and tear. They must be replaced if you have an accident as damage may not be visible. When fitting, the base of the child seat should be in contact with the car seat at all points to give good stability. Follow the manufacturers fitting instructions exactly. You should NEVER use a rear facing infant carrier or child car seat on a seat fitted with an airbag. For forward facing child seats check the manufacturers guidance for use on seats with airbags fitted.

Before each journey check that straps are not twisted and they are properly adjusted to allow for the thickness of the child's clothes. They should be tight enough for the child to be comfortable. Double check the restraints of those old enough to strap themselves in. Be careful of metal parts on car seats on sunny days; they get very hot and could burn a child.

Second-hand Car Seats

Second-hand car seats should be avoided, unless their full history is known and they have had a full safety check, for the following reasons:

❑ You are unlikely to get a seat made to the latest safety standard.
❑ You may not get a copy of the instructions, these are vital if you are to fit the seat correctly.
❑ There may be important safety components missing.
❑ The seat may have been damaged in an accident, damage is not always obvious to the untrained eye.
❑ It may not fit your car properly.

Car Seat Law

It is compulsory for children under three years old to wear an appropriate child restraint. Children over three and under twelve years old (unless they are over 135cm (4ft 5ins) in height) must also wear an appropriate child restraint if the vehicle is fitted with seat belts. Children over twelve years or over 135cm in height can wear an adult seat belt. In Southern Ireland children must be over 150cm in height to travel with only an adult seatbelt. Taxis are exempt from these rules, unless restraints are available in which case they must be worn. Do not allow a child to sit on your lap while a car is moving (even if you are not driving) this is not safe. Never travel with a child on an adults lap or two children sharing a seat belt.

From May 2008 restraints must comply with UN ECE 44.03 standard or higher.

Car Seat Types

Baby and child seats are secured in a car using the adult seat belt or Isofix. Isofix is a new standard for installing car seats being adopted by vehicle manufacturers. If a car has this feature Isofix seats just plug in. A separate three-point harness is used to secure the child into the seat. For older children booster seats/cushions are used. These raise the child in car seat so that the adult seatbelt can be used. As children of the same age can vary in size, weight and height are the most accurate guide to the type of restraint most appropriate for a child.

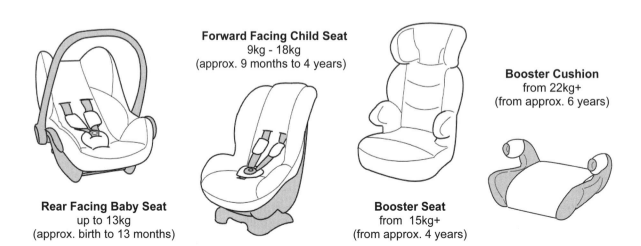

Forward Facing Child Seat
9kg - 18kg
(approx. 9 months to 4 years)

Booster Cushion
from 22kg+
(from approx. 6 years)

Rear Facing Baby Seat
up to 13kg
(approx. birth to 13 months)

Booster Seat
from 15kg+
(from approx. 4 years)

Public Transport

If you are using public transport it can be helpful to check in advance timetables and access issues such as the arrangements for taking pushchairs, buggies or wheelchairs if necessary. You may need to confirm with the transport company that there will be sufficient space for all the children. Allow additional time for catching trains and buses. Before you leave for a journey, call to check for changes to published timetables.

Make sure you make use of any safety precautions provided such as seat belts on coaches. On trains and buses make sure children sit in their seats and don't wander around. If you are using a taxi ensure it has appropriate seats and restraints for the children in your care.

Be careful on the steps up and down on buses and trains. These can be difficult for children to negotiate and if you have shopping or a pushchair keep hold of children whilst these are being stowed away.

Travel/Motion Sickness

Travel sickness is caused when the messages received from the balance organs within the ear and those received from the eyes do not match. For example, if a child is reading a book in the car their eyes are telling them they are not moving, however the balancing organs can feel the motion the car is making. Symptoms are usually sweating, dizziness, nausea and vomiting.

There are several ways of reducing or preventing motion sickness. Reduce motion as much as possible by sitting the child in a seat that is not over the wheels of the vehicle. Encourage children to look out the window so that the pictures from their eyes match the message from their balance sensors. Spotting games or 'I spy' can help as it involves watching out of the window. Games, books or colouring where a child has to focus inside the car can cause motion sickness so try to find alternative entertainment. Music or story cassette tapes can help distract children.

Full stomachs or lots of liquid in a child's stomach can also contribute to motion sickness. Encourage a child to drink little and often rather then lots at once, and not fizzy or milky drinks. Light, easy to digest meals are best if eating before a trip. Do not eat whilst moving, stop the car and allow time afterwards for the meal to settle.

Fresh air is helpful and keep the temperature of the car cool. Car petrol fumes can also cause nausea so close the windows if you get stuck in traffic.

Parents may be able to provide you with the travel sickness medicine that their child usually takes and instructions on when to give it. Dosage and the time administered should be recorded for your records and signed by a parent. If you are travelling you can prepare by carrying plastic bags (beware of shopping bags as these have holes in the bottoms), a container or small bucket, a cloth, spray disinfectant and wet wipes. Children who have been sick will need reassurance, as will the other children present.

Walking

Walking is an excellent form of exercise and less expensive than car journeys. Make sure you and the children are wearing sensible shoes to help prevent tripping or falling. Point out steps and uneven pavements or paths to children, they may not notice these.

Consider using reins or wrist straps, especially if you have several smaller children to ensure that they stay near you and do not get lost. If you are out in the evenings, especially in winter when it gets dark early, wear fluorescent materials. You can buy armbands, waist coats, straps or similar, and these will help drivers see you.

Pushchairs should be fitted with a three point harness, and preferably shoulder straps as well. This is to ensure children do not slide out the bottom or climb out over the straps. They should fit snugly to the child, not be loose. If your pushchair is not fitted with straps you can buy a separate safety harnesses to attach. On hot days an umbrella or hood is helpful to keep a child cool and out of direct sunlight. If using a rain cover, ensure it has adequate ventilation. Make sure you use the brake when stopping or putting the child in. When crossing the road keep the pushchair on the kerb until the road is safe, do not wait with the buggy in the road. Do not overload a pushchair with bags as this will make it unstable and bags on the handles may cause it to tip over backwards.

Where possible use zebra or pelican crossings to cross the road and allow plenty of time. Children will walk slower than you and should not be hurried in case they trip. When walking alongside roads children should walk on the inside away from traffic. If the path is too narrow to walk next to each other children should walk in front where you can see them.

Escalators

Children under six are at the highest risk of accidental injury during escalator use. If you have more than one young child or have a pushchair with you it is safer to find the lifts rather than use the escalator. Before using an escalator simple precautions reduce the risks. These include: identifying the emergency stop buttons; noting their location; and checking children for untied shoe laces, drawstrings, long loose hair and baggy clothing.

Encourage children to:
❑ Pick up their feet when stepping on and off.
❑ Hold the hand rail but, only if tall enough to reach easily.
❑ Not touch the sides below the hand rail.
❑ Stand facing forwards.
❑ Keep feet, long hair and clothing away from the sides of the escalator.
❑ Try to stand near the middle of the step.

Holding toddlers hands prevents them putting them into areas where they can become trapped. When you reach the end it is also a good idea to pick up small children rather than have them step of themselves. They may not have the ability to anticipate and coordinate stepping off.

Road Safety

Children should be taught road safety appropriate to their development, but you should not rely on them always remembering it. Children should not be allowed to cross the road unassisted even on quiet roads. Children will not be able to judge distance and speed of oncoming traffic until they are around twelve years old and may not recognise danger from traffic they can hear but not see. Having lower eye levels, their view may also be reduced.

When crossing the road you should make it clear to children that they must always stop at the kerb and hold your hand. Children will learn behaviour from you so never hurry or cross in unsafe places even if you think there is no danger. From a young age children can learn basic rules such as stopping at the curb, holding hands, checking for traffic and not running. The most popular scheme is: stop, look, listen. You should always stop at the edge of the pavement. Look both ways for traffic (even in a one way street as car may come from the wrong direction) and listen for traffic that might be approaching out of sight. You should cross in a safe place, not between parked cars or where you are blocked from the view of oncoming cars. Encourage them to go through the process of looking both ways and listening even if it takes longer and you can see the road is clear.

Explain to children why you take these precautions, that cars go on roads and that you have to be careful when crossing the road so that you do not get in their way and get injured.

Swimming Pool Safety

Individual pools may have a variety of factors which can influence children's safety. Risks associated with swimming in public pools include the following:

❑ Small children running and gaining access to deep water.
❑ Children running and slipping on wet surfaces.
❑ Weak or non-swimmers loosing their footing in moving water.
❑ Children submerging unnoticed in busy pools.
❑ Children moving from the changing room to pool unaccompanied.

Risks are reduced by close supervision by yourself both in and out of the water. If the child is in the water then you will need to be in the pool too. Whilst in the pool you will need to maintain constant watch over the children for whom you are responsible and stay in close contact with children who are weak or non-swimmers, for whom arm bands or similar floatation devices may be appropriate.

In a traditional twenty-five metre pool with both deep and shallow water many pools apply the following ratios:

❑ Children under four, one child, one childminder.
❑ Children four - seven, two children, one childminder.
❑ Over eights unaccompanied at the discretion of the pool management and the parent/guardian.

Some pools may have special sessions with an increased number of life guards where a childminder may be able to have more children in the water with them.

9. Child Protection / Safeguarding Issues

'Children have the right to be protected from all forms of physical or mental violence, injury or abuse, neglect or negligent treatment, maltreatment or exploitation including sexual abuse by those looking after them.' UN Convention, Rights of a Child, Article 19.

As a childminder you need to provide an environment where children feel secure, are safe and respected, their view points are valued and they are encouraged to talk and be listened to. Childminders need to work with parents to build a relationship where both parties are kept informed of matters relating to the child's welfare and children should be provided with support and guidance and feel able to talk to you if they have difficulties. Children need and deserve to feel loved, cared for and to be protected from harm.

It is good practice to have a written child protection policy to share with parents (see Section 17. Maintaining a Portfolio of Policies and Procedures) so they are aware you record details of injuries and any procedures you implement if abuse, including neglect, is suspected. It is a parent's right to be kept informed of any action taken or intended to be taken on behalf of their child unless to do so puts a child in danger.

Childminders should be aware of the help available if they suspect child abuse, but should also be careful not to jump to conclusions. There may be explanations they are unaware of, for example, a scary story causing nightmares or a playground accident causing injury.

Child Protection or Safeguarding Children are broad terms which describe the philosophies, policies, standards, guidelines and procedures used to protect children from both intentional and unintentional harm and applies to the responsibilities of yourself as the childminder. There are regional variations for the terminology but the aims are universal. Child protection is a part of safeguarding and promoting the welfare of children. In England a universal form, the Common Assessment Framework, has been devised to monitor children's progress where outside help may be required.

Local Safeguarding Children's Board (LSCB) England & Wales; Child Protection Committee (CPC) Scotland

These are statutory mechanisms for agreeing how the relevant organisations in each local area will cooperate to safeguard and promote the welfare of children effectively and that includes protecting them from harm. Organisations working together include social services, education, health, police, probation, voluntary sector and early years services.

Common Assessment Framework (CAF) England

CAF is a Common Assessment Framework with standardised paperwork that can be completed if you are looking after a child who is not reaching the expected achievements for development, socially, emotionally, physically or cognitively, where you believe that an outside agency may be able to help. As a childminder you may be the outside agency used to support a child. It consists of three features: an pre-assessment checklist, designed to help practitioners identify children who would benefit; the process and information required to complete the CAF; and the form to be filled in and shared with others.

The CAFcan be used to help identify needs before they escalate into more serious concerns. For example disruptive and anti-social behaviour, overt parental conflict or lack of parental boundaries or support, poor attendance or exclusion from school, SEN or disability.

Observation and Record Keeping

Having a child protection/safeguarding children policy is good practice and is mandatory in some regions. The policy will familiarise parents with the child protection routine and procedures. Childminders are required to keep accident and incident records. This is where existing injuries, no matter how minor, sustained when not in the care of the childminder and injuries that happen whilst in the childminder's care should be recorded.

Records are kept primarily for the protection of the child, but can also be useful in helping the childminder or parents in cases where abuse is alleged or if an insurance claim is made. These records should be kept with the co-operation of parents. It will help to explain to them the various sections that you will fill in, that it is a requirement of your registration, and why you need to keep them.

Each record should include the child's name, date and time of injury and description of the injury with diagrams if necessary. Include details of how the injury was observed, what the child was asked about it and their response. If the explanation is satisfactory little extra detail may be required, however if the child is upset or concerned or the injury is serious then detailed written notes must be made, remember these should be fact not opinion. An annotated photograph may prove useful, particularly of bruising, slap marks and bite marks which may fade.

You should keep in mind that inexperienced questioning could hamper legal proceedings as the child may answer with what they feel the adult wants to hear. Open questions are best, e.g. who, what , when, where did this happen. Observe and listen to the child but do not probe or ask leading questions. If you feel something is suspicious leave the questioning to a professional. Never promise to keep information a secret. You should explain to the child that some secrets are too important to keep to yourselves.

Parents should be asked about how an injury occurred. Observations and explanations from the parents may provide a rational explanation. Parents explanations should also be recorded, and they should sign the record, enabling them to share what is written about their child.

Having records enables reoccurring problems or patterns to be easily identified. They can become important evidence if child abuse is suspected and later investigated. In your records or any reports you are asked to write, should there be an investigation, it is important to distinguish between directly observed evidence, information gathered from reliable sources and opinion.

Directly observed evidence consists of factual information based on what you have actually seen or heard. You should present this with date, time and full information to include diagrams, a photo if available, a record of events and a record of anything a parent or child has said. Information from reliable sources should be labelled as such and include date, time and source. It could include name, sex, age and address of the child, other children who live in the household, information from a health visitor, doctor, playgroup and of course, you as the childminder. Opinions should be labelled as such and could comprise of an evaluation based on the presented observed evidence and information from the reliable sources.

Your report could be used to determine whether an emergency protection order or an assessment order is required. Should there be sufficient evidence then your report will be needed as evidence during the child protection conference. If there is subsequently a court case then your report may also be required as important evidence for the prosecution.

Observations of a child's behaviour and physical condition should not be intrusive. Regular observations of the child's behaviour whilst playing, or working ensure that significant negative changes of behaviour are noted and any patterns of behaviour that are unusual or not in keeping with their developmental level can be recorded. Naturally occurring opportunities, e.g. changing nappies, taking a child to the toilet, helping change for the swimming pool or dressing up can be used for observing new injuries including bruising and abrasions without being intrusive. If noticed these can be written up as required.

Keeping records on the children is very important as they can also be used to show the growth and development of a child. In sharing these with the parents you will be able to see if there has been a failure of the child to thrive, and they will highlight any negative behavioural changes. If the records show there are any outstanding causes for concern they can be discussed with the parents and (if not satisfactorily resolved) your local child protection team will be able to advise you on the most appropriate course of action. Detailed records can also protect the childminder and their family from allegations of abuse, as childminders frequently work alone which can make them vulnerable to such allegations.

Factors Increasing Vulnerability of Children

There are many factors which statistically make a child more likely to be abused. You should keep in mind however, that not all children / parents will fall neatly into these categories. Child maltreatment is related to factors found both within the family community and wider culture. Certain characteristics of children e.g. prematurity or difficult behaviour, combined with unmanaged parental stress, and isolation from supportive ties to the community and extended family, increase the chances of maltreatment or abuse occurring. When a culture or society approves of force and violence as an appropriate means for solving problems child abuse is promoted.

Parent/Carer Factors

Most abusing parents love their children and desperately need help. They are reacting to all the circumstances in their lives. In addition to unsatisfactory conditions and lack of money, many abusive parents have acute problems with insecurity and inadequacy. They may have suffered psychological damage during their own childhood.

Parents who abuse children do not always belong to any particular socio-economic group or class. Statistically abuse is more likely to occur in families where the mother is young (less than 30) and two or three children are born in quick succession, the mother often becoming pregnant or having another child soon after a 'battering' incident. Fathers of abused children also tend to be young, often being unable to cope with the responsibility. They may have a history of unemployment, illness or criminal activities. Often both parents have suffered emotional deprivation as children.

Parent/carer factors potentially contributing to maltreatment relate to personality characteristics, psychological well being, history of being abused, substance abuse, their attitudes and knowledge and age. Examples include the following:

❑ Lack of knowledge of children's development and needs.
❑ Unrealistic expectations of the child.
❑ Youth of parents and childish, dependant personality types.
❑ Parents are poor decision makers.
❑ Parents find it hard to take responsibility for things they do.
❑ Parents find it difficult to relate to or communicate with others.
❑ There is a family history of abuse or neglect.
❑ Unwanted pregnancy too far advanced for termination.
❑ Disappointment over sex of infant.
❑ Bonding problems, complicated pregnancy, early separation (premature).
❑ Inability to change ideas, learn new parenting skills or repeating own upbringing.
❑ Teenage pregnancy, the stress, lack of knowledge of child development and care required increases the numbers of children with physical, emotional and intellectual development problems.

❏ Parents at risk often suffered material or paternal deprivation themselves and may have difficulty establishing strong bonds with their own children.

❏ Low self-esteem.

❏ Postnatal depression, a very small number of mothers affected with this may have mood swings, forget to feed the baby, leave it unattended or treat it like a toy.

❏ A history of drug or alcohol abuse.

❏ Depression or mental illness in parent(s) (e.g. clinical depression).

Family Factors

Family circumstances and pressures can make it difficult for parents to meet the needs of their children in terms of appropriate food, adequate attention, affection or responsible care. Abuse may often occur during periods of crisis, possibly due to housing, financial or social problems. There is often an inability to cope with the natural reactions of anger and frustration with the child. Parents are often lacking an appropriate role model to follow and have an insensitivity to the babies or young child's needs. These parents may have little idea of babies abilities or needs and are liable to make unrealistic demands for obedience and to have high expectations of progress. When the baby is wakeful at night, refuses food or cries, it is interpreted as ingratitude and rejection of their love.

Family factors include the specific life experiences of some families such as marital conflict, domestic violence, single parenthood, unemployment, financial stress and social isolation. Examples include the following:

❏ There is a great deal of stress in their lives.

❏ Marital maladjustment, separation or divorce.

❏ Difficult financial situation.

❏ Social isolation with no support system.

❏ Stresses of single parent families, e.g. earning a living, caring for children, coping with own emotional reactions to absence of partner and the sole responsibility for the family.

❏ Violence seen as acceptable and a means of resolving conflicts.

Child Factors

While premature babies and children under four years are most likely to be abused or neglected, abuse can occur from birth to late teens. Babies may be abused because their cries of hunger provoke a negative reaction from the adult, who unable to stand the noise any longer, loses self control and shakes, beats or burns the baby. Toddlers may be attacked because they have been 'naughty' and are being 'taught a lesson', with the adult losing self-control, lashing out and beating the child who may be wet or have touched something deemed out of bounds.

Some children may be more vulnerable to abuse than others. Blind babies smile less than sighted infants and cannot show parents a mutual gaze, and this may lead some parents to believe the infant is rejecting them. Other children who are more prone to abuse include step children, sickly children, children who cry a lot, children who do not enjoy eating, premature babies, children with disabilities and children not born a desired sex.

Children are not responsible for being victims of abuse, but some factors can make them more vulnerable. Examples could include:

❏ Inadequate age gap between children.

❏ Child may be different, have physical disabilities or imperfections or learning difficulties.

❏ Twins (one may be abused).

❏ Where there are real or imagined 'problems' with the child, e.g. sleep problems, hyperactivity or disabilities, interfering with bonding.

Environmental Factors

The isolation caused by some types of housing and separation from other members of the family, who in previous generations may have lived close at hand to offer support and advice in a crisis, can be a contributing factor in abuse and neglect. Physical abuse and neglect are strongly linked to multiple deprivation factors, such as poverty, a very unsettled lifestyle or abuse of drugs and alcohol.

Environmental factors can include poverty and unemployment. Other examples could include:

❑ Poor utilisation of medical care.
❑ Bad housing exacerbating tense family situations. Children in overcrowded homes are twice as likely to be delinquent or aggressive, causing more friction.
❑ Disputes with neighbours.

Helping Children Protect Themselves

Children can be encouraged to protect themselves by:
❑ Raising their self awareness;
❑ Building their confidence;
❑ Ensuring they have a range of contacts and strategies to ensure their own protection;
❑ Helping them understand the importance of protecting others;
❑ Teaching them their rights and the responsibilities of adults towards them.

Tip: Ask at your local police/garda station, they should have child orientated leaflets about stranger danger as will the Kidscape charity.

Raising self awareness:
Children are naturally innocent and trusting and need help to protect themselves, such as developing an awareness of their bodies appropriate to their stage of development, with the cooperation of parents, who should be informed of the reasons behind this and be given opportunities to make suggestions and work in partnership. Opportunities occurring during everyday activities can be utilised to help children identify and label parts of their body. Naturally occurring activities may include nappy changing, many toddlers at some point will want to know why a boy has a penis and looks different from a girl. Nappy changing is also an ideal opportunity to answer questions on urination and excretion, the detail and the way in which you answer question will depend on the age and stage of development and the responses you have discussed with the parents. Children should be encouraged to respect their bodies and demand that others comply with this too.

Many stories, action rhymes and games can help children become aware of their bodies and help with identifying and labelling body parts, e.g. 'Simon says', and the song 'Head, shoulders, knees and toes'.

Confidence building:
Children need to be encouraged to develop a level of confidence and the ability to communicate their refusal of certain kinds of adult attention or requests, and how to say NO! They need to understand that they can decide for themselves who is allowed to kiss or cuddle them and that they do not have to do anything against their will if it makes them feel uncomfortable. They need to understand about 'good' secrets, e.g. a surprise present for mummy, and 'bad' secrets, e.g. "come with me, don't tell mum it's our secret". This can be hard to explain particularly to younger children, encourage them to tell if they cannot decide whether a secret is 'good' or 'bad'.

Strategies to ensure their own protection:
Children need to learn who they can trust and with whom they can be safe with, e.g. a teacher, carer, policeman, cashier in a shop if they are lost or a security guard. Children should be taught the definition of a stranger. This could be explained as someone they have not met

before or someone they know but not well, and mummy wouldn't invite them in for coffee. They need to be taught awareness of stranger danger and the tricks and ploys that might be used to entice them. The ability to say no when appropriate will help them protect themselves from abuse.

Discussions such as kinds of secret we do not have to keep, used with books that deal with personal safety and talking to strangers, help to explore the issues of personal safety and give children the ability to express their fears and anxieties.

Understanding the importance of protecting others:
Children should be listened to, they should be taken seriously and helped to develop an understanding of the importance of protecting others. Asking questions during stories which draw children's attention to feelings (theirs and others) and including stories where others need assistance can be helpful.

Children's rights and the responsibilities of adults towards them:
Explaining to children their rights and the responsibilities of adults towards them must be done in language they can understand, with opportunities provided for them to express fears and worries. Children should be encouraged to assert these rights when this is appropriate, i.e. it does not mean they can break the ground rules if they feel like it. Health and safety issues and common sense need to be taken into account.

Making children less vulnerable to abuse is also a good strategy. An example of this could be by encouraging and helping the parents of a blind baby to 'read' hand and body movements, instead of waiting for smiles or eye contact, strengthening the parent to baby bond.

Recognising Abuse

Child abuse falls into four main categories, neglect, physical abuse, emotional abuse and sexual abuse. Abuse may consist of more than one type.

Neglect

Neglect is a persistent or serious failure to meet a child's basic physical needs to the extent that health and development are adversely affected. It occurs in many forms including, exposing a child to cold, not providing adequate food, leaving the child unattended, or failing to seek medical advice or attention. Injuries caused by lack of reasonable supervision and control, such as, having no fire guard or letting young children play in the street unsupervised are also neglect.

A child that is neglected may have poor standards of hygiene, dull matted hair, poor state of clothing, a baby may have persistent nappy rash from infrequent nappy changes. There may be an infestation of headlice or fleas that is not treated. The child may be constantly tired, under weight, hungry, and listless, may lose weight, have growth restriction and in general seem withdrawn and not thrive. Children may have destructive tendencies (e.g. breaking things on purpose), have low self esteem, neurotic behaviour (e.g. rocking, hair twisting and inappropriate thumb sucking). Children may have difficulty with their social relationships, steal compulsively, scavenge for food and may horde food. Parents may repetitively pick them up late and be inattentive to the child. Severe neglect is associated with major impairment of growth and intellectual development.

Physical Abuse

Physical abuse is the most prevalent form of abuse. Physical hurt or injury deliberately inflicted, for example, hitting, shaking, squeezing, burning (including cigarettes), biting or giving of poisonous substances (e.g. drugs or alcohol) are all examples of physical abuse.

A child that has been physically abused may have unexplained bruises, cuts or burns. Injuries may be on areas unlikely to be accidentally injured, including stomach, inner arms and back (Note: bruises are more difficult to see on darker skin, and you should be aware of the naturally occurring Mongolian Blue spot found at the base of the spine). Children may fear parents being contacted or fear returning home. They may withdraw from physical contact or flinch if you make a sudden movement. Their arms and legs may be covered in hot weather (note: this may be culturally appropriate). Physical abuse can cause aggressive behaviour in children, emotional and behaviour problems and educational difficulties. Explanations for the injuries may be unforthcoming, implausible or unspecific. Parents may leave injuries untreated or will attend a different casualty unit each time. Parents may seem very critical of their child and use what appears to be excessive punishment.

Emotional Abuse

Emotional abuse involves constantly failing to show a child love or affection, including severe and persistent rejection, criticising, bullying, harassment, taunting, ridiculing, belittling, frightening, threatening or 'scapegoating'.

A child that has been emotionally abused may have behavioural problems, such as aggression, have a low self esteem and crave affection and approval. Their development may be delayed. It is possible they may develop a sudden speech disorder (e.g. stuttering or pronunciation changes). They may fear new situations and exhibit inappropriate emotional responses to stressful situations (note: so do some Autistic children). Some children will show neurotic type behaviour as in neglected children. There may also be extremes of passive or aggressive behaviour, compulsive stealing, bed wetting or soiling. Underlying emotional abuse can be as important as other more visible forms of abuse in terms of its impact on the child.

Sexual Abuse

Abuse may range from showing pornographic videos or magazines to exhibitionism, fondling, through to masturbation, oral sex or sexual intercourse and may involve an adult using a child for gratification via bribes, threats or physical force. Abusers are not only men,10% of sexual abusers are women.

A child who has been sexually abused may display sexual behaviour to other children or with toys, have inappropriate knowledge for their age or talk about inappropriate behaviour by adults. They may have fear of a specific person or situation (e.g. changing nappies or clothes, bathing or being put to bed). There may be non medical soreness of the genitals or bottom. Children may suffer from nightmares or bad dreams, sadness, depression and a loss of self esteem. This form of abuse has the lowest recorded incidence.

Fabricated or Induced Illness (Munchausen's Syndrome by Proxy)

This is a potentially lethal form of abuse where a care giver (usually the mother) induces or reports imaginary symptoms of illness for the child. The child suffers from the 'carers' actions and may also receive unnecessary treatments, tests or diet. Possible indicators are as follows: repeated visits or stays in hospital with failure of diagnosis; unexplained bouts of puzzling illness; symptoms not making medical sense; symptoms which disappear when the parent is absent and a parent who welcomes medical intervention and testing even when known to be painful.

Behavioural Changes

Depending on the form of abuse, emotional and social behaviour that is abnormal or unusual for a child may be noticed.

Emotional reactions of abused children are damped, possibly in an attempt to reduce their risk of abuse. At the childminders or school they may assault, threaten or harass the caregiver. They may also avoid the friendly advances of children and adults, a reaction that might help to maintain abuse at home.

Abused toddlers instead of reacting sympathetically to the distress of other children, may become fearful or angry, they may even attack a crying child. Older children often seem excessively compliant, passive and obedient, stoically accepting what happens. Some older children may behave more like toddlers, negative and aggressive. These children have not developed a basic sense of trust, part of 'normal' child development.

Behavioural patterns must be taken in context, e.g. aggression or regression may follow the birth of siblings, death of a relative or change in family circumstances. Generally a child's behaviour is a good indication of health and well being. Unhappy, frightened children may demand more attention or isolate themselves. A child flinching from normal contact may have been hit on a regular basis.

An abused child may have low self-esteem and poor social relationships, they may show frozen watchfulness, there is likely to be a delay in developmental areas due to lack of stimulation.

An emotionally abused child mainly exhibits physical signs as body language, there may be withdrawn movements, signs of frustration, anger, sadness in the form of temper tantrums. They may show excessive comfort habits e.g. sucking, biting or rocking. Life for the child does not seem to be fun, self-esteem is low, there is a lack of confidence, in 'having a go' at doing things. An emotionally abused child may constantly seek attention, may tell lies and even steal.

A sexually abused child may be withdrawn, lacking in self-confidence, with poor self-esteem, there may be feelings of being bad or dirty, they may not eat or sleep well. There may be an unusual knowledge of sexual behaviour in things they say, play with or draw.

Other examples of behavioural changes include:

❏ Becoming unusually quiet or aggressive.
❏ Severe tantrums.
❏ Air of detachment, 'don't care attitude'.
❏ Mistrust of adults, particularly those who are close, 'frozen watchfulness'.
❏ Sexually explicit behaviour (inappropriate for age/stage of development).
❏ Over compliance.
❏ Continual masturbation, aggressive or inappropriate sex play.
❏ Child only happy/comfortable with you.
❏ Child often kept away from setting.
❏ Child has few friends.
❏ Tummy pains for no medical reason.
❏ Sleep disturbances, nightmares, bed wetting (if developmentally inappropriate).
❏ Regression, depression, withdrawal.
❏ Child runs away from home.
❏ Relationships with adults/child which are secretive and exclude others.
❏ Loss of appetite/over eating (comfort eating).
❏ Self-inflicted injury.
❏ Suicide attempts (rare).
❏ Very anxious to 'please' care giver.
❏ Over reaction to mild criticism.
❏ Apprehensive when others cry.

Assessing Injuries: Accident or Intentional?

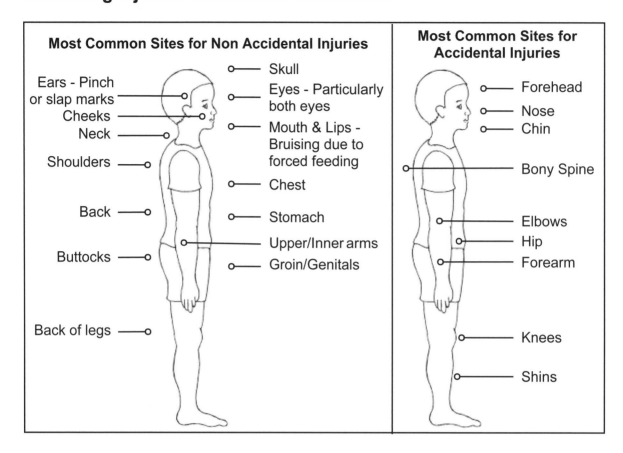

Type of Injury	Non- Accidental	Accidental
Bruises	In a regular pattern Including both old and new bruises (yellow and purple bruising) Reflecting shape of striking implement On lips and mouth, ears and eyes Bilateral (e.g. grasp marks) Finger/hand prints	Few, scattered and irregular distribution. Of same colour and therefore age. Maybe confused with: Birthmarks Mongolian blue spot
Cuts and Abrasions	Large deep untreated scratches Bite marks too large for other children and adult teeth pattern Finger nail scratches Torn (fraenulum in mouth) Incisions (e.g. from razor blade	Minor and superficial e.g. grazes Easily explained Cleaned and treated
Burns and Scalds	Clear outline - may be splash marks around the burn. Position difficult to be self inflicted (e.g. backs of hands or buttocks)Scalds due to being placed into hot water e.g. feet and hands Shaped burns or blisters - e.g. cigarette burns, soldering irons etc.	Logical explanation Medical attention received Sometimes rashes which blister can resemble burns e.g. impetigo and nappy rash where it is severe or become infected.
Fractures	In various stages of healing particularly to skull, nose and face or spiral in nature A delay in seeking treatment. Fractures in young babies, are not common and may be suspicious if child is under 2 years.	Common on arms and legs, ribs are rarely broken unless due to a traffic accident. Due (rarely) to brittle bones.
Injuries to genital areas	Bruising of genital/anal area Bleeding Inflamation Infection	Accidental injuries (seek expert opinion) Soreness due to nappy rash. Anal soreness may be due to constipation or threadworms.

When assessing whether an injury is likely to be accidental or non-accidental (made deliberately by someone) the site and shape of bruises and abrasions are an important factor. Marks on parts of the body that come into contact with the ground when a child falls over forwards are usually accidental, but not always. Any injury to a young baby is more likely to be non accidental. Any injuries that have a pattern, are untreated or do not match the explanation given should raise concerns. When assessing physical injuries, in addition to the injury itself you also need to consider the explanation for the injury, history of previous injuries and the child's behaviour. It must be remembered that alternative medical, psychological or social explanations may exist for some signs and symptoms.

Mongolian Blue Spot

Children of African origin and those of mixed racial origin may have a 'Mongolian Blue Spot' at the base of their spine or buttocks. Occasionally the marking may occur on the shoulders. Marks look similar to a small recently acquired bruise. This is quite normal and it fades as the child grows older. It usually disappears three to five years after birth and almost always by puberty.

Von Willebrand's Disease

This is an inherited bleeding disorder. Children with this condition can present with lots of bruising and may resemble battered children. This condition should have been detailed in your records if known, as internal bleeding, for example into the head, eyes and joints may require treatment.

Brittle Bone Disease

This is a genetic disorder which causes fractures in childhood. Fractures can be difficult to predict, with some occurring during normal handling or with little trauma. The fracture rate diminishes during teenage years. The condition should have been detailed in your records if the parents were already aware.

Effects of Stereotyping on Identifying Abuse

To make accurate assessments of possible abuse there needs to be an understanding that there are wide variations in parenting styles, family structures and relationships. Stereotypes including culture and gender should be carefully avoided when assessing possible signs and symptoms of abuse. For example, the stereotype that boys are always dirtier and untidier than girls, could mean that signs of neglect are ignored.

Practices in bringing up a child vary greatly in different cultures. Though there are general rights such as being fed, sheltered, clothed, to have sleep and affection, that are constant within most cultures there are other things that when taken out of context from the culture that may seem 'wrong'. For example, in some cultures children fast during special religious occasions and within their culture this is acceptable. It will be done in a way that does not have a negative effect on the child however from a western point of view this may seem strange. It is important to remember that for some cultures physical punishment is considered 'normal' and acceptable when used within a loving family context.

Disclosure

Disclosure is where a child directly or indirectly informs of abuse or brings to your attention something which leads you to become suspicions about the possibility of abuse. Children may approach you with a statement or question (open disclosure) or less obviously through their play, art works, body language or a combination of these. Interpretations of these should be made, keeping a sense of proportion. There may be a perfectly reasonable explanation for what has been said or shown. Before any action is taken an evaluation of behavioural symptoms, information from the child, information from the parents and any other information available should be made (unless the child has disclosed sexual abuse, in which case if a parent is implicated, they should not be involved and Social Services notified immediately).

If a child is making a disclosure speak to them gently and slowly, provide them with plenty of time to say what they want to without being pressured. Language used should be appropriate to a child's level of understanding. Younger children will not be able to answer complex questions about experiences they may not understand, they may not have a good perception of time and may not be able to distinguish between past and present events. Never use 'leading' questions e.g. "Did Daddy do this?" Use open questions such as "Who did this?"

A child's ability to cope with the experience of sexual abuse, once recognised or disclosed, is strengthened by the support of a childminder who believes the child, helps the child understand the abuse and is able to offer help and protection.

Remember it is not your job to ask probing questions; Leave that to the trained experts so you do not prejudice the evidence. Record what has occurred straight away. To ensure accuracy do not delay and be careful not to add your own interpretations to the evidence. If there has been a disclosure, or where there is any doubt as to whether there was a disclosure, discuss the event and your interpretations with the Social Services Child Protection Team. Should the disclosure be of sexual abuse (direct or indirect e.g. a child has exhibited inappropriate sexual knowledge) advice should always be sought.

Effects of Abuse Disclosure on Childminder

If you have been present at a distressing disclosure you may require personal help and support to deal with the emotional reactions it may have caused. It can be helpful to talk to someone in confidence about your feelings. This could be a childminding colleague who will be able to reassure you that the feelings are normal. Obtaining further help and advice is not a sign of weakness but a sensible professional approach. Social Services should be able to provide this help.

Taking Action

If you suspect a child is being abused, you are responsible for protecting the child and ensuring the abuse is stopped as soon as possible. You are the child's first line of defence; do not assume someone else will help the child. The child should be listened to, believed and action taken. An abused child's rights and needs are being violated.

Making a Child Protection Referral

If you believe a child may be suffering, or be at risk of suffering, significant harm then your concerns should be made known to your local Children's Social Care Departments Child Protection Team. The police/garda and the NSPCC/ISPCC also have powers to intervene in these circumstances.

Local Authorities have their own specific procedures for making referrals. You can obtain copies via your Children's Information Service (CIS) or childcare development worker. You should ensure you are familiar with your local policies and procedures regarding the reporting of child protection concerns. You should also keep the relevant telephone numbers, including after hours services, where you can access them easily.

When you are making a referral have your information in front of you. Clearly state why you are making the referral. Explain why you are concerned today, provide the most recent information first. State clearly why you think it is a child protection matter.

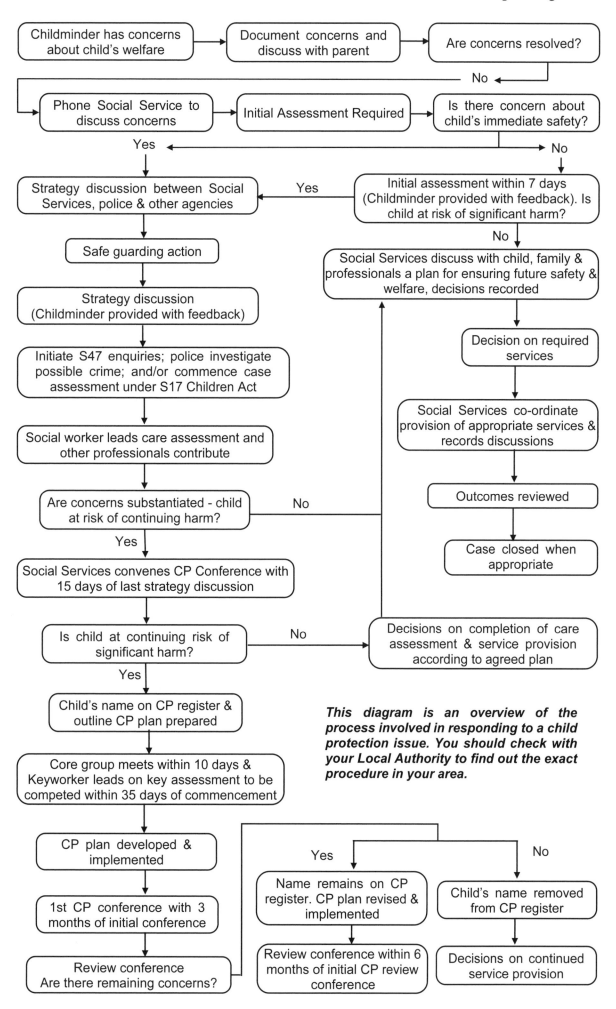

Childminder has concerns about child's welfare → Document concerns and discuss with parent → Are concerns resolved?

No

Phone Social Service to discuss concerns → Initial Assessment Required → Is there concern about child's immediate safety?

Yes   No

Strategy discussion between Social Services, police & other agencies ← Yes ← Initial assessment within 7 days (Childminder provided with feedback). Is child at risk of significant harm?

No

Safe guarding action

Social Services discuss with child, family & professionals a plan for ensuring future safety & welfare, decisions recorded

Strategy discussion (Childminder provided with feedback)

Decision on required services

Initiate S47 enquiries; police investigate possible crime; and/or commence case assessment under S17 Children Act

Social Services co-ordinate provision of appropriate services & records discussions

Social worker leads care assessment and other professionals contribute

Outcomes reviewed

Are concerns substantiated - child at risk of continuing harm? — No →

Case closed when appropriate

Yes

Social Services convenes CP Conference with 15 days of last strategy discussion

Is child at continuing risk of significant harm? — No → Decisions on completion of care assessment & service provision according to agreed plan

Yes

Child's name on CP register & outline CP plan prepared

This diagram is an overview of the process involved in responding to a child protection issue. You should check with your Local Authority to find out the exact procedure in your area.

Core group meets within 10 days & Keyworker leads on key assessment to be competed within 35 days of commencement

CP plan developed & implemented

Yes   No

1st CP conference with 3 months of initial conference

Name remains on CP register. CP plan revised & implemented

Child's name removed from CP register

Review conference Are there remaining concerns?

Review conference within 6 months of initial CP review conference

Decisions on continued service provision

Remember to ask to whom you are talking to and record the name and to ask what they will do next and when you will be informed of the outcome of the referral (do not forget to leave contact details). Remember if you are concerned, persistence is the key.

The Duty Social Worker will need to know the following details if known: your cause for concern; names and addresses of child or children for whom you are concerned; names of parents or carers of the children; the school or nursery or other provisions the child may attend; the family's doctor; any other professional you know to be involved with the family; the planned time for departure; who would normally collect the child and any other information relevant to the investigation.

If you refer a case of possible abuse to the duty social worker of a Child Protection Team, they usually contact you within two hours, with advice on the initial child protection plan. From this point on Social Services will co-ordinate the enquiry and in England will complete a CAF or amend an existing one. Telephone referrals should be confirmed in writing within forty eight hours. Within forty eight hours of your referral a decision will have been made as to whether or not a child protection conference will be called.

Parents, Childminders and Children's Rights

The parents, children and childminder, if applicable, should be fully involved in all stages of the investigation as is consistent with the child's best interests and safety. Investigating officers should explain any allegations and concerns, the investigative process and a parents or childminders legal position and rights. Parents (or if it is an accused childminder) must also be provided with written information.

During child protection procedures and investigations children, parents and childminders have rights which must be observed:

❑ Health visitors and social workers do not have the right of entry into a parent's or childminder's home.
❑ Social workers need to obtain access and permission to see and interview the child. They should use negotiation and persuasion. If they do not get permission they can obtain a child assessment order.
❑ Ofsted and other childminding regulators have the right of entry to a childminder's home. See Section 2. Registration and Inspection Uncovered, for information on investigations.
❑ Diagnosis of child abuse normally requires both medical examination and a social assessment of the family background. Parent's consent to a medical examination should be requested.
❑ A balance must be kept between protecting the child and identifying false accusations, often there is a perfectly reasonable explanation for injury or behaviour and parents and childminders need the opportunity to explain.
❑ Intervention should only occur where 'significant harm' could result, e.g. sexual, physical, emotional abuse or neglect.
❑ Parents can challenge an emergency protection order after seventy two hours if they were not present when it was made.
❑ Parents should be informed of child protection conferences and invited to attend where appropriate.
❑ Parents retain parental responsibility while their child is in care.

Child Protection Procedures

Procedures may vary between the UK regions and for Southern Ireland and this is a general overview.

Procedures usually include child protection conferences, child protection plans, child protection registers or information sharing registers, assessments, child assessment orders, care orders, supervision orders, review conferences, emergency protection orders, police protection order and court intervention. The child protection process begins with the reporting of a concern and is followed by referral, information gathering, planning, investigation, conference, registration and a child protection plan with a review after three months and then deregistration or subsequent reviews. At each stage of the procedures consideration will be given to ascertain the safety of the child and whether emergency protection is required.

When Local Authority Children's Social Care Services receive information indicating a child is at risk of harm they have a legal duty to investigate and take any steps necessary to protect and promote their welfare. 'Harm' is defined as 'ill-treatment or the impairment of health and development and includes seeing or hearing the ill-treatment of another'. For example a child could be conceived as suffering significant harm if they witness domestic violence. Harm is divided into the four categories physical, emotional, sexual and neglect.

Initial Assessment

Within twenty four hours of referral children's services must decide what action if any is required. The decision will be recorded and the referrer notified. If there are ongoing concerns an initial assessment will be carried out within seven days of referral. The assessment is to look at the needs of the child and what actions are needed to protect or promote the child's welfare. Other assessment from any professionals, including childminders, working with the child will be included and the Common Assessment Framework where applicable and feedback to the referrer provided. If the assessment concludes a child is not at risk but 'in need' of support services a core assessment may follow.

Core Assessment

This identifies the child's needs and determines what services would be appropriate to meet them for the best child outcomes. Childminders are often considered as a suitable service. Core assessments are usually completed within thirty five working days from commencement.

Strategy Discussion

If at the initial assessment it was concluded a child was at risk of harm a discussion, within eight working days of referral, involving children's services, the police and other agencies will occur to determine the course of action required. The child's family will not participate and the referrer will be provided with feedback within ten days.
Examples that result in these discussions and an S47 enquiry include:
❑ Child under police protection.
❑ Serious injury to non-mobile baby.
❑ Direct allegations by a child of physical or sexual abuse.
❑ Presence in the household of person who poses a risk to the child.

S47 Child Protection Enquiry

S47 investigations are the initial stages of the core assessment, an enquiry to determine whether action is needed to promote and safeguard a child's welfare. If these enquiries indicate a child is suffering or is at risk of suffering 'significant harm' children's services will arrange a child protection conference. Conferences are normally held within fifteen days of the last strategy discussion/meeting.

Child Protection Conferences

If a conference is not to be held the decision will be sent in writing to the referrer and will include the reasons behind the decision. A copy of this may also be sent, as appropriate to the circumstances of the child and family, to: police, health visitor, doctor, school, nursery, childminder, regulatory body, for example, Ofsted, Education Welfare Officer and relevant hospital staff. If any of these persons or agencies (and that includes childminders) disagree with the decision not to hold a conference, then they have to write to Social Services requesting a conference is held. This will then be held within five working days of receipt of the request.

Where it is established that the evidence suggests child abuse or neglect a decision will be taken to call a Child Protection Conference within forty eight hours of a referral. It will be convened as soon as possible, taking into account the need to protect the child, the need to collect relevant information and to allow for the attendance of key personnel. This will normally be within eight days of the referral.

At a child protection conference professionals involved with the child or family meet to discuss written evidence presented as reports. This is a multi-agency meeting organised by Children's Services which is attended by the family and all the professionals involved with the child. This might include the doctor, health visitor, teacher, paediatrician and childminder. Should care proceedings have been instigated a Children's Guardian of Family Proceedings Officer may attend as an observer. Parents must be informed the conference is taking place and if appropriate they will be invited to attend. Where children have sufficient understanding to participate in the process they will be encouraged to attend too. The conference will be chaired by someone independent from the case and aims to look at all the information about a child's circumstances and if a child is deemed at risk to come up with plans to protect the child and promote their welfare.

As early childhood workers, childminders may be asked to attend. When writing your report have all your information to hand. Use simple language and explain any terminology you use. Write clearly or use a word processor. You will need an introduction including your details, and relationship to the child. Remember to read your completed report to ensure you have not left room for ambiguity or interpretation and do not assume people will understand what you are saying, explain carefully. In most areas a member of the child protection team will support you during this process. It will help if you have submitted a short report to have a copy you can refer to at the meeting. You may also ask for support from your childminding development worker, or your network coordinator if you belong to a network, in producing the report and in accompanying you to the meeting.

At the end of a conference an action plan for the child's protection will be made and the child may be placed on a child protection register. Note: child protection registers are being gradually phased out in favour of the new integrated Children's System and Information Sharing Index. In some cases the family may be offered help and counselling or parental instruction (e.g. in some cases of neglect). Dates will also be set for reviews of the situation.

Children in Need

A child will be deemed to be in need of help if they are unlikely to achieve or maintain a reasonable standard of health and development without intervention or provision of services.

Child Protection Plan

This is a written document explaining the plan and will describe how the child will be helped. There will be an initial assessment of the child and family to 'see how things are' and will be developed into a full plan by a core group to produce specific, achievable, child focused objectives with strategies and activities to enable them to be achieved. The local authority or NSPCC can apply for a child assessment order to give them a seven day window during which the assessment will take place. This is used when the parents do not co-operate, but where there is not an emergency.

The protection of the child will take the form of a care or supervision order. The child protection plan will be reviewed at regular intervals, either six monthly or more frequently if required, at a review conference attended by a multi professional team involved with the family (including childminders sometimes), possibly attended by parents also. A child will be deregistered where support and supervision is no longer required. Records will be kept by the authorities for seventy five years.

Child Assessment Order

This takes the form of a multi-disciplinary assessment in non-emergency situations. The order directs the parents to cooperate with the assessment, but does not allow for the removal of the child. This assessment will be used to determine whether the child is suffering or is likely to suffer significant harm.

Care Order

If a care order has been made the child will be taken into the care of the Local Authority Social Services department who will place the child into a foster or community home. Parental responsibility will then be shared by the Local Authority and the parents.

Supervision Order

Where a supervision order has been made the Local Authority will support and supervise the family and child in their home setting for a period of one year. They may use the support of other agencies or childcare professionals to help with this, for example, the child may be required to attend nursery, playgroup or a childminder.

Protection of the Child in an Emergency

Should there be a concern for a child's safety if they return to their family home then different procedures will apply, these may include emergency protection orders, police protection orders court intervention and resident care orders. Should court proceedings be instigated to remove the child from the parents (known as Court Intervention) there are certain procedures that should be followed.

Emergency Protection Order

An emergency protection order can be applied for by a concerned teacher, childminder or adult. The order has to be applied for to court or to a magistrate and the order will last for up to eight days, this can be extended by another seven days if required.

This order can also be used when access to a child is refused and there is urgent need for protective action. The protection order enables the child to be taken to a safe place. If the parents were not present when the emergency protection order was made they can challenge the decision after seventy two hours have elapsed. Parental contact is maintained whenever possible.

Police Protection Order

Where there is concern for a child's safety a specially trained police team can remove a child into foster care for seventy two hours to ensure their safety. The police must inform the child, the parents or carer and the Local Authority. During this period the parents' retain parental responsibility.

Court Intervention

These proceedings are used to enable the child to be removed from the parents. During the proceedings the parents must be present, this includes everyone with parental responsibility. A guardian ad litem will be appointed to represent the child's interests in court.

The proceedings will take into account the wishes and feelings of the child and they will be involved as active participants in decisions made about them. Where the child is to be placed in care they can be offered the choice of having a resident care order and living with a relative or of going into care with a foster family.

Parents will retain parental responsibility while their child is in care, but they share it with the Local Authority. Parents will be consulted and encouraged to participate and to keep contact with their child.

Residence Order - If the child or the court chooses a residence order they may be able to live with a relative e.g. grandparents. In this instance, the grandparents will assume parental responsibility.

Contact Order - This order ensures a parent's right of contact with the child and how they are to be maintained and monitored. A child however does not have the right to be in contact with their parents.

Specific Issue Order - This order can be made to ensure a parent undertakes a child's specific requirements. This could for example, be used to ensure a child is taken to physiotherapy sessions.

Prohibited Steps Order - These orders are made to prevent something happening, e.g. the child must be kept away from a specific person.

Exclusion Order - This order allows for the removal from the house of a perpetrator instead of removing the child.

Working with Abused Children and Their Parents

Most abusive parents love their children and with support they may be able to stay together. This is usually in the best interests of the child. Recognition of the importance of the child to parent relationship, regardless of whether the relationship has been abusive, is important. Not being judgmental is also important, parents may need help to feel confident with their parenting.

Most abusive parents can be helped to build a more positive relationship with their children. Concentrating on the good intentions of the parents gives them a positive image. You will need to show respect, this will encourage the parent in the idea that children also need respect.

Parents can be helped by demonstrating alternative methods of doing things, e.g. they can learn alternatives to hitting out at a wrong action from their child, giving the parents more choice. Parents can be encouraged to take pleasure in their child's daily achievements. By showing respect for the child's family you will help the child to feel respect and to develop a positive relationship with their parents.

The child should be encouraged to develop a relationship with their parents where they frequently express affection (lots of cuddles), where they can share experiences (including activities and talking to each other). They should be encouraged to be kind to each other and to enjoy each others company.

If you are giving messages of friendship, showing respect for others dignity, valuing people, even if you are rejecting what the parent has done, but not the parent themselves you will be helping to raise a parent's self esteem.

When working with the child who makes contributions towards the activities of other children you should provide praise and attention for joining in. The other children should be encouraged to listen to the child and respond positively, the child's contributions must be valued. You will need to help the child to feel valued, one of the group, listened to and appreciated.

When you are childminding a child who is on a Child Protection Register you should remember to take careful note of the physical and emotional state of the child when they arrive. Any additional injuries, however minor, and any unexplained absences should be notified to the duty social worker. If the placement is part of the help being provided to the family by a Social Services Department then any special arrangements and details of the child's social worker will have been provided to yourself in writing at the time of the placement.

You may not always be told if a child is on a Child Protection (CP) register. In some cases Local Authorities will not inform you. This is to ensure that childcare provision workers do not show bias to children and treat them all with equal concern. A parent may tell you that their child is on the CP register, but they have the right not to do so. It is important to develop a good working relationship with a parent and to make sure you know about access arrangements and if appropriate have a password code for pickups.

Abusers

Children from all cultures are subject to abuse and neglect. It is important to be sensitive to differing family patterns, life styles and child rearing practices that vary across different racial, ethnic and cultural groups. Child abuse cannot however be condoned for religious or cultural reasons. Four to five children die each week as the result of abuse or neglect (NSPCC).

Parents are not the only people that may be responsible for the abuse of a child. Any adult that has access to the child could be the abuser, this could be a family friend, relative, member of staff at a créche or similar.

Abusers may appear pleasant and friendly in your interactions with them, and it is important not to ignore concerns because you feel that 'she/he would never do a thing like that'. Children are abused more often by someone familiar to them, such as a family member, than by a stranger.

A proportion of adults who sexually abuse children will have themselves been sexually abused as children. They may also have been exposed to domestic violence and discontinuity of care. However it would be wrong to assume that most children who are abused will become abusers.

Effects on Children

Abuse can have long lasting traumatic effects which damage a child's development physically, psychologically and emotionally. Abusive parents fail to use reasoning for their rules and regulations this hampers a child's developmental skills in reasoning and problem solving. Abused children may grow up with feelings of being worthless and find difficulty in forming happy relationships. Some may even become abusers themselves. However, one in four people working with children have been abused themselves, they are not abusers but work especially hard to prevent what happened to themselves befalling the children in their care.

10. Equal Opportunities

What is Equal Opportunities?

Equal Opportunities in a Diverse Society

We live in a diverse society. This means that society, the place and the people that are around us, varies a considerably. Society includes a wide range of people with different cultures, religions, economic situations and needs.

Equal opportunities is about ensuring all these people have equal access to care, education, and other basic human rights. The colour of a person's skin, their religion, ability, gender, age or social background, or any other characteristics should not affect the opportunities that are available to them. When they do it is called discrimination.

What this Means for Childminders

As childminders work in a diverse society this needs to be reflected in the care that they provide. This means not only avoiding discriminating against the children and families they work with but also actively promoting equality of opportunity and anti-discrimination so children will grow up respecting other people.

Childminders need to provide opportunities for children to explore and learn about their own and other peoples cultures. By gaining knowledge and understanding of their own culture and background children develop a sense of belonging and strong self image. To accomplish this childminders need to provide a safe and supportive learning environment with toys and resources positively reflecting diversity, for example, cooking utensils, clothes, toys and a range of food available. Childminders can provide opportunities to learn about cultures, history, places, and people during day to day activities. Examples include when cooking, or visiting places such as a museum or market.

Children should be valued as individuals and childminders should discuss with parents their child's culture and beliefs, dietary requirements, dress code, hair and skin care and special needs, and a written record should be kept of these. It is important to meet the needs of all children irrespective of gender, disabilities, social background, culture or religion. As a childminder you are a role model to the children you care for, so it is important you implement your equal opportunities policy and practices successfully.

Early Learning Goals from all regions include aims for children to become sensitive to the needs and feelings of others and show respect for people of other cultures and beliefs, and to respond to relevant cultural and religious events and show a range of feelings such as wonder, joy or sorrow in response to their experiences of the world.

What Equal Opportunities Doesn't Mean

Equal opportunities does not mean that every child must be treated exactly the same. Children are all individuals, and what is right for one child may not be right for another. The opportunities available to children should be equal but the process involved in creating them may vary from child to child. For example, all children should have an equal opportunity to education, but the type of education most suitable might vary from child to child. For some children a special school might be the best educational opportunity.

Tokenism

Tokenism is often mistaken for multiculturalism. It occurs when the provision of equal opportunity toys, books and other materials does not reflect diversity but simply focuses on a single aspect, for example, just including a black doll. The doll has been used as a token of culture. Diversity has not been encompassed and it just serves to emphasise the differences. Another example is when culture or race is used as a novelty or theme, or as something that should be tolerated.

Avoiding tokenism involves choosing play, reading, crafts and displays that do not just include a black doll or a picture of a wheelchair. All materials should reflect diversity. A selection of dolls could be provided of varying appearance, blonds, brunettes, Asian, black, boys, girls, that's not to say you need one of everything to be multicultural. Multiculturalism should reflect real life. Choose materials that show everyday situations not just the stereotypical views of a culture, race or ability. For example, not all Asian people wear traditional Asian clothing and not all wheelchair users have no mobility in their legs. Children are learning all the time so it is important that equal opportunities are fully integrated with day-to-day care.

Taking part in activities, such as, making a traditional meal is not tokenism unless this is your only multicultural provision.

Tourist Curriculum

This is a form of tokenism. It refers to exploring a culture in the way a tourist might, just looking at famous landmarks and traditional customs or festivals. This approach can leave children with a stereotypical view of a culture and without an insight into the day to day lives of people belonging to that culture or religion, e.g. not all African people live in rudimentary villages, there are large cities in Africa.

This does not mean you cannot encourage children to learn about a particular festival but that this should occur as part of a wider exploration of the culture.

Stereotypes

A stereotype is an assumption based on what you consider 'normal' for a person in a particular situation or group. For example, a female stereotype might be that women do the housework, where in fact in some families men do the housework, or it is shared between partners.

Stereotypes can seem both positive or negative but either way they can be detrimental to a child's development. A negative stereotype, for example, would be where you encourage the stereotype that disabled children cannot join in activities. You are preventing them from experiencing a full range of activities and learning a useful skill. A positive stereotype such as all girls are good at knitting is also detrimental, as a girl that is not good at knitting may feel they are 'abnormal' or inadequate.

Legislation Covering Equal Opportunities

UN Convention on the Rights of Children

The UN Convention on the Rights of a Child is an international treaty applying to young people under the age of eighteen. It is divided into articles setting out children's rights, these include the right to play, to be free from abuse and to be free from exploitation. Several of the articles are particularly relevant to equal opportunities:

The Convention on the Rights of the Child (November 1989) states:

❏ Article 23

1. Parties recognise that a mentally or physically disabled child should enjoy a full and decent life, in conditions which ensure dignity, promote self-reliance and facilitate the child's active participation in the community.

Childminders should consider how they will enable children with special needs to participate in all activities and work with parents to ensure they understand and can meet the needs of all children. You could write a policy to explain how you will do this.

❏ Article 29

States Parties agree that the education of the child shall be directed to:

1(c) The development of respect for the child's parents, his or her own cultural identity, language and values, for the national values of the country in which the child is living, the country from which he or she may originate, and for civilizations different from his or her own;

1(d) The preparation of the child for responsible life in a free society, in the spirit of understanding, peace, tolerance, equality of sexes, and friendship among all peoples, ethnic, national and religious groups and persons of indigenous origin;

To meet this childminders should promote respect for all people and cultures and provide opportunities for children to develop the relevant social skills involved. Childminders need to provide a broad range of activities and materials that promote equal opportunities and encourage children to learn about different cultures.

❏ Article 30

In those States in which ethnic, religious or linguistic minorities or persons of indigenous origin exist, a child belonging to such a minority or who is indigenous shall not be denied the right, in community with other members of his or her group, to enjoy his or her own culture, to profess and practise his or her own religion, or to use his or her own language.

Childminders should provide opportunities for children to take part in any cultural or religious practices and respect children's and parent's wishes for example, with regards to diets and dress code. Children who are bilingual or whose first language is not English should have the opportunity to use their home language. Parents will be able to provide you with key words for example; hot, cold, yes, no and other simple words appropriate to your situation and the child.

❏ Article 31

1. States Parties recognise the right of the child to rest and leisure, to engage in play and recreational activities appropriate to the age of the child and to participate freely in cultural life and the arts.

2. States Parties shall respect and promote the right of the child to participate fully in cultural and artistic life and shall encourage the provision of appropriate and equal opportunities for cultural, artistic, recreational and leisure activity.

Childminders need to provide play and learning opportunities that allow children to learn about cultures and people that are different to their own. Activities and materials should encourage development opportunities.

Race Relations Act 1976 (and Amendment 2000)

The Race Relations Act outlaws discrimination on the grounds of colour, race, nationality and ethnic origin. The Amendment Act adds a duty to actively promote equality of opportunity, good race relations and to actively tackle racial discrimination. As a result of the act, the Commission for Racial Equality, a publicly funded, non-governmental body, was set up to tackle racial discrimination and promote racial equality.

Race & Religious Hatred Act 2006

This act makes it an offence to threaten or stir up hatred on religious grounds and amends the laws on encouraging racial hatred. The law applies to believers in any or no religion, both ethically diverse or mono-ethnic where the hatred is against a person or group who do not share the perpetrators beliefs.

Disability Discrimination Act 1995 (and Amendment 2005)

The Disability Discrimination Act outlaws discrimination of a disabled person or child. A disabled person is described as "anyone with a physical or mental impairment, which has a substantial and long-term adverse effect upon their ability to carry out normal day-to-day activities".

The act makes it illegal to refuse to provide, or deliberately not provide, a service which is offered to other people; offering a lower standard or inferior service; or offering less favourable terms. Although service providers are required to make reasonable adjustments for disabled people so that they can use a service they are not, at present, required to do anything that would necessitate making a permanent alteration to the premises.

The Disability Rights Commission is an independent body set up by the Government with the aim of eliminating discrimination against disabled people and to enforce their rights.

Sex Discrimination Act 1975

The Sex Discrimination Act outlaws sex discrimination against individuals in employment, education, and the provision of goods, facilities and services and in the disposal or management of premises.

The law prohibits both direct and indirect discrimination. Direct discrimination is where a person is treated less favourably than a person of the opposite sex in comparable circumstances, such as a boy not being able to join a ballet class. Indirect discrimination is where a condition or practice is applied to both sexes but it adversely affects a considerably larger proportion of one sex than the other, and it is not justifiable, such as a condition that all children must have long hair to take part in a play which would generally make more girls eligible than boys.

The Equal Opportunities Commission was established under the Sex Discrimination Act in 1975. They are an independent statutory body working towards the eradication of sex discrimination and providing assistance to those that have been discriminated against.

Education Act 1996

Part four of this act sets out the process of assessing, statementing, and education of children with special educational needs, from two years of age and before that if the child has been identified by their parents or Social Services as having special needs.

Special Educational Needs and Disability Act (SENDA) 2001

The SENDA came into force in two parts. The first in January 2002 and the second in September 2002. It amended parts of the law governing the education of pupils in school who are disabled. The act also strengthened pupils rights to main stream schooling, making schools legally almost unable to discriminate against children with SEN.

Prejudice and Discrimination

Prejudice means pre-judging, making assumptions about a person or group of people without accurate facts, or in opposition to the facts. Prejudice is often based on stereotypes. Many of us hold prejudices without realising it. The assumption "boys will be boys" is such an example and may mean that the way you treat children will not be providing equal opportunities.

Some prejudices stem from a tradition, some knowledge or actions that have been passed down through generations and have become an accepted way of acting. Such as, in many societies women have traditionally played a subservient role to men, though this may not generally be expected now, traditions are still passed on.

A person's upbringing greatly impacts on any prejudices they may develop. Children learn to respect the views of their parents and often come to hold similar views; if a parent or role model has prejudices these can be passed to the child. Unless these prejudices are challenged the child may in turn pass them on to their children. Children may be ignorant of the facts which would enable them to correct their prejudices.

Ignorance does not mean that someone is 'stupid' or unintelligent, it means that they are lacking the information or have inaccurate information on a particular subject that is important in formulating an opinion. Childminders can help challenge prejudices by providing accurate information and opportunities to learn it.

Prejudice can also stem from superiority, the belief that they are better than someone else.

Challenging Prejudices

Prejudiced behaviour should not be ignored. It is important you make it clear that it will not be tolerated. By ignoring prejudice you encourage children to think that it is acceptable. If a child displays prejudiced behaviour towards another child the first step is to calm down both children, and the victim may need comforting. You need to discuss with the child displaying the unacceptable behaviour why they behaved in that way and the effect it had on the other child using language appropriate to their development.

The behaviour may stem from jealousy or lack of knowledge. If the victim speaks a different language or has special arrangements it can help to explain why to all the children present. Teaching each other words from the other's language or 'have a go' with special equipment can help the children become more accepting of each other's differences. However make sure you are avoiding tokenism and 'singling' out children. For example, if looking at languages, look at many different languages. Not just the different one. The same would apply for disabilities.

Talk to children about discrimination and encourage them to challenge it. Involve them in thinking of ways to address issues such as how activities can be adapted for a younger child or a child with disabilities. Talk about the impact prejudice has and how it makes people feel. Challenge prejudicial jokes. Being a good role model is another essential part of preventing and addressing prejudice. In many situations children will use your behaviour as a guide for how they should behave towards others.

Providing opportunities for children to learn about the things they have prejudices about is the best way to challenge them. Removing the lack of knowledge or incorrect knowledge that leads to the prejudice will help resolve it. Children may ask difficult or complicated questions, and they may ask them at inappropriate times e.g. 'Why has that lady only got one leg?.' It's important that their questions are acknowledged and answered so they know they can talk about and ask questions about these issues. It is also a good idea to talk to parents about the questions that children ask so they can address them to. Never refuse to give a child information. If you are not sure how to answer, suggest they ask their parents when they are collected. Refusing outright to explain leaves a child to form their own conclusions or rely on inaccurate information from other sources which could lead to them developing a prejudice.

If a child's prejudices stem from their parents, care should be taken not to express disapproval of the parents in front of the child. Talking to children about feelings, of themselves and of those shown prejudice, can help them understand how their actions can impact on other people.

Challenging Parents Prejudices

Occasionally you may meet a parent who makes discriminatory remarks or encourages their child to do so. You may have a policy on equal opportunities which will cover discrimination and it may help to share it with the parent reminding them of what you find acceptable/unacceptable. At the very least you should always discuss equal opportunities at your first meeting with new parents. It can also be helpful to encourage such parents to mix with the other parents and children, as prejudice often stems from ignorance and meetings may help alleviate this.

You should challenge all such remarks. If this behaviour is deeply ingrained or cultural do not expect an instant change. You may have to insist they refrain from such remarks or behaviour whilst on your premises as being a starting point to work from. Some parents are not aware what they have said or done is discriminatory and if challenged tactfully and with explanation can be encouraged to change their terminology and sometimes even their behaviour.

Forms of Discrimination

❑ **Direct discrimination -** a person is less favourably treated because of their race, ethnic origins, sex or a disability.
❑ **Indirect discrimination -** where a requirement or condition (without reason) is applied to everyone but causes difficulty to one particular group.
❑ **Victimisation -** this is when a person is treated less favourably because they have complained about discrimination or supported someone who has.

Racism

Racism is the belief that someone is inherently better than another person on the sole basis of their race. It is the suggestion that one race is 'better' than another. It is based on ignorance and it is important not to dismiss it. Racism has been the cause of countless deaths and the destruction of cultures throughout the world and history.

It is important to remember racism is not just about 'white' people being racist towards people with different coloured skin. It can be between any culture or race, for example, it could be aimed towards an Irish person or American. It can also be shown towards a person of mixed race.

Racism is a type of prejudice and should be challenged in a similar way. Children need to be provided with the opportunities to learn why racism is wrong and how to interact with people from cultures and races different to their own.

History: By the late 19th century the world was being divided up between a few powerful countries, imperial powers such as Great Britain, France, Germany and the US. Justification was needed for the domination of the 'non Europeans'. Darwin's theory of evolution was utilized to argue that 'whites' were biologically superior. Labelling the natives as savages and inferior meant that the imposition of British culture and religion was seen as assisting them. This may seem like a long time ago but remember skin colour still affected peoples right to vote right up to the 1960's.

There are many examples throughout history of people from different cultures and races being treated as subservient to others. The slave trade is one example of this. The Holocaust, where Nazi Germany, committed mass genocide against the Jews and Romany's is another example. More recently is the association between anyone of middle eastern appearance and terrorism - irrespective of their actual religious ideologies.

Recent race relation legislation, anti-racist campaigning and multicultural education has made racism unacceptable, unfortunately many of the historical prejudices still remain and must be challenged.

Myths: Non white people are: inferior to white people; less valuable members of society; will achieve less in education.

Sexism

Sexism, discriminating against someone because of their sex, is another form of prejudice. You can help discourage it by providing both boys and girls equal opportunity to activities. Children may need encouragement to try activities that are often associated as being 'boys' or 'girls' activities. For example girls may need encouragement to join in ball games and boys with cooking. Traditional gender roles need to be challenged.

Sexism can be directed at men, not just women. For example, in issues such as the lack of custody rights for fathers or that playing with dolls is not appropriate for boys.

History: Many cultures are based around a patriarchal system, with the family being ruled by a male head of the household. Religions including Christianity, Judaism, Islam and Hinduism all include the patriarchal system. Property and nationality have traditionally been passed down the male line. Until the 20th century women had limited rights to property, no voting rights and were generally under the control of either their fathers or husbands. Images throughout the majority of the 20th century portrayed the stereotypical family image of a working husband and a housewife. In some cultures practices such as confinement of women to the home, female circumcision and abandonment of female children are still found.

Sexuality

Discriminating on the basis of sexuality means treating someone differently because they are gay, lesbian, heterosexual, bisexual, transgender, or discriminating against a person on the basis of their association with or in relation to someone with a particular sexual preference.

Children will be unaware of what the terms, gay, lesbian, heterosexual or bisexual mean in regards to sexual relationships, they will however, depending on age, be observant of emotional relationships, recognising differences to their own family. You may find yourself asked questions like "Why does John have two daddies?" The answers to these questions can be discussed with parents. How they want to explain will vary from parent to parent and on the development of the child. An answer such as "Not everyone has a mummy and a daddy, some people have two mummies or two daddies." can be helpful.

Prejudice could also arise from parents who may worry about the impact on their own children. This generally stems from a lack of information. You should reassure parents that sexuality does not impact on the standard of care that a parent or carer can provide for a child. Offering information or suggesting sources of information can help resolve parents fears. Common misconceptions include: homosexuals have AIDS and that gay men do not make good fathers.

Social Class

During the year 2005/06 there were 3.8 million children living below the poverty line in the UK. (Households Below Average Income, Department for Work and Pensions, 2007)

Poverty is not always just about a lack of food or shelter, it is also relative to other families within the UK. For example, parents may have difficulty providing new clothes, buying expensive toys, or going on holidays. Children may be discriminated against if they are not seen to be wearing the latest 'gear' or have the latest toys. It is important to consider how a child who has not been able to go on holiday may feel when other children discuss holidays they have been on. You should consider carefully things that might cause exclusion to parents on lower incomes such as they may not be able to provide wellies for an outing to the park or fees for a trip to the zoo. You could support parents by having a spare set of wellies for the park or planning activities and venues without entrance fees or paying the fees yourself (note: this would be tax deductable).

History: In the 19th century the poor were considered to be lazy and their situation their own fault. Poor houses were created to house them. Environments within these houses were deliberately harsh to discourage people from seeking assistance. Families were separated, men and women were not allowed to mix and children were separated from their parents. It was decided that those in the poorhouse should only be fed to the standard of the poorest living outside the poorhouse, and this meant that they lived on the edge of starvation.

Age

Discrimination on the basis of age covers all ages not just 'older people'. It occurs when someone feels that a person is too old, or too young to do something. For example, a child may feel that a grandparent is too old to take part in sports or that a younger child is to young to join in a game. It is important to correct any misconceptions and it will help to discuss the feelings of the person or age group the discrimination is directed to. It could also occur in a situation where a child is developmentally ahead of, or behind, their peers.

Physical Appearance

When we meet someone we often form an opinion of them quickly, this may not necessarily be accurate and may alter as we get to know them. The saying 'Don't judge a book by its cover.' is particularly significant here. People may discriminate by forming an opinion based on appearance before they have met or got to know a person, for example, assuming that a physical impairment also means an intellectual impairment. Children may ostracise someone who is different from themselves; the differences could include wearing glasses, having a missing limb or wearing different clothes. It is important to respond to this in the same way as all prejudices, by correcting misconceptions and discussing why this behaviour is unacceptable.

Disability

The term disability covers a broad range of conditions and abilities. Children or adults may be discriminated against because people form inaccurate beliefs about how a disability affects them. Learning difficulties or disabilities that affect communication can be particularly missunderstood.

History: Historically, disability has been treated with little understanding. Disabled people have been treated as outcasts, defective, with their disability a punishment from God or the work of the devil. The ancient Greeks saw epilepsy as a disturbance of the mind and in 355 BC Aristotle said "those born deaf become senseless and incapable of reason." It was believed that deaf people could not learn because communication was essential to learning.

In early Christianity disability, was seen as an impurity that could be purged through prayer and rituals, services were organized by the church to care for disabled people. By the middle ages disability became associated with the devil and disabled people were persecuted.

In 1676 Bethlehem Royal Hospital opened to the public, the inmates were a popular form of entertainment. Soon the hospital became so popular that visitors had to be restricted by a ticket scheme. Public viewing of the patients continued into the early 19th century when public opinion moved against the disabled as a form of entertainment.

In 1913 the Mental Deficiency Act defined four grades of Mental Defectives: idiots, imbeciles, feeble minded and moral defective. Institutions were renamed 'colonies'; their purpose being to separate the residents from society. Under the 1913 Act people could be detained for as long a period as the authorities saw fit. The Board of Control was not accountable to either Parliament or the Minister of Health. The only restriction in place on their power was that the person had to show signs of the deficiency before 18 years of age. Lack of understanding meant many impairments were classed as a mental deficiency inaccurately.

Alexander Graham Bell campaigned for sterilisation of deaf girls and to prohibit marriage between deaf persons in the name of "eugenics" in an effort to control the growth of a "defective variety of the human race".

In Nazi Germany, disabled people were experimented on and gassed. The disabled were seen as defective and their removal necessary to prevent corruption of the human race.

Myths: 'A person with a disability is sick'. Disability is not a illness, though in some cases it may result from one. Seeing disability as an illness falsely suggests that it is something that needs to be cured.

'Disabled people have a poor quality of life'. Disabled people have the same needs and goals in life as all people. The problems they encounter can be rectified by society considering their needs such as accessibility issues.

'A disability means a mental impairment'. Though some disabled people may have a mental impairment, this does not mean that all disabled people do. Disabled people can reach the same academic achievements as non disabled people if equal opportunities are applied to education.

'Disabled people can't have jobs or be valuable members of society'. Many disabled people work and all are valuable members of society.

When teaching children about disability it is useful to remember, 'No one can do everything, but everyone can do something'.

Refugees and Asylum Seekers

Refugees are people who have been forced to flee from their own country because of war, their religion, political beliefs, or race puts them in danger of arrest, torture or death. Many would prefer to return to their home, often this is not possible until the problem has been resolved.

When a person flees their country as a refugee, they apply for the right to be recognised as such in the country they have fled to. This is process is called seeking asylum. If they are granted asylum, they then have the right to be protected by the law and cared for financially by that country. If they are not granted asylum they may be returned to their country of origin.

Equal Opportunities Provision

Helping Children Develop to their Full Potential

Providing equal opportunities not limited by race, culture, gender, or disability, helps children develop to their full potential. It's important your expectations of children are not influenced by prejudice or stereotypes. For example expecting girls to play mainly with dolls, tea-sets and dressing up and boys with cars and building blocks, without challenging this can limit them in reaching their full potential. Different activities have different developmental values, for example, tea-sets and dolls can help children develop social skills and construction toys help children develop mathematical skills. By not encouraging children to take part in a range of activities their development in some areas can be held back. Where possible use gender neutral language. Using language that gives gender specific titles to job roles can also be limiting, for example use police officer instead of policeman.

Children with disabilities should be encouraged to reach their full potential. Having limited expectations and not encouraging children to reach new goals and develop new skills can hamper their development. Having a preconceived idea of what a child will be able to achieve or not achieve could prevent you providing a full range of opportunities. Children should be encouraged to 'have a go' and all effort praised whether the same goal is reached to that of their peers or not. This may mean adapting activities so that less able children can take part in an activity e.g. putting sand in a tray on the table so a wheelchair user can reach it.

Culture or race stereotypes such as 'black children' are better at basket ball than 'white' can cause a child to either focus on basket ball or not consider it as an option at play time. Children should be encouraged to reach their full potential not that of a stereotype.

Take a step back when children are playing and look at the type of toys they are playing with. If there is an obvious segregation between the sexes e.g. girls playing with dressing up clothes and boys with cars consider how activities can be adapted to challenge stereotypes. By encouraging children to take part in a range of activities and not setting stereotypical expectations we help children to develop to their full potential.

Incorporating Equal Opportunities

Promoting equal opportunities does not mean just providing the equal opportunities/ multicultural toys found in toy catalogues. It does not need to be difficult or expensive. It should be fully incorporated into activities not used as a theme.

Diverse Cultural Areas - Dolls not of the typical 'blond, rosebud' complexion are more likely to be available in local toy shops in a diverse cultural area. Charity shops in these areas may have clothes or cooking utensils from a wider range of cultures.

Library - You can borrow cook books from a range of cultures, multicultural children's books, information books or activity books, if you inform the library you are a childminder and hence have lots of children they may allow you to take out extra books. When choosing reading books look out for ones that promote equal opportunities and positive non stereotypical roles, particularly in the images.

Photographs - Take or collect photos and post cards of any multicultural activities you do and stick them on the wall with labels in dual language so the children can read them, examples could include, a multicultural meal (curry, pizza, noodles) local outing to cultural centre, children from different races or cultures, or local supermarket, religious buildings. Pictures can promote discussion and help create an interesting and welcoming environment.

The Internet - There are a wide range of resources available on the Internet, try searching for particular festivals or places. Children should not be allowed to use the Internet unsupervised, picking a few interesting sites in advance helps you control the information available and prevents children becoming bored whilst you search.

TV Programmes - A television guide should list programmes aimed at lower schools that may contain positive multicultural images or children with special needs, many are late at night and will need recording. Clearly label the boxes for ease of identification and to prevent accidentally reusing the tape, before you add them to your collection. You can watch these with the children and discuss them.

Music - Music plays an important part in many cultures, a range of different music, songs, dance and instruments can all be enjoyed by children.

Clothes and Fabrics - Children can look at clothes in shops, or as part of role play. Different fabric and dress styles can be considered in relation to the environments people live in. Different uniforms for job roles can help promote equal opportunities if all children are encouraged to try different roles.

Cooking - Try cooking recipes with the children, and use some of the recipes to provide a variety of food from other cultures for the children's meals. Children may like to bring in recipes from home and you could compile you own cookbook from their favourites. Remember to include different diets (e.g. vegetarian) and ways of eating.

A range of cooking equipment and eating implements can be explored, both real and toy ones. Items like chopsticks can be used for fine motor activities, role play and eating food.

Local Market - Look for unusual fruit and vegetables, these can be discussed with children or purchased and tasted. A range of different cultural foods and foods from various countries may also be available, children could taste these and different shapes, colours, textures and smells can be discussed. Young children will not understand that some foods, such as fruit, come from another country. They do not understand the concept of distance. Avoid saying "this comes from Africa", young children will only understand it comes from the market or supermarket. By school age they will be beginning to understand this concept.

Friends or Family Travelling - If you or someone you know are going on holiday to another country ask them to bring back a piece of traditional clothing or a toy suitable for the children. Post cards from other countries are also popular with children and are good for encouraging discussions. Books written in different languages can promote discussion about writing and language for school age children, particularly if the writing is unlike English e.g. Cantonese or Russian.

Parents - Can be a source of a wide ranges of materials including music, dual language books, artefacts, clothing, photos, traditional foods and recipes, specialised toys and equipment.

Magazines - Cut pictures from magazines that reflect multicultural and equal opportunities diversity positively and make a collage, stick it on the wall for the children to look at and discuss. Early years practitioners magazines often contain posters promoting multicultural issues.

Packaging - Writing from a variety of languages can be found here, most packaging will have instructions in several languages. Empty food boxes can be used to set up your own corner shop, or set up your own restaurant with dual language menus.

Everyday Opportunities - Everyday opportunities can be used to discuss equal opportunities with children. For example, discussing why some shops have ramps helps children become aware of other people's needs. Children may go on to spot things that might cause access problems and even suggest solutions.

Equal Opportunities Toy Ideas

There is an increasing range of equal opportunities toys available from toy suppliers. You should be able to find items such as the following:

❑ Books/CD's of songs and music from other cultures.
❑ Books and posters featuring festivals and places from around the world.
❑ Books on other cultures or religion and reflecting diversity.
❑ A range of dolls of different ethnic origins and some with disabilities.
❑ Small world play people of different nationalities.

❑ Puzzles showing people in non stereotypical roles, such as a man doing the washing or a woman laying bricks.

❑ Cooking sets including equipment used in a range of cultures, such as a wok and chop sticks.

❑ Dressing up clothes featuring traditional dress from a range of cultures, and clothes allowing children equal opportunity to explore roles such as being a builder or police officer.

❑ A map of the world so children can associate where things come from (for older children).

Books and resources that are not good examples of equal opportunities can be used to involve children in discussions about discrimination and how equal opportunities can be promoted.

Welcoming Equal Opportunities Environment

A welcoming environment is one that is inviting to child or adult and one that they feel comfortable in. A welcoming environment is more than just pictures on the wall, it is also about the general atmosphere. People play an important part in the environment, smiling, being friendly and having a positive attitude will all help create a welcoming environment. Children will take cues from other children present, if they are happy and welcoming this will help the child feel at ease in the environment.

The physical environment is also important, children are more likely to feel welcome if the environment caters for their needs. If adaptations are needed, these should be easily accessible or out ready, where possible, rather than a child needing to ask. Reflecting children's home environment by using familiar items will help them feel comfortable in your environment.

A good way to assess how welcoming your environment is, is to pretend you have not been there before. Start at the bottom of your drive, at your front door or just inside. Look around and imagine you are seeing it for the first time, what impression do you get? Can you tell that children are often present? Does it look like a fun place to be? What is the first thing you see as you come in the door is it a child's picture or blank wall? What impression does what you see give you? Once you get inside look around the room, are the toys easy to spot and does it feel welcoming? You do not need to turn your living room into a playroom or children's art gallery. Toys can be packed away when children are not present and displays made on boards so they are easily stored away.

The toys, equipment, activities and visible materials help create a welcoming environment, as will providing a broad range of equal opportunities materials. Below are some ideas:

❑ Use welcome posters in the entrance, children can help with making these and words can be written in multiple languages.

❑ Photos of the children you care for, past and present where provided by parents.

❑ Make sure that books contain a range of positive images including different positive images, showing disabled people, people from different cultures, social backgrounds, situations, and non stereotypical roles.

❑ Display a map of the world so that children can locate family, friends or places where they have lived and visited.

❑ Develop resources which encourage playing different games from around the world or games that help children learn about different people and their needs, role play and similar.

❑ Encourage parents to come in and share stories or festivals with the children, or read in their home language.

Bilingualism

Bilingualism means using more then one language. Often this is used to refer to children whose first language is not English.

Children whose first language is different to the majority in your setting may spend time listening before joining in. You can help them feel welcome and part of the group by encouraging them to share their language. Keywords like drink, toilet, cat, biscuit and toys are easy to learn and children will benefit from learning a new method of communicating. These words are likely to be the first words they will learn in English through repeated daily use. All languages should be valued, encouraging the development of languages has many benefits for children.

It is helpful for a child to learn what language to speak and where. It can be helpful to speak in English even when you understand the child's first language where others will not understand. You should not assume that because a child (or parent) speaks good English that this is their first language, many people speak their second language as well as their first. You may be being spoken to in English as a courtesy.

Positive Images

Every day we see hundreds of images on the television, in books, magazines and billboards, in shops, on the front of packaging or the side of a lorry. We are not always aware how they have impacted on the way in which we think about something. If images are not true representation of diversity they can promote stereotypical ideas.

Displaying positive images of themselves and children that they can relate to can help a child's self esteem and encourage them to reach their full potential. For example, if a child has a disability and they see a person with a similar disability in a positive role it will help them realise what they can achieve. If a child sees a person in a role that is generally considered not that belonging to their particular, class, gender, race or similar it will help the child realise their opportunities are not limited by their class, gender or race.

Positive images should also show people of different races, cultures, classes, abilities and gender in positive roles, generally these are roles that are not stereotypical. Examples include, a man doing domestic activities, a woman builder, an ethnic minority lawyer or a disabled athlete. Positive images can cover any age, race, gender, class, culture, ability in a wide variety of roles from taking children to school to flying an airplane This is because for example, if a child always see images of older people as frail, grumpy, old fashioned or similar stereotypical portrayals, they will assume a stereotypical view, that this is what all old people are like. By introducing the idea, through positive images, that older people can be fit and active, enjoy taking part in sports, be friendly, and generally not just be the stereotypical 'old person' you have challenged the stereotypes a child could otherwise develop.

Language in Equal Opportunities

The language used to describe particular groups of people or to promote equal opportunities can be difficult to master and sometimes there are grey areas over what terms are acceptable and which are not. Avoid stereotypical language that makes assumptions, for example, do not assume that everyone is heterosexual, where possible use gender neutral language such as partner instead of husband/wife. Do not assume that someone belonging to a particular 'group' will necessarily share the same characteristics.

Do not use language like 'ethnic' or 'culture' to describe those from ethnic minorities everyone has a culture and an ethnicity.

Never define anybody by their disability or a medical condition they may have and recognise that individual personal characteristics are far more important, e.g. it is not acceptable to refer to "special needs groups or individuals". Children should not be referred to by their physical characteristics, such as 'the blond girl' or 'the black child', use children's names.

The term coloured is no longer an acceptable term. By definition all people are coloured. If this term is used to describe minority ethnic people it is generally regarded as offensive and insulting. Currently the term black is used to refer to people of African, African-Caribbean and Asian origin.

It is helpful to listen to the ways in which people describe themselves. Using the same terms prevents you from making assumptions or using the wrong language. For example, a visually impaired person may refer to themselves as blind, sight impaired, visually impaired or visually challenged. Individuals may prefer different language. Children should be given the opportunity to express how they want their impairments to be described.

Relevance of Equal Opportunities in Predominantly 'White' Areas

You may feel that if you live in a predominantly white area racism is not an issue. 'How can there be racism if there are no black people?'

Race is not just about black and white. Many British people will refer to themselves as, for example, Scottish, Welsh, Turkish or Asian. Many areas in Britain have ethnic minorities and people from many different cultures, religious and social backgrounds.

The idea that interaction with ethnic minorities is needed to develop racist ideas is inaccurate. Racism is often associated with ignorance of a particular ethnic minority or ethnic minorities in general, children who have had the opportunity to learn about different cultures are less likely to have racist ideas.

Adults are shaped greatly by the things they learn as children, and it is important to equip children with the skills and knowledge they will need as adults. Learning about other cultures and being accepting of other people's differences will help children become good members of society as adults, whatever the ethnic population of the society they live in.

Assessing your Equal Opportunities Practice

It is important to think about and assess how well your equal opportunities policies are working and how well your actions match them. Discrimination can occur without intention, continually re-evaluating where your provision can be improved will help prevent this happening.

It is also important think about any stereotypes you may have grown up with. It is important to admit these to yourself and take steps towards challenging them. Creating an action plan may be helpful.

❏ **Step 1 -** Research facts. This will help you learn accurate information and correct any misconceptions that are contributing to the stereotype.
❏ **Step 2 -** Plan activities that are anti-discriminatory.
❏ **Step 3 -** Put what you have learnt into practice.

Regularly re-evaluate your attitudes and actions to assess how you are progressing. You may also want to consider taking part in equal opportunities training or read and research around the subject.

Admitting your prejudices or finding yourself acting in a discriminatory way may generate feelings of guilt. It is important to admit where you were wrong, to apologise if necessary and to take positive steps to prevent reoccurrence.

Religion and Culture

These are only overviews; you should ask the parents of the children to provide you with details of the requirements for their children. Not all members of a particular culture or religion may follow the same practices and some may adhere more strictly than others.

What is Culture?

Cultures are beliefs, behaviours, languages or ways of life that are shared by a group of people. They use this knowledge to interpret events and people, and to interact with each other. Cultures can be shared by people in a particular location, or by people that hold similar values or beliefs. Not all members of a particular culture will hold identical beliefs and practices, you should remember that within a culture there may be many more sub cultures and individuals. Not all people in one country belong to the same culture, there may be many cultures within a country, and also many different languages may be spoken. Culture and diversity is not just about race, colour, age or sexual preferences. Culture is learnt and not biologically inherited.

Christianity

Most followers of Christianity are Roman Catholic, Protestant or Eastern Orthodox and consider Jesus as central to their religion. Under the heading of Christianity there are many differences in traditions and practices.

Christian homes may have visible symbols of faith such as icons, crosses, crucifixes or biblical texts. Baptism and celebration of Holy communion are the most widely practised rites. Casual use of 'Jesus' or 'Christ' in conversation when used as expressions of surprise or shock can cause offence.

The major festivals of the Christian calendar are Christmas which celebrates the birth of Jesus, Easter a movable festival commemorating his resurrection and Pentecost celebrating the coming of the Holy Spirit.

Catholic

Catholics are encouraged to attend weekly Mass and are under an obligation to attend Holy Communion and Sacraments of Reconciliation (Confession) during the Easter season.

Catholicism revolves around the seven sacraments: Baptism, Reconciliation, Eucharist, Confirmation, Marriage, Holy Orders (joining the priesthood), and Sacrament of the Sick (Last Rites). The importance of receiving Christ's body and blood at Communion is central and there is a great emphasis on moral law.

Protestant

The term Protestant is used to refer to Christian groups developed during the Reformation. Protestant Christians differ in the degrees with which they reject Catholic belief and practice. Most Protestant churches recognise two sacraments: Baptism and Communion.

The Protestant religions include the Anglicans (Church of England), Lutherans, Baptists, Presbyterians, Methodists, Pentecostals and Quakers.

Hindu

Traditional Hindu first names have a meaning. Naming systems can be complicated and a surname may be given before the first name. It is important to check how the parents and child wish to be addressed.

Diet: According to Hinduism, food is divided Into three types - Sattvic, Rajasic and Tamasic. Tamasic is considered not good to eat, food that is left over or contaminated is usually called Tamasic food. Hindu's believe that these foods produce jealousy. Rajasic foods include animal meat, spices, onions, garlic, hot pepper and pickles. Hindu's believe Rajasic foods produce activity and strong emotions. Sattvic foods include fruits, nuts, and vegetables. Hindus believe these foods produce calmness.

Hindu dietary code prohibits the eating of beef and pork. To Hindus, a cow is a sacred animal. Many Hindus do not consume meat, as they believe that killing animals is a sin. Hindu's may generally eat less meat. Rules for eating include being clean before sitting down to eat. Foods may be eaten with fingers.

Festivals: include Raksha Bandhan, Holi, Divali (Festival of Light) and Nararatri. During Raksha Bandhan girls will make silk thread bracelets for their brothers called Rakhis in return for their protection. Boys will wear these on their wrists and they should not be removed. During the spring festival of Holi (February/March) children may wear white clothes during the morning to show off the splashes of red, pink and yellow where they sprinkle or squirt each other with coloured water. They will usually change their clothes during the afternoon. Traditionally sweets and sugary bread are eaten and parents may send some for the children to share. When they go home there may be dancing, music and a bonfire so they may be late to bed for this occasion. During Diwali which falls in October/November they may have candles on their window sills at home. They may have coloured sand or powder sprinkled in their doorway (Rangoli patterns) and Diva paintings to welcome visitors. They may talk about this with you or you may see for yourself if you take children home. Greetings cards are sent and you may receive one or wish to send one to a child's family. Festive foods eaten include sweets and stuffed chapatis and parents may send some to share. Some times for this festival a bonfire will be lit and fireworks enjoyed.

Hindu's believe it is wrong to hurt living things due to their beliefs on rebirth. Sometimes parents may suggest that bad behaviour may cause a child to be reborn as disabled. Some Hindu's also believe disabled people are disabled because they are being punished by God. This view may need careful challenging.

Jewish

Jewish dietary laws require that all food be Kosher. That means animals must be of the right type and slaughtered in a particular way according to their beliefs. To be Kosher an animal must be ruminant (chew its cud) and have split hooves. Kosher animals include cows, sheep and goats. Jewish law forbids the eating of pork, as pigs are not Kosher. Most commonly eaten fowl are kosher, for example chickens, ducks and geese. Animals must also be free from disease to be Kosher. Fish must have fins and scales to be Kosher, so tuna, salmon, flounder and trout are all allowed but shellfish are not.

Jews believe that animal's characteristics are absorbed through eating them. Animals that are Kosher tend to be domesticated animals that are gentle. Carnivores are generally not Kosher as these are associated with characteristics that are believed to be undesirable.

Wine and grape-juice products may only be used if produced by Jews and cheese and milk can only be used if it is from Kosher animals. Hard cheese must not contain rennet. Meat and dairy products are not to be cooked or eaten together and separate cooking utensils should be used to prevent contamination.

Festivals: include Passover (Pesach) held during the spring where each person has a book (Haggadah) and special foods are served. New year, Rosh Hashanah occurs during September, and on the tenth day of the new year Yom Kippur is remembered. Fasting occurs, no work is done, leather shoes must not be worn and makeup is not used, so it might be an idea not to use face paint. During this festival baths are not taken, so avoid messy activities.

Sukkot an autumn festival, Hanukka a winter festival where candles are lit. An eight branched candle stick (Menorah) is used lighting up a branch on each successive evenings. During this festival it is traditional for presents to be given. There will be traditional foods such as Latke (grated potato cakes) which parents may wish to share with the other children and you may receive greetings cards or like to exchange cards with a child's family. Winters end is celebrated by the festival of Purim.

The Jewish Sabbath begins at sundown on Friday and ends at sundown on Saturday. During this time no labour must be undertaken and no fire lit (this includes switching on power).

Muslim

The Muslim naming system is complex. The first name is not always the personal name by which they are addressed. It can be helpful to check which is the first name and which is the family name and to check how parents and children should be addressed.

Story telling is an important part of Muslim tradition. Parents may wish you to include specific books they recommend to enhance this. Remember if they are dual language or in Arabic and children are following the text then the writing will be read from right to left.

Diet: Muslim dietary laws require that meat be Halal. Food that is not Halal and is forbidden is called Haram. To be Halal, meat must be slaughtered in a particular way. Pork and meat from carnivorous animals is forbidden, also fish without fins and scales. Muslims wash and say prayers before and after meals and children will be expecting the eldest person present to start eating first.

The Koran dictates that children should be breastfed for two years, you should respect this and the mother should be encouraged to provide expressed milk or if local arranging for her to call in to feed perhaps at lunch time, may make her feel more comfortable about leaving her child.

Pillars of Faith: There are five beliefs that the followers of Islam base their daily lives on.

Profession of faith - "There is no deity but Allah, and Mohammed is his messenger." Muslims may repeat this phrase several times a day to remind themselves of God's central position in their lives. This should not impact greatly on your childcare provision however other children present may need an explanation of why this phrase is said.

Ritual worship - Muslims are required to pray formally five times a day, at dawn, midday, afternoon, evening and night. If the parent desires you may need to provide a quiet area to allow the children to do this. A child will pray barefoot facing Mecca, so a compass may be useful and somewhere to keep their prayer mat safe will be essential.

Almsgiving - Muslims pay a specified amount of money of their wealth each year to assist the poor and sick.

Fasting - During the month long Ramadan, Muslims refrain from eating and drinking from dawn to sunset. Children under twelve are often exempt from fasting or may fast for shorter periods, perhaps only for one or two days a week. You will need to respect the parents wishes if they require this and you can help by providing alternate activities for the child while any other children present have their meals. Children during this month may be tired due to the change in family routines. They will often wake earlier and go to bed later than usual. On the twenty sixth day of fasting children may be particularly late to bed or be up all night.

During Ramadan there are some activities that may need to be avoided and it is best to check with the parents which of these will apply, and if there are any others you should be aware of. These include strenuous activity if a child is fasting, swimming where a child might swallow water, tasting activities, television, musical and singing activities. It will also be helpful if you are caring for a child who is fasting to have discussed in advance parents wishes should the child become distressed.

Pilgrimage to Mecca - Islam requires every believer to make at least one visit to Mecca in their lifetime if means are available.

Key Concepts: Modesty and Cleanliness. Muslims wear clothes that cover their bodies. Men must cover themselves from waist to knees and women from head to toes except for hands and face. This usually applies to children also. Before prayers and meals, washing of hands face, arms, head, ears and feet are required.

Worship: The building used for communal worship is called a Mosque and their Holy Scripture the Qur'an. The Qur'an must be kept on a shelf higher than any other books. Friday is holy day for Muslims and prayers are obligatory.

Festivals: There are two key Muslim festivals. Children sometimes call Eid-ul-Fitr 'our Christmas' because they have presents and sweets and a celebration meal. Hand painting at this festival is called Mehndi. Greetings cards are sent. When making these cards Arabic words and letters can be used along with abstract patterns. It is against the religion to have pictures of people on them. Eid-ul-Adha is a festival including a sacrificial feast with pastries nuts and raisins, lamb, rice, chicken and fish, to mark the end of the pilgrimage to Mecca.

Sikh

Sikh first names can be unisex. Surnames may include caste and family names, plus Singh (lion) for boys or Kaur (princess) for girls. It is practical to check how parents and children should be addressed.

Sikh do not eat beef. They may eat other meats although some Sikh may be vegetarian. Food may be eaten with the fingers.

Many Sikh believe hair should not be cut and young children may wear special head coverings (patka). From the age of about eleven boys will begin to wear turbans. It is considered an insult to remove a turban as it is a symbol of faith. Sharing and music are considered important and that all people are equal. They believe they should share celebrations and feasts with everyone from irrespective of religion, so you may be invited to join in celebrations or share some of their cuisine.

The Sikh culture has five symbols worn or carried to indicate they are Sikh. Note: not all Sikh will adhere to this tradition. The symbols are a steel bangle, a comb, a pair of white shorts, a curved knife, long hair and a turban or head covering.

Festivals: celebrations include the birth of Guru Gobind Singh (January/February), Baisakhi (April), Diwali (October/November) and the birth of Guru Nanak (October/November).

Buddhist

Buddhists are generally vegetarian, though some may eat some meat or fish. They usually allow milk. The Buddha encouraged vegetarianism, because he considered the killing of an animal an act of violence. In fact Buddhists deplore the killing of all living things and even swatting flying insects will not be appreciated and may upset a child.

Buddhist ceremonies are held on days of full moons and they wear brightly coloured masks for their festivals including Wesak.

Seventh Day Adventist

Seventh Day Adventists like to live life as simply and naturally as possible. Trips to the theatre, and cinema should be avoided. Watching of television and videos should be avoided and dancing is forbidden.

Diet: Their dietary laws forbid pork, and other meats may not be eaten. Most eat eggs, milk and milk products and many are vegetarian. When offering beverages to parents and children remember no caffeine is allowed, e.g. cola, coffee or tea and if drinking socially with the parents, they cannot drink alcohol or partake of tobacco products.

Jehovah's Witness

Jehovah's Witnesses believe the bibles teachings. They actively share with others information about God, referred to as Jehovah and about his son, Jesus Christ. Their beliefs differ from other mainstream Christian faiths in several areas. They do not believe in the Holy Trinity, but believe in Satan as an active force responsible for the worlds problems. Although they do not celebrate Christmas or Easter they remember Christ's death.

Family is important to witnesses. Fathers are seen as the head of the household, but the importance of women is recognised. Children have strict rules to follow.

It is important to be aware of possible breeches of confidentiality as Witnesses are permitted to disclose confidential information to their Witness Elders, should the information be relating to a matter of gross wrongdoing. You may also like to be aware that lying is considered to be wrong.

Witnesses do not celebrate any holidays or festivals belonging to another religion with the exception of Christ's death (Memorial) and this includes Christmas, Easter, Halloween, New Year, Sukkot, Mothers Day, Diwali, Valentines Day, Guy Fawkes etc. Witnesses believe these originate from false religions and that God disapproves of them. Although wishing a Witness 'Happy Birthday' or 'Happy Christmas' may cause offence to some, they respect the right of others to celebrate these holidays. When planning your activities remember children do not celebrate birthdays, this includes eating any birthday cakes or exchanging birthday presents and cards. However, other gifts can be exchanged at different times of the year. Jehovah's Witnesses take a neutral view of politics and this includes not singing the National Anthem.

Blood transfusions are considered wrong, blood is viewed as sacred. Witnesses will decline blood even in an emergency. A Witness who receives blood may be excommunicated. However, blood replacement fluids or blood substitutes are allowed, full details should be recorded for use in emergency situations. A medical directive (information sheet) should be available, outlining both the Jehovah's Witness bibles view and any legal responsibilities.

Diet: Anything that contains blood or blood products such as Black Pudding is unacceptable. Meat from an animal that has been strangled, or shot and not bled properly is also not allowed as it is not inline with the Jehovah's Witness bible teachings.

Paganism

Paganism is a very diverse nature-worshipping religion with many distinct traditions. They may believe in one or many gods. Some groups concentrate on specific traditions, practices or elements such as witchcraft or Celtic traditions. The pagan family includes Wiccans, Druids, Sacred Ecologists, Shamanists and Heathens which include Odinists, Asatru and Vanatru.

The seasonal differences between hemispheres mean solar festivals are celebrated on different dates in the Southern hemisphere. Commonly followed festivals include the following where the pagan year comprises of a seasonal cycle of eight festivals spaced at intervals of six to seven weeks.

Samhain- This festival is Celtic in origin and marks the day of the Dead. It falls between autumn and winter in October/November. For pagans it is a time for honouring departed spirits and reflecting on changes in their lives. It is also a time when children born during the year are welcomed. This festival is regarded by some pagans as the start of the new year, considering it as the time when the goddess is pregnant, she will give birth to the God at Yule. Life begins before birth and therefore the year begins at Samhain. Traditional activities include celebratory feasts and apple bobbing. This festival is not usually followed by Heathens.

Winter Solstice/Yule- This is a solar festival falling in December on the shortest day. This is one of the oldest winter celebrations in the world. The log burns to conquer darkness, banish evil and bring luck for the coming year. This festival is regarded as the new year by followers of the Norse religions.

Imbolc- Also called Oimelc and Candlemas is celebrated in February and marks the start of the farming season. Celebrations are centred around fire and rituals may include making of candles and planting of spring flowers. Celtic in origin.

Spring Equinox- Celebrated in March, part of the solar calendar when both day and night are of equal length. Associated with renewal of life of the earth and the coming of spring. Traditional activities may include planting seeds, egg races, egg hunts, egg painting and egg eating.

Beltane- This Celtic festival falls in April/May on the cusp between spring and summer. It is a fire festival celebrating the fertility of the coming year. Traditional activities include leaping over fire to bring good fortune and maypole dancing.

Midsummer Solstice- Is the festival of mid summer, sometimes called Litha. It is part of the solar calendar and falls in June on the longest day. At mid summer Pagans honour the suns strength and the divine powers that create life. It is a time of plenty and celebration. Pagans may stay up to watch the sun rising on the first morning of summer.

Lughnasadh- Some times called Lammas, is a festival of Celtic origin celebrated in August. It is a thanksgiving for the harvest. Festivities may include sports and games linked to the harvest such as cheeses rolling.

Autumn Equinox- This forms part of the solar calendar and occurs in September when both day and night are of equal length. It is a time for pagans to reflect on the past season. A harvest festival may be held to give thanks for food to last the winter. For many Pagans, this festival honours old age and the coming of winter.

Other festivals you may encounter include the Blot (Bloat) and Symbel/Sumbel. Childminders caring for children from Pagan families could ask parents if there are any specific books they can recommend which will help them in their understanding.

Rastifarian

Rastifarian is a way of life and not a religion. There are links with both the Jewish faith and Christianity. Family and friends are important in this culture as is music. Music tends to be Reggae, the songs containing life stories and beliefs. Rastafarian colours are green, black, red and gold (the colours of the Ethiopian flag). Children's arts and crafts are much appreciated, with natural materials preferred.

Rastifarians may be vegetarian or vegan. They eat 'ital' food, which is food that is whole, or in its natural state. They do not eat pork or scaleless fish and many will avoid preserved and processed foods.

Rastifarians never cut their hair, it is a symbol of strength. Women always keep their hair covered. Where dreadlocks are worn, combs or shampoo may not be appropriate. Parents may prefer the dreadlocks to be brushed gently. They may be tied back with braid or ribbon to keep them out of children's eyes, or they may come with scarves or caps which they can wear to the same effect.

On holy days white clothes will be worn with a knitted hat (Tam). Celebrations include the new year, Haile Selassie's birthday, and the birthday of Marcus Gravey. During prayers children will hold their hands in a special way to represent heart and spear, the symbols of peace and war.

Somali

Children from Somali may speak Somali or Swahili and are mainly Muslim. Children will have Muslim names plus a traditional Somali name. It is incorrect to call them by the prefix. The Somali have a clan system and it should not be assumed that two Somali children will find it easy to become friends. The Somali people have a very strong oral tradition and there is little in writing available on their history or tradition. Many Somali are refugees and may be traumatised and distressed and may be living in large single parent families.

Somali tend to be Muslim and all the usual Muslim festivals will be celebrated. Girls normally keep their legs covered. Some girls will keep their heads covered but it is not compulsory. Boys will wear trousers and not shorts, they may wear a sarong when at home. Diet will be Halal.

Somali children may have difficulties with English. They often feel frustrated and or misunderstood leading to aggressive behaviour. Somali children do not generally instigate conflicts but will retaliate when provoked. Revenge is an obligation of their honour in their culture, all other options are construed as weakness or defeat. If you make a promise to a child or parent it must be kept or they will lose faith and their trust in you.

Chinese

Chinese names are frequently given as the family name first followed by the personal name or names. If a child or their parents have two personal names they should both be used. Note: some Chinese families have adapted their naming system to the Western naming practice.

Much of Chinese food is stir fried with rice or noodles or steamed. Meals often finish with a clear soup to clear the palate. Children learn to use chopsticks at around the same time as those using cutlery.

New year is well celebrated and celebrations last for three days. Houses are traditionally decorated with spring blossoms, fish pictures, silk banners and red and gold. There may be pictures of door Gods to prevent evil spirits entering. During these celebrations they may become temporarily vegetarian. Tangerines, nuts and melon seeds can be served for luck. Special cakes and sweetmeats may be brought for you to share. This is the time for dragon dancing and fire crackers. The main religions in China are Taoism, Confucius and Buddhism.

African-Caribbean

The majority of African-Caribbeans are Christian with a Rastafarian minority. They may not refer to themselves as African-Caribbean so check how they identify themselves. Some cultural factors which affect children's behaviour and our perception of their behaviour can include their avoidance of eye contact and their particularly emotional and physical expression of behaviour when stressed.

Children may be expected to unquestioningly obey their parents requests, taking time to adjust to your required behaviours. Parents may not like their children to address an adult by their first name as this is considered to be disrespectful. Children will use a title to address you or may call you 'aunty'.

Children's hair may need special oils or moisturisers as it tends to be dry. It can break or tear easily and care is needed especially when drying it. If you are combing hair it is helpful to begin combing from the ends and work back towards the roots. Hold the hair to the head just above where you are combing to prevent pulling the hair and to protect it from breaking. The hair is usually washed leaving the braids intact even when they contain beads. Children's skin may also need moisturising to prevent dryness, particularly in winter to prevent chapping.

Traditional foods may include green bananas, pumpkin, avocado, bread fruit, mango, pawpaw, goat or mutton curries, fish, black eye beans, chick peas and corn meal.

Eastern Europeans

Eastern Europe encompasses Belarus, Bulgaria, Czech Republic, Hungary, Moldavia, Poland, Romania, Russia, Slovakia and the Ukraine. Eastern Europeans practice a range of faiths including, Christian, Muslim, Roman Catholic, Jewish and Protestant and encompass a wide range of cultures and languages.

Customs celebrated are often linked to religious festivals and New Years Day, Easter and Christmas are celebrated throughout the region.

Polish families are frequently Catholic. To them Christmas Eve (Vigil Day) is more sacred than Christmas Day and a special dinner of thirteen courses, without meat, is served. All Souls day is for commemorating the dead and a special Kutia, barley porridge is served.

Czech families Christmas celebrations begin on 5th of December with Saint Nicholas day. Christmas dinner is traditionally carp. They also celebrate Witches night on 30th April with bonfires to celebrate the ending of the cold weather.

Czech families are used to taking shoes off when entering a household and would expect you to do the same if visiting. If you give flowers to families ensure they are odd in number. Even numbers of flowers are reserved for funeral bouquets.

11. Caring For Children With Special Needs

Special Needs is an umbrella term encompassing a large number of diagnoses. In the past, special needs have been considered by many to be the more severe or obvious needs that children may experience. These needs generally arise due to conditions or disorders that have a medical diagnosis after assessment by a paediatrician. These severe or obvious needs often result from a variety of syndromes including deafness, blindness, autism or cerebral palsy. However many children may have less obvious or short term special needs that are determined by observation and assessment of a child's learning, development and behaviour.

The Medical Model

The medical model is a more traditional method of looking at disability. It puts the emphasis on the child to adapt or cope with the environment they are in and their attempt to conform with society. In the medical model the impairment is the condition and the disability is caused by their condition. The disability is seen as something that should be treated and made as 'normal' as possible to fit in with society.

The Social Model

In the social model the word impairment is used to describe a loss of physical, sensory or intellectual function in individuals. The word disability is used to describe the ways that a child with impairments is excluded from full participation in society's activities, such as lack of physical access, lack of opportunities, education or denial of rights are the barriers that they face. This way of looking at things shows that it is the environment not the impairment that creates the disability, by removing the obstacles in the environment we are removing the disability.

Social or Medical Model?

It may help to understand the difference between the medical and social model of disability if you consider it for an individual.

Amy has a hearing impairment.

Using the medical model:	Using the social model:
Amy has a problem. How is she going to cope with this problem? She will have to adapt to our setting.	Amy has an impairment. What support or actions can we take to help her overcome possible barriers? We will ask her how we can adapt our setting.
Result : Exclusion Here the problem is seen as being with the child and it is up to them to meet society's rules.	Result : Inclusion With this model the onus is on society to include the individual and adapt to their needs.

The social model is now widely accepted as the correct way to think about disabilities, particularly by those that have an impairment or work with disabled people. Remember impairments may also be temporary. Glue ear causes hearing impairments and a child with a broken limb has a temporary physical impairment.

With all disabilities the child as an individual with their need for love, care and attention is more important than the disability. It is important to think of all children as individuals, whether they have special needs or not. It is particularly important not to assume two children with the same impairment have the same needs. Parents will be able to provide you with information on any more complex needs. Care should be taken to ensure children with a disability are not made to feel younger than their chronological age because they have not reached 'normal' milestones in their development.

Using the Appropriate Language

When working with children with special needs you will hear and use a range of different words and abbreviations, at first it may seem confusing and knowing which words to use in what context will take practice. This is partly because individuals define their own situation and also terminology which is acceptable changes over time. There are words that are no longer acceptable as it is felt they refer to special needs in a negative or derogatory way.

It is important to use the correct language, as the way you refer to a child will convey to the child your feelings about them. If you speak about their needs in a negative or derogatory way you will lower their self-esteem and confidence. The way in which you react to and talk about a child's special needs will also impact on how others treat them. You should always refer to the child first and then the disability. For example, Thomas is autistic and not autistic Thomas. To the other children you care for and to parents you may be a role model particularly if they have not had much contact with children with special needs, they will mimic your responses.

Terminology

As language is constantly evolving this section can only be a guide.

Child with Disabilities - This is not a correct term, children do not have disabilities they have impairments. The environment they are in can cause them disabilities however, in which case, use the term disabled children.

Learning Disability - An individual with an impairment that impacts on 'normal' acquisition, understanding or retention of information. This could interfere with language skills, organisational skills or social skills.

Handicap - This is not generally an accepted term, and can be offensive, use disability instead.

Special Needs - Adaptations, specific to an individual, that can be made to the environment to prevent a child with an impairment from encountering barriers relating to their impairment.

Special Educational Needs - Adaptations that can be made to the learning environment to prevent a child with an impairment from encountering barriers related to their impairment

Special - When used referring to a disabled person can be viewed as patronising.

Ability - The capacity to do something.

Disabled - Implies broken and people with disabilities are not broken.

Cripple - This is not a correct term, instead use physically impaired.

Birth Defect - Babies cannot be returned as defective. A more appropriate phrase is congenital disability.

Mentally Handicapped - This terms become obsolete in favour of learning difficulties/disabilities.

Gifted - A child significantly ahead of his/her peers in a particular or several areas of learning.

Spastic - People with Cerebral Palsy used to be described as spastic due to their difficulties in controlling muscles. However this term has been dropped from use as it has become commonly used as an insult for someone viewed as incompetent.

Sensory Impairment - A loss of sensory function, this is most commonly sight or hearing. The degree of loss can vary from total loss of function to partial function.

Retarded - No longer acceptable, use mentally impaired.

Disorder - Having a disruption of normal physical or mental functions.

Invalid - A person or child made weak or disabled by illness or injury.

Suffers From - Use living with, as 'suffers' implies something to be cured.

Answering Children's Questions

If the children you care for have questions about a child in your care with special needs they should not be told not to ask. Prejudice often arises from a lack of knowledge about a disability. You should reassure them that it is acceptable for them to ask questions as long as it is in a respectful manner. If children have any concerns or misconceptions these should be addressed in language that is appropriate to their level of development.

A child with special needs may be happy to answer questions about themselves or show how any special equipment they use works. You should not assume however that a child will be happy to discuss their disabilities. By discussing special needs even if you do not care for a child who has them you will help children learn about diversity.

Answering Parents Questions

Parents can also have questions if you care for a child with special needs. They may be worried about the impact this will have on their child. You should be reassuring and honest about how it may affect your routine. Discuss the benefits to all the children in sharing time together.

Special Educational Needs

Children are classed as having Special Educational Needs (SEN) if they have learning difficulties that make it significantly more difficult for them to learn than other children of a similar age. Children who are 'gifted' i.e. exceptionally intelligent also have SEN. Special educational needs are not always lifelong and some 20% of children may have special educational needs at some time in their childhood, of these only 2% will be statemented (Alcott 2000). Short term needs may arise for a variety of reasons including illness or accidents and temporary emotional problems.

If you think a child may have special educational needs that have not already been assessed you first need to discuss this with the parents. If you belong to an accredited network a SENCO (Special Educational Needs Co-ordinator) should be available to offer assistance, otherwise it is up to the parents to seek advice from their doctor or health visitor. If the child attends school or nursery the parents will also be able to seek advice there.

Special Educational Needs Codes of Practice

The Special Educational Needs Codes of Practice provide advice to Education Authorities, maintained schools, early education settings and others about carrying out their statutory duties to identify, assess and make provision for children's special educational needs.

In relation to early education settings, such as childminders, they cover the role of the SENCO (Special Educational Needs Co-ordinator), individual education plans, statementing, statutory assessments and provision.

The guidance in the codes usually follow four main principles:
❑ A child with special educational needs should have their needs met
❑ The special educational needs of children will normally be met in mainstream schools or settings
❑ The views of the child should be sought and taken into account
❑ Parents have a vital role to play in supporting their child's education

Children with special educational needs should be offered full access to a broad, balanced and relevant education, including an appropriate curriculum for the Foundation Stage and National Curriculum (Special Educational Needs Code of Practice, Department for Education and Skills, 2001).

Early Years Action / School Action

If a child needs extra or different help you and their nursery or school may be required to show or teach the child things a little differently. Such as providing extra help and monitoring their progress to see if the extra help is working.

Early Years Action Plus / School Action Plus

If the extra or different help is not working you will need to liaise with a SENCO and you may receive help from a speech and language therapist or other specialist. If the child is still not making progress then statementing is the next step.

Statementing

Statementing is the production of a document, based on an assessment and professional opinions, which will set out a child's needs and all the extra help needed by the child which can be provided within the resources normally available e.g. money, staff time and special equipment. If a child is undergoing statementing then a parent may wish to have extra discussions about their child with you. This process may seem a frightening time to some parents, as they will have been given 29 days to say whether they agree to an assessment being made, and they may need your reassurance or ask for help and advice during this time.

The first stage of the process of 'statementing' is a formal negotiation process between the local education authority and the parents. It involves a detailed examination of a child's special educational needs and what additional help may be required. You may find a parent would like some help with considerations when deciding what they think would be best for their child.

The Local Education Authority (LEA) will provide information for the parents about sources available for advice and information, and about the help children can receive in state schools. Parents will also be asked if there is anyone else they would like the LEA to speak to about their child, e.g. the child's childminder or Health Visitor.

The LEA then gathers information and advice about the child's special needs from their school, doctor, childminder, if applicable and an educational psychologist. Parent's are also asked to provide information and views about their child's needs.

During the assessment process the parents have a right to attend with their child any interview, medical test or other test. The child may need to be seen alone at some point during the assessment to enable the difference in behaviour to be noted. Parents may also make use of a named person to help them express their views and offer them support and this can include naming their childminder.

Once all the advice and comments about a child's educational needs are received, the LEA decides whether to make a statement of special educational needs for the child. A proposed statement is then provided for the parent to enable views and alterations before the statement is finalised.

Adapting the Environment

For some children with special needs adaptations may be needed to the environment. Necessary adaptations will depend on the individual needs of the child. Parents will be able to tell you what equipment is used at home, possibly providing you with any specialist equipment needed.

When thinking about adaptations try considering each stage of an activity and how a child with special needs may have difficulties. Usually you will know what the specific difficulties a child may encounter are. If you are thinking about general adaptations try not to assume that difficulties might just arise for those in a wheelchair.

Example: What adaptations might be needed for using a toilet?

Stages with using a toilet:
1. Opening door
2. Reaching light switch
3. Lifting Lid/Getting on to toilet
4. Supporting self in a sitting position
5. Reaching toilet paper/cleaning self
6. Getting off toilet
7. Reaching sink
8. Controlling taps/soap

Once you have broken the activity down into stages consider what problems might be encountered at each stage. How can you assist a child with poor coordination with lifting the seat lid? How will a child with a visual impairment know which tap is hot or cold?

If you are having trouble thinking of possible problems within the environment, think about it from the view of a disabled child. Attempt to move around the bathroom blindfolded, wearing thick gloves or without standing up, what problems do you encounter?

Adaptations could include support bars for the child to hold onto whilst on the toilet, putting the soap on a rope so that a child with poor coordination will find it easier to control or having a large end on a pull chord for the light so it is easy to grab.

General Adaptations

Creative play - Because of the nature of fantasy and creative play most children can take part without special adaptations. They can imagine or create whatever they want to, a disability can become part of a fantasy activity when playing with others.

Care should be taken to ensure a child with special needs is not marginalised or excluded.

Computer Use - Tracker or roller ball mice may be easier to use. Specialist software is also available to meet a range of different needs.

Blue Tac - good for holding toys in place on tables or trays and for holding paper still for drawing or painting.

Self Adhesive Velcro - Used with a fluffy glove can encourage page turning with board books and enable puzzles to be completed.

Dycom - Mats of tacky plastic to hold things still, such as toys and dinner plates.

Limited Mobility - A beanbag or large cushions can help with support whilst doing floor activities or a large cushioned mat for outdoor activities. Suitable chair for support at mealtimes and for activities at a table. Concept activities may need adaptations particularly for positional and relationship concepts as children may not be able to climb over or under equipment, but could pass over or under a sheet for example. Items of equipment should be within easy reach, examples of this could be items suitable to be pulled out and over a wheelchair, raising the sand tray on blocks. Tactile experiences are also good for children with limited mobility as they can explore the environment with fingers, arms and hands. Water can be fun, even if they are only able to dabble hands and feet in a raised bowl of water. Wheelchair ramps may be required for entry if you have a raised step. Large melamine chopping boards can be used to span a wheelchair when cooking and some bowls have a base which can be attached to this board for mixing activities. Puzzle boards are useful, they will sit over a wheelchair and the pieces adhere and cannot fall to the floor. Paint brush handles can be extended for use with an easel. Children may require special cutlery and crockery if they have insufficient grip or uncontrolled movements. Examples of these include, plates with wide rims and deep centres, non slip place mats, angled cutlery and twin handled cups.

Visual Impairment - Increase provision of tactile, scented and noisy toys, larger toys and bright colours. Place the brightly coloured toys on a dark background to increase the contrast. You can use cues such as timers, bells and lights. A hula hoop can serve as a boundary and confine toys assisting children in controlling their immediate play area.

Hearing Impairment - Increase use of vibrations for toys and play, make use of echoes on outings, flashing warning lights.

Speech and Language Impairment - Use clear shortened instructions, possibly with the use of Makaton or Pecs.

Makaton & British Sign Language

Makaton may be used with children who have learning or communication difficulties where recommended by parents or specialists. It is based on British Sign Language and is a pictorial language using hand pictures and shapes to communicate. Makaton is a speech aid and should always be accompanied by speech.

British Sign Language is more complex with its own grammar and regional variations. It is a signed communication involving movements of hands, shoulders, face and head used within the deaf community.

Many colleges and web communities offer courses to help you learn the basics.

Pecs

Pecs may be used where recommended by specialists. It is a picture exchange communication system and not normally accompanied by speech. It is an augmentative system of communication which relies on picture recognition for items or activities a child may want. These are exchanged to receive the desired item, a biscuit for example.

Braille

Braille allows non sighted people and children to read by touch. Braille consists of raised dots that represent letters or words. Each letter is represented by a different pattern of dots within a 2x3 block. Braille can be handwritten or written using a typewriter like machine. It is written from right to left so that when it is turned over to show the raised dots it is read from left to right.

Helping Children Understand Visual and Hearing Impairments

Children may be curious about blindness and deafness. It can be hard to explain to children what this means, letting children experience these can be the best way for them to learn.

Provide a range of tactile items e.g. braille writing, toys, and objects for children to explore with and without closing their eyes. Find braille in the community for children to experience, lift buttons often have braille on as well as numbers, some lifts will have voices announcing the floors.

Provide some noisy toys, musical instruments and a video to be explored with and without ear defenders or material wrapped over ears to muffle sound. These two activities may help children understand their deaf or visually impaired playmates better.

Wheelchairs

Wheelchairs should not be seen as negative or confining. They allow users to gain extra independence and freedom. When you are planning to care for a child that uses a wheelchair it will be important to discuss with the child and parents about access and transportation. You will need to check that the doors are all wide enough to accommodate the chair and bathroom facilities are accessible. A child who uses a chair may also be able to walk short distances and use the chair to conserve energy or to move more freely.

You will need to plan carefully any outings you take and check in advance how accessible they are. You may also be able to acquire a disabled parking permit if necessary. Other children may need help to understand that the wheelchair or other walking aids are not toys to be played with.

Introductions to Specific Special Needs

Physical Disabilities

Children with multiple impairments have complex needs. Physical impairments may mean a child has a physical disability. The impairments may be genetic, congenital or the result of injury or illness. These physical disabilities can be short term, such as having broken limbs, or long term.

Disabilities can delay a child's development both in learning and mobility and may require equality of access for the provision and access to adapted resources to improve their outcomes. For example, a mobile child with a physical impairment can explore even if they are visually or hearing impaired especially if they can reach out for what they want to examine or play with. A child who is physically impaired and not mobile may have to rely on others to keep them supplied with interesting objects to investigate or play with.

Learning Difficulties

A child with significantly greater difficulties in learning than those in their peer group or a disability that impedes learning is described as having a learning disability.

Several factors may combine to cause a learning disability. There are many physical disabilities which may affect children's intellectual ability, these include Downs Syndrome, Autism, Cerebral Palsy, and sensory impairments.

Dyslexia

Early signs of dyslexia may be late speech development, co-ordination difficulties such as trouble getting dressed and putting shoes on the correct feet, tripping, bumping into things and falling over. A school age child may have difficulties with reading and spelling, putting words/letters in the right order, remembering times tables, and take longer than average to do written work. School can be a stressful place for a child with dyslexia. They may be teased or bullied by peers and become frustrated by many things.

Dyslexia affects the learning of a child in one of or a combination of reading, spelling, writing and sometimes numeracy/language. Children may also have weaknesses in short-term memory, sequencing, visual perception, spoken language and motor skills. Children with dyslexia may jumble phrases, or substitute words (e.g. 'lampshade' for 'lamppost'), have difficulty learning rhymes and show little interest in letters or words.

Dyslexia is independent of social background and does not mean that a child has no ability in areas that involve reading or writing, they may have strengths in particular areas.

Dyspraxia

This condition was once called the 'clumsy child' syndrome. Children with dyspraxia have difficulty in planning and carrying out complex movements.

Fine or gross motor skills are hard to learn and they may be hesitant or awkward in performing them. Language development may also be delayed or impaired. Children with dyspraxia have trouble understanding the messages their senses convey to the brain and relating them to the actions required. Children can be intellectually equal to their peers but they have difficulty planning and organising thoughts i.e. they will forget basic essentials for school such as pencils. Some children with dyspraxia have moderate learning difficulties.

A child with dyspraxia may exhibit a number of the following characteristics:

❑ Difficulty with writing or drawing.
❑ Dislike of games, climbing frames and outside play.
❑ Difficulty with ball skills.
❑ Messy eating and drinking.
❑ Slow or has trouble dressing themselves.
❑ Difficulty or inability riding a bicycle.
❑ Difficulty with concentration.
❑ Falls over frequently.
❑ Disruptive (poor concentration).
❑ Cannot stand on one leg, finds difficulty hopping or jumping.
❑ Difficulty copying from text or writing down dictated information.

There may be additional problems with writing, reading, spelling or speech. Children improve in some areas with age and practice.

Attention Deficit Hyperactive Disorder (ADHD)

Symptoms of ADHD include hyperactivity, poor attention impulsive behaviour and social difficulties. Children may fidget if asked to sit still or get up from activities. They may run around and it may be hard to gain their attention or calm them down. A child may have trouble waiting in turn and interrupt other children. They may also be clumsy or accident prone. ADHD can also be associated with delayed language development.

It can be hard to diagnose as these are behaviours found in many young children. Parents may not be given a definite diagnosis until after the age of six or when a child starts attending school.

ADHD is more common in boys and generally improves as a child gets older. Children, usually only those over five, may take medication, usually Ritalin. Behavioural management is usually the main form of treatment for the condition. Reinforcing good behaviour and discouraging unacceptable behaviour. You should get the child's attention before giving instructions and make them in clear, easily understood language. Activities should be short and with regular breaks.

Hearing Impairment

There is a wide range of levels of hearing impairment. Not all children are profoundly deaf, some may just have a mild hearing loss. Some hearing impairments can be temporary such as 'Glue Ear'. Hearing impairments can affect a child's language and communication skills.

Some children may use hearing aids, others employ signing or lip reading to help with communication. The child's parents will be able to explain the communication strategies they use. They may also be able to provide information on sign language, or demonstrations to you and the other children in your care. Mild hearing losses may not interfere with communication, children can be very adaptable and may compensate for it, sitting near you as you read a story, or lip reading.

You can help a child by reducing noise in the environment. Carpets, rugs, and soft wall coverings can help make a childcare environment less noisy. Background sounds such as a radio or television interfere with clear communication. If a child ca not hear speech clearly then they will have more difficulty interacting with people. Noisy environments also can be a problem for children who wear hearing aids, especially in understanding conversation. You should keep in mind hearing aids help the child hear better, but they do not restore perfect hearing. They also enhance all noises around a child which can be very distracting.

When you speak to a child face them so they can see as well as hear what you are saying. Speak normally, without exaggerated lip movement, but also speak clearly. Do not stand in front of bright lights or talk from another room. Using gestures with hands and expression can also help convey your point.

Make sure you have the child's attention before speaking to them. You can touch their shoulder or arm to get their attention if they are busy playing. If you need their attention immediately or you need to gain their attention from a distance try flashing the lights on and off a few times.

Be prepared to repeat things if necessary. If you cannot get the message across one way rearrange the sentence and present it in a different way, perhaps with the key words at the beginning of the sentence. Do not ever say to a child 'Oh, it doesn't matter, it's not important', this can be humiliating.

You also need to plan for emergencies. It is a good idea to add flashing lights to a smoke alarm if you care for a child with severe hearing impairments as they may not hear an audio alarm. You should practice what happens in an emergency so the child knows what is happening if they are unable to hear what you are saying.

Visual Impairment

Visual impairments can vary in severity and the effect they have on the child. Each child is an individual and they and their parents will be able to tell you best what provisions you need to make.

You should take care to keep doors fully open or fully closed, and furniture in the same place, so that the child knows where it is safe to walk. Sharp corners, such as the edges of tables, may need to be padded for younger children. If you have rugs make sure there are no curled up edges. Outside play areas should be smooth with no uneven paving slabs that could be tripped over.

It may help a new child to visit several times so they can become comfortable with the environment before staying on their own for the first time. They may also feel more comfortable exploring if there are less children present.

Children with visual impairments may not be able to see the body language that we often unconsciously use to aid communication. For example, they may not see you looking towards them when you talk, and so not realise it is them you are addressing. Use their name so they are aware who you are talking to. Hand gestures may also not be helpful, in this case you must use spoken directions, for example, 'The red brick is by your left foot'. Visually impaired children may not catch a disapproving look that will alert most children to the fact they are doing something unacceptable, in this case, use your tone of voice to express your meaning.

Children should be helped to develop their sense of touch and hearing as much as possible to help compensate for their visual impairment. The earlier such skills are encouraged the earlier a child can develop a sense of independence. A sense of touch will help children to become independent in dressing themselves, locating themselves and learning braille if required. They will use their fingers to collect information which their experiences and your guidance will help them interpret. Textures are useful for helping little fingers become more sensitive.

Use lots of descriptions when talking about things, describe colours, shapes, the weather, and things that are happening around them. Where possible let children hold an object so they can associate it with what you are talking about.

Children who are blind can sometimes be hesitant about reaching out, touching and exploring. Ensure toys are contained close to the child so they can be reached and cannot roll away. Toys they cannot reach will have gone for good from their point of view. 'Feely' boxes and toys are fun for non mobile children. For toddlers and older children fill a cloth bag with toys and household items. It can be taped open to the floor with masking tape to prevent excess movement and place a child's hands into the opening, or use crates for containing the items. A space blanket can produce sound and visual stimulation. Visual stimulation may be appropriate for some visually impaired children. Rope Christmas lights are an inexpensive visual stimulation and can make a change from the tactile stimulation provided by sand and water.

Speech and Language Impairment

Six percent of the pre-school and school aged population may have speech or language impairments (Afasic 1998). They have problems with articulation, language, fluency, or voice which affects their ability to learn or to communicate effectively with others. Educational help required by these children will depend on the severity of the impairment. Some children will benefit from the one to one conversations with their childminder and others may require more specialised help from experts in special education or speech therapists.

Epilepsy

Epilepsy is seizures caused by a disturbance in the brain function. The severity will vary for each child, from mild and hardly noticeable, causing a funny sensation or loss of concentration, to convulsions and loss of consciousness.

There are many types of epilepsy, and not all include fits. Two types are:

❏ **Generalised Absence** (previously called Petit Mal). A child having this type of fit may have a blank look with a slight twitching or blinking. This usually lasts only for a few seconds, children may not even be aware that it has happened.

❏ **Generalised Tonic-Clonic** (previously called Grand Mal) is the most common seizure type in children. This involves a stiffening of the body, there may be loss of consciousness, eye rolling, and the face and lips may go blue. This is followed by the clonic phase of rhythmic convulsions and usually lasts a couple of minutes. Children may sleep after an attack.

Drugs are often used to control the seizures and if the child's epilepsy is triggered by stimuli such as flickering lights, care must be taken to avoid these.

The first aid course childminders are required to take should give you information on dealing with a fit. The following are the basics. When a child has a fit:

DO - Protect them from injury by moving any sharp or hard objects, and move them away from danger if they are having a partial seizure. Cushion the child's head if they fall down. When the convulsions have stopped, place the child in the recovery position This will also be covered in your first aid course. The child may be upset, so reassure them and talk to them. Stay with them until they have regained full consciousness. Talk with the other children and reassure them about what is going on. Record the fit in your accident/incident book.

DON'T - Try to restrain the child, put anything in their mouth or force anything between their teeth. Do not move the child, unless they are in danger. Do not give the child anything to eat or drink until they have fully regained consciousness.

If a child fits for longer than five minutes, longer than usual for them, is injured (and needs emergency treatment), or does not regain consciousness then call the emergency services.

Cystic Fibrosis (CF)

This is an inherited disease, caused by a faulty gene. Symptoms can include chronic lung infections, liver problems, diabetes, inability to absorb fats and nutrients from food, pancreatitis and gallstones. Children may cough frequently but they are not infectious. Most children with CF can join in with whatever activities the other children are doing. They may tire faster, but will still enjoy exercising.

When caring for a child with Cystic Fibrosis you may have to learn physiotherapy techniques to help keep their lungs free from fluid. They may also need to take vitamin and enzyme supplements and have a diet high in calories and protein. Extra calories ideas include using butter and vegetable oils, mayonnaise, cream cheese, cream, brown sugar, syrup, powdered milk, cheese and peanut butter. All of which can be added to snacks and meals as appropriate. Children with CF need extra salt and especially in hot weather. The parents will provide you with the details of the individual needs of their child and you may need to meet with a physiotherapist to learn the techniques involved in keeping airways clear.

Down's Syndrome

Down's Syndrome is caused by a chromosome abnormality. It may affect the child's development and appearance. Characteristics may include almond-shaped eyes, a small jaw causing the tongue to appear big, poor muscle tone and increased susceptibility to infections. Heart disease is also more common. A child with Down's Syndrome may have delayed speech or never develop speech and you may be asked to use Makaton with a child to help their speech development.

A stimulating environment and positive attitude will help a child reach their full potential. Children with Down's Syndrome do not always see connections between actions. They may need instructions repeated several times to aid their understanding. They may not immediately see how to transfer learning from one situation to another. Repetitions of activities and instructions are most helpful. The child's reaction times are slower, and patience and time is required for best results.

Angelman Syndrome

Angelman Syndrome (AS) is caused by a chromosome abnormality and is commonly diagnosed between three and seven years of age when characteristic behaviours and features are more evident. Children usually have a severe developmental delay, minimal use of words or are non verbal and movement or balance disorders. They may have seizures, sleep disorders and feeding problems.

These are often happy, smiley affectionate children who enjoy laughter. They enjoy 'rough and tumble' games, noisy or musical toys and are frequently fascinated by water. Children often learn to communicate using Makaton or Pecs. Walking may be delayed until they are three to four years old although 10% will not achieve walking.

Autism & Aspergers

The causes of Autism are still under debate. It affects boys more often than girls. Autism varies in severity (spectrum), the milder end of the spectrum is referred to as Aspergers Syndrome. Abnormal behaviours associated with autism usually develop when a child is about a year old. They are usually all present by their third birthday.

A child with autism may not play with other children, avoid eye contact, be upset by a change in routine, repeat back words or phrases, have trouble with both verbal and non-verbal communication, or become obsessed with a topic or action such as flapping arms. Children with autism may be particularly bright in one area, such as music.

Providing a child with structure can be an important part of dealing with this disorder. Routines are important; it helps a child to feel secure. If a big change like starting to attend playgroup is going to happen, then work with the parents to introduce it gradually, take the child on several visits and let them become used to the new situation. Children with Autism can get wound up, so allow for quiet times for example before meals, to allow them to relax, a story or quiet music can help.

Children with Autism may use language literally and may misinterpret what is said due to difficulties reading body language. They often show no sense of fear or danger and may not like being touched. You will need to be firm, it should be made clear that you will not accept undesirable behaviour, set the rules and stick to them. It is also important to praise when a child does well. Try to avoid situations that might provoke unacceptable behaviour unnecessarily.

Cerebral Palsy

Cerebral Palsy (CP) is the term for disorders of movement due to damage to a child's brain during pregnancy or early childhood. Cerebral Palsy is a mix up in the messages being passed between the brain and muscles. There are three types, and children may have a combination of more than one. The degree of effect will also vary between individuals, in some it may be hardly noticeable.

The three types are:
❑ **Ataxia:** unsteady walking, lack of balance, shaky hands and jerky speech.
❑ **Athetoid:** involuntary movements, difficulty with speech due to trouble controlling the muscles involved.
❑ **Spastic:** muscles in one or more limbs are tense and stiff which causes difficulty with movement. Approximately 50% of children with CP will have this form.

In addition to the different types of CP there are classifications for the areas of the body affected.
❑ **Quadriplegia:** affected in all four limbs. Children have difficulty moving and may require a wheelchair. They may also have trouble speaking and eating.
❑ **Hemiplegia:** CP only affects one side of the body while the other functions normally. Children can usually walk and run but may limp or have an awkward gait.
❑ **Diplegia:** CP only affects the legs. Walking or running may be difficult but they can hold themselves upright and have good use of arms and hands.

A child with Cerebral Palsy may also have some of the following:

❑ Poor eye sight or a squint.
❑ Problems judging distances.
❑ Hearing impairments.
❑ Speech difficulties and problems with chewing.
❑ Epilepsy.
❑ Inability to to sit unsupported.
❑ Inability to access toys or activities without physical support.
❑ Learning difficulties (this is not always the case, many children with Cerebral Palsy have abilities equal to their peers.)
❑ Some children may also be prone to chest infections, constipation and have difficulties with body temperature.

Physiotherapy is often employed to help improve muscle control and improve posture. The child's parents will explain what is necessary for the care of their child.

Allergies

Children can be allergic to a wide variety of things, from pets to certain food. You should ask parents if there is anything their child is allergic to and details should be included on the child's record form.

Coping with an allergy can be hard for children. They may not find it easy to understand why they cannot eat certain food or smell the flowers like other children do. From an early age the child should be taught what they are allergic to and also why there are different rules to other children. 'You must not eat chocolate,' is not going to be as effective as 'You can't have chocolate because it makes you feel poorly.'

Some allergies can cause life-threatening reactions; if a child starts having an allergic reaction you should seek help as fast as possible. The mouth, throat, and bronchial tubes may swell and interfere with breathing. The face may also swell. Milder symptoms of allergies are a clear, runny nose and sneezing, itchy or stuffed-up nose or itchy, runny eyes.

Children may have medicine to take. You will need to record parents permission for use, and the doses given for the parents to sign. If the child carries an Epipen you will need to obtain training in its correct usage. Parents will be able to provide details of the care needed for their child.

Asthma

Asthma is a condition in which the airways of the lungs become either narrowed or completely blocked, preventing normal breathing.

Although everyone's airways can constrict in response to allergens or irritants, the airways of a child with asthma are more sensitive. When the airways have become obstructed, it takes more effort to force air through them, so breathing becomes laboured. This results in wheezing and sometimes coughing. An asthma attack (an episode during which shortness of breath occurs) will require either medication or some other form of intervention for the child to breathe normally again.

Bronchodilators are drugs that open up or dilate the constricted airways, while drugs aimed at reducing inflammation of the airways are called anti-inflammatories. In very young children these are administered with a nebulizer, this fits over the child's mouth and nose while they breathe in medication which is in tiny droplets in the air inside. An older child will use an inhaler, which has an opening they place their mouth around, press a button breathe in, then hold their breath for short period. Inhalers need to be available at all times, so it is a good idea to have a spare kept at the childminders in case of forgetfulness.

Milder attacks may be stopped by getting the child to sit quietly and breathe slowly, breathing in and out of a paper bag may help. Parents will be able to explain and demonstrate correct administration of any required medication. Older children will administer their own treatments. Use of Inhalers needs to be recorded in your records.

HIV and AIDS

HIV is an abbreviation for Human Immune Deficiency Virus. This virus damages the body's natural immune system. Over time if the HIV infection becomes advanced it may lead to AIDS. The initials AIDS are short for Acquired Immune Deficiency Syndrome.

There is currently no cure for AIDS, treatment is designed to keep the virus under control in an attempt to prevent further immune damage occurring. It is only prevention that prevents further spread of AIDS as there is no vaccine currently available. Where a non infected person comes into contact with the virus there may be a small window of opportunity in the first few hours or days after exposure where the use of specific drugs may prevent infection.

Myths or mis information about AIDS and HIV can lead to prejudices and discrimination. Many myths regarding the transmission of AIDS have been developing since AIDS was first identified, usually occurring due to lack of scientific knowledge. Common but incorrect myths include the beliefs that the transmission or spreading of AIDS occurs through normal social contact e.g. hugging or by touching, handshakes, sweat, tears, swimming pools, paddling pools, utensils, drinking fountains, prepared food, coughing and sneezing and sharing of toilet facilities. Where a parent believes these stories to be correct they may show their prejudice by encouraging their child to discriminate against a child with HIV or AIDS. As with all discrimination these attitudes should be challenged.

When you are caring for a child who is HIV positive or has AIDS you should be aware of confidential issues. Parents may fear discrimination and the associated social stigma if the information is disclosed. If other parents are aware then you may have to address their concerns about the child's infection and the measures in place to prevent cross infection. Children who are infected or affected by HIV or AIDS are considered as children in need by Social Services and as such they may provide you and the parents with assistance.

Infection is caused or spread via bodily fluids, usually by intercourse, infected needles and syringes, blood to blood contact and infected breast milk. Many other infections including gastro-enteritis and hepatitis are also transmitted through exposure to body fluids including blood, saliva, urine, faeces and vomit.

Standard hygiene precautions minimize risks of all infectious diseases, including HIV. Good practice would be for children not to share cups, plates and cutlery and for these to be washed in hot soapy water or dishwashed between use even though they pose no risk for HIV they can carry other infectious diseases putting those with reduced immunity at risk. Children should not share items of food, toothbrushes, flannels or hair brushes. Cuts and open wounds should be covered with a dressing and although sharing of toys will not transmit the virus, good practice would suggest if it has been in a child's mouth it should be washed in soapy water and rinsed before another child plays with it. Disposable gloves should be worn for changing nappies, or cleaning up bodily fluids and when administering first aid. This is especially important if you have hangnails, cuts, scrapes or rashes on your hands.

Spillages should always be wiped up and disinfected while wearing disposable gloves. Where spillages are contaminated, floors and other surfaces should be disinfected with diluted bleach, recommended concentrations are one tablespoon to one litre of water. Surfaces should then be left to air dry. All waste should be sealed in a plastic bag and disposed of safely. Hands should be washed thoroughly in running water after the gloves are removed and safely disposed of. Where the spillages are on washable items e.g. Clothes or sheets they should be machine washed on a hot cycle. Contaminated articles should be washed separately from other washing.

Children with AIDS are more at risk from general infections caught from the other children, which will take advantage of a child's weakened immune system, than other children are to catching HIV. For example, colds, tonsillitis, chickenpox etc. can easily become serious or turn into pneumonia.

Circumstances or conditions of a child's environment can limit or enhance a child's development. Children with HIV and AIDS need to live a normal life and have contact with other children. If this is not permitted a child's physical and emotional well-being and their social and intellectual development can be permanently limited. Children need opportunities and time to develop in a caring environment, with playmates and with both emotional and developmental support.

Diabetes

The pancreas gland in a child with diabetes provides none or insufficient amounts of insulin. Insulin controls the levels of sugar in the blood, low levels of insulin cause high levels of sugar in the blood and urine. Before physical activities such as sports these children may need extra carbohydrates.

Symptoms may include thirst, frequent passing of urine, tummy pains, headaches and behavioural problems. If insulin levels drop too low a child may become unconscious. Diabetes can also cause kidney damage, visual impairment and circulation problems.

To control their levels of insulin children may have insulin injections, and/or a controlled diet. They will also test and record the levels of sugar in their blood/urine. Depending on the age of the child they may be able to perform these treatments themselves or you may be required to.

The parents will explain the exact routine that their child follows and a nurse will be able to train you in performing injections if they are required.

Coeliac Disease

Coeliac Disease is a metabolic disorder causing sensitivity to gluten, which in the UK affects one in every hundred people. Gluten is a protein found in wheat, rye, barley and oats. Children may have difficulty in digesting food. A diet free of gluten will be required and parents will be able to help in advising you of the most suitable foods. Parents may be prepared to provide you with gluten free bread, biscuits and pasta as they will be able to obtain them on prescription. When feeding a child with Coeliac disorder, check the contents labels of all food stuffs. Manufacturers hide wheat products in the most unlikely foods for example, some yogurts, chocolates and crisps contain gluten. Some manufacturers now label foods 'gluten free'. Diarrhoea is the most common symptom if gluten is inadvertently eaten.

Spina Bifida

Spina Bifida is an abnormality in the spinal column where one or more vertebrae in the backbone fails to form properly, leaving a gap, and damage to the central nervous system. Children may also have bowel or bladder control problems and paralysis of legs and feet due the damage to their spinal cord and may use crutches, braces or wheelchairs to help with mobility. Some children may also have learning difficulties.

Where to Get Advice

The parents should be your initial contact for providing advice on the care of their children. You may want to find out more however. Here are some other places where you may be able to get advice and information.

❏ Doctor
❏ Health Visitor
❏ Children's Information Service (CIS)
❏ Support Groups for a particular Special Need
❏ Schools

Parental Feelings & Needs

For many parents their fist feelings on a child's diagnosis may be denial followed by anger. This sometimes becomes directed at a childminder, not intentionally but it is triggered by feelings of grief and loss of what might have been. This merges into fear. Fear of the unknown and fears of rejection. Some parents can become almost immobilised by this fear and need gentle nudging towards help and assistance.

There can be feelings of guilt and self reproach from questioning the causes of the disability and confusion. Parents may need support and understanding and especially at the outset where you can be the 'light at the end of the tunnel' as you may help them to focus on one day at a time to start with.

Do not pity a parent. What they need most is empathy. By helping them consider their child's positive aspects and achievements you will be supporting the parents as someone who is valuing their child.

12. Child Development and Education

Childminders play an important role in promoting the development and education of the children they care for. There are a variety of methods, techniques and new innovations you will hear mentioned. It can seem confusing and you may wonder if it has any relevance to the care you are providing. It will help you to realise that in many ways you are probably already encouraging the development of the children in your care, informal everyday activities can be just as valuable as planned ones, and your methods may already incorporate the systems mentioned further on in this section.

Child Development

SPICE

Children's development is sometimes categorised into five areas: social, physical, intellectual, communication and emotional (SPICE). This approach separates a child's social development from their emotional development and their intellectual development from their development of communication.

However, there are now many examples of SPICE being translated with the 'C' being used as creative and some times linked as creative and cultural development in order to produce a more balanced curriculum.

PILESS

This is another system of categorising children's development. Six areas of development are defined: physical, intellectual, language and communication, emotional, social, spiritual. This system recognises the importance of biology, linguistics and sociology, providing a focus for study and the planning of activities.

Care should be taken when using systems such as SPICE and PILESS not to apply the categories too rigidly and miss the importance of the child as a whole.

Developmental Stages

As children develop, their needs and abilities change. The following are guidelines only as there is no such thing as a typical child. Ages are only an indicator of normal development, steady development is more important than obtaining a given stage at a certain age.

❑ **6 weeks**
May smile and 'talk' back when spoken to, notices movement, can raise chin from mat.

❑ **3 months**
Can already relate to people, can keep head erect for a few seconds, clasps and unclasps fingers, noticing hand belongs to them. Can reach and miss cradle toys. They can recognise (have concepts of) differing speech sounds and can mimic both high and low sounds and will babble. Babble will include vowels and constants. They have a developed sense of smell and can tell the smell of their mother from that of other mothers. They can tell light from dark and have some colour perception. Their hearing is better than their sight at this stage in their development. Touch senses are mainly using the hands and mouth. They have a full set of tastebuds and can distinguish between sweet and sour, preferring the taste of milk. During this phase they like mobiles and brightly coloured toys which are easily handled, preferring rattles to be placed into their hand and activity type gyms they can kick at.

❑ 6 months

Can sit upright with support. Uses a palmer grip (scoop type grip) and notices their feet belong to them. Everything goes to the mouth for testing. Can roll from front to back and from seven months can also roll from back to front and fall off high surfaces such as beds. At this age they can distinguish emotional tones of voice. Children of this age like to sit on a lap and grasp toys, play with large beads, activity gyms and centres and other similar toys. They find textures fascinating, beginning to recognise what they touch by the feel of it. They will recognise familiar objects, develop favourite tastes and respond to differences in temperature.

During this time period a child becomes able to hold their head erect with a straight back and can raise their head and chest when placed onto a mat. The child will play with their feet and can follow movement with their eyes and can grasp dangling objects, suggesting they recognise and judge distance in relation to the object using depth perception and may also be using prediction. They will use prediction i.e. bib means food is coming. Babies of this age love an audience but it is around this time they will begin to develop an aversion to strangers. A baby of this age will understand that two objects can occupy a space (toy behind a cushion) but they cannot yet appreciate the notion of time or the meaning of temporary. Children of this age like to play "peek a boo", crumple paper and splash water. They like putting things into containers, and noisy toys are favoured.

❑ 9 Months

Between nine and twelve months a child's memory is developing. They can remember the past and anticipate the future. They will begin to understand routine sequences. Their sight is improving and they can follow rapidly moving objects using visual perception. Their tastebuds are maturing and they have a greater ability to distinguish flavours. Around this age children begin babbling to attract attention and communicate, and can understand simple words. They can move around the room by pushing or pulling with their hands, rolling or crawling. They can sit without support. They have a fear of strangers and like to feel secure.

❑ 12 months

At around this age children can pull themselves into the standing position and will stand up while holding onto furniture. The pincer grip is developed and they can drink from a spouted cup. They will understand simple words and commands and will be able to point and wave. Their emotions can change rapidly and lots of reassurance will be required in new situations. At this stage of development, toys they like to play with include bricks, books and push and pull toys. They will enjoy scribbling, the pencil will be held by the end, producing marks on the paper, there will be no strength of grip and poor muscle control, producing random uncontrolled scribbles.

During this first year children develop a sense of trust that familiar people around them are dependable. This trust can be strengthened or undermined in later years. Babies who have received consistent care from familiar, loving childminders, who meet their needs will grow to feel their immediate environment is trustworthy. Your responses to a babies physical and emotional needs will affect their development of a basic sense of trust or mistrust.

❑ 15-18 months

Within this time frame children usually begin to walk and learn to crawl up stairs. Their leg muscles may have become sufficiently developed to enable them to bend and pick up toys from the floor. They will be able to hold a cup themselves and get their spoon to their mouth, they cannot usually get the spoon into the mouth yet, but may lick the contents off. They may begin to use their first words which are usually 'label' words. Children of this age range do not like changes to their routine and will be quick to notice strangers. They can build a tower of two bricks and like to scribble. Their pencil grip is becoming firmer producing to and fro lines on paper. This is still experimental and the pencil is often mouthed.

❑ 18 months

By eighteen months their balance is improving, and they can walk up stairs with help and crawl down backwards. They can use their spoon effectively. They will be able to take off their shoes, hat and socks. Children of this age are very curious. A preference for their right or left hand begins to become evident. They will begin to develop a tripod grip of their pencil and will scribble too and fro on paper with random dots appearing. The dots are very often deliberate and may be poked into holes. Vocabulary will be approximately fifteen words although they will understand many more, and they will often use this vocabulary to label body parts. They can build a tower of three bricks and point at pictures in a book and enjoy finger painting. It is in this phase that they begin to develop a strong willpower.

❑ 18-24 months

This is the phase of declaring independence with the associated temper tantrums. Emotional feelings are very strong and they will need help with the language to describe them. When running the child will be able to stop and start and avoid obstacles. They will use the banister rail when using stairs. They will be able to throw a ball (overarm), feed themselves, turn pages, put on hats and shoes and can turn door handles. Painting is enjoyed and by twenty one months takes the form of streaks. Their drawing is still purposeless scribbling, pleasurable to the child. All the movements for painting and scribbling come from the shoulder as purely muscular movements. By two years scribbling becomes purposeful, coordination is improving and the use of wrist movements has begun. They will use a preferred hand to hold their pencil, drawing circles, dots and lines. They may begin to develop bladder control. They will not understand the concept of sharing but their attention span and hand to eye coordination will be improving. Vocabulary will be in excess of two hundred words and will include two word phrases. Favourite toys and occupations are interlocking bricks, unscrewing things, posting objects, pegs to hammer, crayons and chalks.

❑ 2.5-3 years

Children become more aware of toileting needs and may be fascinated with urination and excretion. Will jump with feet together, kick large balls, paint with a brush and pay attention to the marks made, make random snips with scissors, steer 'sit and ride' toys, pick up threads and 'bits' off the carpet, and may use a fork. When drawing, an important part of their picture is the face, rarely will there be a second circle, arms are infrequently depicted but feet often appear. Children should be encourage to draw these figures. Sometimes children of this age will draw repetitive individual lines to represent movement. Mood swings will vary between clinging and independent. They may have irrational fears and need support and reassurance. However, fear of separation begins to lessen. Their hearing will normally have become as acute as that of an adult in terms of high frequency sound. They will be using action words (verbs), descriptive words (adjectives), sizes (big and small), position words (in, out, under) and will be able to hold a basic conversation. Pretend play will be developing. Favourite activities include sand and water play, threading of large beads, painting, dough activities, cutting and sticking, painting, toy cars and small world activities.

❑ 3 years

Can now walk upstairs independently with alternate feet, peddle a trike, stand on one leg, sit cross legged, cut with scissors, paint with a large paint brush, use their spoon and fork, will carry their own cup, can walk on tiptoes and will have a vocabulary in excess of 800 words. During this period a child's visual skills become fully developed, they have an increase in understanding of concepts and facial expressions but little understanding of the concept of numbers. Hearing development is slowing down and children begin to make more sense of what they are hearing. They will enjoy scribbling and will be imitating circles. Between the ages of three and four figures begin to appear, usually a circle with arms and legs protruding from the head. Odd letters may also begin to appear usually V, H and T. Paintings produced during this period are often of one colour only, which may be overlaid by many single colours, often culminating in black. Increasing coordination makes intellectual development easier i.e. they can grasp bricks to stack without knocking them over and can hence learn the concepts of over, under, on top and how the lower bricks can cause the higher ones to fall if they wobble. Favourite activities will include imaginative play, including small world activities and dressing up; art and crafts; ball games; climbing frames and slides; tricycles and scooters; books and stories. They will have become interested in having friends to talk and laugh with.

During their second and third year, children develop a mind and will of their own. They are becoming aware of themselves and develop a sense of wanting independence. This is the period of "I can do it myself". Children who do not have a chance to make their own choices where appropriate, or adults who are too strict in forcing them to do things or who do not let them attempt to achieve things themselves may cause poor self confidence, creating doubt and possible shame.

❑ 4-5 years

Children in this group are becoming more stable and emotionally secure. They need adult support to enable them to cope with difficult situations and still fear the loss of parents. They can throw a ball with aim, cutting with scissors has become more controlled and will be fairly accurate. Children may form preliminary blue prints of what they will draw, arms are often still drawn from the head with no trunk depicted. Young children do not insist a drawing is realistic, but as cognition and fine motor skills improve they want to produce greater realism and hence produce more complex drawings. Content will still be mainly concerned with people, houses, transport vehicles and flowers. As their visual control progresses, human figures are given heads legs and trunks, a typical house will be portrayed as a square box with square windows. Each child will produce individual symbols and representations. Children will be developing their concept of tomorrow and the future, they will also be beginning to differentiate left from right. Children will also be experimenting more with letters. Children in this period may show curiosity about sexes, becoming aware of being male or female. Children may explore each other's bodies. They may masturbate, with no emotions except pleasure, and no feelings of guilt unless induced.

❑ 5-6 years

Children of this age may be able to read, skip, swing, climb ladders, skate, ride a bike, copy small letters, write their name (although letters may still be large and spreading), hit a nail with a hammer, colour in outlines most of the time, use a pencil sharpener, copy drawings, catch a soft ball or bean bag with one hand, hit a ball with a bat, kick a ball with aim and pour out their own cereal. During their art work there will be much use of colour. Typical pictures depict a yellow round sun, possibly with rays, a narrow blue strip of sky at the top of a piece of paper, green trees and a narrow brown strip of earth at the bottom. People depicted will have head, trunk, legs, eyes, nose and mouth. The human form is drawn quite well, each mark produced having a meaning. Sometimes navels and nipples will be drawn. During their sixth year pictures become more elaborate depicting people and objects in all sorts of everyday situations. Even at this age children do not mirror reality. Drawings will still contain perceptual distortions making their pictures seem inventive and fanciful. Even when there has been no sex/role stereotyping in play, many children of this age still segregate. Favourite activities include adventure playgrounds, bikes, scooters, ball games, computer games, small Lego and Meccano.

During the period from three to six years, children develop a sense of initiative. This develops through their ability to try things and having the confidence to take risks. Within this period children need stimulation of their curiosity, imagination and opportunities to experiment. This is the age where conscience and imagination develop. This may account for the nightmares so common to this age group.

Beyond six years of age the pre-occupation with fantasy begins to subside and they want to be engaged in real tasks they can complete. Feeling successful will encourage their sense of self worth and eagerness to learn more, providing you have selected challenging opportunities at the right level. Children will have developed the concepts of length measurement, distance, time, area, volume, capacity and weight and the appropriate vocabulary, and will be beginning to understand conversion of mass. They will have higher level skills of vocabulary, prediction, why, inferring things, problem solving language, ability to sequence activities and write stories. Children within this age range like consciously putting their language and problem solving skills to use. Care should be taken when setting tasks as feeling defeated will lead to a sense of inferiority that can discourage future learning. The more you can affirm a child's uniqueness as an individual the easier it will be for them to develop a solid sense of self worth.

❏ 7-8 years
During this period children are confident and independent. They can be irritable, self centred and aggressive. They may refuse to share and will show frustration when they cannot achieve their objectives. They are striving for independence, and become aware of the world around them. Writing will have become smaller, aligned and they will be able to draw a diamond shape neatly. During this period children will begin to produce logical drawings and cataloguing of events. They may attempt to draw profiles of faces. There is still no real attempt at solidity, perspective or distance, but there is a real interest in pattern.   The drawings become more realistic as the child develops more control over the pencil and comes to notice and understand more about the world (improved concept development).

❏ 9-11 years
It will not be until around nine years of age that a child will learn how to represent depth in their drawings (Nicholls and Kennedy 1992), they will then begin to record from nature and attempt landscapes. Sometimes a girl of this age may fall in love for the first time, a move away from individuality and a recognition of the need for companionship. Favoured activities are as for those of the five to six year olds, plus magnifying glasses and microscopes, constructional toys and woodwork. Children will also enjoy team games.

This is the age of growing independence, a strong sense of self and the need for social acceptance and to experience achievements. It becomes more emotionally important to have friends, especially of the same sex and complex friendships and peer relationships develop. Peer pressure and academic challenges increase.

Children may feel they do not need adult care or supervision but, left to themselves they may be lonely, unhappy and sometimes frightened. They may enjoy reading fictional stories, develop interests in collections or hobbies and fantasise about the future. They can also understand concepts without hands on experiences.

❏ 12-14 years
This is the period often referred to as early adolescence. It is a time of many physical, mental, emotional and social changes. Hormones change as puberty begins. Boys grow facial and pubic hair and their voices deepen. Girls grow breasts, pubic hair and begin menstruating. Peer pressures that occur frequently involve alcohol, smoking, drugs and sex.

This age range tends to be more independent with their own personality and interests. They can be inwardly focused, moody, short tempered and anxious but, are better able to express feelings through talking. There is usually a strong sense of right and wrong.

❏ 15-16 years
Appetite is great and the need for sleep increases. The rapid growth may cause clumsiness and lack of coordination. Oily skin and acne may be problematical and sexual desires and fantasies increase.

Assumptions and solutions presented by adults may be challenged. Arguing and reasoning skills improve, deductive reasoning, educated guesses and construction of hypothetical solutions and problems evolves. A conscience is developed, fact can be distinguished from opinion and credibility of information sources is evaluated. Personal goals may be set which reflect those set by others. In this phase their emotions may be represented as a pendulum.

Factors Affecting Growth and Development

Growth is the increase in size and weight of a child. Although there may be great variation at birth growth pathways are similar. Development is the process by which the body, brain, abilities and behaviours become more complex. A child's emotional needs are affection, sense of belonging, independence, sense of achievement, approval and self esteem. Without these a child's growth and development will be impaired. A child's ability to explore and discover increases their ability for intellectual development which can be challenged if they are ignored or prevented from learning by over protection. The 'training' children receive will also affect the amount of self control they develop over such things as jealousy and how they deal with worry and frustration. Discipline or lack of discipline will also affect children's behaviour and their social and emotional development.

What Helps Growth and Development?

Included in the factors which help a child's growth and development are good health, a happy child, a child who is conversed with continuously, a child who is encouraged to explore and where there is a high degree of tolerance to infant clutter and disorder.

What Hinders Growth and Development?

Factors which hinder a child's growth and development include poor diet which stunts their growth; severe long term illness which may slow growth; effects of parental smoking which may affect their growth, development and health; a lack of love and interest making a child feel insecure and unhappy, possibly also leading to a failure to thrive physically, and an inability to deal satisfactorily with their emotions; stress may stunt a child's growth, causing them to be excessively thin or over weight; playpens used for long periods; television used extensively; lack of opportunity for talking and playing; nothing of interest to do; constant nagging; bullying; poor health and lack of stimulation.

Gross Motor Skills

These are skills which require co-ordination between the child's large muscles and their brain. The age at which children develop their gross motor skills is very variable and may depend on the opportunities and experiences they have encountered.

Examples of gross motor skills include: sitting, crawling, cruising, walking, hopping, running, jumping, throwing, catching, striking, kicking, whirling, spinning, bouncing, balancing, pushing, pulling, climbing, stretching, swinging, dancing and pedaling.

Fine Manipulative Skills

These skills require coordination between the muscles and the brain and require very precise movements, particularly of the hands and fingers. Fine manipulative skills require a lot of practice and will be developed at varying ages dependent on previously learned experiences and opportunities you offer.

Examples of fine manipulative skills include grasping and holding, picking up, pointing, pre-writing skills such as drawing, painting and mark making, constructing objects as in jigsaws, or cutting, modelling, sticking, sawing, hammering, threading and sowing, fastening buttons, using cutlery and digging.

Intellectual Development

Intellectual development (sometimes called cognitive development) is development of the mind and includes recognition, reasoning, knowing and understanding. Intellectual development is closely linked to a child's communication development, their ability for abstract thoughts and their ability to talk about events that might happen or which they do not wish to happen. The ability of a child to use their cognitive skills will be strongly influenced by the environment and the attitudes of the people encountered.

Sensory Development

A child's sensory development is very important. Sensations lead a child to perceptions so they can make sense of, understand and get feedback through their senses, seeing; smelling; hearing; touching and tasting, and movements of the body (kinesthetics), to form concepts of how and why things react or link in the way they do. Young children may have a gap between the concept they want to communicate and their vocabulary. Talking things through with them and adding additional label words (nouns) and descriptive words (adjectives) helps extend their vocabulary to narrow the gap.

The Curriculum

A curriculum is broadly the activities, experiences and routines a child will be able to access to help them develop and learn during the time they are present with their childminder. Childminding curriculums do not need to be formal, like those used within a school environment, and all activities even laying the table or dusting the television help children to learn.

Young children's time-table or curriculum needs to allow time for activities that are undirected by adults. They need time to develop their play and to experiment, pacing their learning to suit themselves. This approach encourages children to form relationships and friendships with the adults and other children present.

There must be a pattern to the day, a routine, to ensure a feeling of security and some sense of what will happen next. Planning needs to take account of the time frames as appropriate to ensure completion of the activities to the child's, and your, satisfaction. Tight inflexible schedules are inappropriate. Children need time to avoid rushing activities, but not so long that they cannot sustain their involvement and interest.

With long term planning for young children, the more open ended the plan can be, the more chance children will have of being within an environment supportive to their learning and including free flow play.

Activities and experiences need to be balanced to support the child's whole development. This can only occur if implementation generally reflects the plans you have made, preventing omissions of experiences and an unbalanced approach. You should ensure that a wide variety of experiences are provided with a learning progression, continuity and the provision of opportunities for children to practice their new skills. The curriculum should be developed from a blend of children's development, abilities and interests and the intended outcomes. This will ensure it too meets the individual needs of the children within your setting.

The most effective planning will use opportunities from the whole day, it will include care routines and not be solely restricted to activities that seem to be 'educational'. The incorporation of local resources into the plan can also enhance this. For example, visits to the fire station, library or woodlands encourage a child's development of understanding the world, their personal and social development and their vocabulary. Activities should be planned to reflect the social and cultural background of the children present. This will enable them to realise their potential, feel positively about themselves and their achievements while avoiding the limitations of stereotyping and encouraging the value of diversity.

In Scotland, Wales and Ireland curriculum plans should incorporate Desirable Outcomes or Stepping Stones from the Foundation Stage Early Learning Goals (for children from three to between five and six years) and aspects from Birth to Three. In England, from September 2008, the Developmental Elements and Early Learning Goals (EYFS). If your implementation of the curriculum plans, have broadly reflected your planning intentions, then children will have reached and probably exceeded these outcomes by compulsory school. After which children become legally required to follow Government controlled National Curriculums.

Other Considerations

To help children maximise the opportunities for learning you are going to provide, you will need to take into account principles that are significant for their development and education. These include security, autonomy, self image, self-esteem, assertiveness, perseverance, challenge, motivation, independence, choice, responsibility, self control, feelings, relationships and the seven C's (confidence, co-ordination, competence, creativity, communication, concentration and co-operation).

You might also like to remember your school days or courses you have taken, you probably found you learnt slowly or not at all when you were bored and people seemed indifferent. Then paid attention and learned quickly when the topic was interesting, relevant and presented with enthusiasm.

Security - This is crucial for a child's well being. Known and repeated routines help promote this feeling and a secure environment promotes the most effective children's learning. Activities that promote security include: set meal times, collection of other children at routine times, cuddles and attention when required, predictable environment and consistency of care.

Autonomy - Your planned curriculum should ensure children are able to become aware of their own attitudes and feelings and those of others. They will need time and space to learn to moderate and regulate their own behaviour, actions and activities with regards to the needs of others. Activities that promote this include: co-operative play, role play and circle time (group activities where everyone shares experiences).

Self Image - Children need to develop a positive self image. They need to learn to like and respect themselves. The way children see themselves is very strongly influenced by our attitudes and opinions of them, i.e. if criticised or frequently told they are 'silly' they will believe this and enact what they feel is your definition. Activities that promote children's self image include: self portraits and sharing photos from home. Recognition of differences between people and the realisation everyone has a positive side.

Self Esteem - Development of self esteem is contributed to by the response of others to the child. You will need to communicate to each and every child that they are valued for themselves. Developing a child's self esteem is very important because the development of the child's positive view of themselves enhances their ability to learn. A child with good self esteem will believe in themselves. A child with a disability may need help with coming to terms with the disability and how some people may react to it in order to develop good self esteem. Activities that promote this principle include: construction play, homes and families topics, love, security, trust, providing positive images and positive role models.

Perseverance - You will be providing the motivation to persevere when your planned curriculum and environment are designed to take into account the children's experiences and interests together with the current stage of development. You can encourage the perseverance by providing tasks and activities which are motivating and challenging. Children should be encouraged to finish tasks to a satisfactory conclusion when self chosen or given. Activities that help children learn perseverance may also have an element of waiting rather than instant success, such as: making clay pots, cooking or jigsaws.

Challenge - It is important to recognise the value of encouraging children to set their own challenges and within your planned environment it is beneficial to provide activities which challenge the stage of children's learning. This will engage their minds at the highest level of thinking as they advance their knowledge. Activities that promote this include: can I do it by myself activities, how can I do it? what comes next? Giving the 'next stage' of an activity e.g. from ten piece jigsaw to fifteen piece jigsaw.

Motivation - Self chosen tasks provide the best motivation for children encouraging them to develop control over their own learning, helped by an exciting environment, activities and resources which support the children's natural desire for exploration and discovery. Activities that promote this include: learning by investigation, heuristic materials (see Activities and their Value) and easy access so children can choose for themselves.

Independence - This will develop when you provide the children with increasing freedom and personal choice within their environment and encourage them with self help skills, providing them with ample time to practice their newly developing skills without criticism, and without offering help unless requested by them. Activities that promote this include: construction play, tidying up after themselves, choosing activities and asking for help when necessary.

Choice - Providing children with opportunities to choose, e.g. " Would you like apple or orange juice?", enables children to begin to make their own decisions, gradually developing control over their own environment and learning.

Responsibility and Self Control - Children should be encouraged to take responsibility for their own actions and be helped to understand the consequences of any action they take. Children can be helped to develop a sense of responsibility and self control by being given freedom and personal choice within aspects of their own daily routines. It also helps children when you talk about their behaviour and how it makes people feel. This should be for when they have done or said something positive as well as for undesirable behaviour. Activities that promote this include: tidying up after themselves, carrying and delivering messages, setting the table and thinking of others.

Confidence and Assertiveness - Where children are valued, encouraged and have developed good self-esteem in a safe and secure environment they will have the confidence to try new activities. Confidence in themselves (self-confidence) is gained where activities are developmentally appropriate and children are given positive encouragement of their efforts even when not quite correct, and criticism is not used.

Children's confidence in asserting their rights should be encouraged. Letting them make informed choices can help. They should be aware that sometimes it is alright to say no, or refuse to do something they feel is not appropriate e.g. go with a stranger. Children should be encouraged to express their views and feelings, e.g. "I don't want any more dinner", "I would prefer to go to the woods today instead of the park". This helps encourage them to be confident and assertive. Where children cannot have the freedom of decision, e.g. for health and safety reasons, these should be clearly explained to the child. This will ensure that their confidence in being able to choose (asserting their influence) is not damaged.

While you should encourage assertiveness at appropriate times you will need to ensure children do not confuse it with loudness (shouting) or aggressive behaviour. They should be encouraged to stand up for their rights, i.e. "it belongs to me", but without being unpleasant or aggressive.

It is especially important to ensure children who are physically or emotionally challenged and those who have special needs feel they are equally valued and of worth. This will ensure they can develop the self confidence and assertiveness they will require to meet the challenges of life. Activities that promote this include: construction play, sand and water play, arts and crafts and activities where resources are shared, with no right or wrong way to complete them.

Co-ordination - This will eventually become crucial in a child's ability to write and is developed as a child progresses their developmental stages. Providing ample opportunities and encouragement, to practice skills helping a child's co-ordination, will also be indirectly contributing to the child's development of literacy skills. Activities that promote this include: jumping, balancing, walking, posting, painting, threading and puzzles.

Competence - When a child becomes proficient at something their competence will be encouraged because they have the necessary skills and / or knowledge. Competence is the product of practice, praise and guidance. Children can become competent at a whole range of activities and events including self help skills, jumping, threading, talking and stacking bricks.

Creativity - To encourage creativity you will need a rich environment with both natural and man made resources and props. Valuing the children's ideas, creativity and expressiveness and attempts at problem solving as they develop these through play, arts, crafts and experimentation will encourage them to become adept at problem solving by becoming imaginative thinkers. Providing these activities will have provided them with the opportunity to think beyond the obvious and to develop their own ideas.

Point to note: templates, tracing and pre-screwed up coloured tissue paper and similar activities are pre structured and discourage creativity. They can also undermine children's self esteem, hampering a child's chance of becoming a confident active thinker.

Communication - The development of good communication skills will become essential for learning to read and write. The wider the vocabulary and understanding of the vocabulary the easier it will be for a child to learn to read. Children also need to be able to communicate to express their feelings. If this is not possible their self esteem may be damaged, they may also have temper tantrums or exhibit challenging behaviour. Communication skills are not exclusive to sound, they include gestures, body language and signing. Additional support will be needed for children who cannot vocalize.

Concentration - Young children concentrate best when occupied by something they find interesting. The ability to concentrate will help children to learn when they encounter the more structured learning of a primary or National Curriculum. 'Desk bound' tasks for young children do not help them concentrate, boredom may also lead them into developing poor learning habits.

Activities which help them stay focused include those that they have selected for themselves, those where they have been permitted to set their own agenda for play, e.g. role play and those where the equipment provided is attractive, easy to use, developmentally appropriate and can be used in a variety of imaginative ways to extend their play.

You can help a child to concentrate and stay on task by using praise and interacting to provide further challenges. Encouraging children to continue with an activity when it is reaching a natural conclusion or the child is becoming frustrated may make the child resentful and become disinclined to concentrate on similar tasks.

Co-operation - Learning to co-operate with others is a gradual process and a social skill that will be important to children throughout their life. In order to co-operate they will need to learn to share ideas, feelings, resources and to take turns. They must also understand they cannot always do what they want. Language development may affect a child's ability to express their thoughts and take turns. Direction and guidance will be most important to help children grasp the concepts of sharing, after all, to share ones sweets really means to give them to someone else, taking turns with a sweet is frowned upon. This can be very confusing at age three or four years. Early intervention, support and praise prevents conflict and helps children to understand co-operation and take into account the feelings and rights of others. Ideas for practising these skills include floor puzzles, construction activities, board games, simple card games and musical statues.

Feelings - Children will find it easier to integrate with, and respect, others if they can express and understand their own feelings. Children can have such a mixture of feelings that they may find difficultly in expressing them clearly. Children need to be provided with opportunities and the language they need in order to express themselves. Stories can help them to talk about and learn about their own and others' feelings. Imaginative role play or puppets allow them to share their experiences of feelings and act them out.

Relationships - Children within a group form relationships with each other and with the childminder, their assistants and the family members they meet. Introducing a new child to the group may temporarily upset these stable relationships. Talking about the new child before they arrive so they are not a surprise and providing non-competitive activities while they settle can help. Activities which support this include: dough craft, sand and water play, arts and crafts and heuristic play (see Example Activities).

Occasionally the new child will find it difficult to form relationships. Possible reasons include: because they are developmentally delayed, they are acting aggressively because they are nervous, they do not have naturally out-going personalities or there is discriminatory behaviour from the other children. Where they are having difficulty, having eliminated any discriminatory behaviour, it may help if you nominate a special friend to 'look after' them and be their friend.

Types of Play

Solitary Play

Solitary play is where children play alone. Children under two engage in this form of play. Children do not always wish to be sociable and do not lose the need for solitary play. There are some times when children feel the need for personal space, they do not always wish to join in group activities and may wish to play alone. Your curriculum should be flexible enough to allow this.

Spectator Play

This is a developmental phase found in toddlers slotting in between solitary and parallel play. Children will watch each other playing around them but do not join in. This form of play can be found in older children and is common with children new to the childminding setting, those with English as a second language and those for whom the activity is a new experience where they are lacking in confidence. The children watch what the others do as a learning experience. They may choose to join in repetitions of the activities in the future. This is a perfectly valid form of play and a learning experience in itself.

Parallel Play

Parallel play begins as an extension of solitary play. This form of play is where children play alongside other children, but not with them. It is a developmental phase found in children around the age of two. Each child plays their own game quite separately from the other although they may be playing with similar resources. Through this form of play young children begin to share the resources and communicate with each other until play becomes co-operative. True co-operative play evolves at around the age of three years.

Sometimes older children desire companionship of their peers, but do not want to interact with them. This form of play is helpful to new children and those 'under the weather'. Painting is an example, children are together with the same activity but do not have to look at each other and can talk as much or as little as they like.

Associative Play

This type of play is where children play with others. The children share toys and interact with each other. Children are involved in similar activities but without specific organisation. Children play as they like but are part of a larger group. This form of play usually occurs from three to five years of age.

Cooperative Play

This type of play requires organisation. Children are part of a group with specific aims. There are usually leaders who organise or dictate the play format and followers in this form of play. Hangers on are often given the role of baby, dog or cat when younger children begin cooperative play.

Learning Through Play

For children to learn through play they need time, space, opportunities, support and encouragement to help them to experience, explore, experiment, achieve, repeat and concentrate. Among other things, play encourages and is important for developing self esteem, task orientation, attitudes to learning, persistence, flexibility and creativity.

With such an extensive range of outcomes for each play experience you will need to be sensitive to what the child may be exploring within the activity. This will enable you to provide appropriate support and to extend the play and learning experience.

Basic Concepts

Basic concepts are general or abstract ideas required to develop intellectually, socially and emotionally. The more abstract the concept the more difficult it is for children to grasp. The concepts that children are able to grasp depend on their stage of development.

Activities that develop basic concept understanding need to be appropriate for the age and ability of the child. Most concepts can be introduced in play and during everyday domestic activities. Remember unplanned events can be incorporated into their understanding of concepts.

Type of Concept	Area covered includes:	Example Activities:
Mathematical	Numbers, ordering, counting, matching/equals, weight, volume, more than/less than	Dressing, getting ready to go out or pictures. What order do you put clothes on, can you put your shoes on before your socks?
Physical/ Scientific	Properties of objects, colour, shape, growth, heat, light, floating/sinking, change of state	Growing a plant, seeds, water, light, growth, taste.
Position/ Relationship	In, out, near, far, left, right, over, under	Cardboard boxes, are you in the box? Can you get under the box?
Moral	Good, bad, right, wrong, sharing, fairness	Discussing concepts as they occur, through play, e.g. squabble over toys.
Time	Times of day, morning, afternoon, next, before, after, yesterday, tomorrow, day of week.	Discussing events, what did you do yesterday? Today is Monday.

Children need time to take part and finish activities to their satisfaction; completing an activity will give them a sense of achievement. If they become frustrated they are less likely to want to join in with future activities. If a child becomes bored or distracted from an activity they should not be made to complete it. It can be finished at a later date when they are in a more receptive mood. Children are easily distracted so minimise distractions such as television, radio and interruptions.

The aim is not to teach concepts to a child, but to let them learn through play and daily interactions.

Example Activities and their Value

Games

Games with rules are linked to the beginning of literacy and numeracy, rules of vocabulary, turn taking, mathematical concepts and counting skills, labelling and sorting. Board games and card games such as Snakes and Ladders, Snap and Happy Families can be used to encourage turn taking and understanding of rules. These type of games encourage vocabulary of a mathematical nature together with placement concepts, descriptions of the game and differences and occupations. 'Feely bags' or games where an object to be described is hidden for another to find can also be used to promote the use of descriptive language. Ball games and games such as 'Simon Says', can be used to introduce turn taking and associated language, names for actions and the concept of looking and copying.

Stories

Stories introduce and develop book language, helping develop concepts and feelings. The discussions and questions books produce can encourage children to use concepts like past, present and future by helping them recall familiar events in their lives. These discussions can help children develop an understanding of the world, geography, general knowledge, culture and associated vocabulary. Vocabulary and sentence length are encouraged as they discuss books, the content, their likes and dislikes and retell the story. Use of tone and volume of voice can be used to enhance the story and encourage children with poor listening skills to remain attentive. Stories often give children ideas that they subsequently use in imaginative play.

Cooking

Cooking activities where children actively help will encourage concept development, discussion of the senses and naturally introduce mathematical language including weight, volume, temperature. Vocabulary including words associated with taste and smell, flavours, temperature, textures, comparing and contrasting, irreversibility, emotions, and naming of nouns and actions used can be introduced.

Painting

Painting and printing activities may lead into free play when the opportunity arises. Using a variety of media such as brushes, hands, feet, fingers, fruit and sponges on a variety of materials from paper to clay gives the chance to use social and co-operative skills and descriptive speech and develop fine motor skills. Painting can be used to provide a relaxing stress free activity for children with English as a second language, emotional problems or poorly developed social skills, as they can be encouraged to express anxieties and anger through the medium of paint.

Painting may elicit self talk from children reluctant to talk in public as they describe to themselves what they are doing and creating. Children are also learning to express individual feelings and realise their ability to make their own contribution boosting their confidence and self esteem.

Collage activities are helpful for promoting fine muscle control and give opportunities for choice. Choosing helps them learn about appropriate choices e.g. will this stick? They can use collage activities to make and test predictions as to what effect they will create.

Art activities are ideal times to promote words associated with colours, shades, combining colours, rainbows, textures, patterns, size and shape, actions, equipment and methods used.

Gardening

Gardening where children choose seeds at the garden centre returning to plant, nurture and transplant when bigger, encourages the use of a wide variety of descriptive words and understanding of growth and its processes. Vocabulary developed from this are recollections of the outing, counting of and sharing of seeds, descriptive words of items used, the concept of growth and its requirements, hazards to seedlings and descriptions of creepy crawlies encountered. This activity also encourages lots of "why?" and "what if?" questions where children extend their understanding and through this their vocabulary.

Outings

Outings and walks encourage children's language use as they help plan and recollect the event. Children can be encouraged to use past, present and future tenses and descriptive vocabulary which will vary depending on the outing. Play opportunities outside the childminding environment including, parks and play grounds, trips to the library or shops and childminder 'dropins' are also very useful in extending children's knowledge and understanding of the world, providing a wider range of experiences for both intellectual and gross motor development than otherwise possible.

Music

Music is another structured activity children adapt or evolve for use in free play. As children experiment with sound they learn language to help themselves identify and talk about what they are doing, to distinguish between high, low, fast and slow. Music helps children listen with concentration and discriminate more freely between different sounds. This can be especially helpful for children with poor listening skills. Deliberately using incorrect words during a song can also help children listen carefully as they delight in correcting you, e.g. "Mary had a little lamb, its fleece was black as soot". The addition of songs to the music helps build up a rich store of traditional language from various sources and strengthens the children's understanding of rhyme and rhythm encouraging them to play with rhyming words. Songs with actions to match the rhyme help children with English as an additional language join in. Songs can be used to help these and other children identify and name body parts and understand concepts. Concepts are easier to understand as they are enacted while singing action songs.

Music and dance is an area which could be further developed to accommodate children with poorly developed listening skills, poorly developed social skills and English as an additional language. Taking a simple rhythm with simple refrain e.g. "Mary had a little lamb, his fleece was white as snow" and building it up in layers can help children enhance their listening skills.

Children can begin by clapping to the refrain, with the timing to the beat of a drum, followed by singing the words and then by playing percussion instruments. It is advisable to allow a few minutes to familiarize themselves with the instruments, this is noisy at first but they can then be encouraged to settle down on a preset cue. Long lengths of brightly coloured cloth can then be introduced, using these children can be shown how to make Afro-Caribbean hats with some, dressing up with the others. Children can then be encouraged to move around the room swaying, singing and playing their percussion instruments in time to the beat of the drum.

The rhythm encourages listening skills, the dance and the movement with song encourages dual language children to join in something they cannot fail in, children with poor social skills can join in successfully while practising turn taking. The song can be sung in a variety of languages encouraging children with poorly developed listening skills to pay attention and children's home languages can be incorporated. The activity also encourages language with discussions on the instruments and their origins, the brightly coloured cloth and its intrinsic designs and requests for further songs. The dancing encourages children to use gross motor skills in a controlled fashion.

Water and Sand

Water and sand can be used singly or together for both structured activities and free play. Where structured scientific words, concepts and properties can be encouraged with predictions and outcomes, and mathematical properties. Children can be encouraged to describe apparatus used, what they are doing, what is happening and why. When used as free play vocabulary can be changed to holiday words, geographical words and worlds according to props available. Sand and water play can be helpful for children with poor social skills as there is no pressure on them and they learn to share. It also provides clear contexts for language development, especially for children with English as an additional language.

Jigsaws

A variety of jigsaws, including simple tray puzzles and more complex puzzles, chosen according to the age and stage of a child's development can be used to elicit a wide vocabulary. Puzzles can include depictions of festival scenes, non stereotypic images, animals, housing, life scenes and sequencing. Children can be helped where required and language practised. Opportunities for sorting and ordering words, descriptions of the picture content, size and shape through to single word utterances such as 'more' from younger children. Jigsaws also help children to discriminate between similar shapes which will help them distinguish the differences between the alphabet letters and helps their hand eye co-ordination, these are essential pre-reading and writing skills.

Tidying Up

Tidying up games help children with sequencing, deciding what goes next in the process, together with time concepts, what's happening next and the appropriate vocabulary. There are many naming opportunities and plurals can be introduced. Folding of the dressing up clothes can be used to introduce mathematical fractions and descriptive vocabulary.

Role Play

Role play is imaginative play where children play out first hand experiences or ideas from books, television and other sources. Children with first hand experience increasing the vocabulary of the others, whilst playing out their experiences and fears. This form of play also encourages talk about families, extended families, geographical descriptions and encourages recollection, use of past, present and future tense. This play encourages turn taking, negotiation of plans and activities promoting social language and skills. Their choice of role play activity influencing the accompanying vocabulary it develops, providing children with opportunities to describe, label, question, compare and contrast, and practice feelings and emotions. During role play children can also imitate adult speech patterns and assimilate new vocabulary by taking on the different roles. The wider the range of 'equipment' provided the more scope for differing scenarios to be developed, and the wider the range of vocabulary produced. Many of the items interchangeable in the differing roles children devise, the beginning of symbolism, an essential pre reading and writing skill.

Examples of role play scenarios children may develop include, 'house play', shops (various), hospitals and doctors, transport, holidays and outings, castles and kings or fairies. Other role play involves the use of small world miniatures of familiar life experiences. Examples of small world play you can provide includes train sets, dolls houses, farm animals, zoo animals, cars, road mats and garage, fire station and fire engine and play people.

In addition to the learning experience of role play, small world play helps children develop the fine motor skills they will require for using drawing and later, writing implements. It is also providing practise in planning, organisation and problem solving skills.

Role play is very helpful to children with poor social skills it can help with socialisation, there is no competition and they can develop in a 'safe' environment. Role play also helps language development. Provision of role play can be further extended to accommodate children with English as an additional language by including more items important to them at home as these will be the first English words they will want to learn. Parents should be approached for their help in suggesting and procuring appropriate items. Some children hesitant to talk face to face find talking on play telephones easier, successfully utilising it for extending their vocabulary during role play with both your and other children's help.

Outdoor Equipment

Climbing frames, slides, swings, and other outdoor equipment can be used as a multi purpose free play activity. Standing alone they can be used to elicit descriptive and action words, and for the understanding and naming of concepts. Children may also make a den with the addition of a sheet and other props, the language will change to that of the role play scenarios. In warm weather a paddling pool may be introduced, changing again the language opportunities available. Action verbs, descriptions, discussions and scientific experimentation with appropriate language can be encouraged. Physical play helps a child to develop self confidence and physical competence. It encourages the development of both fine and gross motor skills, and gives children the chance to practice their co-operative skills. Outdoor equipment does not need to be in your garden, if you do not have the space, a visit to the park is just as useful. The EYFS suggests children should have daily outdoor access.

Toy Library

Toy library and loan schemes provide a valuable resource for childminders, allowing them to borrow for a small fee a wide variety of items varying from jigsaws to larger items such as ball pools and pushchairs. Alternating toy use with loaned toys and equipment prevents boredom and provides a wider range of activities for a minimal cost.

Borrowing a double pushchair or larger play item from such a scheme may avoid the need for purchases if only required for a short time, or it can be used to check the ease of use or play value of a particular brand before purchase.

Toy loan schemes can also be a good place to meet other childminders and discuss play activities, childminding or seek advice. They often provide a child friendly environment with opportunities for children including those with special needs to play, and choose toys that appeal to them.

Modelling and Construction

Construction toys and activities such as junk modelling, wooden blocks, Duplo and Mega Blocks can be used to increase social and conversational skills. The wider the variety of resources and associated equipment the wider the vocabulary developed. These activities can also be used to introduce mathematical language, colours, shapes and positioning words.

Construction activities and modelling allow children to explore, experiment and create, and help to establish, confidence, independence and self esteem whilst providing opportunities for children to play alone, along side others or in a group where they can contribute to a shared purpose. Children will be able to use the experiences these activities provide for problem solving, negotiating, representing, reasoning, planning, estimating and discussing.

Physical development is promoted during modelling and construction activities because, as they build and create, children move themselves up and down, often crawling under and through as they construct giving them the chance to experience the relationship of body size to available space.

Dough

Using multi coloured dough with a variety of textures produced with wholemeal flour, rice, lentils or glitter, and the freedom to manipulate playdough as desired children can engage in social conversation and skills (particularly helpful for those with poor social skills), describing their actions. Colours and textures promote questions as they experiment and manipulation develops both fine and gross motor skills. This activity is helpful to those with English as an additional language as there is no competition and clear contexts. Dough is also valuable for children needing to express violent emotions and feelings in a safe and acceptable way by destroying and recreating their models.

With both modelling and dough activities there should be no predetermined end product to enable children to develop their own ideas, while you observe, support, value, encourage and praise them for their efforts.

Puppets

Puppets are an ideal medium for encouraging conversation from even the most reluctant child, including those with poorly developed social skills. Using puppets they can communicate ideas and feelings. Talking to the child through the puppet can also be used to extend their vocabulary and develop understanding of feelings and emotions.

Animals

Interaction and learning about animals can be a valuable learning experience for children. That is not to say that childminders need to keep pets, there are many alternatives. Children can study animals in their natural habitat whilst out for walks or exploring a garden or outside area. Visits could also be taken to animal-related venues, such as a local rescue centre, farm, zoo or pet centre.

Animals can be used to encourage learning in all areas of curriculums. Learning to treat animals with care and concern, and learning about animals needs, helps children in their personal and social development. Taking part in role-play with animal themes such as pretending to be animals or making farms helps children in their language and literacy development. Sequencing and matching, such as matching baby animals to their parents or sequencing chicks from eggs, to chick, to chicken helps children with mathematical development. Exploring the natural habitats of animals and discussing their needs helps children in their knowledge and understanding of the world. Making models and grooming animals helps children's physical development. Creative activities such as drawing animals, and painting, and discussions of animals smells, noises and feel helps children's creative development.

Television

Television can be a sore subject for childminders; it is sometimes suggested that children at a childminders will do nothing but sit in front of the television all day. While this is not true it does not mean that children should never be allowed to watch any television. Television is often considered to be a bad thing for children, however, there are advantages when it is used as part of a variety of other activities.

Through television children can enjoy different stories and glimpse cultures and countries they may otherwise not have known about. Television only becomes detrimental to development if children are allowed to watch it for long periods without adult supervision, watch hours of programmes that offer little to their development or, video after video just to 'keep them quiet'.

Children cannot interact with a television screen, however, if you watch a programme with a child it could promote discussion and offer ideas for games or role play to be used later. In this way television can be come a positive learning opportunity. Make sure there are interesting activities, that do not involve the television, available so children do not seek to watch it through boredom. The television should not become "background wallpaper" - switch it off between relevant programmes. The short concentration span of children under 18 months means they can gain little from television so its use should be restricted.

Computers

Like television, computers have their positive and negative points. Children should not be allowed to sit at a computer playing non-educational games for hours on end. Playing educational games, for example, ones that promote literacy and numeracy, typing stories or drawing pictures can aid a child's development when used for short periods as part of a range of activities and help incorporate ICT into children's knowledge.

Heuristic Play

During Heuristic play children discover through their play how everyday objects interact. One example of Heuristic play would be a treasure basket, favoured by non-mobile babies who can sit independently. Objects included can be stored and presented in a wicker basket and should all be everyday household objects such as an egg whisk and keys and naturally occurring items e.g. pine cones and large shells. None of the objects should be bought toys and should include textures and a variety in size of objects. All object must be clean and free from sharp edges. Treasure baskets must always be supervised closely as babies will explore objects with their mouths as well as hands.

Heuristic play can also be successfully used with other pre-school children who in addition to exploring activities may use it for imaginative play and to explore mathematical ideas.

Heuristic play is self-motivated and purposeful with children deriving pleasure from their efforts and their discoveries. Activities children 'invent' include picking up and dropping, shaking, banging, looking through, listening, giving and taking, posting and playing along side, sequencing and pairing, emptying and filling, stacking, differentiating sizes, balancing, rolling, playing together, copying, and participating in adult activities including digging, rubbish collection and sweeping leading into pretend play followed by fantasy play.

Heuristic play helps children discover concepts and increases their knowledge and understanding of the world. This form of play enables very young children to demonstrate their ability to interact and use non-verbal communication. Where mobile children are encouraged to help tidy away the opportunity for sorting, collecting and ordering occurs naturally.

Sessions with an abundance of resources tend to be calm, quiet and relaxing and provide opportunities to observe and assess children's development.

Heuristic Play Time

Six months	Treasure basket - what is it? - mouthing and feeling
Becomes	What can I do with it? - banging, seeing through, giving and taking items, posting, starts non socially, with pleasure from effort and discovery.
Becomes	Sequencing - rings onto poles, people into vehicles Pairing like items Learning about size Stacking - cans, bricks etc. Balancing - stacking items on top of each other Rolling - reels and cans
About 18 months	Children begin playing together and will take on other's ideas and copy them Filling - putting smaller items into the larger ones
About two years	Pretend play - what can it become?- the beginnings of symbolism are emerging

Domestic Activities

Many of the things a child learns through play are also learned through interactions with their childminder and the other children. This will include mealtimes, discussions, outings, visits and household tasks.

Washing up:	Confidence, self esteem, competence, responsibility, sense of community, vocabulary, volume and capacity, properties of water, bubbles, floating, sinking. Extension possibilities include: hygiene, where does water go? drains sewers, where does it come from? Rainfall and evaporation.
Watering Plants:	Confidence, self esteem, caring, responsibility, sense of community and co-ordination. Extension possibilities include: growth and requirements, size and measurements, needs of others.
Dusting:	Caring, responsibility, confidence, self esteem, reliance, co-ordination, sense of achievement and pride. Extension possibilities include: where does dust come from? waste disposal and recycling.
Eating Together:	Sharing a pleasurable experience and learning appropriate behaviour, confidence and self esteem. Extension possibilities include: vocabulary, what do others eat and how? healthy eating and hygiene.
Sharing out Snacks:	Sense of community, responsibility, confidence, self esteem, manners, sense of time, addition and subtraction. Extension possibilities include: healthy eating and hygiene.
Laying the Table:	Sense of community, responsibility, confidence, self esteem, addition and subtraction, mathematical sets and co-ordination. Extension possibilities include: cutlery use when dining out, restaurants, other forms of 'cutlery'.
Note Taking:	Responsibility, confidence, helps children act out use of written language using pre-writing skills, include telephone messages and shopping lists. Extension possibilities include: shopping, references, stories and use of written language.

Domestic activities are very useful in furthering children's understanding of their own environment and furthering their learning opportunities. The following are some of the tasks and activities children enjoy sharing and some of the learning opportunities they provide.

Wall Displays

Displaying children's work or using a display to explore a theme is a positive aid to children's development. Children can help with collecting materials, planning and decorating the display. Displaying of children's work and their helping to produce displays gives children a strong sense of accomplishment and self-worth.

Rather than using existing posters to make a display, encourage children to draw their own pictures or cut them out. Pictures can be labelled with the children's help; if necessary they can be helped to look up what to write in books. Dual language labels can help promote equal opportunities and provide an interesting talking point.

Displays can be put up on a pin board, on the wall with blue-tac, on a table or the window. Bright colours and pictures are attractive to children and writing should be large enough to read once the display is put up.

Worksheets

The worksheet seems to go in and out of favour. It is widely recognised now that children learn best through their interactions with the environment they are in, through finding out things for themselves. For example, playing with magnetic letters on the fridge or adding up the money when shopping is more helpful to children's learning than solving maths problems on paper.

This does not mean that worksheets are not useful, they can still be used as part of a broad range of other learning opportunities. Worksheets can be helpful in reinforcing the things a child is learning through other activities. For example, after a child has spent time playing with letters on the fridge a worksheet can be introduced to help with reproducing those letters, reinforcing what the child has learnt. It is important to carefully choose worksheets which offer opportunities to extend knowledge, are challenging or promote creative development. If a worksheet offers no challenge it has little value.

Worksheets should not be used as a holding activity, just given to keep a child quiet whilst you are busy with another. Interact with the child and discuss what the worksheet is, asking "and how can it be completed?" If a child becomes bored or frustrated do not force them to finish as they will be unenthusiastic when the activity is suggested in the future.

Activity Planning

When planning activities you should consider the ages and development of the children present, adaptations necessary for special needs, alternatives or adaptations to outdoor plans if the weather may affect the activity.

Supervision

Young children and babies will need constant supervision to ensure that they are safe and to avoid accidents. As children become older, supervision may become more general as they learn to abide by activity rules. The type of activity will influence supervision levels. Older children, for example, may not need close supervision when colouring once their development is such that they understand not to colour the walls or table, whereas younger children will need closer supervision to ensure this. Some activities such as those involving water involve constant supervision regardless of children's age.

Day	Activity	Benefits	Possible Adaptations
Monday	Educational computer use. Number or word games, typing stories, drawing pictures.	Helps with numeracy, literacy, keyboard skills and hand eye co-ordination.	A larger keyboard or pointer could help poor coordination. Larger type on screen or speech software for visual impairments. Assistance with reading. Support chair.
Tuesday	Painting. Using a variety of painting techniques.	Expressing feelings, thoughts and emotions. Being creative and using imagination.	If unable to use paintbrush could use hands/feet. Add texture to paint (e.g. sand) for visual impairments.
Wednesday	Musical activities could include making/using instruments, dancing or singing.	Children can express ideas and feelings. Good for physical development.	Vibrations for hearing impairment, e.g. touching drum.
Thursday	Cooking-ginger bread people, reading ginger bread man story.	Helps with weighing and measuring, understanding concepts of volume, and also literacy.	Large display or talking scales for visual impairments. Separate piece of mixture for touching and feeling. Special spoon for grasp problems.
Friday	Dressing up, role play using clothes, hats and their own masks, and 'make believe'.	Develops creative play.	Clothes that are easy to take off/put on e.g. hats, aprons.

Curriculum Planning

If you are receiving the Nursery Education Grant for three and four year olds, working with the EYFS, or are inspected for children's learning and development by Ofsted or similar your curriculum will also need to contain a wide range of opportunities, activities and experiences to cover the Early Learning Goals. You may find it helpful to begin by identifying what the children should learn and how they will be able to learn. You will also have to consider health and safety issues when devising your plans and to ensure your plan will provide an anti-bias curriculum.

You will find your routines with the children and collecting children from school, or nursery are going to affect your planning of activities and you will need to take this into account when devising your plans. Your plans should be used as guidelines and not rules so that flexibility to include spontaneous events and interests can be explored.

When devising your long, medium and short term plans you can consider what a Childminding Inspector, your Network Coordinator or Childminding Development worker will be looking for. They will be looking at your overall planning for your care and educational programme and how you are covering each area of the early years curriculum, relevant to your region, and the progress a child is making. They will want to satisfy themselves that you are making the best use of your equipment and resources in your planning and that activities and opportunities included are appropriate to the age of the children. If you are working in England they will also be looking to ensure the principles of the EYFS are embedded in your practice.

Both the childminding regulator and your network coordinator if applicable will also be looking at the plans to ensure you are using a range of teaching methods e.g. structured learning and freeplay. Plus, you can also demonstrate through your planning an equality of access and opportunity and the involvement of parents where possible.

To ensure you have planned sufficiently to cover all of the goals you will need to plan at several levels, this could include:

Short Term Plans

Short term plans contain lots of detail on a daily basis, are usually produced weekly and outline the activities, experiences and play opportunities you are planning. You may like to include in this plan any additional information from an Individual Learning Plan used to support a child with SEN or meet a child's individual needs. When setting out your plan you may find it helpful to detail fixed routines onto your plan before you add the activities and you can also include opportunities for observation and assessment of the children. These short term plans are then easy to adjust in light of children's achievements, progress and needs that the evaluations have highlighted. Other factors may need to be considered, for example when caring for Muslim children fasting during Ramadan your short term plan should not cause children to involuntarily break their fast or cause them to undertake undue exertion, or partake in inappropriate activities. These short term plans should take account of children's individual needs and be responsive to their ideas and spontaneous play.

Week Plan Start Date:		
Day	AM	PM
Monday	**Visit to Park** **Talk about** animals seen, what they eat, where they live + positioning words. **Count** Ducklings, discuss near & far, big & small. **Barking rubbing:** textures. **Look at** and smell flowers. **Notice** rubbish and talk about litter and bins. **Walking** quietly, running and stamping for troll hunt.	**Construction Toys** Megablocks, bricks and stickle bricks. **Words** - colours, shapes, positions, joining words, counting, numbers, size. **Improve** hand eye co-ordination. Sorting and matching. Sharing out bricks. Vocabulary.
Tuesday	**Role Play** Variety of props chosen by children. To be extended by additional props, vocab & suggestions, e.g. past and present events, stories and make believe. **Songs and action rhymes** Sing, actions, clap to rhythm.	**Beads** Manipulating and threading beads, abacus and counting. Number songs and stories. **Outside Play** Ball games and 'bug' hunt.
Wednesday	**Playdough** Manipulating dough, cutters, knife, rolling pin etc. **'Writing'** Children to take notes for me and read them back later.	**Story Time** Stories told and read, endings to be anticipated words followed and pages turned. **Outside Play**

	Week Plan Continued...	
Thursday	**Feelings** **Read** copycat faces, practice faces and **talk about** sadness, happiness. **Read** jealousy book **talk about** feeling jealous and why. **Draw** happy and sad faces **Listen** to happy and sad music and **dance.**	**Cutting and Sticking** **Collage** variety of materials colours and textures. **Writing** shopping list. **Walk** to local shop to buy list contents, look at money, cost and change.
Friday	**Jobs** **Talk about** peoples jobs. **Watch** man mend washing machine. Read road safety/ stranger danger books and discuss. **Small world play,** people and vehicles; encourage role play with these and cause and effect with reference to story and job roles - anti stereotypes.	**Painting** Free expression. **Talk about** colour, texture, mixing colour, brush control, drips, picture etc. **Sand play** **Think about** volume, size, textures, consistency, construction, shapes, moulding.
	Other activities will take place as the children choose between planned activities or expand on a favourite activity.	

Individual Activity Plan

If you want to plan an activity in more depth or in relation to a particular child you may use an Individual Activity Plan. It is not necessary to do this for all activities. An example follows:

Activity: Visit to Park	**Date:** 21st May 2008
Activity Details: **Talk about** animals seen, what they eat, where they live + positioning words. **Count** Ducklings, discuss near & far, big & small. **Barking rubbing:** textures. **Look at** and smell flowers. **Notice** rubbish and talk about litter and bins. **Walking** quietly, running and stamping for troll hunt.	**Possible Adaptations Needed:** If the weather is wet we will wear wellies and rain coats and stamping in puddles will be incorporated into activities. Instead of bark rubbings we will do rubbings of coins and household items when we get home.

Resources Needed: Paper and crayons for bark rubbing. Bread for ducks.

Evaluation: The weather was good so we adhered to our original plan. The children enjoyed the activities and David was particularly enthusiastic about the animals we saw describing them to his parents on collection. We plan to collect leaves and make a display using them and our bark rubbings about trees. Emma enjoyed counting the ducks and successfully counted up to 9. The children linked our discussions about litter into the effect this might have on the animals we saw, and stated that they would always put their rubbish in the bin.

Extension: Drawing what we have seen Making a display of bark rubbings Sorting our rubbish into different categories and recycling

Note: The evaluation is a brief observation of what happened, children's achievements and progressions. The extension is how the learning can be moved forwards. These notes can be brief.

Medium Term Plan

This would include less detail and would cover a longer period, a school term for example. It should ensure balance to your curriculum and may concentrate on particular concepts, skills, knowledge and attitudes you wish to develop. It should also include any daily routines. An example follows:

Theme: Holidays and Journeys	
Personal, social and emotional development Safety issues. Suitable clothing. Picnics - healthy eating. Hygiene. Behaviour.	**Knowledge and understanding of the world** Locating places on maps and globe. Varieties of transportation. Seat belts and harnesses. Places of interest - details. Foreign lands - cultures and foods.
Communication, language and literacy Stories. Songs. Travel games - I spy, animals beginning with... Looking at brochures. Recollection of past holidays and trips.	**Physical development** Stepping stone paths and trails. Mimicking transport. Awareness of space.
Mathematical development / problem solving, reasoning & numeracy Making maps. Calculating how far. Counting.	**Creative development** Posters. Role play. Weaving.
Notes: need travel brochures, find photos of trips and outings and borrow some from parents to help with recollections.	

Plans do not have to be theme orientated. You may prefer to use a Medium Term Plan such as the following example:

Personal, social and emotional development	Knowledge and understanding of the world
Caring & sharing Expected behaviour Listening to others Healthy snacks Domestic & gardening tasks - sense of belonging Caring for animals - awareness of needs Visit new places Self confidence Self esteem Dressing ourselves	Nature trails Woodland walks Canal visit Outings to shops, garage, market, vets Road safety Planting and growing flowering plants and vegetables
Communication, language and literacy Vocabulary Communication skills poems & stories Songs Action rhymes Captions and labels Descriptions Pictorial time table	**Physical development** Outdoor games - gross motor skills Enacting big, small & locomotion Enacting animal / bird movements Running, walking, stairs, climbing Pencil control Hand eye coordination Construction activities Health & hygiene
Mathematical development / problem solving, reasoning & numeracy Reasoning & numeracy Shapes, size & growth Measurement of growth - height charts (children & plants) Shopping & money Weighing fruit & vegetables at supermarket Patterns and sequencing Counting, more than, less than Number songs & rhymes Pairs - animal ark & socks	**Creative development** Songs & music Musical movement Musical instruments Role play Modelling- junk, arc & animals Painting & drawing Collage Dough & gloop activities Planting pots / tubs for patio area Photography Den construction Cooking

NOTES:
Bedding plants
Parental permission slips
Healthy treats cornflour
Photographic paper for printer.

Long Term Plan

This plan could cover four to twelve months. It should contain broad outlines of activities, outings, themes, required attributes, visitors and routines. It should be appropriate for the age and stage of development of children present. Your plans can also include the use of local environments and events such as seasons, weather and festivals. It can be of benefit to link the overall activities and opportunities to the Early Learning Goals and children's development to ensure full coverage. Long term planning gives you time to ensure you can make use of resources and equipment available and obtain other resources needed by purchase, borrowing or from a loan scheme or toy library.

There is no right and wrong way to set out your plans providing they are clear and easy to use and understand. The amount of detail you show on the plan is your choice, but they should be able to be followed by outside agencies including regulatory bodies such as Ofsted. The short term plans for example could be set out as a timetable or produced in detail to show key learning intentions, Stepping Stones or the ELG's for each activity; the target language you hope children will achieve; and may also contain annotations for the resources you will be using.

SUMMER TERM 2008				
Areas of Learning	**Themes Linked to the Areas of Learning**			
	Making a Garden	**The Woods**	**Wheels**	**Holidays and Journeys**
Personal Social and Emotional Development	Caring for plants and the environment.	Keeping safe, caring for others, environmental issues.	Looking after our property and respecting other peoples.	Safety issues, suitable clothing, picnics.
Communication Language and Literacy	Vocabulary and using reference books.	Vocabulary, stories, reference books.	Vocabulary, stories, rhymes and labels.	Stories, songs and travel games.
Mathematical Development / Problem Solving, Reasoning & Numeracy	Growth charts.	Numbers and shapes in the environment.	Shape, number, position, and size.	Making maps.
Knowledge and Understanding of the World	Visits to garden centres and gardens.	Wildlife, tree variety, season, wardens.	Outing to tyre specialist, bus stop and car park, tyre tracks.	Locating places on maps and globe, varieties of transport.
Physical Development	Effects of exertion.	Walking, running, outdoor ball games.	Riding bikes, scooters etc, awareness of space.	Stepping stone paths and trails.
Creative Development	Photography, painting, paper flowers.	Bark rubbing, leaf prints, plastercasts of paw prints.	Collage of wheel shapes, junk models, role play.	Posters and role play.

Themes

There are many themes appropriate for using with children in the three to four year age bracket. These include: what we eat, self, growing, where we live, homes and shops, buildings, the garden, people who help us, opposites, water, animals and pets, nursery rhymes, festivals and celebrations, countries, seasons, weather, holidays, transport, wheels, colours, shapes and time. Themes such as these can appear in your long term plans, but each can be divided up to appear in more detail as smaller topics in your short term plans.

It is not essential to use themes but for some people they can aid planning. However, all themes used must be of interest to the children and be able to be adapted to allow full participation by all of the children.

Individual Education Plan

Whilst curriculum planning should be undertaken with each individual child in mind it may not be possible to encompass all the strategies some children require in order for them to progress and they may need an Individual Education Plan (IEP). Individual plans are produced for children who have special needs and may cover both educational or behavioural needs. They will contain actions or targets which are different to the experiences within your standard curriculum.

Childminders may be involved in the process of producing an IEP either because they are accredited childminders, working with the EYFS, or because they care for a child who is having a plan produced at another educational setting.

An IEP will need to contain strategies to help a child progress and include short term targets for the child. It should include the teaching strategies for how these targets will be worked towards. The targets are usually related to behaviour and social skills, communication, literacy and mathematics.

People involved in devising an IEP may include: the parents, the child, the childminder, Special Needs Coordinator (SENCO) and the teacher. IEPs should always be discussed with the parents and child. Children must be involved at an appropriate level using language appropriate for the child's development, understanding and needs. It will be helpful to ask them about their difficulties and explain about targets.

When planning an IEP it is best to choose 3-4 targets with the aim of progression from what the child can already achieve. For example if the child can listen for two minutes extend this with a target of five minutes. Always set targets in small steps.

It can be particularly helpful to discuss with all those working with the child what their preferred way of working towards the set targets is. Choosing the correct approach for the child will help elicit a better response and co-operation from the child.

You should consider how often and how long you will spend with the child working towards their targets. Children can tire easily and it is better to plan for short frequent sessions, rather than longer sessions. Lots of repetition will help a child learn and consolidate their learning before you move on to the next step.

The IEP should have a set review date. This should be long enough for targets to be met but not too long that new targets are not set as the child progresses. You may find three months is a good starting point. The length of time between reviews can always be altered at the next one. A regular review should also be held if the child meets targets in advance of the review date. At a review both children's and parent's views should be sought on the progress being achieved.

When working with a child, remember to praise any success. You should be honest because they can tell if they have reached a goal. Non success should be addressed in a positive way by suggesting alternative ways of achieving and praise being given for efforts.

The IEP will become a working record of progress; children's achievements should be recorded together with any difficulties and any strategies that worked well or failed. Children may like to help in recording success, such as by using star charts. If the IEP is not working well a review is needed. This should become apparent by comparing previous progress to current progress. The monitoring of IEP's and their evaluation can be used during the process of statutory assessment should this be required.

The following is an example of the long term objectives set for a non verbal child with motor skill below those expected of children of a similar age where lack of eye contact made communication difficult (Luke has ADHD, is Autistic and has Mosaic Downs Syndrome).

Objectives:

- Luke engages in activities requiring hand-eye coordination, for example jigsaws, when encouraged by an adult seated with him, everyday, midmorning.
- Luke will move with more control and coordination, both individually and in a group situation, supported by an adult or his peer group, everyday and whenever possible.
- Luke will hold eye contact while communicating between himself, adults and peer group on 50% of occasions.

These objectives are then broken down into smaller steps. Each week the steps are evaluated before planning the next weeks targets with repetition and reinforcement included as necessary. The steps were developed over an eight week period for the two days attended by the child so that by the last week the objectives were reached. The following example shows week one.

Child's name: Luke	Week beginning: 5/5/08
Weekly targets: To show interest in shape sorters To walk outdoors without tripping To respond when called	**Teaching arrangements:** One-one support, range of sorters, bright colours Childminder to hold hands and peer group to join in Reinforce Luke's name as personal to him, peers and childminder
Daily evaluation:	
Monday: Luke showed some interest in shape sorters, easily frustrated and temper tantrums when shapes don't fit. Walking- drags feet and shuffles toes down, this may be causing tripping. Responding on his terms only.	
Tuesday: Prefers to transport shapes than post. Walking - encouraged to pick feet up when walking, less stumbling occurred. Responding - still on his terms	

Recording Children's Progress

You may like to record children's progress as you follow their development and progression through the Foundation Stage, Birth to Three or the EYFS. This will help your future planning and show you the children's developmental stage and help you make future curriculum plans. One way to depict progress is to use a pictorial representation. This is easily filled in and can be fun for the children to help with. It will demonstrate to both network staff and regulators the progress being made and will make sharing the information with parents simple and provide them with a permanent record they can keep and/or share with the next education provider. Other methods include observations, daily diaries and child profiles. See Section 14. For Observation, Assessment and Evaluation.

Child Profiles

A child profile demonstrates the uniqueness of a child and illustrates their physical development, experiences, interests, learning and achievements. There is no right of wrong way to produce your profile; however, it must be manageable, clearly understandable by outside agencies and always reflect the child positively. It is inappropriate to include any sensitive or confidential information within the profile.

The profile can be used to extend planning for the child, show patterns in children's learning and behaviour, plot children's progress, reveal schema's, provide a memento for a parent,

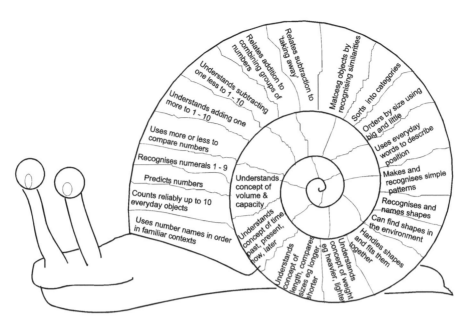

Evaluation Criteria for Mathematical Development

help children with recollections, demonstrate to a regulatory body, network coordinator, early years advisor or childcare development officer how effective your planning and observation cycles have been.

Children should be allowed to develop a sense of pride and ownership of their profile and encouraged to choose work or photographs to include. Encouraging parents to share their child's profile with yourself and the child at regular intervals enables reflection on development, learning and achievements and demonstrates working in partnership with parents and helps children develop self esteem and self worth.

A profile is considered to be formative assessment as it demonstrates how a child progresses and develops. When a child reaches the end of a developmental phase or will be concluding their time with you, you may find it helpful to summarise the information collected. This summary would be referred to as a summative assessment (the sum of assessments made) and can indicate areas which need further consideration.

Profiles can be organised by areas of learning, aspects or as a continuous diary like record highlighting areas of children's learning in the summary completed termly. The diary style profile shows more clearly play preferences, personal interests and schemas that evolve, and provides a more holistic child centred record, but it can make picking out areas of learning more difficult without practice.

Scrapbooks may be suitable for diary style profiles or you may prefer to use loose leaf and a ring binder, particularly if you are including computer produced records such as plans. The following are suggestions for possible inclusion in a profile. It is not an exhaustive list and the contents will be dependant on the child in your care.

Pen pictures: Profiles may be accessed by a range of adults so an introductory page can be helpful. This could take the form of a pen picture of the child and could include name, age, date of birth, position in family, cultural heritage, likes, dislikes, routines and current abilities. Information can be collected from the child, parents and records.

Baseline assessment: This is an overview of where the child is developmentally for example in motor skills, socially and emotionally and in language.

Monitored communication: This could include words or signs in use and sentence length. The use of this will be dependent on the age and stage of development and is not always essential.

Parental contributions: This could include written or verbal comments or reports from parents, observations and photographs.

Observations & evaluations: These can be both brief notes and longer observations of activities, learning, development and progress made.

Planning: This can include both long and short term objectives or intentions, curriculum planning, routines and IEP's.

Reports: These might include reports from other professionals such as physiotherapists and speech and language therapists.

Photographs: These should be given a descriptive title and can be annotated to tell the story where required and might include children taking part in activities, achieving a first or pictures of children's creations particularly those which will not keep, like sand castles, piles of bricks and dens and those which they would prefer to take home.

Samples of children's work: These could include samples of proto writing, art work or sewing.

Summaries: These are produced by processing the content of the observations, evaluations, photographs and samples of work and show the progress made within the relevant curriculum.

Permission forms: It can be helpful to include a copy of relevant permission forms such as permission for observations and use of photographs.

Early Years Foundation Stage (EYFS)

In England, from September 2008, the following Birth to Three framework and Foundation Stage together with the National Standards are combined to form the EYFS. This framework is compulsory for all children from birth to the August after their fifth birthday, including those with childminders and other Ofsted registered provisions. Childminders should follow the statutory guidance to ensure they are following all the legal requirements. An overview is provided in Section 1. Childminding: An Overview, English National Standards/EYFS Overview.

The practice guidance, provided to all practitioners, shows how you can meet the children's welfare needs, how the four themes: a unique child, positive relationships, enabling environment, learning & development, must be embedded in your practice. The guidance demonstrates good practice for care and learning with suggestions for planning and resourcing and the developmental steps children are likely to make in each of the areas of learning and development.

There are Principles into Practice Cards which can be used as pointers to encourage observations, effective practice, play and support opportunities, planning and resourcing and ideas for combating challenges or dilemmas you may encounter and a CD Rom containing a range of resources, which will also be useful for assignments.

Children are grouped into six basic stages which overlap to allow for differing developmental rates. The age groups are only an outline with the stage of development more important when providing for each individual child. The age groups used are: 0-11, 8-20, 16-26, 22-36, 30-50, and 40-60+ months.

❑   A Unique Child

This theme reflects on the importance of planning around the individual child. Children are individuals and competent learners from birth, confident and self assured. To ensure this theme is embedded in your practice focus on having a good working knowledge of each child's developmental stage, their individuality, their potential to become self assured and confident. Consider the importance of children's well-being within a secure, safe and inclusive environment (see Section 7. Health, Hygiene & Safety, Section 10. Equal Opportunities, Section 11. Caring for Children with Special Needs and Section 13. Childcare Unravelled for ideas).

A unique child links to the Every Child Matters outcomes : Making a Positive Contribution, Stay Safe and Be Healthy.

❑   **Positive Relationships**
Children learn to be strong and independent from having secure, loving relationships. To embed this theme focus on having a good working relationship with parents and developing children's attachments to yourself to achieve the seven C's detailed in Other Considerations within this chapter.

Positive relationships links to the Every Child Matters outcomes: Making a Positive Contribution, and Stay Safe.

❑   **Enabling Environments**
Environment plays a key role in supporting and extending children's development and learning. This theme reflects the importance of planning around resources and the environment to promote learning rather than producing schedules of adult led activities. Remember the environment you provide and the wider the environment you visit impacts on learning. Regular assessments and observations of children's progress enable planning to extend learning and adapt the environment as required (see this chapter and Section 14. Observation, Assessment and Evaluation for more ideas).

Enabling environments links to the Every Child Matters outcomes: Making a Positive Contribution and Enjoy and Achieve.

❑   **Learning & Development**
Children develop at different rates and in different ways; all areas of learning are interconnected and important. This picks up on the Birth to Three aspect, A Competent Learner. To include the Learning and Development theme in your planning focus on providing learning experiences that are developmentally appropriate, stimulating and challenging that will promote the acquisition of a wide range of skills and knowledge in a holistic manner (read the rest of this chapter for ideas).

Learning and development links to the Every Child Matters outcome: Enjoy and Achieve.

The six areas of learning and development and their accompanying Early Learning Goals are taken directly from the previous Foundation Stage and the pointers included under the Foundation Stage heading are equally applicable to the EYFS.

Minor changes under the area Communication, Language & Literacy were made to update the previous Foundation Stage before incorporating it into the EYFS.

❑   Hear and say initial and final sounds in words, and short vowel sounds within words. Has been replaced by:
❑   Hear and say sounds in words in the order in which they occur.

Mathematical Development has been renamed Problem Solving, Reasoning and Numeracy, but the Early Learning Goals remain the same.

To use the EYFS effectively a cycle of observation, planning and assessment should be used reflectively to ensure individual needs and current interests of the children are met. It is also good practice to document children's learning journey as they progress through your childminding setting using a diary, scrap book or child profile.

Much of childminders existing practice has naturally been incorporated into the EYFS requirements, making it easier to achieve than some settings. For example childminders already gather information about children and their families using child record sheets to include children's language and cultural requirements, likes, dislikes, allergies, health problems and many make notes or observations regarding children's development and learning, involve parents in supporting their child's development and take children out of the house on a regular basis and engage in messy play. They also undertake health and safety audits and regular risk assessments, promote equality of learning and work in partnership with parents.

Birth to Three

This is not a curriculum. It is a framework which encourages a focus on the child and how they learn, emphasising the importance of seeing the whole child and understanding how each aspect of a child's development impacts on other areas. It does not divide learning into distinct areas or skills but it identifies four aspects of early learning: strong child, skilful communicator, competent learner and healthy child. The aspects are subdivided into four components. In Scotland, Birth to Three's key features are relationships, responsive care and respect, and developing a sense of self. It is also a less prescriptive framework.

Birth to Three in all regions stresses the importance of the environment, experiences and relationships.

A strong child:
❑ Me, myself & I   (awareness of self & own abilities)
❑ Being acknowledged & affirmed   (include friendships)
❑ Developing self-assurance   (includes self-confidence)
❑ A sense of belonging   (includes being a member of a social group)

A skilful communicator:
❑ Being together   (positive relationships & conversation)
❑ Finding a voice   (using language)
❑ Listening & responding   (observing and responding to language)
❑ Making meaning   (understanding and being understood)

Babies are born with the ability to learn language and their verbal communication begins with their very first sounds. These sounds are gradually changed to fit the language they hear the most, i.e. 'the mother tongue'. Children learn how their 'mother tongue' works by hearing it used by 'experts' around them and by using it for themselves. Children practice talking and will often generalise rules e.g. "one sheep, two sheeps." They will gradually refine what they say until they learn the conventions of their 'mother tongue'.

There is a strong link between a child's development of language and their ability to think and understand. Talking is an important thinking skill. When we talk we work out what we think, and as the vocabulary increases so does the ability to make sense of the world around us. We can then use the language to engage in symbolic thought and reading becomes possible.

A competent learner:
❑ Making connections   (making sense, includes discovery and early maths)
❑ Being imaginative   (includes the beginnings of symbolic play)
❑ Being creative   (movements, touch, music,art, crafts)
❑ Representing   (includes symbolism and early mark making)

Sharing books, stories and rhymes with children is important for helping them develop their language and communication skills. It is important to match books to the development level of the child. For example, at one year a child will prefer a brightly coloured picture book that they can look at, to a book containing mainly text. A wide range of books should be provided from soft vinyl books with brightly coloured pictures and no text to story books with pictures.

A healthy child:
❑ Emotional well-being   (including emotional stability and self help skills)
❑ Growing and developing   (including physical development)
❑ Keeping safe   (including discovering boundaries, limits and
                                               rules and saying no)
❑ Healthy choices   (including making choices and personal hygiene)

When planning for children in the 0-3 year age range it is easier to plan developmentally appropriate traditional play based activities and excursions within a supportive environment which value children's individuality efforts and achievements. Then you can see which components are not obvious and add them. This will ensure plans can flow with the children's needs and be adaptable enough to take in unplanned experiences and develop according to the interests and needs of the child, while covering the full range of aspects and components and you will not become 'bogged down' by over planning. Brief observations and evaluations will indicate what children achieve and what plans should develop towards.

Effective practice within the Birth to Three includes the following:

❑ Treating children as individuals when planning
❑ Time for interactions as you talk and play with the children
❑ Developmentally appropriate experiences and activities
❑ Developmentally appropriate resources and environment
❑ Effective and responsive relationships with children and family
❑ Equality of opportunities
❑ Being enthusiastic and motivating
❑ Using observation to extend and respond to children's interests

The Birth to Three framework can be used to encourage children's all round development and guide your practice helping produce positive outcomes for children as you record and share their progress.

Foundation Stage/Phase & EYFS

Note: In England the Foundation Stage has been incorporated into the EYFS under the theme Learning and Development.

Foundation Stage curriculums are for children aged from three and ending at five years old in England, six years in Scotland and Northern Ireland, seven in Wales. They put the emphasis on activities being fun, relevant and motivating for each child and learning being carefully planned and structured. This stage should be play-based, child centred and holistic.

"Learning for young children should be a rewarding and enjoyable experience in which they explore, investigate, discover, create, practise, rehearse, repeat, revise and consolidate their developing knowledge, skills, understanding and attitudes. During the Foundation Stage, many of these aspects of learning are brought together effectively through playing and talking" (Curriculum guidance document, Department for Education and Employment)

Foundation Stage curriculums are organised into four areas of learning in Southern Ireland, five in Scotland, six in England, seven in Wales and Northern Ireland. The areas of learning are:

❑ Identity & Belonging (S. Ireland).
❑ Well-being (S. Ireland).
❑ Personal, Social and Emotional Development (Scotland; England)
❑ Personal, Social and Emotional Development & Well Being (Wales)
❑ Personal Development & Mutual Understanding (N. Ireland)
❑ Language, Communication and Literacy Development/Skills (England; Wales)
❑ Language & Literacy (N. Ireland)
❑ Communication (S Ireland)
❑ Communication & Language (Scotland)
❑ Problem Solving, Reasoning & Numeracy (England)
❑ Mathematical Development (Wales; not applicable in Scotland)
❑ Mathematics & Numeracy (N. Ireland)
❑ Knowledge and Understanding of the World (England, Scotland; Wales)
❑ The World Around Us (N. Ireland)
❑ Thinking & Exploring (S. Ireland)
❑ Physical Development (England;Wales)
❑ Physical Development & Movement (N. Ireland; Scotland)
❑ Creative Development (England & Wales;
❑ Expressive & Aesthetic Development (Scotland)
❑ Expressive & Aesthetic Development & Arts (N. Ireland)
❑ Bilingualism & Multicultural Understanding (Wales)
❑ Religious Education (N. Ireland)

In school the 'reception' class can be the final year of the Foundation Stage, therefore many children should already be working towards the Foundation Stage before they start school. Childminders belonging to a Accredited Network may be able to access funding for 3-4 year olds for provision of the Foundation Stage Curriculum. Note: Foundation stage curriculums are continually evolving and your local childcare development team should supply you with the latest guidance. The following is a summary of the latest information at the time of publication.

Personal, Social and Emotional Development and Well Being

This includes development of independence skills, particularly important for those who are highly dependent on adult support for personal care. Children with behaviour disorders and vulnerable children will require extra support and a structured approach to achieve successful social and emotional development.

Children need positive examples and materials that will challenge their thinking, with opportunities for play and learning which take into account and value children's particular religious and cultural beliefs and promote self esteem.

Children should be encouraged to negotiate and settle differences while becoming aware of the ethos of right and wrong and the feelings of themselves and others. Positive encouragement and experiences help children gain and retain the disposition to learn.

By the end of the Foundation Stage, (DfES Statutory Framework for the EYFS, Early Learning Goals (ELG's),
most children in England will:

❑ Continue to be interested, excited and motivated to learn;
❑ Be confident to try new activities, initiate ideas and speak in a familiar group;
❑ Maintain attention, concentrate, and sit quietly when appropriate;
❑ Have a developing awareness of their own needs, views and feelings and be sensitive to the needs, views and feelings of others;
❑ Have a developing respect for their own cultures and beliefs and those of other people;
❑ Respond to significant experiences, showing a range of feelings when appropriate;
❑ Form good relationships with adults and peers;

❑ Work as part of a group or class, taking turns and sharing fairly, understanding that there needs to be agreed values and codes of Behaviour for groups of people, including adults and children, to work together harmoniously;

❑ Understand what is right, what is wrong, and why;

❑ Dress and undress independently and manage their own personal hygiene;

❑ Select and use activities and resources independently;

❑ Consider the consequences of their words and actions for themselves and others;

❑ Understand that people have different needs, views, cultures and beliefs, which need to be treated with respect;

❑ Understand that they can expect others to treat their needs, views, cultures and beliefs with respect.

By the end of the Foundation Stage, (Scottish Executive) most children in Scotland will:

❑ Develop confidence, self esteem and a sense of security;

❑ Care for themselves and their personal safety;

❑ Develop independence, for example in dressing and personal hygiene;

❑ Persevere in tasks that at first present some difficulties;

❑ Express appropriately feelings, needs and preferences;

❑ Form positive relationships with other children and adults, and begin to develop particular friendships with other children;

❑ Become aware that the celebration of cultural and religious festivals is important in peoples lives;

❑ Develop positive attitudes towards others whose gender, language, religion or culture, for example, is different from their own;

❑ Care for the environment and for other people in the community.

By age five of the Foundation Phase, most children in Wales will:

❑ Feel confident and be able to form relationships with other children and adults;

❑ Demonstrate care, respect and affection for other children and adults;

❑ Begin to show sensitivity to others and to those with difficulties;

❑ Concentrate for lengthening periods when involved in appropriate tasks;

❑ Explore and experiment confidently with new learning opportunities;

❑ Acknowledge the need for help and seek help when needed;

❑ Begin to take responsibility for personal hygiene (for example washing hands after using the toilet, before handling food);

❑ Dress them selves, if given time and encouragement;

❑ Take turns, share and begin to exercise self control;

❑ Understand that all living things should be treated with care, respect and concern;

❑ Respond positively to a range of new cultural and linguistic experiences.

By School entry at four, most children in Northern Ireland will:

❑ Show sense of personal worth;

❑ Increasing self confidence, self control and self discipline;

❑ Enjoy relationships with other children and adults and can work independently and as part of a group;

❑ Learning to share, take turns, follow and lead;

❑ Becoming sensitive to the needs and feelings of others and can demonstrate consideration for others;

❑ Some understanding of rules and routines and engages in acceptable behaviour;

❑ Some independence in dressing and personal hygiene;

❑ Eager to explore new learning;

❑ Increasing awareness of the importance of healthy food, hygienic habits, exercise and rest;

❑ Persevere with tasks and seek help when needed enjoying their achievements;

❑ Learning to treat living things and the environment with respect, care and concern.

In short the goals for personal, social and emotional development should help children develop confidence, social skills and a desire to learn.

Language, Communication and Literacy Development

As a child becomes more competent with text they rely less on the pictures to follow a story, and can cope with fewer illustrations. As they progress the text can be reduced in size, the amount of text increased and the length of story as their attention span increases. You should not always rely on age to choose suitable books, developmental level is more important.

Books should be enjoyable and stimulating to children. Children often enjoy books that reflect their own experiences. Books should represent all groups of society positively, including those with special needs, and of varied cultures, shown in non-stereotypical roles. The children may also find it interesting to explore dual language books.

A trip to the local library so they children can choose their own books is often very popular. Reading books can promote discussion and imagination; children who cannot yet read will often make up their own stories from the pictures.

It is through play that children become aware their gestures and actions can represent real things and develop ways of representing their experiences through these symbols. Recording and sharing their experiences symbolically through drawing, painting, constructing and play helps them learn about the more abstract system of signs - written words.

The more you encourage children to talk about themselves, events, ideas, objects and experiences the greater a child's vocabulary will become. You will also find they have the chance to practice language conventions. Children like to practice words with favourite sounds, rhythms and patterns, poems and singing provide excellent opportunities.

Mark making by children is their first attempts at writing and should be encouraged. Give them a purpose such as your shopping list to write, a motive (such as we can go and get the shopping), and they will begin to give meanings to their marks. As they practice they will begin adding shapes and squiggles in their writing, copying what they have seen you do, with recognisable letters appearing soon afterwards. Usually those you have demonstrated when you write their name on everything. Mark making should be fun and part of play, not a set task.

By the end of the Foundation Stage, in England, (DfES Statutory Framework for the EYFS, ELG's), most children in England will be able to:

❑ Enjoy listening to and using spoken and written language, and readily turn to it in their play and learning;
❑ Explore and experiment with sounds, words and texts;
❑ Listen with enjoyment and respond to stories, songs and other music, rhymes and poems and make up their own stories, songs, rhymes and poems;
❑ Use language to imagine and recreate roles and experiences;
❑ Use talk to organise, sequence and clarify thinking, ideas, feelings and events;
❑ Sustain attentive listening, responding to what they have heard by relevant comments, questions or actions;
❑ Interact with others, negotiating plans and activities and taking turns in conversation;
❑ Extend their vocabulary, exploring the meanings and sounds of new words;
❑ Retell narratives in the correct sequence, drawing on the language patterns of stories;
❑ Speak clearly and audibly with confidence and control and show awareness of the listener, for example by their use of conventions such as greetings, 'please' and 'thank you';
❑ Hear and say sounds in words, in the order in which they occur;
❑ Link sounds to letters, naming and sounding the letters of the alphabet;
❑ Read a range of familiar and common words and simple sentences independently;

❑ Know that print carries meaning and, in English, is read from left to right and top to bottom;

❑ Show an understanding of the elements of stories, such as main character, sequence of events, and openings, and how information can be found in non-fiction texts to answer questions about where, who, why and how;

❑ Attempt writing for various purposes, using features of different forms such as lists, stories and instructions;

❑ Write their own names and other things such as labels and captions and begin to form simple sentences, sometimes using punctuation;

❑ Use their phonic knowledge to write simple regular words and make phonetically plausible attempts at more complex words;

❑ Use a pencil and hold it effectively to form recognisable letters, most of which are correctly formed.

By the end of the Foundation Stage, (Scottish Executive) most children in Scotland will:

❑ Have fun with language and making stories;

❑ Listen to other children and adults during social activities and play;

❑ Listen with enjoyment and respond to stories, songs, music, rhymes and other poetry;

❑ Listen and respond to the sounds and rhythm of words in stories, songs, music and rhyme;

❑ Pay attention to information and instruction from and adult;

❑ Talk to other children or with an adult about themselves and their experiences;

❑ Express needs, thoughts and feelings with increasing confidence in speech and non-verbal language;

❑ Take part in short and more extended conversations;

❑ Use talk during role play and retell a story of rhyme;

❑ Use language for an increasing variety of purposes, for example to describe, explain, predict, ask questions and develop ideas;

❑ Use books to find interesting information;

❑ Recognise the link between the written and spoken word;

❑ Understand some of the language and layout of books;

❑ Develop an awareness of letter names and sounds in the context of play experiences;

❑ Use their own drawings and written marks to express ideas and feelings;

❑ Experiment with symbols, letters and, in some cases, words in writing;

❑ Recognise some familiar words and letters, for example the initial letter in their name.

By age five of the Foundation Phase, most children in Wales will:

❑ Listen to a good story;

❑ Relate the broad thrust of the story;

❑ Listen, respond to and recall songs, nursery rhymes, poems and jingles;

❑ Communicate needs;

❑ Ask questions and listen to responses;

❑ Re tell their own experiences, broadly in the order in which they occurred;

❑ Discuss their current individual and group play and refer to their intentions

❑ Express opinions and make choices;

❑ Identify and explain events illustrated in pictures;

❑ Choose a book and hold it the right way;

❑ Understand that written symbols have sound and meaning;

❑ Understand some of the functions of writing;

❑ Enjoy marking and basic writing experiences- using pencils, crayons etc;

❑ Use marking implements for a range of purposes: painting, drawing, writing, scrubbing.

By School entry at four, most children in Northern Ireland will:

❑ Show evidence of growing vocabulary;

❑ Show development of listening and conversational skills;

❑ Express thoughts, ideas and feelings with increasing confidence and fluency;

❑ Talk about experiences, ask questions and follow directions and instructions;
❑ Sustain attentive listening and respond to stories, nursery rhymes, poems, jingles and songs;
❑ Show an awareness of rhyme;
❑ Engage in role play, using appropriate language to express feelings;
❑ Enjoy books and be aware print has meaning;
❑ Recognise own name;
❑ Create pictures to convey thoughts or ideas;
❑ Use symbols and patterns engaging in attempts at writing in a variety of media.

In short the goals for language, literacy and communication mean children should learn about reading and enjoy listening to and telling stories.

Mathematical Development, Early Mathematical Experiences

Mathematical concepts are formed through children's interaction with the environment and these concepts will increase in complexity as you widen their experiences through the use of appropriate activities and conversations.

Children prefer activities which are imaginative, enjoyable and practical. If you talk to children about what they see you will be underpinning their oral development of mathematics.

Children using means of communication other then spoken English will need additional help in developing and understanding specific mathematical language.

By the end of the Foundation Stage, (DfES Statutory Framework for the EYFS, ELG's) most children in England will be able to:

❑ Say and use number names in order in familiar contexts;
❑ Count reliably up to ten everyday objects;
❑ Recognise numerals 1 to 9;
❑ Use language such as 'more' or 'less', 'greater' or 'smaller', 'heavier' or 'lighter', to compare two numbers or quantities;
❑ In practical activities and discussion begin to use the vocabulary involved in adding and subtracting;
❑ Find one more or one less than a number from 1 to 10;
❑ Begin to relate addition to combining two groups of objects, and subtraction to 'taking away';
❑ Talk about, recognise and recreate simple patterns;
❑ Use language such as 'circle' or 'bigger' to describe the shape and size of solids and flat shapes;
❑ Use everyday words to describe position;
❑ Use developing mathematical ideas and methods to solve practical problems.

By age five of the Foundation Phase, most children in Wales will:

❑ Use mathematical language in relevant contexts: shape, position, size and quantity;
❑ Recognise and create basic patterns;
❑ Recall a range of number rhymes, songs, stories and counting games;
❑ Sort, match, order, sequence, compare and count familiar objects;
❑ Begin to understand mathematical concepts such as 'less' and 'more';
❑ Begin to understand the mathematics of money;
❑ Begin to recognise numbers and begin to match number to sign and sound.

By school entry at four, most children in Northern Ireland will:

❑ Begin to understand early concepts of size and quantity;
❑ Use mathematical language such as, heavy, light, full, empty, long, short, more, another, big and little in relevant contexts;

❑ Show awareness of time through talking about daily routines, seasonal events and turn taking;

❑ Begin to understand and use positional words such as, in front of, behind, above and below;

❑ Talk about shapes in the environment;

❑ In the course of play question, predict and experiment, sort, match, order, sequence and count;

❑ Learn number rhymes and songs and listen to stories with mathematical elements.

In summary, these mathematical development goals are about numbers, patterns and comparisons.

Knowledge and Understanding of the World, The World Around Us

This is promoted by providing activities based on first-hand experiences that encourage exploration, observation, problem solving, prediction, critical thinking and discussion. The environment inside and outside should be interesting to children and have a wide range of activities which are imaginative and enjoyable.

Children should be supported in developing the appropriate vocabulary and assisted if they would like to record information. Children with sensory impairments will need to be provided with supplementary experience and information.

By the end of the Foundation Stage, (DfES Statutory Framework for the EYFS, ELG's) most children in England will be able to:

❑ Investigate objects and materials by using all of their senses as appropriate;

❑ Find out about, and identify some features of, living things, objects and events they observe;

❑ Look closely at similarities, differences, patterns and change;

❑ Ask questions about why things happen and how things work;

❑ Build and construct with a wide range of objects, selecting appropriate resources, and adapting their work where necessary;

❑ Select the tools and techniques they need to shape, assemble and join the materials they are using;

❑ Find out about and identify the uses of everyday technology and use information and communication technology and programmable toys to support their learning;

❑ Find out about past and present events in their own lives, and in those of their families and other people they know;

❑ Observe, find out about, and identify features in the place they live and the natural world;

❑ Begin to know about their own cultures and beliefs and those of other people;

❑ Find out about their environment, and talk about those features they like and dislike.

By the end of the Foundation Stage, (Scottish Executive) most children in Scotland will:

❑ Develop their powers of observation using their senses;

❑ Recognise objects by sight, sound, touch, smell and taste;

❑ Ask questions, experiment, design and make, and solve problems;

❑ Recognise pattens, shapes and colours in the world around them;

❑ Sort and categorise things into groups;

❑ Understand some properties of materials for example soft/hard, smooth/rough;

❑ Understand the routines and jobs of familiar people;

❑ Become familiar with the local area;

❑ Become aware of everyday uses of technology and use these appropriately (scissors, waterproof clothing, fridge, bicycle);

❑ Be aware of daily time sequences and words to describe/measure time, for example snack time, morning, first, next, clock, bedtime;

❑ Be aware of change and its effects on them, for example their own growth, changes in the weather, trees and flowers;

❑ Care for living things, for example, plants, pets at home;

❑ Be aware of feeling good and of the importance of hygiene, diet, exercise and personal safety;

❑ Develop an appreciation of natural beauty and a sense of wonder about the world;

❑ Understand and use mathematical processes such as matching, sorting, grouping, counting and measuring;

❑ Apply these processes in solving mathematic problems;

❑ Identify and use numbers up to ten during play experiences and counting games;

❑ Recognise familiar shapes during play activities;

❑ Use mathematical language appropriate to the learning situation.

By age five of the Foundation Phase, most children in Wales will:

❑ Talk about homes and where they live;

❑ Begin to understand about different places, such as the countryside and the town;

❑ Have a basic understanding of the seasons and their features;

❑ Begin to understand the idea of time: meal times, time of the day (morning, bedtime), sequencing (yesterday, today, tomorrow);

❑ Identify some kinds of workers by characteristics of work: for example, dentist, doctor, farmer, teacher,postal worker, factory worker, mechanic;

❑ Have a basic understanding of the purpose and use of money;

❑ Begin to find out about outcomes, problem solving and decision making;

❑ Begin to understand the use of a variety of information sources (for example: books, television, libraries, information technology);

❑ Begin to appreciate the importance of the environment;

❑ Begin to understand about food and where it comes from;

❑ Begin to appreciate the differences in and uses of a range of materials;

❑ Make choices and select materials from a range, exploring their potential, cutting, folding, joining and comparing.

By school entry at four, most children in Northern Ireland will:

❑ Observe, explore, investigate and select materials in a range of situations;

❑ Ask why things happen and how things work;

❑ Cut, stick, fold, pour, construct using a variety of materials;

❑ Begin to recognise body parts and identify familiar sounds;

❑ Talk about observations and make simple predictions for example, what happens if water is added to sand;

❑ Be learning to care for and show interest in the environment and are aware of environmental issues;

❑ Show care and respect for living things;

❑ Talk about themselves, their homes and families, the preschool/childminder setting and the wider environment, and events in their lives both past and present;

❑ Know about people who work within the local community;

❑ Begin to show awareness of time through interests for example, seasonal and festive events, stories and routines.

These knowledge and understanding goals are about children learning about the environment that they live in.

Physical Development & Movement

Gross motor skills are whole body movements and cover the stages a child goes through while developing control of their body. These include supporting their own head, crawling, hopping and riding a bike. Gross motor skills require stamina, strength and suppleness. As children have the opportunity to practice these skills their stamina and strength will increase. These skills develop hand in hand with their co-ordination, judgement and balance.

Manipulative movements with the hands are described as fine motor skills; they are coupled with increased co-ordination with the eyes referred to as hand-eye co-ordination. This skill is essential for tasks such as threading, use of chopsticks and cutlery, pencil control and tying laces. Children need to spend time practising and refining this skill.

There should be sufficient space inside and outside to set up relevant activities that offer appropriate physical challenges, and the time for children to use all the equipment without feeling rushed.

Resources that can be used in a variety of ways are most cost effective, but those that support specific skills are also essential. Children should be encouraged to use their imagination and have fun.

Some children will require additional support to encourage increased independence with physical activities and to develop physical skills, particularly those with physical disabilities or motor impairments. You may be able to gain helpful advice and information on this from the child's parents, possibly in conjunction with the child's physiotherapist.

By the end of the Foundation Stage, (DfES Statutory Framework for the EYFS, ELG's) most children in England will be able to:

❑ Move with confidence, imagination and in safety;
❑ Move with control and co-ordination;
❑ Show awareness of space, of themselves and of others;
❑ Recognise the importance of keeping healthy and those things which contribute to this;
❑ Recognise the changes that happen to their bodies when they are active;
❑ Use a range of small and large equipment;
❑ Travel around, under, over and through balancing and climbing equipment;
❑ Handle tools, objects, construction and malleable materials safely and with increasing control.

By the end of the Foundation Stage, (Scottish Executive) most children in Scotland will:

❑ Enjoy energetic activity both indoors and out as well as the feeling of well being that it brings;
❑ Explore different ways in which they can use their bodies in physical activity
❑ Use their bodies to express ideas and feelings in response to music and imaginative ideas;
❑ Run, jump, skip, climb, balance, throw, catch with increasing skill and confidence;
❑ Cooperate with others in physical play and games;
❑ Develop increasing control of the fine movements of their fingers and hands;
❑ Develop an awareness of space;
❑ Be safe in movement and in using tools and equipment;
❑ Be aware of the importance of health and fitness.

By age five of the Foundation Phase, most children in Wales will:

❑ Have an awareness of their own bodies and their growth;
❑ Move confidently, with increasing control and coordination;
❑ Use a range of small and large equipment with increasing skill and confidence (for example: bikes, balls, climbing frames);
❑ Handle small tools and objects with increasing control and for appropriate purposes (for example: pencils, paint brushes);
❑ Understand, appreciate and enjoy the differences between running, walking, skipping, jumping, climbing, hopping;
❑ Understand and respond to suggestions about spatial relationships (for example: behind, underneath and below, on top of and above).

By school entry at four, most children in Northern Ireland will:

❑ Enjoy physical play and the sense of freedom it brings;
❑ Begin to use space imaginatively with awareness of space and of others;
❑ Move confidently with control and coordination;
❑ Use a wide range of large and small apparatus with increasing control and coordination;
❑ Understand simple rules and can use tools and equipment appropriately and safely.

These physical development goals all encourage children to be active, healthy and to enjoy exercising.

Creative Development/Expressive and Aesthetic Development/Arts

To encourage creativity and expressive aesthetic development you will need to provide a rich environment in which creativity and expressiveness are valued, together with a wide range of activities giving the children the chance to use a variety of senses. Children will need sufficient time to explore and develop their ideas and to complete the experience, they should not be rushed.

It is important for children to express their creativity freely. In other words offer opportunities for children to experiment with form, texture and different materials. Provide activities with no "end result" (avoid activities suggesting "make one like this") so children have the opportunity to express themselves and extend their imagination.

You can stimulate different forms of creativity by providing resources from different cultures and encouraging art forms and methods of representation from children's home cultures and religions.

Children with visual impairments will need physical contact and guidance to access materials, spaces and movements. Children with hearing impairments will need to experience sound through physical contact with instruments and other sources of sound. Children who do not communicate verbally should be encouraged to respond to music in different ways, such as body language and gestures.

By the end of the Foundation Stage, (DfES Statutory Framework for the EYFS, ELG's) most children in England will be able to:

❑ Explore colour, texture, shape, form and space in two and three dimensions;
❑ Recognise and explore how sounds can be changed, sing simple songs from memory, recognise repeated sounds and sound patterns and match movements to music;
❑ Respond in a variety of ways to what they see, hear, smell, touch and feel;
❑ Use their imagination in art and design, music, dance, imaginative and role play and stories;
❑ Express and communicate their ideas, thoughts and feelings by using a widening range of materials, suitable tools, imaginative and role play, movement, designing and making, and a variety of songs and musical instruments.

By the end of the Foundation Stage, (Scottish Executive) most children in Scotland will:

❑ Investigate and use a variety of media and techniques such as painting, drawing, printing and modelling with fabrics, clay and other materials;
❑ Express thoughts and feelings in pictures, paintings and models;
❑ Use role play of puppets to recreate and invent situations;
❑ Use verbal and non-verbal language in role play;
❑ Listen and respond to sounds, rhythms, songs and a variety of music;
❑ Make music by singing, clapping and playing percussion instruments;
❑ Use instruments by themselves and in groups to invent music that expresses their thoughts and feelings;

❑ Move rhythmically and expressively to music;
❑ Participate in simple dances and singing games.

By age five of the Foundation Phase, most children in Wales will:

❑ Respond to and enjoy rhythm in music-making with a range of instruments and with their voices;
❑ Use a range of materials to create representational images (for example: pictures, drawings, constructions);
❑ Make choices about colour and medium;
❑ Respond to suggestions for dance and imitate movements;
❑ Discuss work in progress and completed (for example: painting, instrument-making);
❑ Begin to enjoy role play and imaginative drama;
❑ Begin to observe and appreciate the work of others;
❑ Begin to differentiate sounds without visual clues (for example: animals, instruments, voices).

By school entry at four, most children in Northern Ireland will:

❑ Explore a variety of materials;
❑ Appreciate colour, texture and sound;
❑ Express ideas and communicate their feelings through role play;
❑ Use imagination and make simple representations using a range of materials;
❑ Develop manipulative skills as they handle appropriate tools and instruments;
❑ Begin to value own and others work;
❑ Learn songs, listen and respond to music;
❑ Make own music by singing, clapping and playing simple percussion instruments.

These creative, expressive and aesthetic goals are about children using their imagination.

Bilingualism and Multicultural Understanding

This theme should be carried across all activities. By the age of five most children in Wales will:

❑ Develop positive attitudes and understanding of who they are, within the family and the different communities that they belong to;
❑ Become increasingly aware of and accept the cultural backgrounds of others and treat people from all cultural backgrounds in a respectful and tolerant manner;
❑ Understand that people have different preferences, views and beliefs and know that each person is different but understand that all are equal in value;
❑ Begin to challenge stereotyping and anti racist comments and behaviour;
❑ Explore cultural differences between their own communities and others across Wales and to share unfamiliar and familiar experiences with their peers;
❑ Experience and begin to develop an understanding of the different routines, customs and events that are important aspects of the cultures within Wales;
❑ Appreciate the different languages, images, objects, sounds and tastes that are integral in Wales today;
❑ Gain a sense of belonging to Wales, understand the Welsh heritage, literature, arts and religious backgrounds as well as the language.

These goals are about appreciating difference, a sense of belonging to Wales and appreciating their heritage including the language. Although these goals form part of the Welsh curriculum they could be equally valid for encouraging children to appreciate their own heritage in other areas.

13. Childcare Unravelled

Choosing Equipment

Childminders need a wide range of equipment suitable for the age, size and stage of development of the children they care for. Equipment may include a push chair, cot, stair gate, fire guard and potty among many others.

Information on choosing safety equipment such as fire guards is in Section 7. Health and Safety, here we deal with more general equipment. Car seat safety is discussed in Section 8. Out and About with Children.

Cot

All cots should meet current safety standards, so check the labels. If you are buying second hand make sure it is still a relatively new cot and is from a smoke free environment. Current safety standard for children's cots and folding cots with an internal length of 900 - 1400 mm is BS EN 716-1:1996.

When choosing a cot, important things to consider include:

✓ The age range of the children it will be used for.
✓ How easy it is to get the child into and out of the cot. There should be a minimum depth of 495 mm to stop the baby falling out.
✓ How durable it is. Will it stand up to the amount of use you are expecting to put it through?
✓ How easy it is to clean? This is particularly important if several children may use the cot, so you can maintain good hygiene standards.
✓ If the cot has bars they should be between 45-65 mm apart to prevent the child getting caught in them. If you are out shopping for a cot a good tip: a fizzy drinks can should not fit through the gap.
✓ The mattress should fit securely without a gap around the edge, make sure the mattress also meets current safety standards. A waterproof covering may be useful.

If you are using a cot infrequently you may want to opt for a travel cot that can be easily stored away when not in use. If you do choose a travel cot check how easy it is to put up and pack away. Specifications for travel cots with a base length of 900 mm or more are those of BS 7423:1999.

You also need bedding; you should have enough spares to enable you to change the bedding between children if you have several using the cot. Quilts, duvets and pillows should not be used for children under one year. Avoid using cot "bumpers" as these can restrict ventilation.

High Chair

When choosing consider:

✓ How comfortable is the seat? If it has padding how easy is it to clean, is it waterproof or will it need removing to be washed?
✓ Will it cater for the range of ages and sizes of the children you care for, or may care for in the future.
✓ Does it have restraining straps? A five point harness is best to keep the child secure and prevent them climbing out. If it doesn't come with a harness, is it easy to attach one brought separately?
✓ Will the tray capture spills and is it easy to keep clean? Can it be removed for thorough washing?

✓ Check that the chair has a stable base which prevents it from being tipped over.
✓ Will storage be a problem? Consider a folding highchair.

Current specification for high chairs is BS EN 14988-1:2006.

Prams/Pushchairs

A pram or pushchair is a useful piece of equipment for transporting children, alternative sleeping arrangements, somewhere to sit while being fed or somewhere safe while you take another child to the toilet. They come in a wide range of shapes and styles, so it is important to find one that will meet all of your needs.

Points to consider include:

✓ Weight - can you lift it easily to get up steps, put it into the car or on to a bus?
✓ Size - will it fit down narrow paths, through doorways, in the boot of the car and into the space you have for storage?
✓ Does it have good brakes which are easily to put on?
✓ Is it easy to steer? If so is it still easy once the weight of a child and shopping are added?
✓ Is the handle at the right height for you to push it comfortably without stooping down or stretching up?
✓ Are the wheels suitable for the type of use? Large wheels are helpful for outings to the woods or park whereas smaller wheels are fine for shopping.
✓ If you are caring for a young baby it will need to lie flat. A range of different seat positions may be helpful to cater for children as they grow and for different children who may use it.
✓ It should has a five point safety harness to keep the child secure.
✓ Does it come with accessories such as a rain cover, sun shade or basket to put shopping or a nappy changing bag in?

Caring for Children

Caring for Babies

Caring for babies can create more demands on the childminder and also additional responsibilities. Babies cannot tell you what is wrong, what they need or where they hurt. They will be relying on you to anticipate and act on their every need. Additional responsibilities incurred when caring for babies can include them being susceptible to crises in health and suffering other baby related problems, for example incidences of 'cot death', reflux, stopping breathing, febrile convulsions, choking, colic and nappy rash. Most of these problems will be 'grown out of'.

Caring for babies will require more of your time and attention than an older child. A baby cannot amuse itself in the same way a toddler or school age child can. Babies require considerably more interaction to prevent accidents and to ensure they have ample opportunities to develop both physically and mentally.

Routines for babies and toddlers are much more important than for school aged children and need careful planning. Babies and toddlers equipment and toys are more expensive to purchase than toys and activities for school aged children and you may wish to take this into account when choosing which age range to care for.

Caring for School Age Children

When caring for school age children it is likely that you will be taking them to and from school. When deciding which children will combine well, school collection and dropping off times will need taking into account. Some schools have staggered finishing times making collecting younger and older school aged children much easier, others all finish at the same time.

Introducing yourself to the teacher and explaining your role helps them become aware of you as a source of information and as a means of communicating to parents. With school age children parents may only visit school premises for open days relying on you to ensure all communications from the school are received. Lower or primary schools may supplement letters with messages on the classroom door and it is important to make sure this information is passed on. Where parents give children messages for the school or their teacher you may need to check this is done when children have trouble remembering to hand in letters. Having a good working relationship with both the parents and the school is beneficial to all parties, and this three way communication helps ensure all parties are kept up to date. Having established a good relationship teachers will be able to feel confident you will pass on worries or concerns and in return may supply information on the child's day, helping you to plan the evening activities or rest periods accordingly.

When children attend school, as well as learning the curriculum they also learn from their class mates, unfortunately not all the things they learn have a positive impact on their development. Children can acquire discriminatory attitudes, 'bad' language or habits from copying other children. They may be copying these to be 'in with the crowd' or because they do not fully understand what they are doing or saying. All prejudice and discriminatory behaviour should be challenged (see Section 10. Equal Opportunities). It will also be necessary to deal with any bad language or behaviours that are picked up (for help see Section 15. Managing Children's Behaviour).

Some children may attend after school clubs or local evening activities, such as sports, ballet, Cubs and Rainbows which may mean you have to collect them at a later time. These activities help children socialise and are particularly good for their self-esteem. Where childminders find collection difficult a parent may agree to another childminder collecting the children and dropping them off (remember ratio's still apply). Arrangements for pick up and fitting activities into your routine will need to be discussed with parents so a suitable agreement can be made. Your contract should make clear whether you are paid whilst the child attends the club. It is also important the club or activity venue have your contact details in the event of an emergency.

Activities

Suitable activities for before school will depend on the child's arrival time. Time will be required to prepare for school, and breakfast may be needed if they have not already eaten at home. Activities chosen will need to be short in nature or such that they can easily be left and continued later. Suitable before school activities might include, reading, tiddly winks, card games, drawing or sewing. Complicated board games are not usually suitable before school. Activities chosen will need to take into account the child's age and stage of development and other children present.

Activities after school need to take into account a range of factors including the child's age and stage of development; the needs of younger children; constraints of space; the need for preparation and eating dinner or tea and homework requirements. Some children like to rush into activities on their return from school, others like to sit quietly with a drink and a snack while they unwind.

Children may need somewhere away from the younger children where they can begin or even finish their homework and will probably appreciate help and/or encouragement with their tasks. A seat at a table is often required and possibly the loan of a pencil and other writing equipment. Suitable after school activities can include board games, card games, painting, drawing, reading, fantasy and role play, modelling, dough activities, cooking, sewing, ball games and outside play. Children may be tired after school and require quieter activities.

You will also need to plan suitable activities for school holidays. Activities can be allowed to develop further and be extended as time will no longer be a constraint. Activities need to be fun and varied. Children will have lots of energy and outside activities and outings will be needed as well. Children who are bored or frustrated are more likely to exhibit unacceptable behaviour.

Combining Care of School Age and Younger Children

When combining the care of school age children with younger children you will need to ensure you can provide the attention school age children will require without adversely affecting the care for the younger children. You will also have to ensure the routines of both older and younger children merge successfully, remembering children have differing requirements at different ages and stages of development. You will probably find you will need to be very organised for a successful combination.

There are many difficulties which can arise when mixing age groups. You will need to be careful to ensure they do not cause a problem. These might include:

❑ Competition for your time and attention.
❑ Items that are suitable for older children such as small beads must be kept away from younger children.
❑ Dietary requirements for meals and snacks may be different.
❑ Older children may make noise and disturb younger children's sleep.
❑ Younger children may 'interfere' or interrupt games and activities older children are doing.
❑ Different activities may be needed to cater for each age range.
❑ Outings that interest older children, such as museums, may bore younger children.

Childminders are often seen as a more 'home' style environment, and many parents like the way in which mixed aged children are cared for together, in a similar way siblings grow up together. Younger children can learn from watching older children and all children will benefit from learning to interact with children of different ages.

Caring for Children from Vulnerable or Distressed Families

Vulnerable families are those experiencing difficulties coping with the pressures of society, such as those with few labour market skills, less mobility, single parent families, teen parents, those who are poorly educated, adult survivors of childhood abuse or neglect, substance abusers, those in social isolation, with mental illness or low income. These families may include travellers, asylum seekers and refugees. Distressed families are usually undergoing a temporary misfortune or stress, such as coping with a divorce, bereavement, illness, stress, child protection issues, financial or housing problems.

Working with families that are distressed or vulnerable may require more tact and diplomacy. They may be under a large amount of stress and you will need to be understanding and consider their feelings. Communicating with parents is covered in Section 4. Working in Partnership, and information on working with families affected by HIV, AID's or child protection issues are also covered in the relevant sections.

Families may require help with filling out forms to claim benefit entitlements and a budget plan to help them meet your childcare costs, e.g. a fixed fee each week balancing out holiday payments for school aged children. They may also look to you for examples of parenting skills and advice.

Children from vulnerable families may be behind their peers both developmentally and in growth. Children may also need additional help in achieving feelings of security, autonomy, self-image, self-esteem, motivation, independence, confidence and assertiveness, communication, emotions and relationships (see Child Development and Education Section

12). Children may also engage in spectator or parallel play (watching others play or play alongside rather than with other children) while their confidence develops. Choosing suitable activities will help them develop and become more confident and join in (see Section 12. Child Development and Education for information on Activities and their Value and types of play).

Sometimes children from distressed families or vulnerable families will take time to adjust to what you consider acceptable behaviour, some useful strategies can be found in Section 15. Managing Children's Behaviour.

Working with children and seeing them develop is very rewarding and parents can benefit greatly from your support.

Meeting Children's Needs

Settling Children

This section considers settling in from a child's perspective. There is more information on settling children from a parents perspective under Section 4. Working in Partnership, New Mums and Dads.

When you introduce a new baby or child into an established group you need to be aware of existing children's feelings. They may feel jealousy, a form of sibling rivalry, or rejection of the newcomer. There is more information on these factors in Managing Children's Behaviour Section 15.

Children with secure attachments will separate easily from their parents. Others with poor attachments to their parent find it more difficult. Young babies usually settle more quickly than those around eight to fourteen months who may feel anxious and need coaxing until they become familiar with you and form an attachment. At this age they miss their mothers and become very aware of strangers, developing both stranger and separation anxieties. However, the more days a week they attend after the introductory period the shorter the period of adjustment will be. For example attending only on one day a week a baby of eight to fourteen months may take six to eight weeks to settle. A baby of this age range attending five days a week may only take two weeks to settle.

Settling in can be less stressful for all concerned if there has been time to organise an introductory settling in phase. This can be effective for all age ranges but, the younger the child the longer this introduction should be for effective settling in. Ideally introductory sessions should be a series of short, regular visits initially with a parent present, perhaps staying for coffee. This demonstrates to the child/infant that the parent is relaxed and at ease helping them to feel safe and secure.

These visits give children time to become familiar with your home environment, your own family and the other childminded children. They also give you the chance to get to know the child and their family, and the opportunity to offer bottles/meals while a parent is present. Some children have difficulties taking a feed or eating at a strange location. Having a parent present relaxes them and you can learn about any special methods parents use such as the correct temperature or favourite colour plate.

Before a child starts their regular attendance a short unaccompanied session can also be beneficial. Ensure you have all the relevant information from a parent including likes, dislikes and routines. For older children it can also be particularly helpful to know what activities they enjoy and what their interests are.

When parents leave a quick exit is best as long drawn out goodbyes tend to make children more upset. Do not allow parents to sneak out either; they need to say goodbye. Sneaking off makes the children more insecure and mistrusting. Ensure parents inform the children that they will return in terms they can understand such as, "I will be back after your lunch".

With new children you will need to spend extra time and attention, provide familiar routines and activities, favourite activities and foods. Allowing treasured toys and comforters as transitional items from home will speed the adjustment period. Some new children may demand physical contact ranging from holding hands or your clothing to needing cuddles, although not all children appreciate cuddles from non family members.

Crying

Before a child is able to express themselves with words they use crying to communicate. Children may cry because they are hungry, lonely, bored, angry, afraid, or in pain or discomfort. You need to be able to work out why the child is crying and what attention they require. This can be done by a process of elimination. Crying for short periods will not harm a baby, but crying for longer periods can be very distressing for both you and the child and can affect their emotional development and ability to form secure attachments.

Hunger/Thirst - Children may cry or become irritable when they are hungry or thirsty, consider the time since they had something to eat/drink. You should check with the parents when they drop them what time they had their last bottle or meal. In hot weather children drink more.

Loneliness - If the child is unused to the new environment or needs some attention, it may feel lonely and cry. Pick the child up and give them a cuddle and lots of attention. Talking or singing a song can also be reassuring if you go out of a child's line of sight. Until they are about nine months old babies are unaware that something they cannot see still exists, so if you're out of sight they'll think you are gone. If the child is new to the setting distraction can help. Try going for a walk or do something special with the child.

Boredom - If a child is unable to reach a toy as it has rolled away, or they have become bored playing with the current toys they may cry through boredom. Older children may become disruptive when bored (see Behaviour Section 15). Provide different toys or activities and more stimulation, adding music to the environment can provide added stimulation.

Anger - A child that is stopped from doing something they want, perhaps because a toy is unsuitable or an activity is not safe, may cry in anger. Try distracting the child by finding a different activity that is more suitable and fun.

Fear - Children can be afraid of various things, often dependant on their previous experiences and age, for example they may be scared of the dark, the cat or loud noises. If a child is afraid of something comfort them and help them deal with the fear, for example, explain how they should turn the light on in the cloakroom before they let the door close.

Pain - If a child cannot explain what is wrong it can be hard to find out why they are crying. If there is no obvious reason you should consider they may be unwell. Symptoms with crying due to illness may include irritability, finding it hard to settle and being abnormally clingy. Illness is often accompanied by a raised temperature. Unusual patterns of crying such as a high pitched moaning can be a sign of meningitis.

Discomfort - A child may cry through discomfort if they have a wet or soiled nappy, they are too hot or cold, they are laying in an uncomfortable position or have wind. Solutions to this would be to change the child's nappy, offer a blanket or remove spare clothing, or move them to a more comfortable position. Crying or drinking from a bottle can cause wind (air in the stomach) which is uncomfortable. Rub or pat the child gently on the back.

Teething - Children may cry if their teeth are growing and making their gums sore. They may drool more then usual, be irritable and chew on toys. Parents may provide teething gel to help soothe gums, and you can provide suitable toys designed for being chewed on.

Tiredness - When children become tired they may cry, even when put down to sleep, other symptoms may include rubbing eyes and nuzzling. It can help to play soothing music and remove any interesting distractions from the room. They may need to be rocked to sleep; however avoid it becoming a routine where the child will only sleep when cuddled to sleep, this can cause problems for parents at bedtime.

Sleep

Sleep and rest periods need to be incorporated into your daily childminding routine. A child's physical requirements for sleep change as the child grows. Good daytime sleep has important health benefits and should be maintained if possible until children are 4-5 years (Wessbluth, 1996). Wessbluth also maintains children allowed an afternoon nap will be less fussy, more adaptable and sleep better at night. Some children will give up their daytime sleep at around two years of age if they have long night sleeps, others will still need a sleep or quiet resting period until they are four or five years of age.

Sleep patterns should be discussed with parents. Some parents will prefer their children to sleep in a confined position with the child feeling more safe and secure, e.g. a pram or pushchair. Others prefer their child sleeps in a cot, on the sofa, or floor. The choice will often depend on age. A baby should not be able to fall out of the pram/off a sleeping area. Whichever is chosen the child should have room to stretch out. Each child should have their own bedding. It can help children settle if they have their own blanket they can identify with, and if you choose blankets of different colours or designs this will also help you keep them separate. Taking blankets with you if going out can mean they will settle more easy in a strange place because the blanket is familiar.

Young babies should be placed on their backs to sleep with their heads turned to one side until they can turn over for themselves and move around. It is recommended that they are placed with their toes touching the end of the cot to prevent the risks of suffocation and over heating. Pillows, duvets and sleeping bags should not be used with babies. Sleeping areas should be cool, between 16°C and 21°C, to prevent a child over heating as young babies cannot control their own temperatures.

Although somewhere quiet to rest or sleep is recommended there are a few children who will not settle if it is too quiet. Putting the radio on low can help. Discussion programs can be effective, so children hear voices, or soft music. There are also some children who prefer to sleep on a sofa or the floor in the midst of other children. They may sleep soundly despite the noise around them; this can help reassure them they haven't been left alone and they may open their eyes occasionally to check you are still there. If they awake refreshed and have settled happily there is no need for concern. Children each have their own sleep routines that suit them best.

Children with poor sleep habits may give the impression they do not need much sleep when in fact the reverse is true, and they might not be getting enough sleep. Children who do not get enough sleep may be irritable, easily frustrated, fall asleep during activities, dinner or every time you use the car. Children learn best when well rested. An Italian study found that in children between 3 and 5 years old who slept less then 10 hours per day they had a 86% increase in their risk of injuries (National Sleep Foundation, 2002).

Children need more sleep than often expected. The average amount of sleep for a 3 month old baby is 15 hours and of that almost 5 hours will be during the day time. At 12 months old children will sleep for approximately 11 hours at night and still need 3 hours in the day time. A two year old needs, on average, thirteen hours of sleep, including night and day, and even 3-4 year olds need 12 hours sleep which if not covered during the night will be caught up on during the day.

Problems with children not sleeping at night are rarely due to daytime sleeps. If a child is overtired they may find it difficult to settle at night. Poor sleeping at night is frequently caused by poor sleeping habits or the lack of a good bedtime routine.

Nappy Changing

The choice of real nappies or disposables should be discussed with the children's parents. They may have preferences possibly for environmental or cultural reasons. In most cases parents will be supplying the nappies. If parents are supplying real nappies they may wish to take them home to wash or use a nappy supply service. If you are washing the nappies you should consider the additional time and costs when calculating fees and expenditure.

Hygiene implication of choice of nappies and changing children are covered in Section 7. Health, Hygiene and Safety. Nappies need to be changed when wet or soiled. The frequency will vary between children, generally the younger the child the more frequently the change is required.

Before beginning to change a nappy it is most practical to assemble all the items you will require, including changing mat, nappy, wipes or similar, barrier cream if required, nappy bag for waste, disposable gloves and lastly the child to be changed. If you are using nappies that require folding, fold these before you encourage the child onto the mat. Real nappies are best used with a one way liner to prevent nappy rash and to make soiled nappies easier to deal with.

Using a changing mat on a firm surface is more hygienic and leaves both hands free for changing the nappy. Ensure the mat is not where a child can roll off. Some children do not feel they have time to stay still and distraction with a small toy can help. Children will learn to cooperate if you are firm and gentle. Talk to a child whilst you are changing them and make it fun.

When you have removed the nappy wiping with wet cotton wool or baby wipes will neutralise the ammonia produced by the urine and help prevent nappy rash. If the nappy is soiled remove matter with wipes or the corner of the nappy before cleaning.

Babies and small children will be interested in what you are doing and you may have to redirect their hands while changing to prevent them feeling the nappy and contents. This is a natural exploratory action. Try offering a toy or book to distract them. Some babies and toddlers whilst lying down like to stamp their feet on the mat while you change them. Its fun and it makes a nice noise, just be careful to whisk away soiled nappies before they have a chance to stamp in them so you do not have socks to change too.

If parents have supplied you with nappy cream this should be applied as directed. Remember if you get creme on the nappy tabs of disposable nappies they may not stick properly. Too much creme also prevents one way nappy liners and one way disposable nappies from working as effectively.

After changing, all waste including gloves, should be disposed of safely and the mat disinfected ready for next time. Remember to wash your hands thoroughly.

Toilet Training

Toilet training requires a joint effort and parents will need to have considered their role and have agreed or have suggested that their child is ready. Toilet training does not work well if it is only done at the childminders, for example with the child wearing pants at the childminder's and a nappy at home. Children may wear a nappy at home during the night however, as becoming dry at night takes longer than during the day.

Children are quick to realise toileting is important to adults. If adults continually make too much fuss about it then they may show non compliance with their wishes either by holding in the contents of their bowel which can cause constipation or by soiling themselves. Adverse adult reaction to their lack of urine or bowel control can affect their learning ability as guilty feelings or a desire to please may reduce their independence.

Bladder and bowel control is achieved with a wide variation of ages, boys tending to be slightly later than girls. There is no point in attempting toilet training before a child is ready, this will only frustrate those concerned and may put the child off toilet training when they later become ready. Children are rarely ready for toilet training under the age of two. Children need to relieve themselves when they feel the urge. Childminders and parents are trying to train children to control themselves and delay the relief until the toilet or potty is reached.

If this becomes a conflict rather than a natural progression then personality problems could occur both in the short term and on into adulthood. According to Freud (1915) children where such conflict occurs, may become adults who are over possessive, obsessive about such things as tidiness, punctuality, cleanliness and they may become sadistic and generally miserable.

To be considered ready to commence 'potty training' a child must know whether they are wet or dry. Before this concept is fully understood using a potty is futile and any potty training success will be down to good timing rather than the child knowing they need the potty. They must be able to walk to the potty and tell you they need the toilet or potty.

Stressing children by insisting on potty training is unlikely to be effective, gentle encouragement is most likely to produce the desired outcome. Potty training should be fun. It does not hurt to play with the bricks while they sit on the pot or listen to a story. It can help the child to be happy, relaxed and cheerful.

You can help a child learn whether they are wet or dry by discussing this when you change them. For example, on finding them wet saying 'Look your nappies wet, time to be changed' in a positive way or discussing the fact that the nappy you have just put on is dry. This is also a good way to give children the vocabulary needed so they can tell you whether they are wet or dry. Once a child is aware of feeling wet then sitting on the potty at regular intervals can be helpful. Suggested times are before and after meals, before and after naps, before and after outings. Choice of pants or training pants should be discussed with the parent, remember some 'puddles' are inevitable.

If a child does not wish to sit still a distraction may help. Let them look at a book or have a drink. If the child successfully performs praise should be ecstatic, the child may wish to tell everyone or even phone their parent to tell them. If there is no success, no irritation should be shown and the child could be told 'never mind perhaps next time'.

Potty training can make outings difficult. Children first using the potty and learning to ask have very little impending warning of needing a 'wee' and cannot wait or 'hold on'. Take the potty with you or check there will be one where you are going. Ensure the child knows one will be available and show them where it is located. You may find it helpful to place a folded towel onto the car seat before strapping the child in if you are using the car. You can also place a disposable nappy under the towel to collect 'accidents' without alerting the child to its presence.

It is best for boys to start by sitting on the potty. If they do not sit to wee, it may be harder for them to learn to sit for bowel motions. They can learn to wee standing up later on.

Tip: If boys continually miss the toilet when they start to wee standing up, and hit the floor try putting a ping pong ball in the toilet bowl for them to aim at. It will remain in place even after the loo is flushed (a piece of toilet paper can also be used to aim at).This can be effective for older boys too.

Bowel training is more successful from around two and a half years. It is sometimes easy to spot when a child is filling a nappy, and commenting on this will help a child recognise the sensation and they may start to tell you they are doing it. Children can sit on the potty after meals or at a time you think they are likely to 'perform'. Again providing a distraction may help them to sit still. Gently remind them what you are waiting for, do not show any signs of frustration or impatience. Do not make a child sit longer than five minutes and remember even if they dirty their pants five minutes later you must not show annoyance. However you could suggest you would be pleased if next time they could do it in the potty.

When the child is using the potty successfully you could introduce them to the toilet. Sometimes it can be helpful to move the pot closer to the cloakroom or bathroom in small steps if it is not already in the room. Take it slowly and ensure they are happy to continue using it in each new location before you move it. This will also be helping the child practise 'holding on' a little longer. Some children will be happy to go straight to the toilet, others will take more time and require this adjustment.

Remember the toilet is big, scary and noisy. Who knows what could be hiding in there and swallow up a small child if they fell in. Hold on to them or use a trainer seat and make sure they feel safe and comfortable. Some children prefer a step to rest their feet on, or to stand on when they learn to wee standing up. Sometimes it is easier for boys to learn to wee standing up by, watching their father or an older boy.

Routines

Time	Monday	Tuesday	Wednesday	Thursday	Friday
8-9	Arrival(M, J, T) Schl drop(M, T)	Arrival(M, J, T) Schl drop(M, T)	Arrival(M, J, T) Schl drop(M, T)	Arrival(M, J, T) Schl drop(M, T)	Arrival(M, J, T) Schl drop(M, T)
9-10	Toddlers group	shopping	activity/play	activity/play	activity/play
10-11	snack	snack	snack	snack	snack
11-12	activity/play	activity/play	activity/play	activity/play	activity/play
12-1	Lunch time Arrival(C)	Lunch time	Lunch time Arrival(C)	Lunch time Arrival(C)	Lunch time
1-2	Nap(J)	Nap(J)	Nap(J)	Nap(J)	Nap(J)
2-3	activity/play	activity/play	activity/play	activity/play	activity/play
3-4	Schl pickup(M, T) Home(C)	Schl pickup(M & T)	Schl pickup(M & T) Home(C)	Schl pickup(M & T) Home(C)	Schl pickup(M & T)
4-5	Tea time Home(M & J)	Tea time Home(M & J)	Tea time	Tea time Home(M & J)	Tea time Home(M & J)
5-6	Home(T)	Home(T)	Home(M, J & T)	Home(T)	Home(T)

If you have complicated routines or several children, you can plan your routine using a table. This can be used for 'normal' routines marking pickups, mealtimes, school drop offs and play times or a detailed weekly plan marking the activities and routines for a particular week. For plans with activities see Section 12. Childcare and Education.

Your plan should include any activities that follow a routine (things that do not vary greatly from day to day). It can help you to easily view what time is available for activities on a certain day for example, at what time you need to finish shopping. Parents may also be interested in what your routine is. Having a written plan can help when you are discussing fitting their child's routine into the routines you have for current children.

Routines in Relation to Children's Development

As children grow and develop their routine will change. As children get older they require shorter naps and playgroup or similar activities may be introduced. The time that mealtimes take and allowance for getting children ready to go out may alter. Once a child starts to put their own shoes and coat on you may have to start getting ready earlier than before to allow time for this without rushing. In general the time for different activities will vary as children develop. Playgroup, preschool and school hours will alter and the location of these may change affecting travelling times.

A school age child's routine will need to adapt so children can begin to meet their homework commitments. They will need access to a table where they will be able to sit quietly and they may need your help and attention for some of the tasks they will be set. They will prefer different activities to the younger children and you will need to be able to provide these without detracting from the care you provide for the younger children.

Working with Parents to Establish Routines

Many childminders care for children from different families. This involves the difficult task of making sure routines can co-exist. For example it is not possible for a child to be fed at the same time as another child needs to be taken to playgroup. When a potential customer visits one of the things you should discuss is routines. If you explain in advance any commitments you have such as school runs and toddler groups. Parents can decide whether they feel their child's current routine can be incorporated into your fixed commitments.

Attending a childminders alters a new child's routine and children will take time to adjust to it. Working with parents you will have to develop a routine that accommodates both the parents wishes and the other children in your care. You may find you will need to adapt the routine initially to enable you to give additional time to the new child in order to ensure they settle in both happily and quickly.

Communicating with Children

Communication is an essential part of childcare. Childminders need to communicate in order to guide children, encourage their development, set boundaries and explain their needs. Children need to communicate their feelings, needs, wants and to express themselves. Communicating is not just about speech; your tone of voice, body language and facial expression, and actions are also aids to communication.

Language is probably one of the most important factors promoting intellectual growth. The quality of the child's language environment is essential and not only how much they are talked to, but how relevant, distinctive and rich the conversation is. Language helps with learning to think and reason and in the making of relationships.

The information you are communicating may influence the methods you use. In an emergency or to prevent an incident you may need quickly gain a child's attention by shouting or making a loud noise. If a child is upset you may communicate using body language such as a cuddle and using softer speech.

Children at different stages of development require differing approaches for effective listening and communicating. At any age, time should be provided for them to have quiet conversations without interruptions. Younger children may have difficulty expressing themselves and may prefer to sit on a lap, care must be taken to show any child you are listening and are taking them seriously by appropriate comments. Children should always be allowed plenty of time to get their point across.

Young children may have a gap between the concept they want to communicate and their vocabulary. Talking things through with them and adding additional label words (nouns) and descriptive words (adjectives) helps extend their vocabulary to narrow the gap.

Communicating with children is not always easy. Sometimes it can be hard for a child to understand what you are explaining to them and likewise a child may have difficulty in understanding what you are asking of them. If there are problems with communication it is easy for you or the child, or both of you, to become frustrated. If children have trouble with communicating, think of other communication methods that do not just involve talking face to face. Children may be more comfortable talking to a puppet or soft toy, on a toy telephone or during role play activities they may also communicate through drawing or writing. Encourage children to express their feelings and wants. Let them know that this is acceptable, at the same time you may have to guide them into acceptable ways of expressing their feelings, for example, a tantrum is not an acceptable way to communicate frustration.

When communicating with children it is important to listen to them as well as expect them to listen to you. Allow them time to finish what they are saying and do not rush them if it takes several attempts for them to explain what they mean. Once they have finished it may help to check that you have understood them correctly by repeating back what they have said.

Imaginary Friends

Around one in four children under five have an imaginary friend at some point. Some children keep their friend longer than this. Imaginary friends take many forms including make-believe children and animals.

In the main these friends are an expression of their imaginative skills used for imaginative play. Imaginary friends should not be ignored or dismissed out of hand. They are useful for a variety of reasons including the following:

❑ As playmate and companion.
❑ To help children to both release and practice feelings.
❑ To help children practice life and social skills.
❑ Be used for positive self talk boosting their self belief.
❑ For practicing language skills.
❑ They allow children to be in control.
❑ They provide a confidant.
❑ They mirror thoughts, ideas and fears providing an insight into children's feelings.
❑ They help children see things from another's perspective.

Some children may use their imaginary friends in a manipulative way using their friend to ensure they can get their own way and can use their playmate in controlling those around them. For example, "I can't sit down, I'm following my dog". This can be solved by suggesting the dog might like to sit down to eat his biscuits. Imaginary friends can also be used to shift blame, a variation on Mr Nobody did it.

Occasionally an imaginary friend can dominate a child's life. This extreme reliance may indicate the child has considerable concerns for example, abuse or bereavement for which further investigation will be required.

Discussing Death

Loosing a family member, friend or pet can be a difficult and traumatic experience for children. Many families avoid talking about death hoping to protect children from fear and anguish. Children with an understanding of death are more likely to be able to cope emotionally with death preventing their confusion and anxiety.

Children under two react to the emotions of fear, anxiety and anger in others. Keeping to a normal routine and spending time with the child will be beneficial.

Children between two and five try to categorise and relate death to their existing experiences. They may view death as reversible, temporary and impersonal. For example, of a dead hamster - "change the batteries". Keeping to a normal routine and allowing time for questions and plenty of reassurance are most practical.

Children between five and nine are beginning to realise death is final and that all living things die. Children may personify death as a person or monster, as in the angel of death, and this may cause nightmares in some children.

Children from around ten begin to understand death is irreversible, that all living things die. Some teenagers will develop philosophical views on life and death and may become intrigued with finding the meaning of life. Some children may react to the fear of death by risk taking in an attempt to establish control over their mortality.

Although children go through stages in the way they perceive death as in all developmental phases ages are only a guide and each child will have their own ways of expressing and handling their feelings and emotions.

Any discussions about death should ensure that you are not contradicting what parents has said. You should always discuss how to deal with questions with parents. A parent may not feel able to talk to a child about death when it happens, because they are too upset and it may become part of your childminding role. When talking about death you need to consider a child's and their families religious and cultural beliefs. Some children will ask questions, others may appear outwardly unconcerned, some may act out their beliefs and feeling through art or during role play. Children may express anger if they loose someone close to them. Anger is part of grief, children can be helped during this phase by accepting their feelings and offering reassurance. It may take time for a child to understand fully the ramifications of death and its emotional implications.

Suggesting a pet or relative has gone away or is sleeping is both confusing and frightening. This may make children afraid to sleep or afraid a parent wont return from work. Be aware if you tell children illness was the cause of death without reassurances this too may cause concern. A preschool child cannot tell the difference between temporary and fatal illness.

Funerals can be explained as an opportunity to say goodbye. It is not harmful for children to witness grief; it will help them understand that it is an acceptable feeling.

14. Observation, Assessment & Evaluation

Observation

Observation is an important concept in your work as a childminder. Observation is a tool for gathering information that helps us learn about each child, our environment, our resources, our experiences and our relationships with families and children. Observation is watching to learn. Reasons for observing a child include the following:

- ❑ To help understand and get to know a child.
- ❑ To enable a positive relationship to be developed.
- ❑ To inform discussions with parents.
- ❑ To produce a baseline assessment.
- ❑ To plan developmentally appropriate play and learning experiences.
- ❑ To identify next steps for learning and progression.
- ❑ To identify concerns about a child's development.
- ❑ To identify triggers for behaviour issues.
- ❑ To inform practice.
- ❑ To reflect on practice.

Children are very routine orientated and may become upset if their preferred routines are disrupted for observations. Methods of observing and recording data should be kept unobtrusive to avoid disturbing a child's natural pattern of behaviour. You should organise observations to fit their preferred routine and take time to ensure they feel relaxed and secure. Children below 30 months of age are unlikely to be aware they are being observed providing you have arranged for their needs to be met. By the time children have reached approximately 40 months of age they are naturally inquisitive and may want to know what is being done, with this age group it will help to explain to them before beginning that you will be sitting writing notes. It is possible that some children will become self-conscious and reluctant to try new activities if they feel you are watching them.

Observations should include a means of identifying the child (either name or initials), the date, time, duration, location, context and details of other children and adults present. Observations must be comprehensive to provide valid, representative (typical/characteristic) descriptions of the aspect of behaviour in question. You must take care to be sensitive to a child's existing social relationships when observing interactions.

You must record observations as they happen together with the context in which you are observing. Accuracy is paramount. Remember observations only produce a sample of behaviour or development, and should not be used for planning for the child until you have confirmed your findings by several further observations to ensure you have a total picture. Occasionally for some observations other professionals (e.g. psychologists or teachers.) may need to be involved. They may have input to add or may see things from a different perspective.

Before formally observing a child the parents written approval should be sought, the reasons behind the observation should be explained, and encouragement to become involved offered. Parents need to be assured records made from the observations remain confidential, accessed only by other professionals with a 'need to know' and the parents themselves. It should be emphasised to parents that the observations are not for producing a negative list of things a child cannot do but to produce a positive record of a child's progress and achievements.

Childminders working with the EYFS have a legal requirement to observe and plan for children's development. They are required to make ongoing observational assessment to inform planning in order to meet children's individual needs. However many such observations will be brief and can be noted on sticky labels and transferred to a child's records or profile (see Section 12. Child Development and Education, Recording Children's Progress).

Observation Types

When observing you need to decide whether a naturalistic or structured observation would be most appropriate.

❑ **Naturalistic -** Observations of children in their usual surroundings, doing what they would normally be doing, with no attempt to structure the situation. Useful for looking at behavioural triggers, social grouping and other developmental activities.
❑ **Structured -** A situation organised to observe a particular activity or for gathering specific information, such as organising a posting game to observe a child's fine motor skills. These forms of observation can be useful for checking on developmental aspects and baseline assessments.

During the preparation for a structured observation period care must be taken to select tasks and activities consistent with the child's level of development and their physical capabilities to ensure they can perform to their full potential. These must also be appropriate for the objectives of the observation.

It may be necessary to encourage the child to show what they can do, so in this case 'facilitative techniques' may be used to provide guidance or direction. Facilitative techniques include: questioning to obtain further information, prompting either verbally or by showing how to start something, and suggesting actions. Care should be taken that the use of a facilitative technique does not significantly affect a child's performance and that it is consistent with the objectives of the observation.

When taking an observation you can perform a snapshot or longitudinal observation.

❑ **Snapshot -** A description of what a child is doing at a particular point in time. For example, recording a child's behaviour and interactions during a mealtime to gain a 'snapshot picture' of their behaviour.
❑ **Longitudinal -** Observations carried out over a period of time. For example observation and recording of a child's language development each month for a year.

Observation Methods

❑ **Time Sampling -** Recording of what a child is doing at regular intervals during a set period of time. For example, every 20 minutes during the morning.
❑ **Interval Recording -** Similar to time sampling but a specific behaviour is watched over a short time.
❑ **Event Sampling -** Observation and recording of particular events as they occur, for example temper tantrums.
❑ **Duration Recording -** Plotting how long a particular behaviour or activity lasts.
❑ **Diary -** Less formal recording method to trace developmental changes such as vocabulary and favourite activities.
❑ **Flow Chart -** Using a diagram of the activities and equipment layout and drawing lines on it to show which activities a child uses. Lines can be colour coded to indicate sex or age of children.
❑ **Trail/Movement Records -** Using a diagram as above and plotting the movements of a particular child's use of facilities or for monitoring safety issues.
❑ **Participative -** Joining in as you observe. This method has both advantages and disadvantages.
The advantages include: you can encourage children to do the things you want to observe; you can ask questions to discover the meaning behind children's actions and you can

incorporate check lists. The disadvantages include: it can be difficult to record your own words and actions and children's behaviour may alter.

❑ **Non Participative -** trying to be as unobtrusive as possible, with other adults giving the children care and attention as required, while you observe.

Advantages include: your own words and actions are not recorded; it is easier to be objective and it is suited to free description and target child methods. Disadvantages include: it is difficult to avoid being intrusive and you are unable to encourage children.

❑ **Target child -** Focusing on one child whom you may have chosen, or who may have been selected at random. It may be helpful to use code or a form of shorthand to enable all the significant information to be recorded.

Recording Observations

Records of observations help you to check on a child's progress; they can be used to help plan future care and identify any problems or potential problems. They are not intended for testing or grading of children. Several methods of recording follow:

❑ **Free Description -** A narrative record describing events as they happen, including:

Circumstances: The activities/learning involved, the underlying current of play, the position in the play room, the time of day, the equipment present, what is done, what is said i.e. the kinds and quality of conversation generated.

Social context: The number of people/children present, children's ages and sex, their interactions and whether an adult makes a difference to the play or conversation.

Where the event was activity based, it will help to reveal the kind of play and learning most often produced (promoted), the record should include whether the activity lent itself to long stretches of play linked to a single theme or a short one of actions. Also include what triggered and sustained interest and concentration and what brought it to an end.

These free description observations tend to be short because they require intense focus. They are ideal for recording in the EYFS, Birth to Three and Foundation Stage and require little or no practice. They can be hand written or typed or even presented in notebooks, diaries or on sticky notelets.

❑ **Structured Description -** Events are classified and described in categories, including for example, fine manipulative skills and gross motor skills.

❑ **Pre-Coded Categories -** Records are kept using a system of codes, for example, E= eating, S= sand play and V= vocabulary.

❑ **Check Lists -** Records are kept using a series of checklists to regularly monitor development and are particularly effective for babies and toddlers. These lists can be completed over a period of time using natural observations. Participant observers can ask older children to carryout specific tasks or lead activities to encourage participation. For example 'Simon Says' could be used to see if children can hop or stand on one leg. Observation comments such as, 'stands on one leg' and the date are helpful.

❑ **Sociogram -** Detailed records kept of how the children relate to each other and friendship patterns.

❑ **Pie, Bar Charts and Graphs -** Constructed after the observations and are pictorial representations of the collected data.

❑ **Grid Bases -** Pre selected things, such as, uses a specific activity, toy, or performs an action are marked onto a chart. This is a very quick method of recording but it is more limited than the narrative observations and some important information may be missed if it does not fall within the grid.

Observation records such as checklists and grid bases may be completed while observing. Others, including free description, will require notes to be taken, with abbreviations or shorthand used to prevent omission of details, enabling a full report to be written up later. Whichever method chosen for recording your observations there should be no delay in the writing up, records must be produced while information is still clear in your mind. Where records of specific or general events are to be taken over a period of time a diary or log book will be required.

Only facts should be written up as observations, opinions based on the observations should only be recorded if they are clearly labelled as such for example, evaluations. Judgmental remarks should be avoided. 'Off task' behaviour should be recorded if of interest, this may enable other aspects of behaviour other than those being focused on to be observed. If there is a lot of talking be selective. Pick out key phrases demonstrating development, knowledge or social understanding.

With some observations, technology more advanced than a pen and paper may be used. A video camera, camera or tape recorder may be used to record a session, however these are more obtrusive and with some children this may cause them to alter their behaviour as they 'play' to the camera.

Factors Affecting Validity

When observing you should be aware of factors that may affect how accurate a picture an observation gives you including the following:

The occasion or situation in which the child is observed: Behaviour will vary depending on the situation, time of day or night, behaviour of other children, whether a child is hungry, thirsty or tired and these may be times to be avoided. Observations of behaviour may need to be repeated on a number of occasions and in different situations to get a representative picture.

Social, cultural or gender-based influence: Care should always be taken to consider these, for example, a child avoiding eye contact with you or other adults when spoken to may be socially correct for their own culture, it should not be taken as an indicator that a child has not heard, or is being rude. Other examples might include, not observing knife and fork use for fine motor skills in children used to using chopsticks or expecting boys to be better than girls at kicking or catching a ball.

Context in which observation occurs: If, for example, your observation was while on a trip or at a party, the children may have been over excited, more boisterous and noisier than usual. Children may also display uncharacteristic behaviour where there has been a major upheaval, such as, a new sibling, or change of school. Some children may be unsettled, this will affect their behaviour.

Other factors that may affect the validity of your observations include: Insufficient observations to provide an accurate picture, the chosen activity did not reflect what was being assessed, variations in the observation methods used when a variety of children were given the same developmental test, or too many distractions disrupting the child's concentration on task performances.

Assessments

These are your reflections of the information collected during observations, taken in context of background knowledge of a child's development and behaviour, (including parental input).

Discussion with children's parents, colleagues and other professionals where appropriate is recommended. They may have information or comments to add, for example, a child, who is very quiet within the setting, may be found on discussion with their parents to be more lively at home and just overwhelmed by the situation.

Assessments are divided into two parts:

Initial Assessment: This assessment is also referred to as a baseline assessment and should only be based on evidence that is relevant, significant and meaningful. You need to be certain what was observed was not accidental and can be repeated, i.e. it is truly representative.

Final Assessment: This should comprise of a written descriptive account, including a structured profile (with headings for various sections). It may contain a pre-coded system of recording with key, charts, diagrams and other visual representations of the data collected.

Through your regular observations and associated assessments you will be able to gain an understanding of:

❏ A child's development, needs and well being.
❏ A child's abilities and the extent of their skills and knowledge.
❏ How the child is interacting with the other children and any adults present.
❏ The child's developmental patterns.
❏ The child's typical childhood behaviour patterns.
❏ What makes each child unique.
❏ How different experiences of a child's social and cultural background have contributed.

The results of your assessment are essential for forward planning. These results can indicate the nature of a child's care may need changing, for example they may need finger food, or for leaving the current plans and routines for child care or learning unchanged e.g. satisfaction with their progress or development. If you are applying for accreditation Ofsted, or your regulator, will be looking at your assessment process to see how you monitor and assess individual children's progress and they will be hoping to see how parents have been involved in the monitoring and assessment of their children. This will also be particularly important for all childminders working with the EYFS.

Planning and Evaluation

The results of a final assessment or longer observations can be used to develop and amend plans for a child's individual care and education. They can be used to help in the establishment of goals and strategies for play and other learning activities and experiences to help a child progress and develop, or to enable a child to change their behaviour.

Using the final assessment you can devise optimum environments for the children which will promote a child's holistic development, whilst responding to their needs.

You should be able to use the information gained to enable appropriate action to be taken should any aspect of the child's development, health or behaviour be causing you concern as they are not typical for the age and stage of expected development. The assessment process can also be used to monitor, evaluate and improve the service you offer, and help when devising your curriculum.

What can you Plan

Planning can be used for a wide variety of reasons including:
❏ Inside and outside provision.
❏ Resources.

❑ Time.
❑ Learning goals, aspects, outcomes.
❑ Language development.
❑ Thinking and reasoning.
❑ Curriculums.
❑ Observations.
❑ Assessments.
❑ Records.

Implementation

This will mean putting your plans for goals and strategies into action and will require assistance from parents. This may mean introducing a behaviour modification program e.g. to reduce aggression, providing individual help in specific aspects of learning e.g. a 3 year olds' speech development, or helping to build up a child's self esteem.

Evaluation

Through the evaluation process you will identify the child's achievements and the direction of future progression. Ensuring that children can reach their full potential by the elective planning of their future activities. The evaluation will include the use of your observations to assess how successfully your plans were implemented.

Remember, planning and evaluation should be a continuous ongoing cycle. There is more about planning, evaluation and child profiles in Section 12. Child Development and Education, Curriculum Planning.

Child Evaluation

Child evaluations can be used for judging how much progress has been made while taking into account knowledge of a child's past experiences. Evaluation needs to be systematic and continuous.

All areas of a child's experiences need to be continually evaluated to ensure they meet the changing needs of the child. Areas to evaluate should encompass the whole learning environment including the use of materials, space and time and could include the following criteria:

❑ Are the children interested?
❑ Are they concentrating?
❑ Are they playing together?
❑ Are all areas of learning catered for?
❑ Are materials and equipment well maintained?
❑ Are the children encouraged to work independently?

There is no formal assessment of pre school children. They are individually evaluated. You may like to read the section on Child Profiles in Section 12. Child Development and Education for more details. The expected Early Learning Goals will be followed by the key stages of National Curriculums.

Where Key Stage 1 is used, children will undertake a series of standard assessment tasks (SATS) which together with a teachers assessment and evaluation is designed to indicate a child's individual progress through the curriculum. This evaluation of the students attainment of educational goals indicates the outcomes of their formal education. Giving accountability and providing evidence of the quality of instructional materials.

Evaluation criteria will vary according to the purpose of evaluation. An example could be criteria set for reading. The child is heard to read. The criteria to look for might include:

❑ **Fluency** - Satisfactory to child's development.
❑ **Phonic use** - Trying of new words.
❑ **Comprehension** - Understanding of story.
❑ **Enjoyment** - Willing or not, enjoyment of story.
❑ **Difficulties** - lack of concentration, no progress.

Evaluation of difficulties and where appropriate helping with mistakes, and of a child's understanding of a passage and their enjoyment will give a good indication of a child's progress. The ultimate goal for reading is for the child to be able to understand written material, to evaluate it and use it for their own needs. Whether for recreational, educational or life experiences.

For some evaluations it may help to state which goal or aspect describes the current stage of development and subdivide the criteria being evaluated for each topic/subject/event into the following headings:

❑ Introduced
❑ Worked on
❑ Consolidated
❑ Progression/next steps

Ongoing evaluations of children should be reflected in long, medium and short term planning. For recording purposes you might like to look at Section 12. Child Development and Education, Recording Children's progress and Child profiles.

Self Evaluation

Self evaluation helps in evaluating your own practices, the curriculum content and its effectiveness pertaining to the children. It will help with reflection on personal, teaching and management skills. Self assessment can be made at a number of levels. including:

❑ About own work and achievements for a long term plan.
❑ About own work and achievements for a short term plan.
❑ About how you are working with individual children.
❑ Are you differentiating tasks to cater for all age ranges?

There are several methods of self evaluation, which can be used to help you reflect on your practice. These include both subjective evaluations and evaluations against a preset plan. Systematic evaluation procedures demonstrate self effectiveness by evaluation of your own actions and performance ensuring you are a reflective practitioner.

Subjective self evaluation is about how other people feel about you, your practices and their effectiveness. This can be achieved by inviting an outsider (or other childminder) to produce an evaluation of yourself. You can also encourage parents to provide evidence by giving them and older children questionnaires about your service or asking for references. Children can also provide subjective evaluation by showing or telling about their likes and dislikes through pictures and writing which can even be dictated by younger children. Regulators including Ofsted will produce an evaluation of you and your practices in their inspection reports.

Self evaluation can also be carried out by asking yourself specific questions, using a preset plan, about such things as purposes, planning, preparation, methods used, relationships to assistants, children and parents. It could be set against a job description, questions could include are you fulfilling the job description? meeting points? keeping to time scales? targets? If not, why not? Decide what help or action is required and produce an action plan with steps towards meeting your goals.

Your self evaluation may have headings like those from the Every Child Matters and demonstrate how effective you are at meeting each heading evaluating your practice within that theme. You could include a short pen picture saying where you work and how you meet relevant standards linked to the theme and include a short summary paragraph at the end of each heading.

You might like to include some of the following suggestions as appropriate to your circumstances. You may have others to add.

Organisation:
- ❑ Records, policies and procedures.
- ❑ Daily register.
- ❑ Diary.
- ❑ Accident records.
- ❑ Contracts.
- ❑ Child record forms.
- ❑ Complaints.
- ❑ Training undertaken or to be taken.
- ❑ Paragraph about the children.
- ❑ Prospectus.
- ❑ Certificates & insurance documents.
- ❑ Self evaluation.
- ❑ Action plan.

Helping Children to be Healthy:
- ❑ Policies such as sickness, exclusion, medicines, notifyable diseases.
- ❑ Child records such as medical, dietary needs, permission for accidental treatment including emergencies.
- ❑ How you discourage sick children.
- ❑ Hair, tooth brushes, flannels, paper towels, liquid soap.
- ❑ Toileting, moist paper, step stools, potties, toilet seats.
- ❑ Washing hands after toileting, handling pets, before meals.
- ❑ Promotion of good hygiene practices.
- ❑ Hygiene for changing mat, work tops, bed linen, sell by dates.
- ❑ First aid box.
- ❑ Sample menus.
- ❑ Drinks.
- ❑ Meal times.
- ❑ Sleeping.
- ❑ Physical development.
- ❑ Health & safety checks.
- ❑ Relevant training.
- ❑ Health promotion.
- ❑ Working in partnership with parents.

Protecting Children from Harm or Neglect & Helping them Stay Safe:
- ❑ Checking premises inside and out for safety.
- ❑ Risk assessments.
- ❑ CRB.
- ❑ Road safety, fire drills, stranger danger, water hazards, hazardous plants.
- ❑ Car servicing, equipment safety.
- ❑ Suitable, accessible toys.
- ❑ Accident & emergency policies.
- ❑ Child protection/safe guarding children policies.
- ❑ Relevant training.

Helping Children Enjoy & Achieve:
- ❑ Planning of activities.
- ❑ Developmentally appropriate resources.
- ❑ Outings.
- ❑ Positive self esteem & right from wrong.
- ❑ Positive images.
- ❑ Planning, observations, evaluations, recording of children's progress.
- ❑ Sharing records with parents.
- ❑ Liasing with outside agencies e.g. Physiotherapists, health visitors.
- ❑ Relevant training.

Helping Children Make a Positive Contribution to the Setting & Wider Community:
- ❑ Equal opportunities policy.
- ❑ Special educational needs policy.
- ❑ Behaviour policy.
- ❑ Working in partnership with parents, including contracts, sharing policies, talking to them.
- ❑ Daily diaries.
- ❑ Photography to share with parents.
- ❑ Open door policy.
- ❑ Children sharing responsibility.
- ❑ Borrowing equipment, books from library, toy library, networks, other childminders.
- ❑ Sharing child profile.
- ❑ Inclusion officers.
- ❑ Social & emotional development records.
- ❑ Resources & activities which reflect diversity.
- ❑ Inclusive practice.
- ❑ Relevant training.

Many childminding regulators are now expecting to find evidence of regular self evaluation because self evaluation confirms good practice and enables modification of those aspects that may require some change. Self evaluations should be checked against other evidence to ensure you have not been too self critical.

Action Plan

An action plan is a framework used to improve aspects of your practice. It can record any aspects of practice you have identified through evaluations as requiring improvement or additional development and can include recommendations from regulators or childcare development officers. Your plan should set out concisely how you plan to address aspects for improvement.

Your plan should only contain a few targets or actions with realistic time scales for improvement. Resources must be already present or readily available. There needs to be a means of identifying success. Action plans need to impact on childminding practice and become a feature of continuous improvements which are reviewed and built upon.

15. Managing Children's Behaviour

What is Unacceptable Behaviour?

Unacceptable behaviour is behaviour which may harm other people, either physically or their feelings, damaging other people's belongings, or any behaviour that is considered anti-social. There has been a move away from referring to this behaviour as naughty as children may display behaviour which is not deliberately naughty but which is unacceptable in particular situations.

There are some things that can be mistaken for 'naughtiness' but are in fact normal behaviour for children. It is not 'naughty' for young children to wet or soil themselves. Children under eighteen months cannot control their bowel movements, and children do not generally start potty training until two and a half to three years. It is not 'naughty' for children to feel jealous. It is natural for children who may have been the centre of attention to feel jealous when having to share toys or attention. It is not 'naughty' for a child to cry, and children use crying to communicate their feelings to you. It is not 'naughty' if a young child accidentally hurts an adult, e.g. pulling your hair. This is natural curiosity, they want to see what happens.

Encouraging Acceptable Behaviour

Encouraging acceptable behaviour is more effective than punishing unacceptable behaviour. Children need to feel that their 'good behaviour' is appreciated so they repeat it. There are many ways to reward children for acceptable behaviour. Approval can be indicated by smiles, hugs, 'well done', tone of voice and body language. Approval must be sincere and will help develop children's self-confidence.

Behaviour	How to Encourage
We were getting ready to go out and Rachel fetched the younger children's shoes.	The childminder thanked her and told her how helpful she was.
Alex hit David. Instead of hitting Alex back, David told him he was naughty.	The childminder praised David and told him how not hitting back was the right thing to do. She gave David a cuddle.

Praise and Rewards

Effective praise and rewards will vary, some children will thrive on cuddles, smiles and being told they have done the right thing, others may enjoy rewards such as a special activity or stickers. Avoid using good/bad, clever/stupid as these label the child not their behaviour.

These rewards should coincide with the positive behaviour, if they are delayed children may not understand the link and they will not be effective in encouraging repeated good behaviour. Children over six may understand the promise of rewards later, for example, an ice cream later. Promises should always be kept or they cease to be effective.

Reward	Examples
Social Reward	Praise, cuddles, smiles, clapping.
Activity Rewards	Reading a story, playing outside, visiting the shops.
Primary Rewards	Biscuits, fruit, sweets, magazines, comics.

Quality Time

Children need and want attention. They may use unacceptable behaviour in order to gain your attention; this is called attention seeking. By giving a child quality time you may help to prevent them feeling the need to seek attention through unacceptable behaviour.

Quality time does not mean you ignore the other children and focus on one child. Quality time does not have to be at set times or for long periods to be beneficial. Small things such as asking the child's opinion or pointing out their picture on the wall to visitors in front of them, are all giving the child quality time. Playing and talking with the children also gives them quality time. If you have had a busy day take some time to talk or interact with the child so they realise you still have time for them and they do not need to seek your attention.

Setting Ground Rules

All parents and childminders have some form of ground rules, even if these are not written down. Rules may include things like always taking your shoes off when you come in, saying 'please' and 'thank you' and sharing toys with the other children.

Making the ground rules clear and keeping them consistent will encourage children to display acceptable behaviour. You should stick to the rules. If a child is allowed to get away with something once it encourages them to ignore the rules in the future.

Displaying the rules on the wall or encouraging children to make a poster of the rules and why they are in place helps children to acknowledge the rules and why they are there. Older children may like being involved in setting the rules or limits to behaviour.

Helping Children Learn Positive Behaviour

Examples of positive behaviour include, helping others, remembering not to scream when you want your own way, concentrating and answering questions.

There are several ways to help children learn positive behaviour.

❑ **Talking** - Explain in language appropriate to their stage of development what they should do and why. e.g. "Help me put your shoes on please, then we can go outside to play".
❑ **By Example** - Provide positive behaviour yourself, that children can copy. e.g. Saying 'please' and 'thank you'. Praise other children when they show the required behaviour.
❑ **By Demonstrating** - Encourage them to watch what you are doing. e.g. wash your hands before cooking, then help them wash their hands before they help you cook.

Responding to Undesirable Behaviour

You should respond to undesirable behaviour in a calm and controlled manner. It must be appropriate to the nature of the behaviour and the child's needs at the time. Responding appropriately is easier if there is an understanding of the circumstances and the factors which may provoke children into displaying negative or difficult behaviour. What the child did and what happened may be obvious, but the trigger may be more difficult to ascertain, especially if the child was not being directly observed at the time.

Children must realise it is their behaviour and not them which you do not approve of. If you respond calmly you are setting an example by your positive behaviour, showing that yelling or violence is not a option and that negotiation is more suitable, thus providing a good role model.

Children need to be able to return to normal activity as soon as possible, some children like to watch angry adults, they may find it funny and deliberately annoy you to achieve this reaction. If they are rebuked in a calm, controlled manner they have not achieved their expected result and the behaviour may lessen or disappear.

Sanctions and Strategies

It is a good idea to discuss sanctions and strategies with parents, find out what they use at home and how they would like you to deal with inappropriate behaviour.

Sanctions, a last resort, should be given immediately following unacceptable behaviour, and should be supported by teaching and rewarding new and appropriate or desirable behaviour. They are more effective for older children who can understand that the sanction is a result of their behaviour. If a particular sanction is not working then it should be changed. Sanctions should not lead children to avoid desirable behaviour e.g. avoiding adults through fear. Children also need to be assured it is their behaviour, and not them, that is disapproved of.

Examples of sanctions might include turning off the television, a toy being removed from use or removing a child from an activity.

Strategies

Strategy	Implementation
Changing Routine	Remove the trigger for behaviour.
Behaviour Modification	No attention when behaving unacceptably and reinforcing behaving in an acceptable way with more attention.
Redirection	Direct the child's attention to a more appropriate activity.
Time Out	Withdrawal from activity.
Special Time	A time when they have special attention, prevents the needs for unwanted attention seeking.
Playing	Extend play, child may play out fears or worries with toys.
Ignore	Temporary phase e.g. initially with some tantrums.
Professional Help	For severe behavioural problems.

Setting Goals and Boundaries

Goals and boundaries help children develop relationships with other children and adults, become aware of and then avoid everyday hazards, develop acceptable behaviour and develop consideration for others. Boundaries can also make children feel more secure. Once children are aware of what the boundaries are they will become more relaxed with the environment.

Boundaries, which can be in the form of rules, provide limits for children's behaviour, they also protect children from dangerous consequences of uncontrolled behaviour, and can prevent oppression and discrimination. Boundaries safeguard children's emotional well being and physical safety.

Goals and boundaries must be realistic so children are able to achieve them. They should contribute to their emotional and physical well-being and that of others. They will need to be appropriate to the age and development of each individual child and to move as they progress in understanding and development.

Suggested boundaries for encouraging children's behaviour are included in the following chart:

Age	Boundary
1 year	To Understand 'No'.
2 years	Biting, kicking and throwing toys is not acceptable.
3 years	Tantrums are not acceptable.
4 years	Toys should be shared.
5 years	No teasing or name calling.
6 years	Problem solving for conflicts instead of fights.
7 years	Consideration for others, no discrimination.

Changing Goals and Boundaries

If your goals and boundaries are not effective then you should consider applying them more consistently, revising or adjusting them.   Boundaries will also need to be revised inline with children's age and stage of development.

Behaviour Charts

If there is a particular area of a child's behaviour that needs addressing or a particular behaviour needs reinforcing a behaviour chart may be a useful tool. The appropriateness of this method will depend on a child's development: and whether they can understand the purpose of the chart and how it works.

To implement a reward chart first choose the behaviour you are aiming to promote. A chart is not about noting bad behaviour but drawing attention to good behaviour. An example might be washing hands before dinner. A chart can then be made with a space to mark each time the child washes their hands before dinner. Stickers, stars or colouring in a shape can be used to mark the times they remember. The aim is that the good behaviour is rewarded by attention as everyone can see how well the child is doing. Sticking on stickers is also a fun activity so a child will be encouraged to wash their hands so they can have a sticker.

Once a goal is consistently achieved a different one should be set so the child does not become bored. An extra reward for continual good behaviour, such as visiting the park if the child remembers to wash their hands for a whole week can provide extra incentive. Praise for each achievement will help encourage the child to produce continual 'good' behaviour. The child will want to show the chart to their parents and this can encourage working in partnership with parents.

Unable to Cope with Children's Behaviour

If you have tried all the usual methods of behaviour modification and the child shows little or no improvement you have two options:

❑ Persevere, enlist the help of the parents and present a united front. The parent may wish to consult their Health Visitor for advice and to check if a referral is necessary. You have a much greater chance of improving behaviour if there is consistency between the home and the childminding setting for both the ground rules, what is considered unacceptable and the methods of dealing with unacceptable behaviour. These should be as similar as possible.

❑ The second option is to accept that there are some children that will not be compatible with your childminding regime. For your own, your families, and the well being other children present, and to reduce your stress it may be preferable to give parents notice of termination of the contract.

When giving notice explain that you feel it is in the best interest of the child and where possible offer to work the notice period while they find alternative care.

Parents Undermining your Behaviour Management

Parents rarely deliberately undermine your behaviour management strategies. Children may take advantage of the grey area during the hand over period and many are adept at manipulating parents especially when parents are tired after work and just want to get home and relax. Some children's behaviour changes markedly when parents arrive. Firm but fair management will help tremendously.

Share your behaviour management strategies with parents, they may find them useful and try them out. In turn they may have others that you can use. If you have a policy, share it with the parent, give them a copy and discuss it, also discuss it with the children. You might like to suggest that your 'rules' apply until the child leaves the house, this eliminates the grey areas where no one is sure just whose rules apply and removes the chance for children to play the parent off against the childminder with regard to their behaviour.

Where parents allow children to run 'rampage' while they are there you will need to enforce your behaviour management strategies and make the child and parents aware that you will not allow them to be changed or undermined.

Unacceptable Forms of Behaviour Management

There are some methods of reacting to 'bad' behaviour that are unacceptable including the following.

❑ Naughty Chair
Making a child sit on a chair or stand in the corner in sight of others is a form of humiliation and should never be used. It will not help a child calm down it will encourage feelings of resentment. Children may also go and sit on the 'naughty chair' and feel this means they can still do the unacceptable behaviour as it is negated by sitting on the chair. Having a 'time out' in a quiet corner or room where a child can calm down in private is an acceptable and helpful behaviour management strategy.

❑ Smacking and Physical Punishments (Corporal Punishment)
It is not acceptable to smack children or administer physical punishments. There are no good reasons for smacking a child or administering physical punishment of any form. This includes shaking, biting, pinching, stamping on toes or similar. You are only reinforcing that it is acceptable to hit, bite or show violence to others. Children have the same rights to be protected from physical violence as adults have. If you are using positive methods it is not necessary to use any form of physical punishment.

Meal Time Problems

When looking at problems to do with eating you might like to first consider whether the problem is real or perceived. Sometimes what adults see as a problem could also be related to tradition or culture and may not be a problem to the child concerned. In some cultures it is customary to eat with fingers or chopsticks, rather than fork and spoon. Other eating habits may also vary, such as times of meals, types of food and where it is eaten. These types of cultural preferences may not have been mentioned specifically by parents as to them it is normal behaviour. Children's individual food preferences or 'peculiarities' such as not wanting pudding, may also be seen as problems. Unless they are affecting the child's well being, such as preventing a balanced diet, there may be no need to attempt to alter them.

Toddlers may be stubborn and want their own way and many children have discovered the power they can wield over adults by not eating on request. An adult may resort to begging, bribing and providing highly entertaining antics (such as 'train noises') in order to persuade them to eat. Adults who are caring for children who are underweight or have been premature may particularly employ these methods as they are very keen to have the children gain weight and grow.

A small child will eat when hungry. It may be customary to eat three times a day and as adults we tend to follow this pattern even if not particularly hungry, however children do not see the logic in this. If children refuse to eat at certain times it is often regarded as being stubborn however the child may just be following the 'eat when hungry' rule which to them seems logical. If a child is energetic, curious and generally has a 'zest for life' they are probably getting sufficient amounts to eat.

Refusing to Eat

If a child refuses to eat they may genuinely not be hungry. They may have filled up on fluids, e.g. milk or juice, or snacks between meals. If this is the case, in future provide less between meal snacks and provide water rather than milk which is more filling. Milk can be offered after meals.

If refusing to eat is unusual they may be unwell, so check for symptoms such as a raised temperature. They may also be tired, especially if they have had a busy day. Eating may seem like just too much effort. If this is the case gentle encouragement may help. The child may also have realised the power they can wield, over adults, through food.

Whatever the reason behind a child refusing to eat trying to insist is unlikely to have much effect, however children may be swayed by gentle encouragement. If it is obvious the child does not wish to continue eating, then let them leave the table. Displaying anger does not help. Allow the child to see you place the food into the fridge or the waste bin depending on the reason for not eating. If the child is genuinely not hungry then they may request the food later. Where children are using food and meals as a source of power having ensured that the child has had enough to eat, putting the remaining food in the waste bin after an advanced warning can be helpful in demonstrating that this form of behaviour is not tolerated. It may also help to be relaxed about meal times. Often because the childminder is not stressed by the refusal to eat a child will eat their meals as there is no conflict to 'win'.

Lack of Variety

Children may not always appreciate variety. A wide range of home cooked meals, foods from different cultures and with different tastes and textures will seem wonderful to some children, however others would rather eat the same few meals day after day. You should not enter into an argument with a child over what you feel they should eat or demand that they eat different foods. Aim to introduce small amounts of new foods, flavours and textures to children gradually, in a way that makes them attractive.

It may help if the child watches other children or you eating the new food first, remember too, food from your plate or bowl tastes far nicer than from their own. Foods can be made more attractive by making them more interesting, for example, if a child only wants to eat sausages and mashed potato, add two peas for eyes and a piece of carrot for a nose. This introduces the new foods in a way that's more likely to encourage the child to eat them than demanding they eat a whole portion of peas and carrots. You can also encourage children to help with preparing meals. They are more likely to eat cakes if they have made them, or sandwiches if they helped butter the bread.

Don't Eat Enough

Some children and toddlers may not appear to want much to eat at meal times, this may lead you to feel that they are not eating enough. First consider whether they are eating food throughout the day that increases total food intake. Extra foods might include a handful of raisins while you are baking, a share of your breakfast, or drinking milk between meals.

If you feel the child may be eating less because they find mealtimes boring and are eager to get back to playing try making food look interesting. There are many different shapes to cut sandwiches into instead of squares or triangles. Decorations such as cheese cubes, cucumber butterflies, grapes, raisin faces and carrot sticks can also make meals more fun and promote discussions as well as providing a wider variety of foods.

Small portions of food are more readily eaten and less threatening to a child, point out that they can always have more afterwards. For some children snacks can be their main source of nourishment and they should be chosen appropriately. Avoid sugary foods with little nutritional value, instead try cheese cubes, cold cooked chicken, fresh fruit portions and raw and cooked vegetable sticks, bread or toast.

Sometimes fresh air, having been for a walk, is a good appetite stimulant. Eating picnics in the garden or even using a cloth on the floor can also encourage children to eat, offering novelty value. If you are worried that the child's well being is suffering through lack of food you should discuss this with the parents and suggest they seek advice from their doctor or Health Visitor.

Refusing Lumpy Foods

There are some young children who do not chew and the slightest lump will cause them to gag. This is frequently due to having been fed on smooth baby foods for too long.

It can be quite difficult to rectify this problem. It can help to reduce their milk intake encouraging them to have more solids. Adding small amount of mashed home cooked foods to jars of baby food or pureed foods gradually, will help to wean them on to more lumpy foods. The amount of mashed rather than pureed food should be increased gradually until the whole meal become mashed. The process is then continued by adding finely minced or chopped home cooked foods. Gradually increasing the 'lumpiness'. Converting children to 'lumps' may take several weeks or months.

Refusing Vegetables

Vegetables come in a wide variety of forms, baked beans are vegetables even if they do not resemble such to a child. Children may be fussy over what vegetables they eat or only eat a select few.

Offer a range of different vegetables in a range of different states and see if there are any the child prefers. Some children prefer raw vegetables as snacks and not as part of a meal, e.g. carrot sticks, cucumber slices, courgette sticks or circles. They may like vegetables cooked or uncooked, or cut in a particular way. They may only eat them as part of other foods such as carrot cake, stew or pizza topping. Remember vegetables do not need to look like vegetables!

Vegetable eating should not become a battle-ground, tempt children with decorative small quantities at mealtimes and as snacks, colour can also be quite tempting. If children really do not want to eat vegetables they can always get fibre and vitamins from other food sources, such as fruit and cereals.

Refusing Fruit

Very few children do not eat any fruit at all. Some varieties of fruit are more palatable than others. For example, they may find some varieties of apples too hard or sour.

Fruit shopping is great fun; take the children to the market or supermarket and let them look at the wide variety, the colours, smells and textures available. Let them choose something to take home to try, but make sure the fruit is ripe. Often supermarket fruit is not ready to eat yet.

Some children prefer soft fruits such as bananas, mango and strawberries others prefer more 'solid' fruits. Children may also turn down fruit as they dislike getting sticky fingers, if this is the case offer a spoon or a fork. Fruit such as apples, strawberries, blackberries and black currants can also be stewed to form a hot or cold sauce to serve with icecream.

Eating Implements

From around 15-18 months a child will begin to use a spoon, but it is not until a child is approximately three that they begin to use a knife. Unless food is soft a young child will have insufficient coordination and strength to cut food themselves, and you will need to cut food into mouth sized pieces for them.

It is not until approximately five that a child will be competent using both and knife and fork or chopsticks. Children can practice using cutlery and chopsticks in their play, without the fear of accidents, encouraging them to become more proficient. Play chopsticks and cutlery or the real thing can be used with play dough or pretend food to great effect.

Eating with fingers is very efficient, but some cultures and traditions may require the use of implements. Time to practice and gentle encouragement are the answer. Remember a child who is tired or unwell may revert to using fingers. In these situations rather than insisting it may be better to let it pass.

Lunch Boxes

There are occasions when parents may provide packed lunches or dinners for their child to eat whilst in your care. Problems can arise if there are other children present for which you are providing different food, or if you feel that the foods provided are unsuitable.

Providing other children present with their meals also in a box can help prevent arguments over differences, checking what the lunch box contains in advance and providing similar may also help. If bringing lunch separately is causing problems you should discuss it with the parents and perhaps offer to provide lunch, either as part of your inclusive fees or at an additional charge.

If you think the lunch provided for a child is unsuitable you should discuss this with the parents. Be careful to offer advice rather than dictate. You could offer suggestions of alternatives, parents may not be used to providing a packed lunch and be short of ideas for contents. Any very unsuitable items, such as boiled sweets, could be removed and sent home with the child along with an explanation of why they are unsuitable.

Bullying

A bully is an adult or child who deliberately intimidates or persecutes someone with the intention of causing distress. It takes the form of an attack, whether physical, psychological, social or verbal. Some children are more readily intimidated than others, i.e. what some may laugh off as a joke others may find very upsetting.

Examples of bullying behaviour include: teasing, taunting, racial remarks, sarcastic comments, pulling hair, pinching, punching, kicking, damaging or theft of possessions, cyber bullying including text messages and postings in network communities.

Recognising a Victim of Bullying

Children often indicate they are being bullied by changes in their behaviour. If you are concerned a child in your care is being bullied you should ask them about it, and also discuss it with their parents.

Symptoms exhibited by children who are being bullied may include some of the following:

❑ The child cries themselves to sleep or has nightmares.
❑ The child is unwilling to go to school, nursery, playgroup or similar.
❑ An older child prefers going to school in the car or refuses to walk on their own.
❑ A older child who travels home from school on their own may alter their route, coming home quickly or late after other children have left.
❑ An older child who deliberately leaves their mobile phone at home or ceases to visit their favourite Internet networking communities.
❑ Possessions including books, bags, clothing is frequently 'lost' or damaged.
❑ School work deteriorates.
❑ Child has unexplained cuts, scratches or bruising.
❑ Comes home hungry (has lost dinner money or lunch food).
❑ Asks for, or steals, money.
❑ Becomes distressed, withdrawn, starts stammering and/or stops eating.
❑ Attempts to harm themselves.

The symptoms exhibited may vary with the age of the child. Children who are bullied may refuse to say what is wrong or may give improbable excuses to explain things, e.g. frequently says they have lost their dinner money when in fact it is being taken.

Bulling should be taken very seriously. A child who is bullied will find difficulty in learning at school and the effect can remain with the child for life. Kidscape offers many helpful publications for dealing with bullying.

Taking Action

If a child in your care is being bullied you should give them a chance to talk about their feelings. You should not agree to keep what they tell you secret instead suggest you will tell as few people as possible (i.e. only those who need to know). You will need to discuss the bullying with the child's parents and if it has occurred at school the parents may wish to discuss it with the teachers. It can also be helpful to check the child is not unintentionally provoking the bullying through antisocial habits such as spitting.

You may find that the parent requests you accompany the child to or from school if this is the problem situation. This may be a temporary measure until the bullies become bored. They may also enlist your help in finding other children for their child to walk home with, as bullies are less likely to pick on a group than a lone child.

You can also help the child take positive steps towards preventing bullying. Encourage them not to think like a victim, to walk with confidence even if they do not feel confident. Help them to smile and pretend they are not frightened, to keep walking and ignore the bully. They should not stop and get into a confrontation with the bully. Suggest they laugh at, or ignore, comments or teasing. Bullies hope to provoke a reaction and will become bored if it is not forthcoming. Also provide a sympathetic ear and encourage the child to talk about their feelings and how their day has been.

The Bully

Children often become bullies because of a problem within their own lives. They may have been through a parental break up, the death of a family member, or because they themselves have been bullied or abused. Children may also become bullies through boredom, frustration, insecurity or because they have trouble making friends. Bullies may also have been spoilt and feel that everyone should do exactly as they say and enjoy the feeling of power that it gives.

It has been suggested by Kidscape that when bullies grow up and become adults they are more likely to be violent, have poor relationships and possibly to become abusers. It is therefore in the bully's best interests their behaviour is not ignored.

If you are caring for a child that is a bully you will need to discuss with the parents how to handle the behaviour. Bullies need to achieve some success to make them feel good about themselves. Channelling the success they feel through dominating other children into other areas may help deal with their behaviour. Help them find alternatives that they are good at. This could be a sport, music, art, organising a display or a subject in school.

Remember to remain calm when dealing with a bully, as in dealing with any behaviour you should make it clear it is the behaviour and not the child you disapprove of. You should discuss if possible why they bully. You could also discuss the effects it has on their victims. Be careful you do not 'bully' the child in return. Together with parents you need to set firm guidelines and rules to help them control their behaviour. Ensure they apologise in person or in writing to the person/people they are bullying.

Particularly if the situation is serious the child's parents may wish to seek professional help. This can be done by asking at the child's school if they will approach the educational psychologist or the parent can contact their local child guidance centre, details of which can be obtained from your CIS, Health Visitor or local library.

Screaming Children

There are very few children who scream for absolutely no reason. Whilst screaming is highly stressful on the childminder and other children, the screaming child usually wants or needs something. Deducing what a screaming child wants can be difficult. To resolve the problem the childminder needs to be a detective.

First check for obvious reasons: is the child hurt, ill, wet, dirty, hungry or thirsty. Next consider whether they are tired, bored or frustrated. Other causes include tantrums, communication and anxiety. Some children communicate by screaming. This can be quite common where language development is delayed and in this situation can be very wearing.

If you have covered all the basic needs, this is where you will need to convince the child that screaming is not effective and break the pattern of screaming for no apparent reason. Distraction may work, or taking the child out in a car or pushchair if they have worn themselves out this may encourage them to fall asleep. Visit another childminder; the change of scenery, different children and adults can break the screaming pattern and give you a break.

If the child is screaming to shock or get their own way you need to wear a big smile and not show that the noise upsets you, otherwise this may encourage the child to scream more as they feel the behaviour is working. Depending on the child you will have to assess whether also showing displeasure with the noise will be helpful, consider whether the child already knows that screaming is not acceptable and is screaming anyway or whether they need to understand that screaming is not a behaviour that is acceptable.

If a child is screaming to get their own way you could try suggesting they should 'scream louder' this surprising reaction from you may make them stop or even refuse to scream as this is what you want. You can also try channelling their noise making into more appropriate behaviour, such as getting out musical instruments and putting on music this can also help other children present who are upset or becoming stressed at the noise.

Music can also soothe a screaming child, choose something calming and melodious. If all parents approve you could also try burning lavender oil (out or reach) which is purported to have a soothing effect on children and adults.

Destructive Children

There are few occasions when a child will be wantonly destructive. Small children are by nature inquisitive and messy, and cannot always comprehend or consider the consequences of their actions and are often 'accident prone'. They have no understanding of the adult sense of monetary value and will not understand the difference between breaking an old saucer and breaking the best dinner service.

When dealing with an act of destruction or damage you should consider whether the child should have had access to the item in question or to the implement that caused the damage.

Whilst artistic endeavours should be encouraged there should also be clear guidelines in place, e.g. drawing on paper, not on walls; indelible pens are not for children and lipstick is not for drawing with. If inappropriate items have been used you should revise your storage or access arrangements to prevent the child from repeating the behaviour.

Some children discover that breaking things has a profound effect on parental behaviour. They may deliberately try to provoke parents or break things through spite. If this is the case you will need to be very firm and apply the 'not in my house' rule. Remember withdrawal of privileges is only effective for over five's and most effective for children over seven.

There are also a small portion of children who's destructive tendencies are used to mark your home as theirs. These children usually come from an insecure home, there may have been a parental breakup, they may have come from an abusive situation and be in care with foster parents. You should be 'honoured' they consider your home and presence so desirable because it offers them the feeling of security. Marking can include writing their name or initials on items of furniture and walls. If this is the case becoming cross is not helpful, though you should explain that it is not acceptable. One solution may be to help them mark the place as theirs in acceptable ways, such as writing or pictures to put on the walls for display, labelling a coat peg, or a clothes peg to keep their wellies together.

Lying

Children tell lies for a variety of reasons including:
❑ To avoid difficulties or stressful situations.
❑ To escape punishment.
❑ To avoid disapproval.
❑ To avoid hurting someone's feelings.
❑ To make things easier.
❑ Because they mistakenly believe what they said.
❑ To boost self esteem.
❑ Wishing - sometimes they say what they wish is true.
❑ To protect others.
❑ Over prediction of your reaction.
❑ Attention seeking.

Teenagers may also lie because:

❑ If they tell the truth they will not be allowed to proceed.
❑ They need to keep some things private and may lie to protect their privacy.
❑ They wish to cover up serious situations such as drug or alcohol addiction.

Factors to consider when children lie include the following:
❑ Do they understand about lying.
❑ Are they aware of the distress it causes.
❑ Are they aware of the consequences of a lie.
❑ What do they think happens when lies are discovered.
❑ Telling the truth is learnt over time.
❑ Young children's lies are transparent, as they get older lies are more convincing.
❑ Children under three do not understand the concept of honesty.
❑ From three to five children combine reality with fantasy and may experiment with the truth.
❑ From five children begin to comprehend cause and effect and may lie to affect this.
❑ By eight or nine children have some understanding between truth and fantasy.
❑ By nine or ten their sense of right and wrong usually develops.

Practicalities

Openness and honesty should be acknowledged, praised and rewarded. Children should be encouraged to explain what happened if for example something is damaged and to apologise and consider others feelings. If the damage is deliberate at least you can praise them for their honesty. Children then learn through their experiences and begin to realise honesty is the best policy.

Trust is also an important concept. Children need to learn that when they lie it stops people trusting them on other occasions.

Pay attention to the lies children tell. This can highlight patterns and may help in finding solutions. For example, if lying to boost their self esteem, look at strategies to increase self esteem.

Allow older children and teenagers some personal privacy. Ask what you need to know to protect them without prying.

Who did it?

Do not use closed questions when investigating who the culprit was. You may frighten children and restrict their answers. It is better to ask what happened, from a child's level and in a calm voice, to allow a child to explain. Should they lie and you are aware, it can be helpful to allow them the time and opportunity to change their story and be honest. If the explanation sounds fishy it can be productive to give them additional time to think about what happened and to respond later.

If they are trying to shift the blame, explain this may get them and others into trouble. Remind the child telling lies will not solve the problems and could make things worse.

Too Honest

Many childminders will have encountered these types of comments from children; 'that man's pregnant', 'she's fat', 'his head is shiny', where children are telling the truth as they see it, merely stating a fact.

It is important when discussing honesty to cover feelings. For although you know that telling white lies can save someone hurt, a child may not have grasped that concept.

Repetitive / Compulsive Lying

Older children and adolescents who otherwise seem responsible can fall into a pattern of lying repetitively. They may feel this is the easy way to cope with the demands of parents, childminders and teachers. They are not bad or malicious but it can become habitual. Giving the child an opportunity to retract the lie without fear of consequence may help break the cycle.

Compulsive lying may also occur in children with social behaviour disorders such as ADHD where it may be accompanied by other problem behaviours such as impulsivity and an inability to link consequences with behaviour.

Stealing

Stealing is inappropriate behaviour in school aged children. While some severe cases can indicate a more serious psychological problem most of the time it is a behaviour that will be outgrown. It is more common among boys and occurs most often between five and eight years of age.

Children under three - cannot differentiate between 'mine' and what does not belong to them.

Children between three and seven - begin to respect things belonging to others. They will however trade property without regard to monetary values, if they want something else, and do not view this as stealing.

By the age of nine - children usually respect the property of others and understand stealing is wrong. Children of this age may continue to steal for a variety of reasons including:

❑ Peer pressure and the need to fit in.
❑ Low self esteem.
❑ Lack of friends and they try to 'buy' friendship.
❑ If they lack achievements and steal successfully it can be pride.
❑ Impulse.

Stolen, Borrowed or Swapped

It can be helpful to clarify the difference between stealing, borrowing and swapping. Explain about asking permission before borrowing and that if taken without permission it is stealing. This helps teach respect for other peoples possessions and the manners to ask before taking. If you are sure an object has not been swapped but stolen it can be helpful to encourage the child to restore it to the rightful owner and encourage the child to apologise. Do not humiliate the child but make it clear stealing is not acceptable and should not be repeated. Make sure the child does not benefit from the theft in anyway.

Stealing as a Concern

If the following apply, outside help may be required from for example, a child psychologist:

❑ Older child with no remorse.
❑ Older child constantly stealing
❑ Stealing combined with other behavioural problems.

Reasons for Unacceptable Behaviour

Attention Seeking

Attention seeking behaviour is produced when a child wishes to attract attention to themselves for a variety of reasons. It may be because you are busy with another child and they are jealous, because they are bored or are used to one to one attention.

Examples of this behaviour include: tugging at your clothing, hitting other children, kicking walls, slamming doors, screaming, stopping a video or turning off music, tantrums, refusing to eat, throwing toys, breath holding or deliberately making themselves vomit.

When you react to the attention seeking demands ensure you are not rewarding unacceptable behaviour as this encourages the child to repeat the behaviour. Highlight to the child the attention they receive on other occasions. It can help to reassure them they are important to you, for example, being your special helper, but ensure other children do not feel left out or jealous, or they may start similar attention seeking behaviour.

Regression

Regression is where a child reverts to a more immature behaviour pattern. Usually this is a normal developmental phase. It is important not to be reproachful as this adds to the stress causing the regression. Some children will regress if they are tired, overwhelmed, unwell or under some form of stress. Common forms of stress might include a new baby in the family, a death or divorce.

It is often the child's latest achievement that is first to go and toilet training regression is one of the most common examples, with whiny or clingy behaviour being almost equally common. Other examples include, extra aggression, destructiveness and becoming extra messy.

If it seems to be part of the normal development you may find it helpful to sympathise that things seem difficult but will soon return to normal. Expressing sympathy helps from the child's point of view as it implies acceptance and understanding and helps a child to feel more in control.

You may decide it is helpful to temporarily indulge the child and give extra cuddles and attention if you are confident in the child's ability to progress. While doing this you should continue to offer age/developmentally appropriate play at the same time, this will avoid further regression. It may be that you will have to address the reasons for regression. Where the child is struggling with something at home it will be helpful to discuss this with the parents.

Regression can be a very useful tool to children in attracting adults attention to arrangements that need rethinking, such as sleeping routines. Also to events that need discussing with the child, that may seem frightening or that they may not understand, they may not require details but rather a simple explanation or reassurance, for example, in the case of death or divorce. Regression is an important form of communication in young children and should not be ignored.

Boredom

Children become bored when their activities are restricted or they are frustrated with the availability of suitable activities (or what they deem suitable). Boredom may result in unacceptable behaviour or attention seeking behaviour.

To prevent boredom provide interesting things to do. Some should be new and exciting and some should be challenging. These activities should be in addition to the comfortable and familiar things you normally offer. Joining a toy library or loan scheme is an inexpensive way of providing increased choice for the children and also provides them with the fun of choosing items to borrow.

Jealousy

Jealousy occurs when a child is envious of someone else's possessions, achievements or advantages, or is resentful of someone they see as a rival. Both children and adults can become jealous. There are a variety of reasons that can make children feel jealous, these include sibling rivalry (also between your own children or others in your care), jealousy of other children using their possessions, other children possessing something they want and other children winning games or being shown attention.

Children may display their jealously through anger or frustration, for example, if they are jealous of your praise for another child's work they may refuse to talk to you, draw pictures but scribble them out again, stamp their feet or take revenge by hitting out or damaging the other child's work. Children may find strong feelings such as jealousy hard to control or deal with. It can be helpful for you to assist them with putting their feelings into words, allowing them to express their feelings verbally rather than becoming aggressive. Simple phrases such as 'you're leaving me out', 'that's not fair' or 'do you think he's better than me?' help a child express their feelings so you can deal with any problems rapidly.

Remind children of past accomplishments, 'good' things that have happened to them or 'good' things they have. Encourage them to be happy for their playmates and enjoy what they can share. You may like to point out future positive events also.

If the child is able to understand that others have feelings too, encourage them to think about how other children may be jealous of them, for example, if they have a new toy. Toddlers and younger children are egocentric and cannot understand the feelings of others and will have little control over the jealously they feel. From a young child's view point, 'What's mine is mine, if I want yours it's mine and if I have one at home then it must be mine!'

Avoiding situations that might cause jealously to develop can help prevent problems from occurring. Treat children with equal concern, remember also that this has to be equally through the eyes of the children. Children are more likely to perceive attention given to others than that given to themselves, remind them of attention they are getting. If you ask a child to help you, such as with setting the table, give other children the opportunity to help you too and thank them all for their help. If you are introducing a new child to the setting prepare the other children first and be careful not to leave the current children out.

Sibling Rivalry

Sibling rivalry is a form of jealousy, usually found where a child believes that their siblings are getting more attention or treats. It can also occur between your own children and minded children, as well as siblings or a group of minded children from different families.

When you introduce a new child to the household there will be a period of adjustment to the new social situation. Preparing the existing children by letting them know about the new child, reading stories about new additions and short visits from the new child can help make the settling in period easier. In this situation sibling rivalry may occur if the existing children do not feel they are being treated in the same way as the new child.

It is important you do not over protect new children or babies, existing children may see this as an unequal division of care and attention which will lead to jealousy. Children should be encouraged to talk to new babies and play with them if they are careful.

It is important to treat all children with equal concern in terms of attention and praise, include all children if you are setting tasks and the rivalry is likely to pass.

16. Networks and Accreditation

The Role of Childminding Networks

Many childminders belong to informal childminding networks supporting existing or potential childminders. These are often organised by local childminding groups and may be supported by childminding advisory officers or childminding development workers. The benefits of such groups include:

- ❏ The chance to meet others working in the same profession.
- ❏ Sharing of experience and knowledge.
- ❏ Access to training and information sessions.
- ❏ On going support and advice.
- ❏ Links to other professionals.
- ❏ Holiday and sickness cover.
- ❏ Swapping vacancies.
- ❏ Socializing for both childminders and their children.
- ❏ A louder voice as a group on childminding issues.

In England, Wales and Northern Ireland, in addition to these informal networks, there are formal networks, such as the Children Come First Quality Assurance Network Scheme developed by the NCMA in partnership with the Department for Education and Employment (DfEE) and the Office for Standards in Education (Ofsted). When a network operates to specific quality standards it can be approved under the NCMA Children Come First Scheme and so become an NCMA approved network.

Benefits of Being a Formal Network Childminder
Benefits include:

- ❏ Receiving information, advice and support.
- ❏ Filling vacancies more quickly.
- ❏ Being identified with a network shows higher standards achieved.
- ❏ Coordinator support.
- ❏ Ongoing training opportunities.
- ❏ Access to network resources, e.g. libraries for books and toys.
- ❏ Discounted materials.
- ❏ Access to like-minded childminders.
- ❏ Access to a Special Educational needs Coordinator (SENCO).
- ❏ Quality assurance.

Within a Children Come First Network a coordinator is employed to assess registered childminders and regularly monitor them using the NCMA/NICMA's Quality Childminding Charter. The coordinator also ensures that childminders receive appropriate training to develop their skills and will provide a link between parents and childminders. Each Children Come First Childminding Network is customised to meet the diverse and changing needs of its catchment area and any funding or governing bodies involved. This scheme is intended to ensure an extra high quality of childcare and education service is provided and maintained for families and their children. These networks are becoming more widely available in both urban and rural areas.

Some childminding networks may be subsidised by employers to reduce the cost for working parents, or by other organisations while parents train for work or return to school. They are seen to provide a family friendly childcare option, offering the flexibility to cover changing employment patterns, shift work and the ability to offer overnight care for nightshift workers.

What Networks Provide

A Children Come First Childminding Network, or Local Authority designed network may specialise in one type of service, or combine a variety of services, specific to local needs including:

- ❑ Out of school places.
- ❑ Community childminding places for children and families with special needs.
- ❑ Educational places within the Foundation Stage, EYFS, Sure Start Initiatives and children's centres.
- ❑ College based childcare.
- ❑ Safety, fewer 'latch key kids'.
- ❑ Sure Start childminding places.
- ❑ Childcare and support for teen parents.
- ❑ Care for children 'in need' and support for their families.

As a childminder you can be a useful provider of educational places enhanced by a variety of factors including the following:

- ❑ The low numbers of children create ample opportunities for individual attention. This is a key factor in supporting early learning.
- ❑ The home-base setting together with the surrounding environment provides a rich source of opportunities as well as structured play, other learning activities and experiences. Providing nursery standard education within a home setting.
- ❑ Continuity of care is a key factor in supporting children's emotional development. Emotional well being is an essential pre-requisite for early linguistic and cognitive development. Childminding is the only form of provision providing continuity through the various stages from babyhood to full time school and beyond.
- ❑ Childminding is age-integrated, children are at varying stages of development. Children benefit from the interaction and the enhanced learning opportunities this provides.

Network coordinators within formal networks undertake a variety of roles including the following:

- ❑ Recruiting registered childminders to the network whose current practice meets the NCMA quality childminding charter, or if Local Authority networks their own childcare standards.
- ❑ Visiting you regularly, monitoring to ensure you are maintaining standards.
- ❑ Provide and arranging training opportunities, practical support, advice and information.
- ❑ Matching childminders and families.
- ❑ Liasing with the local Education Authority over the provision of education by accredited childminders.
- ❑ Helping parents find alternative care at short notice because of sickness or holidays.
- ❑ Organising continued training for childminders.

Accredited Childminders

In England and Wales childminders can become accredited if they are part of an NCMA Children Come First Approved Childminding Network and are able to meet the additional criteria in the NCMA Quality Childminding Charter (concerned with the promotion of ELG's or desirable learning outcomes, for the Foundation Stage or EYFS, within a planned curriculum). They will then be eligible for education grants paid through Early Years Development Plans as education providers for three and four year olds.

Childminders who are accredited as part of educational provision must be prepared to receive longer visits from an Ofsted/CSSIW Nursery Inspector than non accredited childminders.

Additional criteria in the NCMA Quality Childminding Charter includes:

❑ The ability to assess the achievements and stage of development reached by a child through interaction and observation of the child and through discussion with the children's families.
❑ To be able to set goals for children's progress, plan activities and experiences to suit each child's stage of development, building on their achievements.
❑ To draw up written curriculum plans, using evaluation of the effectiveness of such plans as they are used to develop plans for the next stage.
❑ To ensure the activities and experiences provided as their early years curriculum enables the children to progress by the age of five towards all areas of the Early Learning Goals.

Accredited childminders are required to have equal opportunity and anti-discriminatory practices and to have regard to the code of practice on the Identification and Assessment of Special Educational Needs and to the additional guidance. All childminders in England, including non accredited childminders, will be expected to achieve this criteria in implementing the EYFS from September 2008. It is anticipated that only those who are accredited will be able to offer the funded free early years sessions.

Process Involved in Joining a Network

If you are in an area where a network is being formed or exists you may be approached and offered information, or you may apply through a recruiting advert or hear by word of mouth. Networks often hold information evenings which childminders can attend and find more about their local network and whether they would like to become involved. Some networks also have a waiting list to which your name can be added or passed on should another network be planned in the local area. In some areas, local may mean within walking distance or an hours drive. It may also depend on the type of network.

If you are to be assessed to join a network you will be supplied with relevant information and helpful tips. Do read these as they will help you understand what is required. Information supplied may vary between types of networks. If the network is a formal one such as the NCMA Children Come First or a Local Authority network before you are invited to join the coordinator will need to understand and know about the childminding service you currently provide. In order to do this, they will need to visit you and your premises on several occasions including when you have minded children present and when you have a quiet time so you will be able to discuss your current practices and show the coordinator the environment which you use for childminding. Typically this will require several visits, with approximately three being the average.

In addition to these initial visits you will also receive regular visits, depending on the network these may be every six to eight weeks. Visits will be made by your coordinator who may occasionally be accompanied by a representative of their senior management team such as an NCMA assessor.

Networks
During your initial visit most network coordinators will allow some time for you to get to know each other and the details of your provision to be discussed. This is also a good opportunity to ask questions. The initial visit may also be used for examining relevant paperwork; producing details of your service; supplying standards and in the case of an NCMA network the Quality Childminding Charter; health and safety checklists and risk assessments. The coordinator may also check to see if you currently meet the network standards or if you would like training to enable you to meet the standards.

Commonly requested information includes:

❑ Current Registration Certificate.
❑ Latest inspection report from your regulator.

❑ Details of Public Liability Insurance.
❑ Details of you car insurance and MOT if applicable.
❑ Your incident/accident book.
❑ Details of relevant qualifications and attendance of relevant training.
❑ Information kept on current children.
❑ Information on how you run you business, e.g. blank contracts, attendance records and financial records.
❑ Children's progress reports if kept.
❑ Policies including children's behaviour, equal opportunities and special needs, if you have them.
❑ Example menus including meals and snacks.
❑ Names and dates of birth of currently minded children.
❑ Details of household members.
❑ Details of childminding assistants if applicable.
❑ Details of backup childminding cover in case of illness or emergencies.
❑ Details of livestock or pets which children come into contact with.
❑ Whether you have a smoke-free environment.
❑ Details of outings and opportunities provided to enable children to mix and join in with larger groups of children, for example, childminding group events.
❑ NCMA or other professional childminding membership if applicable.

During the subsequent visits the coordinator will be looking to see if you are working to their quality charter which may be NCMA's or the local authorities own. They will also be looking at the health and safety issues of your business probably on a room by room inspection checklist.

It may help to make notes in advance on how your practices meet the quality standards for when the coordinator comes. There are details in Section 2. Regulations and Inspections Uncovered, Preparation for a Visit and in Section 7. Health, Hygiene and Safety that will help you check your home is safe, healthy and on reducing risks.

You are likely to be asked for a variety of other opinions and methods you employ covering a variety of points. You should be provided with details of these in advance to enable you to prepare for the visit. It can be helpful to make notes on these details to remind yourself to mention or cover certain points or aspects during the visit.

Commonly raised topics include:

❑ Children Act 1989, Care Standards Act 2000, Disability Act 2001.
❑ Child development.
❑ Play and activities, and their relevance to age and stage of development.
❑ Play and activities provided.
❑ Outside resources used.
❑ Toys, equipment and resources available to support play and learning.
❑ How parents are involved.
❑ Who else you get advice from.
❑ How you share information with parents.
❑ Confidentiality.
❑ Child protection/safeguarding issues.
❑ Behaviour management.
❑ Risk assessments.
❑ Health, hygiene and cross infection.
❑ Emergency plans.
❑ Menus and dietary needs.
❑ Business practices.
❑ Equal opportunities.
❑ Anti discriminatory practices.
❑ Inclusion of children with special needs and disabilities.

❑ Promotion of positive images including those often discriminated against.
❑ Promotion of self-esteem.
❑ Cultural provision.

You may find your network uses check sheets or relevant points information sheets to produce a points system to identify childminders who are most suited to joining the network. The system often allows a score for a partially met point and a higher score for a mostly met point and the highest score for a fully met point.

Your network may have a minimum score you need to obtain to be admitted. You should be issued with details of your performance and all networks should have an appeals procedure you can use if you are unhappy with the results of your assessments.

If your score is not quite high enough you may still be admitted if you agree to undertake relevant training to ensure the network continues to maintain a high standard of childcare and education.

Process of Being Accredited

When a childminder belonging to a network has developed their practice to cover the additional standards including attaining NVQ level 3, DHC level 3 or higher in Childcare and Education they can become accredited. This can also be done at the same time as joining a network if these standards are already met.

Once there are two or more childminders belonging to a network who are accredited the childminding regulator will become involved to accredit the network itself. They will inspect the network and may visit the childminders. If this inspection is passed the accredited childminders will be able to participate in Local Authority plans as providers of education for three and four year olds and in England draw from the government funding to provide this.

The inspection process to become an accredited childminder typically takes 3-4 assessments, they are usually undertaken by a coordinator who is already familiar with you and your practices.

The coordinator is looking for standards over and above those required by childminders belonging to the network but not accredited. They will want to see a brochure, portfolio or prospectus used to provide parents with information about your service and will be particularly interested in any information you supply parents with details of how you will promote their child's learning, e.g. through play, planned and unplanned activities.

The coordinator will want to see evidence of any written records you are keeping of children's progress, this might include diaries, reports, pictorial displays, examples of children's 'work' or progress charts.

The coordinator will want to see evidence of your curriculum planning including activities and experiences you are providing to help children learn and progress through the Early Years Foundation (EYFS) (in England) or the Desirable Learning Outcomes (in Wales). They will be looking at your short term (e.g. weekly), medium term, (e.g. termly/monthly) and long term plans (e.g. yearly). They will be checking that the experiences you have planned will give priority to the three areas of learning, personal, social and emotional development; communication, language and literacy, and mathematical development. You will also be required to demonstrate your plans cover all areas of learning and will also include opportunities for physical and creative development and opportunities to expand on children's knowledge and understanding of the world.

Your coordinator may also like to discuss key areas within the areas of children learning and check your plans will include these. They will look for evidence during their visits that children have the opportunities and activities to achieve these key areas. For example, writing activities could include playing instruments, threading and cutting for hand eye coordination, strengthening of large muscles by using climbing frame, throwing balls and painting, practising fine motor skills by pouring sand and finger rhymes, practising drawing in sand or with bubbles, holding a pencil correctly and paper/pencils being readily available, playing writing for lists and notes. These are all activities which will contribute to a child's development of writing skills.

Your network coordinator should provide you with details of what they will be assessing at each visit to help you prepare. They should also offer you further training if necessary in order to successfully complete your assessment. Your coordinator will also need to satisfy themselves that you have sufficient resources to implement your planned curriculum. Resources include your equipment, toys and materials including arts and craft provision.

You will also need to have some knowledge of the Code of Practice for Identification and Assessment of Special Educational Needs and the guidance for private, voluntary and independent sectors. Your network should include someone with SENCO training and they will be able to advise you on this code. You will also require a statement on your inclusion policy for children with special needs. Your SENCO or network coordinator can help you formulate your policy, you may like to include the completed policy in your brochure or prospectus for parents.

You will be informed of your assessment results and of any actions you need to take and a timescale to complete them in order to become a accredited childminder. After you have been accredited the network will need to have be inspected by a childminding regulator, such as Ofsted before the Local Authority will accept you into its range of provision for Early Years Education grants and for it to count you amongst those supplying early education.

17. Maintaining a Portfolio of Policies and Procedures

Creating Your Portfolio

A portfolio is a collection of documents that support your work as a childminder. They set out in writing how you run your business and what parents can expect from you. Your portfolio is also an opportunity to demonstrate your professionalism and experience: to show what makes you a good choice for parents looking for childcare.

Having an organised collection of information about your services is useful for several reasons. It is helpful when prospective customers are visiting, as it provides all the information they are likely to need in one place guiding you through the information you need to give them. It can give a professional image to the services you are going to provide and reassure parents you are committed to the welfare of their children. When you have an inspection it will help to demonstrate the ways in which you comply with National Standards so you can achieve a higher inspection grade. It will also be helpful when you complete course work or if you want to join a childminding network and become accredited to provide early years education.

Documents

Your portfolio is a good place to keep documents relating to your business such as the following:

Safety Certificates
- ❑ Fire Safety (not compulsory)
- ❑ Car MOT
- ❑ Car Seat Safety (not compulsory)
- ❑ Equipment Maintenance Records
- ❑ Gas and Electrical Safety Checks
- ❑ Environmental Health Reports (if available)

Insurance Documents
- ❑ Public Liability Insurance
- ❑ Car Insurance
- ❑ Legal Insurance (not compulsory)

Example Forms
- ❑ Contract
- ❑ Parent Permission Forms
- ❑ Children's Record of Information

Other Documents
- ❑ Useful addresses and telephone contacts
- ❑ Local area Child Protection Procedures
- ❑ References and thank you letters
- ❑ Training/qualification certificates
- ❑ Planning permission (if applicable)
- ❑ Registration Certificate

Confidentiality

Your portfolio should not contain any documents with confidential information, such as the contracts or payment records of individual customers.

Policies and Procedures

Your portfolio should include copies of your policies. These explain the rules, guidelines and plans for how you run your childcare service and how you would deal with specific situations that you might encounter. Some policies may also include procedures; these explain what steps you take to achieve the goals set out in your policy. For example:

Policy: I will ensure parents are kept informed about matters relating to their children's care.

Procedure: To achieve this I will keep a diary shared between parents and childminder to document children's routines and achievements, and I will schedule regular meetings to discuss any problems or issues parents may have.

The following table indicates which policies are compulsory. You may not have all of these policies, or several may be combined into one document. You should check the applicable National Standards for the exact requirements for your area and note these can be subject to change. Although not all policies are compulsory, you may still find them useful to explain to parents what to expect from your service.

Required Policies	England	Scotland	Wales	N. Ireland	S. Ireland
Child Protection	✔	✔	✔		✔
Complaints Procedures	✔	✔	✔		
Confidentiality		✔			✔
Emergency Procedures		✔	✔		
Accident Procedures	✔	✔			
Health & Safety					✔
Sickness & Exclusion			✔		
Fire Procedures	✔		✔		✔
Parents Failing to Collect	✔				
Lost Child	✔				
Behaviour & Sanctions			✔	✔	✔
Equal Opportunities			✔		✔
Partnership with Parents					✔

Writing Policies and Procedures

It is important that policies can be easily understood. Use simple language rather than attempting to make them sound like a legal document. Try using bullet points, short sentences, flow charts, diagrams or pictures to make your point clearer. For example, your fire escape plan could include a diagram of your premises with the exits marked.

You will find information under the relevant sections throughout this book that will help you decide on your policies and give you ideas of what you need to cover. Your policies do not need to cover every eventuality, they should be an overview of what you would do. The steps below outline how to write a policy using a 'Meals and Nutrition Policy' as an example.

Step 1: Research

Most childminding policies reflect the rules set by National Standards or other legislation. The first step in writing a policy is to check what rules are compulsory for all childminding settings. Then you can add any additional rules specific to your setting. Rules for food and drink include the following:

Requirements from the Early Years Foundation Stage (EYFS) England (Food & Drink)
❑ Meals, snacks and drinks must be healthy, balanced and nutritious.
❑ Fresh drinking water must be available at all times.

Rules from the Statutory Guidance to the EYFS Framework.
❑ Childminders should record information from parents about a child's dietary needs.
❑ Childminders should be aware of food hygiene legislation.
❑ Inform parents what can be stored safely and appropriate food content for packed lunches.

Department of Heath (England) Guidelines
❑ Children should have 5 portions or fruit or vegetables per day

Your Own Rules (Example)
❑ Children will not be given sweets or high sugar treats

Step 2: Topic List

Make a list of the topics you need to cover to incorporate all the rules and guidelines you have found from your research.

❏ The types of meals and drinks you provide, including special dietary requirements
❏ Meal time routine
❏ Whether parents have to provide any items
❏ Food hygiene

Step 3: Write Your Policy Statement

Write a summary of the rules and guidelines that you apply to your setting. Your policy should show how you comply with the rules and guidelines you identified from your research into legislation. The meals policy needs to explain to parents what they can expect from the meals you provide and how responsibility for nutrition is shared between parent and childminder.

> ### Meals and Nutrition
>
> As part of my service I provide healthy nutritious meals, essential to children's well-being, incorporating any special dietary or religious requirements.

Step 4: Write Procedures

Explain how you will implement your policy. To write your procedures, try to imagine yourself in the situation in your policy and then write down what you would do. For example, imagine that it is dinner time, what happens and what rules do you have for children while eating. Think about what other considerations you may need to make in a particular situation.

> **Drinks:** Children are offered drinks (water, milk or fruit juice) at regular intervals during the day, after naps or energetic play and at meal times. They are also encouraged to ask when they want a drink. I have a range of cups and mugs for different ages and development stages or parents may supply their child's own preferred style.
>
> **Menu:** I can provide breakfast (e.g. cereal, fruit or toast), a cold lunch (e.g. sandwiches or cheese & crackers) and a hot home-cooked evening meal (e.g. shepherd's pie, mild curry, or spaghetti) depending on the time your child is at the setting and your requirements. I can also provide snacks as required such as fruit. Meals take into account the governments guidelines of five portions of fruit and vegetables a day.
>
> **Special Diets:** As part of settling a child into the setting I discuss with parents their children's food likes and dislikes and any cultural or dietary requirements. These are noted on the Child Record Form you complete before your child attends. I am happy to provide home-made pureed baby food, alternately you may provide your own pureed food. Please provide formula or made up bottles as required.
>
> **Mealtime Routine:** Before meals children are asked to tidy away the toys and activities, visit the toilet and wash and dry their hands. They may be asked to help lay the table or prepare food. Children sit together at the dinner table to eat, booster seats/high chairs are available as necessary. During mealtimes good manners are encouraged such as please and thank you and not talking with a full mouth. Children are encouraged to try foods that they have not encountered before and the social eating environment provides support and encouragement for this.
>
> **Food Hygiene:** I have registered with the Local Environmental Health Department as a provider of food and have a Foundation Certificate in Food Hygiene.

Step 5: Review Policy

Once you have finished writing your policies, ask parents to read them and comment on how well they understood them and whether there is anything you may have missed. You could also ask other childminders or people in the appropriate field for the policy you are writing. For example, a Fire Safety Officer may be able to give you advice on your fire safety policy.

You will need to review your policies and procedures regularly to take into account new legislation, developments in knowledge and your experiences. You should date your policies and remember to keep copies of old policies incase you receive a complaint so you can reference the policy document that was current at the time.

Your policies form part of your childminding contract with parents and this should be acknowledged by making them sign copies or adding a line to your contract such as '*I have received a copy of the following policy documents...*'.

Presentation

Your portfolio should reflect your services positively so take time to make it as neat and professional as possible. Consider a ring binder or folder for putting the information in and plastic wallets to keep pages neat. You will find you add new information to your portfolio as your service develops, so consider how you will be able to add or update your portfolio when you are designing it. If possible, type up your policies using a computer as this can help make them look extra professional. If you do not have access to a computer make sure your writing is neat and easy to read.

If you have lots of information in your portfolio it may help to divide it into sections. You can use a blank piece of card or paper for this. Sections could include, policies, documents, example forms, training certificates and references. You may like to make your first page a contents page, this will make the information in your portfolio easier to locate.

You may find it helpful to provide prospective customers with a copy of some or all of your portfolio, particularly the pages relating to your policies. These could be photo copies of your original portfolio and be stapled or paper clipped together.

Example Policies

Policies and procedures are unique to each childminder, so although reading example documents will help give you ideas you should write a document that is specific to your childminding service.

Working in Partnership with Parents

This policy should set out how you will ensure important details about children's needs and care are communicated between parent and childminder.

Topics to cover:
❑ Why you feel communication is important.
❑ Methods of communication.
❑ Times for communication.
❑ The types of information that needs communicating.

Working in Partnership

I believe that good communication is essential to a successful working relationship between parents and childminder. The following steps are taken to encourage this:

- When you first place your child in my care you'll receive an information pack with copies of all my policies and other helpful information.
- A 'Record of Information' form is filled in alongside the contract with detailed information about each child's needs, likes, dislikes and routine.
- A diary is shared between parents and childminder detailing the daily routine, eating and sleeping habits and any other helpful information.
- Parents are encouraged to chat informally and share information when dropping off/collecting children.
- If at any point you feel a longer discussion is needed or a more private chat we'll arrange a mutually convenient time to meet or call.

Collection of Children

This policy should explain to parents what you expect from them in relation to collecting their child and what you will do in cases when a child is not collected as expected.

Topics to cover include:
❑ Who is to collect a child.
❑ Arrangements needed if a alternate person is going to collect a child.
❑ Late pickups.
❑ What happens if a child is not collected.

Collecting Children

Collection of children should be punctual and by the appropriate person unless by prior arrangement. Please remember that I may have commitments arranged to fit in with your contracted hours. If you are late it can have a knock-on effect for school collection etc. If you are early you may well find that I am not at home.

If you need to change a collection/drop off time to meet your circumstances please give me as much notice as possible so that we can agree a mutually acceptable arrangement.

There may be times when I will not be able to meet the collection times. In the majority of cases this will be due to pre-planned activities, in which case I will seek your approval. In other cases, I will endeavour to inform you of the delay, and the reason for it, at the earliest opportunity. In these circumstances I will normally deliver the child home and, of course, no additional fees are charged.

In the Event of a Failure to Collect a Child

Every effort will be made to contact you. If you cannot be contacted then the emergency person nominated on your child's Record of Information would be contacted while the children remain in a safe and familiar setting. If all attempts to contact a parent/guardian/emergency contact fail, a reasonable time will be allocated before the local authority duty social worker is informed of the situation. They will then decide what happens next, and whether the police need to be involved in helping to trace a parent/carer. Please ensure if you are running late that you phone and inform us to prevent false alarms.

Complaints Procedure

Your complaints policy should explain to parents what they should do if they have a problem with the service you are providing.

Topics to cover include:
- ❏ Discussing the problem.
- ❏ Time scale for investigation.
- ❏ Ofsted or your regulators complaints procedures.
- ❏ Child protection issues .
- ❏ How parents can contact Ofsted or your regulator with complaints.

Complaints Procedure

I aim to always provide a high level of service to parents. If you do have any problems with my services as a childminder, please discuss the issues with me at an early stage so that any difficulties can be resolved quickly.

I am required by Ofsted to record any complaints together with information on their investigation and will be shared with parents on request. All outcomes will be notified at the earliest opportunity and no later than 28 days from the complaint.

Please note, you can only terminate your contract without notice if I fail to provide reasonable and safe care for your child. In the unlikely event that you feel this is necessary, and you terminate your contract on these grounds, you should state your reasons in writing as soon as it is practical and advise Ofsted of your action and reasons. Please note if the allegations prove to be unfounded I will reserve the right to recoup fees, costs and interest via the courts.

The telephone number for Ofsted's Complaints and Enforcement unit is: 08456 404040.

Business Practice and Confidentiality

This policy should explain to parents why and how you keep records, and how you ensure confidentiality.

Topics to cover:
- ❏ What records you keep.
- ❏ How they are kept.
- ❏ Who they are available to and in what circumstances.

Confidentiality

As part of providing a professional childcare service I am required to keep records relating to the children in my care. These include copies of contracts, contact information for parents and emergency contacts, information on children's allergies and preferences and records of accidents and injuries. I treat all information I receive/record about the children in my care, and their families, as confidential.

- All records are kept securely in compliance with the Data Protection Act. Written records are kept in a locked filing cabinet and computer files are password protected.
- You may request to view the records relating to you and your child at any time.
- Records will only be shared with parents permission or in the case of a child protection issue (see my child protection policy).
- My records are subject to inspection by Ofsted.

Payment & Fees

This policy should explain your rules on payments, deposits and other matters relating to money.

Topics to cover include:
- ❑ In what circumstances you ask for a deposit and how much it will be.
- ❑ In what circumstances you will change a retainer and how much it will be.
- ❑ Whether fees are payable in advance or arrears.
- ❑ Whether you charge an overtime fee for late parents.
- ❑ What fees include/exclude.

Payment & Fee's Policies

Payment

Fees for the contracted hours are normally payable in advance on the due date, as specified in the contract. Overtime payments are normally paid in arrears, with the advance payment for the next period. Written confirmation of charges can be provided on request. All payments are recorded in the Accounts Book; receipts will be provided on request. If payment may be delayed for any reason please inform me in advance.

Working Families Tax Credit

If you are claiming this tax credit against your childminding costs then please be aware the Inland Revenue will check the amount and period for which you are claiming with myself at regular intervals.

Deposit

If there is a period between signing the contract and the date the first payment is due I may ask for a deposit (usually 50% of the first payment). This is to reserve your space and will be deducted from your first payment. The deposit is non refundable. If you decide not to take the place after signing the contract the deposit will not be returned.

Retainer Fees

I normally charge a retainer fee to reserve a place for future use by a child. The retainer fee is a proportion of the normal fee (usually 50%) and is to be paid on the same basis (monthly/weekly etc.) as the service to be provided. A contract will be needed to cover any retained period. The purpose of the retainer is to recompense me for potential loss of earning during the retained period. This is not a credit against future fees. Whilst I am being paid a retainer I will not fill the slot and will therefore provide childminding during the contracted hours if so requested provided that sufficient notice is given. The full childminding fee is payable for any such period. Without a retainer fee I will not guarantee a place for your child at any time in the future.

Please note that where a retained place is not taken up by the parent the retainer fees are not refundable.

Other Fees

Parents are responsible for the payment of playgroup fees. It should be noted that where I am responsible for the child during this time, e.g. if the session is cancelled I will care for them, there is no deduction from the contracted fees.

Equal Opportunities

This policy should explain how equal opportunities applies to your setting and ways in which you ensure equal opportunity for the children in your care.

Topics to cover include:
- ❑ What equal opportunities is and why it is important.
- ❑ The ways in which you promote equal opportunities.
- ❑ How you will address discrimination.

Equality of Opportunities

I offer every child equal access to opportunities to play, learn and develop to their full potential. In order to meet children's diverse needs I provide a safe and supportive learning environment. Within this environment there is an active promotion of equality of opportunity and anti discriminatory practice in which the contribution of all children is valued.

Children have the right to feel valued, develop a positive self image, and be free from discrimination. No person or child will be discriminated against on grounds of skin colour, gender, ability, religion, lifestyle or culture. I shall challenge racist and discriminatory remarks, inappropriate attitudes and behaviour from both children and adults, including parents. I will help children to develop positive attitudes towards people who are different from themselves and help them to avoid prejudices, aiming for children to become sensitive and respectful of the needs and feelings of others. I will help children to develop a sense of their identity within their own cultural and social group as well as offering the opportunity to learn about cultures which differ from their own.

The toys and resources available challenge stereotypes and show positive images of a wide range of people with different genders, cultures and abilities.

Special Needs

This policy should include an explanation of what special needs means and how you ensure that children with special needs have their needs met. This policy might be included as part of your equal opportunities policy.

Topics to cover include:
- ❑ How you will include children with special needs
- ❑ How you will gain an understanding of individual children's needs

---

Special Needs Policy

Any requirements, for example, dietary, cultural, religious or other special needs should be discussed and entered on the Record of Information for a Minded Child to ensure the best care possible can be given to your child.

I will liaise with parents to ensure children's Records of Information contain sufficient information to enable appropriate care to be given. Where children have been identified as having special needs, steps will be taken to actively promote their welfare and development and ensure equality of opportunity. This means that activities will be adapted and extra support provided to allow children of all abilities and developmental stages to participate.

Fire Safety Policy

Your Fire Policy should explain what precautions you take to minimise the risk of fire and a plan for what you will do if a fire occurs.

Topics to cover include:
- ❑ What precautions you have taken to prevent a fire.
- ❑ Your fire escape plan.
- ❑ A record of fire drills.

Fire Safety Policy

Fire Safety Information

- **Smoke Alarms:** These are interconnected and fitted on three levels (including the loft). Smoke alarms are tested regularly, and the batteries are replaced annually.
- **CO Detector:** A Carbon Monoxide alarm is fitted midway between the gas fire and the central heating boiler. It is tested regularly. The combined sensor and battery unit are replaced in accordance with the manufacturer' instructions.
- **Fire Blanket:** This is located in the kitchen and is large enough to wrap a child in. It conforms to BS6575.
- **Gas Fire:** This is not used while minded children are present.
- **Matches:** This is a non smoking household and there are no matches on the premises.
- **Exits:** The Main exit is unlocked. All other doors and windows suitable for exiting in an emergency have keys on adjacent hooks. Parents are requested not to block exits with buggies, bags etc, and children are discouraged from playing in doorways as a safety issue.

Emergency Evacuation

In the unlikely event of a fire occurring the following procedures will be observed wherever possible.

- The door to the fire location will be closed, where possible.
- A phone will be collected.
- The children will be gathered together and we will exit the building by the front door, carrying children who cannot walk.
- If access to this exit is blocked by fire, we will exit by the back door or back patio window.
- The Fire Brigade will be called using the phone. If this was not accessible due to the fire a neighbours phone will be used.

Please note: We will not re enter the building for children's records or possessions until cleared to do so by the Fire Brigade.

Fire Survival Training

Practice evacuations will be organised on a regular basis. Fire safety issues will be incorporated into learning activities through stories and games. Issues covered will include:

- What constitutes a fire hazard.
- Safe exit in a smoke filled environment.
- If the door is hot, leave it shut.
- Stop, drop and roll for burning clothing.

Safe Guarding Children / Child Protection

Your Safe Guarding Children Policy, formally known as child protection, should explain how you ensure children in your care are protected against physical, emotional, sexual abuse and neglect.

Topics to cover include:
❑ What your responsibilities are under current legislation.
❑ How, when and why you keep records of injuries.
❑ Who may see these records.
❑ What the procedure is in cases of suspected abuse.

You could also add:
❑ Contact information for the Social Services Department you report to.
❑ Records of courses you have taken covering child protection.
❑ A copy of your Criminal Records Bureau check .

For more information contact your Local Social Services Department or the NSPCC.

Safe Guarding Children / Child Protection Policy

One of my main responsibilities is to ensure your child's welfare and well being. The nature of care I provide and my interaction with the children means that should children show significant changes in their behaviour or physical appearance it will become quickly apparent. If this happens then further information or explanation may be required to ensure the best possible care is provided for your child. Please note, such incidents will be recorded in the accident/incident book. Any details you provide about your child can be read and checked for accuracy when you counter sign the record.

As a Registered Childminder I am required to keep records of accidents and incidents occurring on my premises and instances of when a child arrives with an injury (however minor). Detailed records include parents, child's or my explanation of events as applicable, date and time with details of injury and treatment if these have occurred. These records are a statutory requirement and are there to protect the children from any danger of abuse. These records are confidential. Records are open to inspection by Social Services and Ofsted as part of the statutory requirements.

Should explanations for accidents, incidents, significant changes in behaviour or appearance sound implausible or a pattern of injuries or events occur then suspicions will be shared with the Bedfordshire Area Safeguarding Children Board as set out in their guidance procedures. Where a child has been placed by Social Services then their placement officer will also be notified.

Health, Hygiene and Safety

This policy should explain what procedures and precautions do you have in place to ensure the health and safety of children in your care.

Topics to cover include:
❑ What procedures you follow to ensure hygiene.
❑ What safety precautions you have taken.
❑ Smoking.

Health, Hygiene and Safety Policy

Every consideration is given to protecting the children from harm and promoting their health and well-being. I regularly subject the premises to risk assessments and safety audits to ensure hazards are minimised both inside and in the garden areas. Risk assessments are also made while using the surrounding community.

The following procedures are in place to promote children's safety, health and well-being:

- Harmful substances including cleaning products and medicines are inaccessible to children.
- Socket covers are in use.
- Safety gates are used when needed for younger children in accordance with the manufactures recommendations.
- Gates and fences are checked for damage and secure while children are present.
- Toys and equipment are regularly cleaned and checked for damage.
- Appropriate car seats are used.
- Safety monitoring devices are regularly tested.
- Spills of bodily fluids will be disinfected and soiled pants and clothing will be returned for your attention.
- Children's hands will be washed with soap after using the toilet, touching animals, messy play, garden activities and before snacks, drinks and meals.
- Paper towels are available to reduce infection risks.
- A box of tissues is always available and children will be helped to wipe their noses when required.
- Individual bedding is supplied for each child.
- Children with infectious conditions will be excluded. Please see Sickness Policy.
- Healthy drinks, snacks and meals will be provided as required. Please see Nutrition Policy.
- The kitchen will be kept clean and hygienic.
- Good practice will be used when storing, preparing and serving food or formula milk.
- Fire safety precautions are in place. See Fire Safety Policy.
- Safety in the sun precautions are undertaken.
- I will not smoke in house or in the children's presence, nor will I let any visitors do so.

Exclusion and Sick Children Policy

This policy should explain to parents how their child being ill effects their use of your service and what you will do if their child becomes ill in your care.

Topics to cover include:
❑ What you consider a sick child to be.
❑ Under what circumstances you will/would not care for a sick child.
❑ What happens if a child becomes ill.
❑ Communicable diseases and exclusion periods.

Administration of Medicines Policy

This policy should explain the procedures you will follow if a child needs medicine administered.

Topics to cover include:
❑ Permission forms.
❑ Prescription and non-prescription medicines.
❑ Special cases.

Exclusion, Sick Children and Administration of Medicines Policy

Please let me know if your child has been ill within the last twenty four hours before they are due to attend. When children are ill they can be cared for best at home with their family, rather than here where other children may be noisy and they may need to go out on school pickups. I do not normally care for children that are unwell but I make make exceptions for minor or non contagious ailments. Children who are unwell with an infectious disease should not attend while they pose a risk of infection to others. The decision whether or not to accept a sick child is mine.

If your child becomes ill while in my care I will contact you and, according to the severity of the illness, may ask you to take your child home.

Medication

When you sign the contract you will also be invited to sign a form giving permission for be to administer non-prescription medications such as teething-gel or Capol.

Please let me know if your child has medicine prescribed by their doctor. Additional written permission is required if you would like me to administer prescription medication. Medication should be in the original container and in the name of the child it is to be administered to. If your child requires an inhaler for asthma please arrange for a spare to keep here in case it is forgotten.

If your child requires medication that needs training to administer, such as insulin or adrenalin injections for an allergy, please let me know in advance so we can arrange this.

Each time I administer medicines it is recorded and you will be asked to sign the entry.

Missing Child Procedure

This policy should explain what you will do if a child goes missing from your care. It will help you plan a head so you will be able to remain calm and logical if this should happen.

Procedure for a Missing Child

If your child should be collected from school and is not awaiting collection, I will inform the school. The child will be deemed to be under the care of the school and it will be their responsibility to locate the child. To prevent false alarms please ensure you phone if your child will be absent from school and does not need collecting.

Children on outings conform to expected behaviours according to their age and stage of development. These include holding hands, wearing reins and staying close. Children receive stranger danger training and what to do if separated from a carer. In the unlikely event that your child goes missing on an outing the immediate area would be searched and where applicable a Tannoy message relayed to locate them. If they are still not located then the police and parent/guardian(s) would be contacted immediately. Notes would be provided of the circumstances surrounding the disappearance, clothes and distinguishing features, in order to help the police with their investigations.

Ofsted would also be informed.

Accident and Emergency Policy

This policy will set out what you will do if an emergency occurs.

Topics to cover include:
- ❏ Procedure you will follow in an emergency.
- ❏ How you will contact parents.
- ❏ The record you will keep.

Accident & Emergency Policy

Your child's safety is of the up most importance and I will take all reasonable precautions to minimise potential risks. My setting is regularly inspected for safety by Ofsted and maintained in accordance with the National Standards. I hold an up to date First Aid Certificate and maintain a first aid box.

If an accident occurs whilst your child is in my care you will be informed and an entry in the accident book will be completed which will require your signature. These records are a statutory requirement and are open to inspection by Ofsted and the local Social Services Department. In the event of a serious incident Ofsted, the local child protection agency and RIDDOR will be notified.

In the event of an emergency:

- I will deal with the situation calmly, reassuring the children present and ensuring children are safe while the problem is resolved.
- Depending on the exact situation, I will administer basic first aid and/or contact the emergency services.
- If I am unable to contact the parents, I will contact the emergency contacts they have provided.
- If it is necessary to attend hospital then parents will be contacted to meet me there. I will try to place other children with a backup childminder otherwise I will take them with me.
- I will share any relevant information you have provided on any medical problems or allergies with emergency medical service and doctors. It is essential you inform me of any changes to the medical information you have provided.

Existing Injuries

Where a child is delivered with an injury you should notify me and an entry will be made in the accident/incident book to be counter-signed by yourself.

Daily Routines

This policy should explain what your daily routines are and how these can be integrated with the routines parents have.

Topics to cover include:
- ❏ What time school/playgroup pick ups are.
- ❏ Your daily routine.
- ❏ How will you integrate parents routines with your own.

Permission for outings as shown on the contract is for day to day routine and local excursions, using public transport, car, or on foot (eg school/nursery runs, feeding the ducks, park visits, shopping trips etc.). If outings outside the normal area are planned separate permission will be sought.

Settling Children In

This policy should cover how you and parents can work together to ensure children settle into their new setting successfully.

Topics to cover include:
- ☐ How you arrange for the child to meet you.
- ☐ Whether you offer a short term contract for settling in.

Settling in Policy

Leaving your child in the care of someone else, for what may be the first time, can be a difficult experience for parents. An introductory settling in phase can help make this less stressful for all concerned. The younger the child the longer the phase should be. Once a place has been contractually confirmed arrangements will be discussed for this settling in phase.

Ideally introductory sessions should be a series of short, regular visits initially with a parent/carer present culminating with short unaccompanied sessions. I will work with you to support both yourself and your child through this important transition period.

These are no set limits for the number of settling in sessions as this will be dependant on the age and development of the child and parental confidence. Some children have difficulties taking a feed or eating at a strange location and so these events will be included in settling in periods. A child is considered to have settled when they have formed a relationship with myself and is familiar with where things are, the routines and are happy to participate in activities.

Sessions with the Parent Present:
These sessions will provide you and/or your child with the opportunity to:
- Ask questions.
- Provide further information about likes, dislikes, favourite activities, best methods of comforting your child and home routines.
- Become familiar with the setting practices, childminder and other children in the setting.

Unaccompanied Sessions:
- When you leave your child I am happy if you find it helpful to phone and check your child has settled.
- Parents are can help the transition by bringing comfort items from home such as favourite toys, blanket or dummy.
- Progress reports will be offered verbally on collection and through children's daily diaries.

If there are any problems or concerns I will of course ring you and you are free to ring me at anytime to see how your child is progressing.

Points for your Consideration:
Babies 0-8 month tend to settle more quickly than those from 8-14 months. If your baby is in the latter age range you may require more settling in sessions to enable them to form an attachment/bond with the childminder and assistant.

- Long drawn out goodbyes tend to make children more upset.
- Do not sneak out - this makes children more insecure and mistrusting.
- Inform children when you will return in terms they can understand.

Provision of Basic Play and other Activities

This policy should let parents know what their child will be doing whilst they are in your care.

Topics to cover:
- ❑ What outings you might take children on.
- ❑ The range of toys you have, whether they are age appropriate.
- ❑ An example of the activities you offer (e.g. art and crafts).
- ❑ Outdoor equipment you have (e.g. slide or swing).
- ❑ How activities are adapted to meet special needs.

Play Policy

For children to learn through play they need a safe and caring environment; time; space; appropriate resources and encouragement to help them experience, explore, experiment and achieve. Through play they will learn to concentrate, develop self esteem and the attitudes important for learning when attending school full time.

I will ensure a safe and caring environment where your child has access to a wide variety of experiences both indoors and outside by using suitable developmentally appropriate resources and planning suitable outings into the wider environment. Activities will be adapted to meet developmental and special needs if this is applicable.

I will provide activities that support the learning outcomes of the EYFS.

Activities will include:

- Role play, including dressing up clothes and hats, doctors/vets kits, tea set and play food.
- Small world toys such as cars, garage, trains, farm/zoo animals and people.
- Construction toys such as Stickle Brix, Lego, Duplo and wooden blocks.
- Puzzles and board games.
- Water and sand play.
- Arts and crafts.
- Messy play such as cornflour, dough and painting.
- Cooking.
- Gardening, care of small animals.
- Outdoor play and equipment such as den building, play house, trampoline, ride on toys, roller skating, ball games, pond dipping and bug hunts.
- Outings to local parks, woods and the canal.

Please note: I am happy to support activities or events from home where children would like to explore these further.

Anti Bullying Policy

This policy should let parents know bullying will not be tolerated in your home.

Topics to cover:
- ❑ Definition of bullying.
- ❑ Examples of what constitutes bullying.
- ❑ Procedures you follow if a child is bullied.
- ❑ Procedures you follow if a child is a bully.
- ❑ Open communication.

Policy against Bullying / Anti Bullying Policy

Bullying in any form will not be tolerated.

A bully is an adult or child who deliberately intimidates or persecutes another adult or child with the intention of causing distress.

Bullying includes the following:

Teasing, excluding, taunting, racial remarks, sarcastic comments, pulling hair, pinching, pushing, kicking, biting, damaging or theft of possessions.

If your child is being bullied I will:
- Provide them with opportunities to discuss their feelings and provide reassurance.
- Promote their self esteem.
- Work with you to help the child take positive steps towards preventing bullying. Such as suitable techniques to use when approached by the bully.

If your child is the bully I will:
- Discuss the matter with you to ascertain possible triggers.
- Ensure they are not bullying due to boredom or frustration.
- Discuss with you how we will address the behaviour to present a united front.
- Ensure bullies have the opportunity to achieve, channelling the success they feel through dominating others into other areas.

If you have concerns regarding your child bullying or being bullied please discuss your concerns with me and likewise should I have concerns I will bring them to your immediate attention. I should like to remind you that minor problems are best dealt with before they have a chance to escalate.

Behaviour Management

Your behaviour management policy should set out clearly the behaviour you expect from children and what strategies you use to encourage this. In some areas a policy on bullying is also required.

Topics to cover:
- ❑ What behaviour you expect, your 'house rules'.
- ❑ How you encourage children to follow these rules.
- ❑ What you consider unacceptable behaviour.
- ❑ How you will respond to unacceptable behaviour.

Behaviour Management Policy

This behaviour management policy is designed to ensure the well being of the children in my care, and to help them to develop self-discipline and self esteem in an environment of mutual respect and encouragement. Children benefit most where their behaviour is managed positively and consistently. There is no such thing as a bad child, however a child may exhibit unacceptable behaviour. We should all be aware that behaviour may be affected by outside influences, such as a new baby, bereavement, illness, lack of sleep, change of routine, or arise from a child's special needs. Please inform me of these or similar circumstances that may effect children's behaviour.

Ground Rules

I have tried to establish a framework of clear boundaries and limits for behaviour so that children know what is expected of them. I emphasise positive expectations for that behaviour. This frame work is for sharing with both parents and the children. The framework will be applied firmly and consistently.

- Children will treat each other and adults with respect.
- Children will respect each others, and the childminder's belongings.
- Children will treat the animals with respect.
- There will be no name calling, teasing or offensive language.
- Children will not hit, kick, pinch or bite, or in any way hurt each other or adults present.
- There will be no standing on the furniture.
- Children sit down when eating or drinking.
- Running is not permitted in the house.
- Children do not play outside unsupervised.

I also like to emphasise the importance of good manners. Children will be encouraged to practise good table manners and to use the phrases please, thank-you and sorry in appropriate situations.

Behaviour Management

I provide a positive discipline policy focusing on prevention, redirection, consistency and firmness within a loving environment. My dealings with behaviour will be sensitive, appropriate and take into account children's level of understanding and maturity. Adults present provide positive role models for children with regard to friendliness, care, courtesy, respect and good manners.

I give praise and encouragement when children live up to expectations and respond to unwanted behaviour according to a child's stage of development and understanding. Attention, approval and praise build self esteem. A child who feels valued tends to behave well and does not need to seek attention by misbehaving.

Where unacceptable behaviour has occurred, it will be stressed that it is the behaviour which is unacceptable and not the child. Where the stage of development is such that the child can respond to reasoning we will discuss the incident, highlighting what was inappropriate and why, focusing on how to behave more appropriately.

Behaviour management strategies are very dependent on the age and stage of a child's development, and will vary from distraction, ignoring bad behaviour while rewarding good behaviour, disapproving looks or tone of voice, in extreme cases time out will be used.

Please note: I have a no smacking policy.

18. Courses & Qualifications

Childminders must take a first aid course and a childminding introductory course as part of registration. There is no requirement to complete further training courses as long as you have the necessary knowledge to meet the National Childminding Standards. However, many childminders do go on to do so. Training can help you extend your knowledge on subjects such as special needs or child development; develop new skills such as business management; or update your knowledge of current guidelines and regulations. Qualifications also provide formal recognition of your experience which may be useful if you want to work in other areas of the childcare sector in the future.

Worried About Becoming a Student?

Considering becoming a student can be very daunting, particularly if it has been a while since you last studied. Most adult students will be in the same situation and your tutor should help you plan how to study and explain how to complete your course work. You may be offered a Key Skills course which covers key skills such as maths, IT (using a computer) and problem solving that will help with your further study. You could also consider starting with a short day or evening course. If you are nervous about being in a classroom setting with other students then distance learning might be for you or you could invite a friend to join you.

Distance Versus Centre Based Learning

Many courses can be taken either as distance learning or centre based. Distance learning usually involves course material being sent to you by post and you returning your assignments in the same way. Centre based learning involves you attending an education centre, for example, a college or school for meeting with your tutor and lessons. Each have their advantages and you must decide which is best for your situation.

The choice between distance and centre based learning is a very personal one and will depend on your circumstances and the courses you are considering. You will need to weigh up the pro's and con's of both before you commit yourself. Discussing the options with your local college, learning centre or distance learning provider will be helpful.

Distance Learning

Distance learning offers great flexibility. You can study any time and at your own pace. You can work when time permits and fit study in around a busy schedule. You do not have to keep up with your class, you can work faster or slower. Deadlines are often more lenient. You can use the opportunity to develop your computer skills by typing your essays on a computer. You may be able to meet other childminders studying in your area through your local group. It may give you a wider choice of courses, if a course is not available locally, distance learning may allow you access it.

To study through distance learning you will need to be more disciplined about studying and not leave assignments to build up. You will not meet regularly with a group taking the same course so you cannot discuss problems or share books and you will not have access to a college library or other facilities. There may not be as much tutor support as centre based learning, but you may be able to talk online to like minded students.

Centre Based Learning

Classroom learning involves regular meetings, usually at your local college. You will be able to discuss the work with your tutor and class mates, allowing you to share information and experiences and make new friends. You will also receive tutorials on the subjects you are covering, giving you guidance on what you need to study. There may be access to a library and computer facilities.

Course times may not be compatible with your work, finding alternate care for your customers may lower your income. Courses may be in the evening so you can attend after work, however this makes for a very long day as they are often several hours long. You will often need to do work at home between tutorials. This type of learning is less flexible, the pace of learning is set by the tutor and you will need to complete assignments for specific deadlines.

Courses Available

There are a wide range of courses available for childminders. Courses such as food hygiene, business management and multicultural cooking, although not specifically for childcarers may also be useful. Some courses result in formal qualifications recognised nationally such as NVQ's, others, particularly day training courses, have a certificate of attendance.

Qualification Levels

The National Qualification Framework sets out five levels of qualification. Level 1 (also known as foundation level) is equivalent to GCSE grades D-G, and foundation level GNVQ's. Level 2 (intermediate) is equivalent to GCSE grades A*-C and intermediate GNVQ's. Level 3 (advanced) is equivalent to A levels and advanced GNVQ's. Level 4 and 5 correspond to higher-level qualifications such as degrees.

NVQ levels are based on this framework e.g. NVQ 3 is a level 3 qualification. Childminders generally take level 3 qualifications or above (as they supervise themselves at work), though you may feel you would prefer to start with a lower level first.

Diploma in Home-based Childcare (Level 3)

The Diploma in Home-based Childcare (DHC) is a nationally recognised award from the Council for Awards in Childcare and Education (CACHE) and NCMA. It replaced the Certificate in Childminding Practice (CCP) in January 2006. The CCP contained three units: Introducing, Developing and Extending Childminding Practice. If you have completed part of the CCP you may be able to count this towards the new DHC - ask your college for more information.

The DHC is made up of five units:
Unit 1: Introduction to Childcare Practice (home-based).
Unit 2: Childcare and Child Development (0-16) in the Home-based setting.
Unit 3: The Childcare Practitioner in the Home-based Setting.
Unit 4: Working in Partnership with Parents in the Home-Based Setting.
Unit 5: Planning to Meet the Children's Individual Learning Needs in the Home-based Setting.

As you complete each module you will receive a certificate, and on completion of the full course a diploma. The units also provide all the underpinning knowledge needed if you decide to go on to do an NVQ Level 3 in Early Years Care and Education.

Unit 1: Introduction to Childcare Practice (12 hours study)

This course is ideal for childminders beginning their career and is usually undertaken as childminders undergo the registration process. Some childminders take the ICP course as a mandatory part of their Ofsted registration process.

The training programme includes:

❑ Establishing a safe and healthy childcare environment in a home-based setting.
❑ Establishing routines for home-based childcare.
❑ Providing play and other activities for children in a home-based setting.
❑ Introducing children and their families to your childcare service.
❑ Managing children's behaviour in the home-based setting.
❑ Inclusion and anti-bias practice.
❑ Child protection in the home-based setting.
❑ Starting a home-based childcare service.

Unit 2: Childcare and Child Development (0-16) in the Home-based Setting

❑ Promoting children's rights.
❑ Working with disabled children and their families.
❑ Children's development and well-being.

Unit 3: The Childcare Practitioner in the Home-based Setting

❑ The reflective practitioner.
❑ Assertiveness and valuing yourself.
❑ Marketing and managing your childcare service.
❑ Policy writing.
❑ Inter-agency working and other professionals.
❑ Child Protection.
❑ Continuing Professional Development.

Unit 4: Working in Partnership with Parents in the Home-based Setting

❑ The childcare practitioner and the community.
❑ Families and cultures.
❑ Promoting positive relationships with parents and the importance of valuing the child's primary carer.
❑ Confidentiality, data protection and the law.
❑ Contracts and complaints.
❑ Communication.

Unit 5: Planning to Meet the Children's Individual Learning Needs in the Home-based Setting

❑ Observation and assessment of children's development in a home-based setting.
❑ Prepare, implement and evaluate plans for home-based groups of children of different ages and abilities.
❑ Meeting individual learning needs in the home-based setting.

NVQ 3 in Children's Care, Learning and Development (Level 3)

NVQ Level 3 in Early Years Childcare and Education, previously known as NVQ 3 Childcare & Education, is a nationally recognised qualification in all areas of Early Years and is designed to be taken whilst working as a childcarer. Whilst courses such as the DHC focus on theory and are assessed using written responses, the NVQ encourages you to put theory into practice. This means that as well as submitting written work, part of the assessment is done by an assessor who will visit you to observe you at work with children in your own home.

The course consists of eleven mandatory units:
❑ Contribute to the protection of children from abuse.
❑ Establish and maintain relationships with parents.
❑ Observe and assess the development and behaviour of children.
❑ Plan and Equip environments for children.
❑ Plan, implement and evaluate learning activities and experiences.
❑ Promote children's language and communication development.

❑ Promote children's sensory and intellectual development.
❑ Promote children's social and emotional development.
❑ Promote the physical development of children.
❑ Provide a framework for the management of behaviour.
❑ Provide for children's physical needs.

There are also three units to be chosen from the list below: (To give a total of fourteen units.)
❑ Care for and promote the development of babies.
❑ Create effective working relationships.
❑ Develop structured programmes for children with special needs.
❑ Establish and maintain a childcare education service.
❑ Inform and implement management committee policies and procedures.
❑ Involve parents in group activities.
❑ Manage admissions, finance and operating systems in care and education settings.
❑ Manage yourself.
❑ Plan, implement and evaluate routines for children.
❑ Promote the care and education of children with special needs.
❑ Support parents in developing their parenting skills.
❑ Support the development of children's literacy skills.
❑ Support the development of children's mathematical skills.
❑ Visit and support a family in their own home.
❑ Work with other professionals.

If you have completed a previous course such as the DHC or CCP you will be able to use this work towards the NVQ assessments so you do not have to repeat previous work.

First Aid Training

All registered childminders must obtain a first aid certificate within six months of registering. The British Red Cross runs a course called 'First Aid for Childcarers' and there are also similar courses run by other organisations. Childminders need to take courses specifically covering first aid for children, as there are differences in first aid given to adults and children. Resuscitation, for example, varies for baby's, children and adults. Applying resuscitation techniques on a child designed for an adult, can cause the child harm.

First aid courses are valuable qualifications, the information you learn and practice could help to save a life. We all like to think that serious accidents will never happen to the children in our care, and we take all the possible precautions to avoid them. Part of these precautions is a first aid course, as it also gives the knowledge to prevent an accident becoming more serious. If an accident should happen you need to know how to deal with it.

A typical course will include:

Accidents
❑ How and why they occur
❑ How they can be prevented
❑ Safety in the child's environment

Causes of Unconsciousness
❑ Head injuries
❑ Electric shock
❑ Foreign bodies

Management of the Unconscious Casualty
❑ Recovery position
❑ Hypoxia
❑ Resuscitation

Fractures
❑ How bones break
❑ Recognition of fractures
❑ General treatment

The First Aid Kit
❑ Contents of the first aid kit
❑ Dealing with blood loss and shock
❑ Dealing with burns and scolds

Minor illness
❑ Recognition and management
❑ Administration of medication

Safeguarding Children and Young People (Level 3)

This qualification is awarded by City & Guilds. There are eight mandatory units plus an additional unit you can choose:

❏ The context for safeguarding children and young people.
❏ Legal and policy frameworks for safeguarding children and young people.
❏ Understanding children and young people's developments needs and their right to express themselves.
❏ The family and environmental context of safeguarding children and young people.
❏ Recognising signs of abuse, harm and neglect of children and young people.
❏ What to do when there are concerns about children and young people's safety and welfare.
❏ Communication and working relationships in safeguarding children and young people.
❏ Creating safe environments for children and young people to prevent abuse, harm and neglect.

One unit from:
❏ Development and the implementation of policies for safeguarding children and young people.
❏ Good practice in recruitment, employment and deployment of staff and volunteers for safeguarding children and young people.
❏ Supporting children and families after abuse has been disclosed.
❏ Safeguarding children and young people in a home-based setting.

Child Protection

There are many child protection courses run by different organisations. They will typically cover:

❏ What is child abuse?
❏ The effects of abuse
❏ Myths and facts about abuse
❏ Managing your own feelings
❏ Recognising child abuse
❏ Responding to a child who needs your help

❏ Reporting child abuse
❏ Why should you report?
❏ What action should you take?
❏ What happens next?
❏ Good practice issues
❏ Your own responsibilities

Basic or Foundation Food Hygiene Certificate

Most local colleges offer this course or it can be done via distance learning. It covers the basic principles of food hygiene and will give you a recognised qualification. Topics covered include:

❏ Food poisoning and its prevention.
❏ Food borne illnesses.
❏ Food handling practices.
❏ Pest control.
❏ Personal hygiene.
❏ Food legislation.

Other Courses

Your local college will be able to provide you with a prospectus. As well as childcare specific courses and those for updating existing qualifications such as the Cache certificate in Early Years Foundation Stage Practice, there may be others that could be of help to you, for example, you may like to take a course on Chinese cookery to help you promote multiculturalism. If you are caring for a child with English as a second language you may want to take a basic course in their first language to help with communication.

Grants and Funding

Training courses are tax deductible, but they can still be expensive. You may be able to get grants to cover the cost of part or all of your training.

The EYDCP, or your childminding development officer, should have details of grants available in your area, they may include:

❑ European Social Funding.
❑ National Lottery Grant.
❑ Start up grants.

Completing Course Work

Reading

When reading a book, use the index to find chapters or sections particularly relevant to the topic you are studying. You can skim through chapters and use headings or look for keywords to locate relevant information. Decide in advance what information you are looking for. Do you need a general overview of the information or detailed information on a particular subject for an assignment? Remember to keep a list of the books you read so you can reference them at the end of your assignment.

Note Taking

Whether listening to a lecture, film or reading from a book, it is likely at some point you will need to take notes. When taking notes the idea is not to set everything down on paper just the important details. Notes should not be full sentences, as these take too long to write down. If you have learnt shorthand you could use this or develop your own. Make sure that you can still understand your notes when you come to read them back.

Example: 'An increase in exercise results in greater fitness', could be written as:

↑ exercise → > fitness

↑ increase
→ results in (or leads to)
> greater

it could be simplified even further to

exercise → fitness

Words are often shortened to, for example (e.g.), children (chldrn.), advantage (adv.). Initials may also be used for common phrases, such Special Educational Needs (SEN).

When taking notes it is very helpful to jot down the book and page number so you can easily go back for more information or to clarify a point later, for example you could use the authors name and the page number - Brown (p20).

Highlighting

If you have brought your own copies of books or have been given large amounts of written information you may find highlighting or underlining in a coloured pen helpful. You need to be selective as you do this, only underlining a few words or a sentence per paragraph. Aim to highlight the point made in that paragraph. Once the point is highlighted you will be able to skim quickly through the text to find the sections you need.

Example: This is information for an essay asking: Why is play important?

Vygotsky (1930's) said that "play is not the predominant form of activity, but in a certain sense it is the leading source of development in pre-school years." I think in many ways he was very forward thinking and I feel that play is a holistic form of learning. Vygotsky believed that play helped children put life into perspective. In my experience this is very true of all children, and especially so for those children coming to my setting as a place of safety. Vygotsky and Piaget (a Swiss psychologist and expert on children's intellectual development) thought that play encouraged children to enjoy games through which they could learn. According to Smith, Cowie and Blades, Vygotsky saw play as the "leading source of development in the pre-school years" because he believed the nature of pretend play meant the child freed its self from the now and actual objects into the world of ideas and what they could represent." The child is liberated from situational constraints through his activity in an imaginary situation" (Smith, Cowie, Blades 1998) It is a transitional stage to operating with meanings. According to Vassilopoulou (2000) Play is still considered a driving force for children's development. I would agree with this as in my experience children deprived of play are developmentally behind their peer group and lacking in social skills.

When first reading it is a lot to take in, but by skimming through looking for particular references to the importance of play we can extract:

"helped children put life into perspective"
"games through which they could learn"
"driving force for children's development"

So we can summarise that play is important for children's development because it helps children put life in to perspective and they can learn through the games they play.

Tables

Tables can also be a good way of making notes, especially if you are comparing things.

Example: What are the pro's and con's of centre based and distance learning?
If you have a table prepared you can fill it in as you work through a chapter in a book or piece of writing. The table may be an acceptable way to present your work or you can then use the information in the table to write an essay.

	Centre Based Learning	Distance Learning
Pros.	Access to library & computers. Classmates for support.	Fits around other commitments.
Cons.	Doesn't fit around work, study at set times.	No tutorials. More expensive.

Flow Diagrams

If you are looking at the process of something, it may help to present your work as a flow diagram.

E.g.   Wash hands → cut bread → butter bread → add ham → cut in half → put on plate

Spider Diagrams

These are often used to collect information about a subject, or 'brain storm' ideas. Spider diagrams are useful for getting your ideas down quickly. E.g. What does a childminder do?

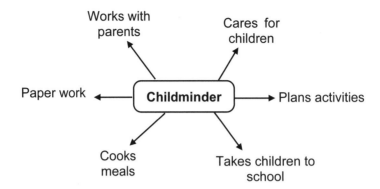

Essay Writing

Writing an essay can be very daunting! The best place to start is with the question itself. Make sure you understand what you are being asked to do and if there is more that one part break it down into smaller sections. It may also help to write it down in your own words.

Firstly look for keywords that explain how you should tackle the question - a list of common ones and their meanings are below. It may also help to look them up in a dictionary.

Keyword	Meaning
Analyse	Look closely at the subject. Look for assumptions they may have made and ask how and why.
Critique	Evaluate something. Ask questions such as why? and how well? It doesn't just mean find the problems.
Describe	You should include a description but you may also need to evaluate as well.
Discuss	Write about the arguments for and against a point of view - look at things from more than one perspective.
Evaluate	Make a judgement on how valid or accurate and statement is. Is it right or wrong or a bit of both? You should explain your reasons and use evidence to support it.
Explore	Examine the topic carefully and analyse all areas of it.
Investigate	Look at all areas of the subject.
Justify	You must argue for and find evidence to support the subject.
Summarise	You must break the subject down into the main points - usually this is quite a brief answer.
Illustrate	Give examples.
Compare	Find the similarities and differences. It might help to start by making a list of things you are going to compare.

Next consider the topics and ideas you need to cover and write a few notes on what to include in the essay. You can use these notes to start looking for information in books and other source material. Take careful notes from these, the notes will become the basis of your essay. Once you have made notes read them through and add any further comments. Organise the notes into topics to form sections in your essay and start writing them up in full sentences.

Any essay should have a beginning (introduction), a middle and an end (conclusion). The introduction should explain what the essay is about, like the blurb on the back of a book or a programme summary in a television guide (remember do not give away the ending, that is for the conclusion). You will find it easier to write the introduction after you have finished the main part of the essay - it is difficult to introduce something before you have written it! The main part of your essay should be divided into paragraphs each focusing on a topic. It contains the information and reasoning you used to answer the question. The conclusion summaries your points and the answers you came to.

Once you have written your draft, read it through and make sure that you have clearly explained all your points and most importantly that you have answered the question. Check it against the word count if you have one. If you have too few words you may need to include more detail, to few and you need to cut out anything irrelevant or reword things to write more concisely. It may help to have a friend read it or put it away for a day and then reread it.

Finally you should check the spelling and grammar. Theses are important so that the marker can understand what you have written and they also count towards your grade. Check whether there are any presentation rules you need to follow such as double spacing lines or only writing on one side of the paper. Keep a copy of your essay when you hand it in in case it gets lost or goes missing in the post.

When you get your essay back read the comments carefully as they will let you know how you can improve ready for your next assignment.

Word Counts

You maybe given a word count when completing assignments. This is a guide to the amount of words that are needed. This does not mean you must count every word, which can take a long time if you have to write a few thousand words! If you are writing by hand, find an average line from your essay and count the number of words and multiply that by the number of lines to give you an approximate word count. Remember your tutor will count in the same way, they do not have time to count every single word either. Most computer programs have an option to view a word count - try searching the help file.

Try not to worry if your assignment asks for a lot of words, you will find 1000 words is not as many as it sounds. If you have researched your topic and understand it well you will find writing longer essays easier.

Plagiarism and Referencing

As you write essays you may use ideas or even quote phrases from other people or books. To show that you are not trying to pass these off as your own, you need to reference where they came from. If you do not reference text or ideas that belong to someone else then its called plagiarism as you imply that the ideas are your own.

You can reference other people's work by putting their name and the date they said/wrote it on the page after you have used their ideas or a quote.

E.g. The child is liberated from situational constraints through his activity in an imaginary situation (Smith, Cowie, Blades 1998).

Bibliography

At the end of an essay you write a bibliography. This is a list of all the sources of information you have referred to in your essay. It should include the authors' name, date they said/wrote it, the title of the piece of work, where it was published and the publisher's name.

The bibliography or reference list for the paragraph used in the highlighting example would be:

Smith, P, Cowie, H & Blades, M (1998) Understanding Children's Development, Oxford, Blackwell.
Vassilopoulou, C (2000) Imagination in Action, NATD Broad Sheet.
Vygotsky, L, (1962) Thought and Language, Cambridge, M.I.T. Press.

Different colleges may have slightly different rules on how you should write your references so check with your tutor for examples.

Organising Your Work

If you do not organise your work you will find it quickly becomes muddled and you will spend needless time looking through it trying to find what you want. You can take notes in a book or on loose paper which can then be stored in a file. Individual sheets stored in a file may be easier if you are doing a long course so you can add pages in or other references like photocopies. Use paper or card dividers to divide up units or topics. Give your work page numbers and add an index to the front of each section so you can tell at a glance what information is stored inside.

Organising your Time

Taking courses, especially those with assignments due at specific dates, can require a lot of discipline. It is very tempting after a long days work to put your feet up and think 'I'll do some tomorrow'.

If you find you are getting behind, or you do not think your doing as much work as you should, set yourself goals. It usually helps to write them down on paper so they are harder to ignore. Plan what work you are going to do during the following week, you can even set daily goals, for example, reading a chapter of a book, or taking notes for a essay. It can also help to organise times that you will have free when you can sit down for a while and concentrate.

Monday	Tuesday	Wednesday	Thursday	Friday
Read through Chapter 1	Re-read chapter 1 taking notes	Write first draft of assignment using notes	Check first draft and make corrections, then finalise	Post essay to tutor and have treat for getting all work done.

When you are organising your time it can also help to set yourself rewards. Studying is hard work and can become a chore if you do it all the time. Give yourself a few days off when you have finished an assignment, or just easy work like organising your folder. If you successfully complete a piece of work then give your self a treat, after all you deserve it!

Getting the Most from your Tutor

Whether you study long distance or at a centre you are usually assigned a tutor. Your tutor is there to provide you with any guidance you may need.

If you are studying long distance your contact will be through telephone or email. When you plan to phone your tutor write the questions you need answered down in advance to help remind you. Have notepaper and a pen handy to take down any information your tutor gives.

If you meet your tutor regularly, it helps to have a spare sheet of paper or a notebook handy as you do your work through the week to jot down any questions that arise so you can remember everything you need to ask your tutor at the meeting.

If you do not think your tutor is providing you with the support promised or you have another problem (e.g. work being returned late) first bring it up with your tutor. If you do not feel comfortable doing this face to face then write a letter or phone. If you still do not feel your tutor is doing everything then you should talk to the college or centre you are taking your course through.

Finding Resources

Books

Your tutor may supply a booklist. This will guide you towards the books that have information relevant to your course. These can seem very long but you will not be expected to read every book or to read cover-to-cover. If you have not been given a book list try asking your tutor or childminders that have previously done the same course what books they recommend. Your local library may be able to help you find books and in some cases order them in for you from other library services. You may also be able to access books from the college or university library for the institution you are studying with. Librarians are usually helpful if you need to find books on a particular subject but do not have a list of titles. Your local childminding group may have a selection of books for you to borrow, or they may know someone who has taken the course previously and is willing to sell the books on. Some colleges have a second hand book scheme where you can buy at a discount. Books can be an expensive part of the course so ask your tutor to recommend which books are most important before you buy any. Your tutor may suggest that you purchase one or several key books that you will use most and borrow the rest.

Specialised Organisations

For some topics specialist organisations or support groups may be a good source of information for example the National Society of Prevention of Cruelty to Children (NSPCC) are a good source of information on Child Protection or for special needs you may have local support groups. These specialist organisations may have leaflets and books, run information events, hold meetings or offer short courses which may help in your studies.

Schools

If you need help with early years education try visiting your local lower or primary school. They may be able to provide you with example curriculums or suggested reading. If your course involves a study of children the school may also allow you to observe lessons, or help as a teachers assistant.

The Internet

The Internet provides access to a wide range of resources. Your college may offer access to online journals and articles as part of their library scheme. When using the Internet you should keep in mind that anyone can publish information on it and the information may not necessarily be accurate or it maybe opinion rather than fact. This means it is important to consider the source of information, for example information from a well known organisations website is more likely to be reliable than from an individuals online diary. The large amounts of information available online can make finding what you want difficult. Try looking for the 'advanced search' option this can help you narrow down your results. Use several words or a phrase and be specific in what you are looking for e.g. "child development learning through play". To find pages matching a phrase exactly surround it in quotes.

Section 19: Useful Organisations

Childminding Support Groups

By working together a group of childminders can support each other, share information and resources and provide back up care in emergencies. In some areas grants may be available to help support groups. If there is not currently a childminding group in your area consider starting your own. It does not have to be big; you can start with just a few friends joining together for a coffee or to take the children on an outing. These events allow you and the children to socialise and give you the opportunity to discuss childminding with other childminders.

Fundraising

Raising money for the group to organise events or fund a newsletter can be an issue. Fundraising can be combined with events so you can have fun at the same time or it may involve applying for grants or asking local businesses for sponsorship.

Here are some ideas:

❑ Raffle - Local shops may donate prizes or childminders may have something to donate, tickets can be sold at an event or handed to childminders to be sold to customers and friends.
❑ Stall - You may be able to hold a stall at a local fete, you could sell cakes, second hand toys or similar.
❑ Grants - Your childminding development worker, local council or CIS will have details of grants. These are useful for particular purposes rather than general running costs. You could apply for money for a toy library, newsletters or to fund an event. You may also like to look at www.grantsnet.co.uk which provides information about grant schemes available to businesses and charities in the UK.

Newsletters

Many groups put out a newsletter to keep members informed of childminding issues, events and training. Home computers can be used in their production. Once a copy has been made local print shops will be able to photocopy them for you relatively inexpensively. You can save money on postage by asking the childminders to deliver a few newsletters each to the other childminders living near by and by emailing copies where possible.

Organising Events

There are many events childminding groups organise, these can be for childminders and children, or an after hours evening event just for childminders, parents may be invited to events too.

Committee

If you are raising money and organising events you will need a committee to keep everything organised. This will include a chairperson to head the meetings, a secretary to take notes about what was decided on and a treasurer to do the accounts and keep track of the money. It will also include committee members who may also be given particular tasks, for example, producing the newsletter, writing press releases or running a vacancy list.

The committee can be nominated by the members of the group then voted for. The childminding professional bodies may be able to provide sample constitutions and details of how to organise committees, or you can create your own.

Training

When you are working as a group you can organise training for members. There are many organisations that will provide training for free, though you may need to arrange a venue. These include the local fire service, paramedics, tax office and speakers from special needs support groups, all the telephone numbers should be in your local telephone directory.

You may also find you can participate in training being provided to local pre-schools or playgroup staff in exchange for sharing the venue costs. There may also be courses at local colleges the group may like to attend. Often people may feel more confident in attending if they can share the experience with other childminders. Relevant courses might include first aid, food hygiene, child development, cooking and childcare.

Press

Publicising your group in the local newspaper can help inform parents of childminders existence and give a positive impression of your services, and this can help generate new customers.

When you hold an event send a press release to the local newspapers in advance. Press releases should include who you are, what you are doing, and when. Also include a contact for more information. Do not worry if no one from the press turns up on the day, you can still send your own photos and a description of how the event went to the newspaper they may still print it. To encourage more publicity consider inviting a local dignitary for example the local mayor, an MP or the head of the local childcare team.

Child Care Related Organisations

Childminding Organisations

Childminding Ireland
This Southern Ireland organisation provides support, advice and information. Website: www.childminding.ie

NCMA
The National Childminding Association is a national charity and membership organisation for childminders in England and Wales. Membership is also available to parents and to other persons or organisations committed to quality childcare. Website: www.ncma.org.uk

NICMA
The Northern Ireland Childminding Association provides a range of services to support parents and childminders. Website: www.nicma.org

SCMA
The Scottish Childminding Association, offer support and advice to everyone involved in childminding provision. Website: www.childminding.org

Regulatory Bodies

England - Ofsted website: www.ofsted.gov.uk
Scotland - Care Commission website: www.carecommission.com
Wales - Care Standards Inspectorate for Wales website: www.csiw.wales.gov.uk
Ireland South - The Health Service Executive website: www.hse.ie contains links to each of the thirty-two Local Health offices and their inspection teams.
Ireland North - The Health, Social Services and Public Safety website has links to the Health and Social Services Boards for each region at www.dhsspsni.gov.uk/indx/dhssps_links

Other Information Sources

Early Years Development and Childcare Partnerships (EYDCP) & Early Years Childcare Partnerships (EYCP)

There are 150 partnerships spread across England. Partnerships encourage training on childcare issues often arranging courses themselves including SEN training, literacy, numeracy, planning, assessments, appropriate curriculums, learning through play and first aid. These courses are frequently free or at a minimal charge and can be accessed by Registered Childminders. Partnerships offer funding opportunities and may have their own Business Finance Support Officer, who will also help childminders. A few partnerships have produced local directories or booklets to help understand the various funding sources available from them.

Children's Information Service (CIS)

The CIS includes a national internet site providing detailed information and advice on child care and child related topics for parents, childcare professionals and employers www.childcarelink.gov.uk to which all EYDCP's and CIS's in England, Wales and Scotland subscribe.

The CIS is a source of information for parents requiring childcare and education, family support services and child related information. The information provided covers children and young people between 0-19 years and will include details of providers, toy libraries, playgroups, toddler groups and parent support groups.

The CIS also includes childminder's childcare services and will promote your vacancies, they can also advise you of training sessions for childcare workers. Some CIS's help with recruitment and retention of childcare workers including childminders. They also promote working families tax credit to help parents to be better able to afford childcare.

The Department for Children, Schools and Families (DCSF)

In England and Wales, the DCSF leads work across government to ensure children and young people achieve the five 'Every Child Matters' outcomes. Web site: www.dfes.gov.uk

Daycare Trust

The Daycare Trust is a national charity that promotes 'high quality affordable childcare for all'. They provide information to a wide range of people on childcare, including parents, childcare workers, employers and Local Authorities. Website: www.daycaretrust.org.uk

Surestart

This organisation brings together early education, children's health and family support. Their website: www.surestart.gov.uk contains a wealth of information much of which will be relevant to all childminders regardless of their location.

Equal Opportunities

Information on equal opportunities, discrimination and rights are available at www.equalityhumanrights.com

Tax Issues

Links to tax, benefits and self assessment for childminders in England, Scotland, Northern Ireland and Wales can be found at www.hmrc.gov.uk, for childminders in Southern Ireland links to tax relief and self assessment can be found at www.revenu.ie

Advice for Specific Special Needs

Allergies
The British Allergy Association website www.allergyfoundation.com contains information on allergies, intolerance's, diagnosis and common food allergies. There is a UK help line on 01322 619898.

Angleman Syndrome
The following website has information including cause and effects, communication and learning. Help sheets are also available: www.angelmanuk.org

Aspergers / Autism
The website: www.nas.org.uk contains information on definitions, diagnosis, education from preschool to higher education, bullying, exclusion and sources of help. There is a helpline available on 0845 0704004.

Asthma / Hayfever
The National Asthma Campaign website www.asthma.org.uk includes information on Asthma triggers, medicines and treatments, controlling Asthma and hayfever and contains links to English, Irish, Welsh and Scottish Asthma Campaigns.

Cerebral Palsy
The website: www.scope.org.uk has a range of downloadable information leaflets. They also have an information telephone line on 0808 8003333.

Coeliac's
The website: www.coeliac.co.uk includes information on the definition and diagnosis. It includes gluten free recipes and product information to enable you to avoid gluten. They have a help line on 0870 4448804.

Cystic Fibrosis
The website: www.cftrust.org.uk contains information on causes, symptoms and treatment, nutrition and education. Their contact telephone number is 020 84647211.

Diabetes
The website: www.diabetes.org.uk has information on signs, symptoms, causes, treatments, food and recipes, and covers tots to teens. The information is also available in a wide range of languages.

Downs Syndrome
The Downs Syndrome Association website at www.downs-syndrome.org.uk has information including cause and effects, health, education, speech and language therapy. They have a helpline on 0845 2300372.

Dyslexia
The website: www.dyslexiaaction.org.uk, has information on definitions, assessments, specialist teaching and research.

Dyspraxia
The website: www.dyspraxiafoundation.org.uk has information on diagnosis, preschool and school aged children and ways of supporting children with dyspraxia. There is a helpline available on 01462 454016.

Epilepsy

This website: www.epilepsynse.org.uk contains information on epilepsy, seizures, treatment, leisure activities, behaviour and education. There is a helpline available on 01494 601300.

Hyperactive inc. ADHD

The hyperactive children's support group website www.hacsg.org.uk includes information on ADHD, recognising hyperactivity, additives and diet.

Sickle Cell Anaemia

The Sickle Cell Society website www.sicklecellsociety.org.uk contains detailed information on traits, diagnosis, health and supporting children with the condition. There is a telephone helpline available on 0800 0015660.

Spina Bifida and Hydrocephalus

The Association for Spina Bifida and Hydrocephalus (ASBAH) website www.asbah.org has information and advice and includes causes and treatments.

Vegetarian / Vegan

The vegetarian Society website www.vegsoc.org includes recipes and has helpful advice on which foods and additives contain hidden meat or meat products.

Animal Related Organisations

Royal Society for Prevention of Cruelty to Animals (RSPCA)

The RSPCA website at www.rspca.org.uk provides information on animal care and has a comprehensive education section with free educational resources available in English and Welsh.

Scottish Society for Prevention of Cruelty to Animals (SSPCA)

The SSPCA website at www.scottishspca.org contains information on animal welfare requirements and links to websites with information on a wide variety of commonly kept pets.

Irish Society for Prevention of Cruelty to Animals (ISPCA)

The ISPCA website at www.ispca.ie contains information on a wide range of animal matters including pet care and pet behaviour.

Ulster Society for Prevention of Cruelty to Animals in Northern Ireland (USPCA)

The USPCA website at www.uspca.co.uk contains downloadable booklets on cats and kittens, dogs and puppies, and rabbits. There is also an education pack which you can send for.

Peoples Dispensary for Sick Animals (PDSA)

The PDSA website at www.pdsa.org.uk has educational resource packs on dogs and cats and health related issues. Information on choosing suitable pets and information on rabbits, gerbils, guinea pigs, hamsters, rats, mice and budgerigars is also available. There are educational resources at http://www.schoolspdsa.org.uk for children from five to fourteen.

Child Protection/Safeguarding Children

Kidscape

This UK charity provides information and advice on bullying and protecting children from abuse. Much of the information is available on their website www.kidscape.org.uk. The telephone number is 020 77303300.

NSPCC/ISPCC
The National/Irish Society for the Prevention of Cruelty to Children (NSPCC/ISPCC) allow you to discuss concerns about a child anonymously by calling their child protection helpline. They are also empowered to make enquiries into the welfare of children at risk and to consider initiating care proceedings.This society works in England, Wales and Northern Ireland. Their website www.nspcc.org.uk contains lots of useful information and links to related research. Their contact number from all regions is 020 78252775.

Children First
This is the Scottish Child Protection Society whose website www.children1st.org.uk contains information and links to fact sheets and their available services across Scotland.

Social Services, Social Workers and Child Protection Teams
These agencies will be able to offer you guidance and assistance before any decisions are made. They have a duty to make inquiries in all cases of suspected child abuse. They will require written reports as evidence to help them decide whether to issue a police protection order, an emergency protection order or a child assessment order. They are trained in the questioning of small children to ensure evidence is not prejudiced. They will also do everything in their power to keep children within their own family group where safety issues are not paramount. They do not have the right of entry and will refer matters to the police if entry is refused. If in doubt always contact these agencies for advice.

Police/Garda
The police have a duty to investigate crime and a general responsibility to protect life. Acts of child abuse frequently amount to criminal assault and together with the Social Services teams they share primary responsibility for child protection often working together on cases.

Health Visitors
The Health Visitor is uniquely placed to recognise and confirm suspected abuse and to help abusive parents with education into the needs and development of their children. They do not have the rights of entry and will present any case to the police before a warrant is issued for the police to enter should children be at risk.

Education Service
The education service includes teachers, education welfare officers and support staff with daily contact with children. They are often the first to see or suspect abuse. They can also help to support an abused child and to help with the education of the parents.

Childminding Associations
Many of the childminding organisations have dedicated child protection officers who can provide advice. See childminding organisations for details of website contacts.

Bibliography

Childcare Unravelled:
Freud, S. (1915) *Essentials of Psychoanalysis.* London, Vintage Classics (2005).

Child Protection:
Berk, L. (2002) *Child Development*, USA, Allyn and Bacon.
Briggs, F. & Potter, G. (1999) *Early Years of School*, Melbourne, Longman.
Bruce, T. & Meggitt, C. (2002) *Child Care and Education*, London, Hodder and Stoughton.
Fanily Rights (2007) *Child Protection Procedures*, London, Family Rights Group.
Geraghty (1996) *Caring for Children*, Oxford, Bailliere Tindall.
HMSO (2006) *Working Together to Protect Children,* HM Government.
Hoffman, Paris and Hall (1996) *Childcare and Education*, London, Hodder and Stoughton.

Curriculum Planning and Child Development:
Abbott, L. & Langston, A.. (2005) *Birth to Three Matters : Supporting the Framework of Effective Practice.* Maidenhead, Open University Press McGraw Hill Education.
Berk, L. (2002) *Child Development*, USA, USA, Allyn and Bacon.
Blenkin, G. & Kelly, A. (1996) *Early Childhood Education.* UK, Paul Chapman.
Brain, J. & Martin, M. (1984) *Childcare and Health*, Cheltenham, Nelson Thornes.
Bruce, T. & Meggitt, C. (2002) *Child Care and Education*, London, Hodder and Stoughton
Geraghty (1996) *Caring for Children*, Oxford, Bailliere Tindall.
Harding, J. & Meldon-Smith, L. *(2000) How to Make Observations & Assessments.* London, Hodder & Stoughton.
Minette, P. (2001) Child Care and Development, London, John Murray.
NSF (2002) *Children's Sleep Habits,* National Sleep Foundation.
Siraj-Blatchford, I. & Clarke, P. (2005) *Supporting Identity, Diversity & Language in the Early Years.* Berkshire, Open University.
Smith, P., Cowie, H. & Blades, M. (1998) (Third Edition) *Understanding Children's Development.* Oxford, Blackwell.
Tassoni, P. & Hucker, K. (2000) *Planning Play and the Early Years*, Oxford, Heinemann.
Vygotsky, L. (2000) *Thought & Language.* London, MIT Press.
Wessbluth, M. (1996) *Healthy Sleep Habits, Happy Child,* USA, Ballantine Books.

Risk Assessment:
(1994) *Keeping Kids Safe*, The Child Accident Prevention Trust.
Lindon, J. (2003) *Too Safe for their Own Good?* London. National Children's Bureau.

Standards and Legislation:
DfES (2007) *Statutory Framework for the Early Years Foundation Stage.* Nottingham, DfES Pubs.
DHSS (2006) *The Care Standards Act 2000 & the Children Act 1989 (Regulatory Reform & Complaints) (Wales) Regulations 2006,* DHSS.
DoH (1997) *The Children Act 1989 - Guidance & Regulations.* London, Department of Health, HMSO.
(1998) *Data Protection Act 1998,* http://www.opsi.gov.uk/ACTS/acts1998/19980029.htm *accessed Sept 2006.*
HMSO. *Guidance to the Sex Discrimination Act* (1997) accessed February 2007 at http://www.womenandequalityunit.gov.uk/legislation/discrimination_act/sda-guide.pdf
HMSO *Race Relations Amendment Act* (2000) accessed February 2007 at http://www.opsi.gov.uk/acts/acts2000/00034--e.htm
HMSO. *Special Educational Needs and Disability Act* (SENDA) (2001) accessed February 2007 at http://www.opsi.gov.uk/acts/acts2001/20010010.htm
UN General Assembly Document (A/RES/44/25). *The United Nations (UN) Convention on the Rights of the Child.* (1989) accessed February 2007 at http://www.cirp.org/library/ethics/UN-convention/

Behaviour:
Hayes, E. (2001) *Behaviour*, London, National Society for the Prevention of Cruelty to Children.

Assertiveness:
(1996) *Assertiveness*, University of Illinois.
(2001) *Assertiveness Tip Sheet*, Organizational Development and Training, Tufts University.

Regulators & Registration:
DHC (2006) *Childcare (Pre School Services) Regulations 2006*, Dublin, Stationary Office.
HSS Trust (2007) *Regulations and Guidelines for Childminders,* Northern Ireland, H & SS Trust.
Ofsted (2007) *Framework for the Registration and Inspection of Childminding and Daycare*, London, Ofsted.

Health, Hygiene and Safety:
Babies, Top Safety Tips for Parents and Carers, Child Accident and Prevention Trust.
(2005) *Food Safety First Principles*, London, Chadwick House Group.
(2005) *Fire Prevention Handbook*, Office of the Deputy Prime Minister.
(2005) *Passive Smoking,* Royal College of Physicians.

Special Educational Needs:
DfES (2001) *Special Educational Needs Code of Practice*, Nottingham, DfES Publications.
Alcott, M. (2000) *An Introduction to Children with Special Educational Needs*, London, Hodder and Stoughton.
Greenstein, D. (1998) *Caring for Children with Special Needs: HIV and AIDS*, National Network for Childcare, NNCC.